DEMOCRATIZATION AND HYBRID REGIMES

International Anchoring and Domestic Dynamics in European post-Soviet States

edited by

Elena Baracani

European Press Academic Publishing
2010

This book is one result of the research project on Euroization and Democratization at the Eastern Borderline of the EU, funded by the Jean Monnet Action, and has benefited of the international conference organized in Florence, in June 2008 by the Italian Society for the Study of the Diffusion of Democracy (SSDD), to which most of the contributors to this volume participated.

ISBN 978-88-8398-061-9

©2010 by European Press Academic Publishing, Florence, Italy

www.e-p-a-p.com

Printed in Italy

CONTENTS

List of Tables

List of Figures

Abbreviations

AA	Association Agreement
AFPDC	Alliance of the Popular Christian Democratic Front
AMN	Our Moldova Alliance
BCDTU	Belarusian Congress of Democratic Trade Union
BFTU	Belarusian Free Trade Union
BISS	Belarusian Institute for Strategic Studies
BOP	Moldovan (Barometrul Opiniei Publice)
BPF	Belarusian People's Front
BTC	Baku-Tiblisi-Cheyan
BTI	Moldovan Peasant's and Intellectuals Block
CDM	Moldovan Democratic Convention
CEECs	Central Eastern European Countries
CES (CEES)	Common (European) Economic Space
CFF	Compensatory Financing Facility
CFSP	Common Foreign and Security Policy
CIB	Comprehensive Institution Building
CIS	Commonwealth of Independent States
CPA	Compact Program Assistance
CSDP	Civil Society Development Programme
CSLS	Confederation of Free Trade Unions in Moldova
CSOs	Civil Society Organizations
CSRM	Confederation of Trade Unions in Moldova
CUG	Citizens Union of Georgia
DCFTA	Deep and Comprehensive Free Trade Areas
DEAF	Domestic and External Actors and Factors
EBRD	European Bank for Reconstruction and Development
EaP	Eastern Partnership
EC	European Community
ED	Executive Directors
EFF	Extended Fund Facility
ENP	European Neighbourhood Policy
ENPI	European Neighbourhood Partnership Instrument
ESAF	Enhanced Structural Adjustment Facility

ESDP	European Security and Defence Policy
EU	European Union
EurAsEC	Eurasian Economic Community
FOM	Ukrainian Public Opinion Foundation
FSA	Freedom Support Act
FSU	Former Soviet Union
GDP	Gross Domestic Product
IDA	International Development Association
IDIS	Institute for Development and Social Initiatives
IFI	International Financial Institutions
ILO	International Labour Organization
IMF	International Monetary Fund
IMFC	International Monetary and Financial Committee
IPP	Institul de Politici Publice/Gallup
IR	International Relations
IUD	Industrial Union of Donbass
JCC	Joint Control Commission
MCC	Millennium Challenge Corporation
MFA	Ministry of Foreign Affairs
MoIA	Georgian Ministry of Internal Affairs
MP	Member of the Parliament
NATO	North Atlantic Treaty Organization
NBG	National Bank of Georgia
NBM	National Bank of Moldova
NED	National Endowment for Democracy
NGO	Non-Governmental Organization
NIS	Newly Independent States
NRB	New Russia Barometer
ODA	Official Development Assistance
ODIHR	Office for Democratic Institutions and Human Rights
OSCE	Organization for Security and Cooperation in Europe
PCA	Partnership and Cooperation Agreement
PCM	Moldovan Restored Communist Party
PCRM	Moldovan Communist Party
PDAM	Moldovan Party of Agrarians
PDM	Moldovan Democrats

PFD	Moldovan Party of Democratic Forces
PM	Prime Minister
PMDP	Movement for a Democratic and Prosperous Moldova
PP	Privatization Program
PPCD	Moldovan Christian Democrat Party
PPP	Power Purchasing Parity
PRGF	Poverty Reduction and Growth Facility
PSL	Moldovan Social Liberals
PSMUE	Socialist Party and the "Unity-Edinstvo" Movement Bloc
SBA	Stand-By Arrangements
SCM	System Capital Management's
SES	Single Economic Space
SME	Small and medium sized enterprises
SRF	Supplemental Reserve Facility
SSDD	Italian Society for the Study of the Diffusion of Democracy
SSR	Soviet Socialist Republic
STI	State Tax Inspectorate
STF	Systemic Transformation Facility
SU	Soviet Union
TACIS	Technical Assistance to the CIS
TAIEX	Technical Assistance and Information Exchange
TEU	Treaty on the European Union
TPA	Threshold Program Assistance
UCPB	United Civil Party of Belarus
UES	Unified Energy System
UN	United Nations
UNM	Georgian United National Movement
US	United States
USAID	US Agency for International Development
USSR	Union of Soviet Socialist Republics
WB	World Bank
WTO	World Trade Organization
YES	Yalta European Strategy

Notes on the Contributors

Elena Baracani received her Ph.D. in Political Science from the University of Florence in 2006, and is currently Research Assistant and Lecturer in European Union Foreign Policy at the University of Florence. In 2008 she won a post doc research grant in the framework of the "European Foreign and Security Policy Studies" programme funded by the Compagnia di San Paolo, and a European Union Institute for Security Studies Fellowship. She is the tutor for the PhD Programme in Political Science at the Istituto Italiano di Scienze Umane, and coordinator of the Italian Society for the Study of the Diffusion of Democracy.

Eugenia Baroncelli is Lecturer in Political Science at the University of Bologna. Between 2001 and 2006 she worked at the World Bank in the Development and Economic Research Trade Group in Washington, DC. Her most recent publications include: 'Aid, Trade and Development: World Bank's Views on the EU's Role in the Global Political Economy', in S. Lucarelli and L. Fioramonti (eds), *External Perceptions of the European Union as a Global Actor*, Routledge, London, 2009; and *Alle radici della globalizzazione. Una indagine sulle cause politiche del commercio*, Bologna: Il Mulino, 2009.

Valerie Jane Bunce is Professor of Government and the Aaron Binenkorb Chair of International Studies at Cornell University. She has also served as Vice-President of the American Political Science Association and President of the American Association for the Advancement of Slavic Studies. She received her Ph.D. in political science from the University of Michigan in 1976. She is the author of *Do New Leaders Make a Difference?* (Princeton University Press, 1981) and *Subversive Institutions: The Design and Destruction of Socialism and the State* (Cambridge University Press, 1999)-and the co-editor (with Michael McFaul, and Kathryn Stoner-Weiss) of, *Democracy and Authoritarianism in the Post-communist World* (Cambridge, 2010, forthcoming).

In addition, she is the co-author (with Sharon Wolchik) of a book now under review at Cambridge University Press: *Defeating Authoritarian Leaders in Mixed Regimes: Electoral Struggles, U.S. Democracy Assistance, and International Diffusion in Post-communist Europe and Eurasia.*

Roberto Di Quirico is Lecturer in Political Science at the University of Cagliari. He defended his Ph.D. at the European University Institute in 1998. He was Jean Monnet fellow at the Robert Schuman Centre for Advanced Studies and Post doctoral fellow at the Istituto Italiano di Scienze Umane in Florence. He published on various topics of International Economic History and European Politics. His latest publication is *L'Euro, ma non L'Europa*, (Il Mulino, 2008).

Mara Morini holds a doctorate in Political Science and is an Assistant Professor at the University of Parma and Genoa. She has lectured in several Russian Universities and she has been Visiting Professor at the European University of St. Petersburg. Her fields of research include party politics and political institutions in Russia, the consolidation of democracy in post-communist countries and the relationship between Russia and the EU.

Leonardo Morlino is Professor of Political Science at the Istituto Italiano di Scienze Umane (Firenze) since 2006 and director of Graduate School in Political Science at the same Institute since 2005. He is also the President of International Political Science Association (IPSA). He has just concluded a research on "The Influence of External Actors in the Processes of Democratization in Romania, Serbia, Turkey, Ukraine" and is directing another comparative research on "The quality of Democracy in Europe: a quantitative and qualitative analysis" on Western Europe and Latin America. He is the author or co-author of 25 volumes and more than 160 chapters in books or articles in journals, published in English, French, Spanish, Portuguese, German, Hungarian, Japanese, and Mongolian.

Manuela Moschella holds a Doctorate in International Studies from Trento University and an MA in Banking and Finance from the Institute on Banking Studies in Lucca. Her research work has focused on the role of the IMF in ensuring global financial stability, international financial regulation, and the relationship between economic ideas and policy making. Her most recent publication is titled 'When Ideas Fail to Influence Policy Outcomes', in the *Review of International Political Economy*.

Anastasia Obydenkova is a Garcia Pelayo Researcher at the Centre for Political and Constitutional Studies (Madrid). She has received her PhD in Political and Social Science from the European University Institute (Florence) and MA from the Central European University (Budapest). Her recent book is *Democratization, Regionalization and Europeanization in Russia: Interplay of National and Transnational Factors* (VDM Verlag: Germany Publisher, 2008).

Alessandra Pinna is enrolled in a Ph.D. programme in Political Science at the Istituto Italiano di Scienze Umane in Florence. She is working on her dissertation, titled *Democratization through Domestic Push and International Pull. A Comparison between Croatia and Serbia*. In 2009, she was at the Yale Graduate School as a full-time Visiting Assistant in Research at the Political Science Department. Previously, she spent a research period at the University of Belgrade, Faculty of Political Sciences, as visiting student.

Rosaria Puglisi is currently serving as political advisor in the EU Monitoring Mission in Georgia, and she has previously worked in different EU foreign policy structures in Western former Soviet Union and Kosovo. She holds a PhD from the Centre for Russian and Eastern European Studies of the University of Glasgow and she has been publishing on the economic and political transition in Ukraine and Russia.

Alina Stanciulescu has a Ph.D. from the University of Florence. At present she is a Post-Doc Researcher at the University of Cagliari. She is currently publishing 'Romania. A Personalistic Approach to Accountability' in L. Morlino and W. Sadurski (Routledge, 2010). Her interests include democratization, accountability and elections in Central and Eastern Europe.

Jonathan Wheatley is a Senior Researcher at the Centre for Research on Direct Democracy (c2d). He is also Lecturer at the University of Zurich and the Swiss Federal Institute of Technology at Zurich (ETH). In addition to publishing a number of scholarly articles, he has also published a book entitled *Georgia from National Awakening to Rose Revolution: Delayed Transition in the Former Soviet Union* (Ashgate, 2005), an analysis of the political regime in Georgia from 1988 to 2004.

Sharon Wolchik is Professor of Political Science and International Affairs at the George Washington University where she teaches comparative politics. She is currently completing a book on democratizing elections in post-communist Europe and Eurasia with Valerie Bunce.

INTRODUCTION

Elena Baracani

While the final quarter of the twentieth century has been characterized by extraordinary advances in the spread of democracy worldwide, during the first decade of the twenty-first century this spread has come to a halt and there have been signs of democracy erosions, even if, however, the third wave of democratization has not yet given way to a third reverse way. On the whole, it can be observed that while transitions to electoral democracy have largely been a success story, this has not been the case for the consolidation of democracy, leading to the instauration and consolidation of a growing number of different called regimes, that combine democratic and non-democratic characteristics[1] [for different labels and definitions coined for these regimes see Morlino, this volume], or to the return of authoritarianism.

This edited volume addresses the main reasons of this phenomenon looking at the empirical reality of European post-Soviet states – Belarus, Georgia, Moldova, Russia, and Ukraine. These case study countries have been selected on the basis of four main reasons. First, they are all post-Soviet countries, which have experienced since 1991, with the dissolution of the former Soviet Union (SU), a process of democratic change that, rather than leading to the consolidation of democracy, has led to the creation of hybrid regimes or to the return of authoritarianism (see Figure 1 for the regime trajectories according to Polity IV data). Second, these countries are not only still part of Russia's "near abroad", which means that Russia wants to continue to exert its political and economic influence on them [see Malfliet, Verpoest and Vinokurov, 2007], but they are also strongly dependent on gas

---

[1] In the following chapters these regimes will be called alternatively hybrid regimes [Morlino, this volume] or mixed regimes [Bunce and Wolchik, this volume].

imports from Russia, and, as a consequence, they might be attracted by this actor. Third, these countries can be defined also geographically and culturally as European, which involves that they could be attracted by the democratic or "normative power" model represented by the European Union (EU), and that, in the future, they might be offered the possibility to join the organization – even if this option is now excluded. Fourth, the EU's policy towards these countries is strongly affected by its relations with Russia, which are conditioned by its member states strong dependence on Russian gas imports.

Figure 1. Polity IV scores of Polity in the case study countries (1991-2007)

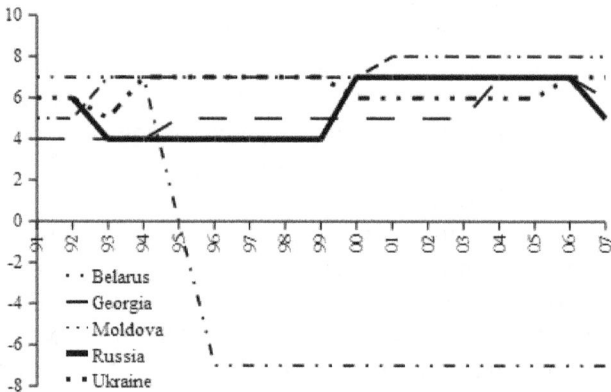

Source: Polity IV, *Political Regime Characteristics and Transitions, 1800-2007*

Note: The Polity indicator provides a single regime score that ranges from +10 (full democracy) to -10 (full autocracy). This indicator is derived by subtracting the Autocracy (AUTOC) value from the Democracy (DEMOC) value. Both the Democracy indicator and the Autocracy indicator are an additive eleven-point scale (0-10).

This edited collection is divided into three parts. The first part is dedicated to the definition of hybrid or mixed regimes and to the presentation of some main hypotheses on the paths and reasons that have led these European post-Soviet countries to the instauration of hybrid or authoritarian regimes. The second and third parts of the volume are dedicated to the role played respectively by external actors and domestic dynamics in favouring a certain regime change. These two parts are motivated by the fact that, even if democratization is mainly a domestic driven process, in a global context characterized by a growing interdependence, external actors have to be taken into consideration,[2] and these actors – as the EU, the United States (US), Russia, and the International Monetary Fund (IMF) – are presented in terms of the anchoring they realize with European post-Soviet countries.

Some economic and politological academic literature [Francois, 1997; Berglof and Roland, 1998; Ugur, 1999; Gros, 2001; Tovias and Ugur, 2004; Featherstone, 2004; Dodini and Fantini, 2006; Berger *et al.*, 2007; Di Tommaso *et al.*, 2007; Önis and Bakir, 2007; Coricelli, 2007; Magen and Morlino, 2008] has used the concept of external anchoring to evaluate whether and how an external actor has a positive impact on macroeconomic or democratic reforms of developing or transition countries. In the only systematic analysis of the impact of the EU's anchoring on democratic reforms of different countries at the Union's borders, external anchoring has been defined as a process in which national political regimes are subject to variably dense external linkages, pressures and stimuli influencing the conditions of democracy [Magen and Morlino, 2008: 28]. The chapters on external actors' anchoring analyze the most important empirical dimensions of this process, as institutional or political ties and economic links, which can positively or negatively influence the other conditions of democracy. It is shown that while the democratic anchoring exerted by the EU, the US and the IMF [see Baracani, Pinna, and Moschella respectively, this volume] on European post-Soviet states has at least the potential to have a positive impact on democratization dynamics, the authoritarian anchoring exerted by Russia [see Morini, this volume] aims at

---

[2] This means that external actors (and factors) are not the decisive ones in explaining regime change, but they are important as long as they contribute to transform domestic actors and factors in ways that can be conducive to less or more democratization.

hampering democratic developments.[3] It is interesting to observe that also a neutral actor on domestic political issues as the IMF can be considered as an anchor to democratization process by: (1) providing financial assistance and advice to its members, in particular on monetary and fiscal measures that help stabilize domestic economies setting the foundations for economic growth, which is usually associated with democratic forms of governance; and (2) strengthening domestic institutions, promoting good governance, fighting corruption, and reducing social inequalities, all activities which favour not only economic but also democratic developments [see Moschella, this volume].

As there is not a single general theory of democratization [O'Donnell and Schmitter, 1986],[4] I suggest first, to develop our research question – that is why some countries have not transformed their political regimes into democracies and have remained authoritarian regimes or have become hybrid ones? – into two more specific questions: (1) what are those domestic and external actors and factors (DEAFs) that, in each country and in a specific temporal period, prevent a successful democratization of the political regime? And (2) what happens when some of these

---

[3] We define the anchoring exercised by the EU, the US and the IMF as democratic as the linkages these actors have with European post-Soviet states favour, at least potentially, domestic democratization dynamics. While the anchoring exercised by Russia is defined as authoritarian as the ties this actor has with post-Soviet states hamper, rather than facilitating, domestic democratic developments. This is obviously also due to the different nature of Russian political regime, which is not a democracy and which has other priorities rather than the promotion of democratization in its near abroad.

[4] Huntington [1991] observed that each country, in a specific temporal period, can present a peculiar combination of conditions which favour or hamper democratization. Bunce [2000] proposed to distinguish between big and bounded generalizations on democratization. Grilli di Cortona [2009: 123-124] lists some general domestic and external conditions which favour democratization. A similar list is offered also by Somaini [2009, 71-75]. More specifically, the academic literature on hybrid regimes usually identifies a number of arenas crucial for the maintenance of this type of political regime: the electoral arena, the executive and legislative arena, and the judicial arena [see Ekman 2009: 8; Levitsky and Way, 2002: 54-58; 2009: 6-14].

DEAFs interact with each other?[5] Second, I hypothesize that the most important interactions (in terms of reinforcing or weakening democratization) are those combining domestic and external levels of analysis (see Figure 2).

Figure 2. DEAFs' interactions

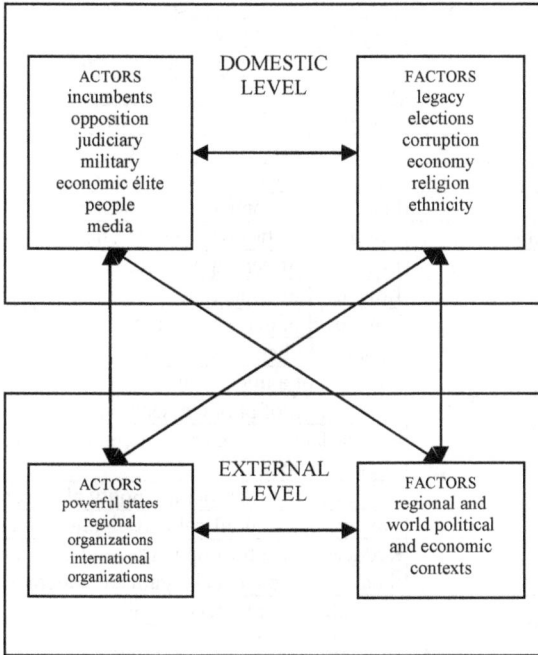

The following table lists the main domestic actors and in particular the specific obstacles they can pose – when certain conditions are present – to a successful democratization. These actors are: the incumbent political élite (the ruling executive or the ruling party), the political opposition, the judiciary (mainly the constitutional court), the military, the economic élite, the

---

[5] This elaboration of domestic and external actors and factors and their interactions is the result of a reflection together with Leonardo Morlino and of a joint presentation made during the 11th meeting of the SSDD on the obstacles to democratization.

people (ordinary citizens), the middle class, the civil society, and the media. And what are the specific obstacles they can pose to a successful democratization?

Table 1. Obstacles to a successful democratization of political regimes – domestic actors

Domestic actors	Obstacles
Incumbents	People's legitimacy to rule the country
	Ability to circumvent the opposition
	Not divided
	Granting of minor democratic reforms
Opposition	Weak and ineffective: unable to attract voters
Judiciary	Very low or lack of independence
Military	Lack of civil control of the military
Economic élite	Absence of a business entrepreneurial class
People, middle class, and civil society	Low level of per capita income
	Low level of education
	Low level of access to information
	Poor civil liberties situation
	Absence of a middle class
	Low or lack of public discontent
	Low or lack of support for democracy as the best form of government
	Low or lack of democratic political culture
	Low or lack of political participation and mobilization
	Reduced space for opposition and civil society groups (backlash or pushback against democracy)
Media	Not independent (freedom obstacles)

The incumbent (authoritarian) political élite may become an obstacle to democratization when it is legitimized by the people to rule the country, when it is able to circumvent the opposition, when it is not divided, and when it uses to grant minor democratic reforms in order to preserve its political power.

The loss of legitimacy of authoritarian regimes is considered by Huntington [1991] as one of the main causes that determined the third wave of democratization, and Diamond [2008] affirms that democratic transitions are made possible by a crisis of legitimacy – or moral title to rule in Lipset words [quoted by Diamond, 2008] – among authoritarian regimes. A regime can be defined as legitimate when "its people believe it is the most appropriate form of government for their country – better than any alternative they can image – and therefore it has the moral right to make laws, collect taxes, direct resources, and command obedience" [Diamond, 2008: 88].[6] This suggests that, in a hybrid regime, if the authoritarian incumbents' rule is perceived as legitimate by its people, it is very unlikely that the regime will move towards more democratization.

An example of the incumbent political élite ability to circumvent the opposition is offered from the Russian President Vladimir Putin [Baroncelli, this volume], who gradually got rid of several potential competitors, by closing media channels owned by Yeltsinites, reforming the upper chamber in the Parliament as an arm loyal to the Kremlin, controlling votes in the Duma, introducing the practice of appointing the governors of the regions (which used to be elected by the people), and making harder for small parties to enter the political arena by (1) raising the electoral threshold from 5 to 7 per cent, (2) raising the number of members each party should have to run candidates in the elections (from 10.000 to more than 50.000), and (3) establishing that a party must have branches in more than half of Russia's regions to be registered and participate in the Duma elections. Another example is offered by Moldova where the Communist Party engaged in a series of activities aimed at reducing the salience of political opposition, as the short banning of the opposition party – Christian Democrat Party – which had promoted the mass manifestations against the regime in 2001, and the threat of lifting immunity for the members of the Parliament that led those manifestations [see Stanciulescu, this volume].

According to O'Donnell and Schmitter [1986: 19], "there is no [democratic] transition whose beginning is not the consequence – direct or indirect – of important divisions within the authoritarian regime itself", and Diamond [2008: 90-91] agrees that divisions

---

[6] However, the lack of legitimacy can take place not only at the level of the people, but also at the level of powerful states and at the level of global public opinion.

within the authoritarian leadership constitute a central factor in democratic transition. Therefore, it can be hypothesized that a united and cohesive, and thus strong, authoritarian leadership is an obstacle to democratization. This seems to be confirmed by Wheatley statement [this volume] that in Shevardnadze's Georgia the emergence of a hybrid rather than an authoritarian regime was predicated by the fragmentation of the political élite. Moldova provides additional evidence to this hypothesis, as with the rise to power in 2001 of a united party – the communists – under a strong leadership – Voronin – there was a concentration of power into the hands of Voronin, who was at the same time President and leader of the Communist Party which had an absolute majority of seats in the Parliament, and the regime moved towards more authoritarianism [see Stanciulescu, this volume]. Another example of a united and strong political leadership that poses an obstacle to real democratization is offered by Georgia, where President Mikheil Saakashvili managed to have a compliant parliament and more or less control over the bureaucracy through his own informal networks and through his ruling party, and this situation allowed him to take unilateral steps that were not in the best interests of the country, as the decision to intervene militarily in South Ossetia in August 2008 [see Wheatley, this volume].

The granting of minor and/or cosmetic democratic reforms is another instrument used by the incumbents to legitimize themselves internally and externally and thus to preserve their political power and to continue to benefit of external support. An example of this is offered by Moldova, which has, in many areas, adopted laws according to European standards, but these laws have not been implemented [see Stanciulescu, this volume]. In a similar way, Wheatley [this volume] argues that in Georgia democracy has been a kind of "selling point" that the authorities use to portray the country as a western-leaning republic deserving international financial assistance and support against Russia.

The political opposition can also be an obstacle to democratization when it is weak, ineffective, or unable to attract enough voters. It can be weak and ineffective for many different reasons; one of these is when it is divided. The weakness and ineffectiveness of political opposition may be measured by the gap between the winner of the elections and the main opposition party or candidate, or the electoral difference between the incumbents and the opposition. For example, in the case of Russia presidential elections, from 2000 to 2004 the gap between the winner and the main opposition candidate increased from 24 percentage units (Putin received 53% of the votes while Ziuganov 29%) to 58 percentage units (Putin received 71% of the votes while Kharitonov 14%).

Another obstacle to democratization can come from the judiciary, when the formal judicial independence combines with some executive control, through, for example, the appointment and dismiss of judges, or when the constitutional courts behave as advocates of the current regime rather than as arbiters. An example is offered by the case of Belarus, where the Constitutional Court has the power to declare any law unconstitutional. This means that it could, potentially, cancel the laws passed by the President Lukashenko and thus balance his power. But rather than acting as an arbiter of the regime, the Belarus Constitutional Court has always been supportive of any law passed by Lukashenko [see Obydenkova, this volume]. Moldova provides another example of the executive control on the Constitutional Court through its politicization. Indeed, while in the period 1994-2000 the Court played an important role in mediating conflicts between the different branches of the government, this role ended since 2001 when the communists gained control over appointments to the court as, of the six judges, two are appointed by the Parliament, dominated by the Communist Party, two by the President Voronin, leader of the Communist Party, and two by the Superior Council of the Magistracy [see Stanciulescu, this volume].

The civilian control of the military is part of the main features of any democratic political regime.[7] Therefore, the lack of this

---

[7] For example, the civilian control of the military is one of the main dimensions of democratic rule of law according to Magen and Morlino [2008].

condition constitutes an important obstacle to democratization, as shown by the autocratic regresses occurred in Argentina, Brazil and Chile between the Sixties and the Seventies, and also by the experience of Turkey, where the military has in the past intervened in political affairs to protect the secular nature of the state. Among our case study countries an example of such an obstacle to democratization is represented by Russia which is characterized by a collusive system between the Kremlin, the army, and the intelligence [see Bunce and Wolchik, this volume; and Baroncelli, this volume].

The existence of a business entrepreneurial class is usually considered as a domestic condition which favours democratization [see for example Diamond, 2008: 98]. In European post-Soviet regimes this business entrepreneurial class is mainly represented by oligarchs who should be considered, potentially, as the main domestic agents for democratic change or at least as the only internal actors able to contain the transformation of the hybrid regime into a fully authoritarian one. The reason for this is that oligarchs after having collected enormous richness need to protect it, which is in danger when the winners gain unlimited power. In Russia, for example, the need of oligarchs to legitimate themselves made them fund opposition parties and movements to support pluralism. Another example is offered by Ukraine, where the oligarchs decided to coexist with the new regime emerged by the Orange Revolution and started to lobby for the consolidation of the rule of law. According to Puglisi [this volume] this shift in the oligarchs' position from supporters of the Kuchma regime into supporters of the new regime is motivated by their twin purpose of attaining social legitimation (as they were faced by public contempt for the murky methods used to accumulate their capital under the previous regime), and legal protection for their ownership rights.

The public is an actor that has been somewhat neglected in the literature [Ekman 2009: 8], but it seems to be the real motor behind any long-lasting process of democratization, as when ordinary citizens lack some of the characteristics listed in Table 1, it is very hard for new democracies to consolidate. As argued

11

by Diamond [2008: 20 and 27], following Mahatma Gandhi's words, the people represents the "spirit of democracy", as "democratic structures are mere facades unless people come to value the essential principles of democracy". This means that if democracy is not really valued by the people, it either won't emerge or won't last.

Civil society organizations (as trade unions, student organizations, churches, professional associations, women's groups, human rights organizations, ethnic associations, underground media, groupings of intellectuals, journalists, merchants, peasants, etc.) when present, independent, active, broadly supported, and mobilized by reformist élite, usually play a crucial role in the evolution towards democracy.[8] This is not the case of Russia, where current political élite have started a strategically managed rally of social consensus by creating and co-opting state-guided groups from civil society under the flag of "sovereign democracy". Specific examples of this are the creation by former President Putin of the Public Chamber in 2004 and the adoption of the law on NGOs in 2006 [see Baroncelli, this volume].[9] A similar situation has also characterized Moldova with the advent to power of the communists in 2001 which have created "parallel" civil society organizations to ensure themselves the support to government policies, and have discredited and discouraged participation in the independent ones [see Stanciulescu, this volume].

However, in his contribution to this volume, Di Quirico argues that, on the whole, civil society organizations – as in particular

[8] Diamond [2008: 158] affirms that "[a] spirited civil society plays a vital role in checking and limiting the potential abuse of state power, but it also sustains and enriches democracy. Civil society organizations provide channels, beyond political parties and election campaigns, for citizens to participate in politics and governance, to air grievances, and to secure their interests".
[9] The Public Chamber which should be a consultative body intended to channel inputs from civil society to state institutions in areas of public relevance, has ended up in being a mechanism to increase the visibility of non-political issues and an additional information gathering tool in the hands of the executive. Then, procedural and substantial requirements of the 2006 law on NGOs have drastically reduced the number of NGOs that are officially active on the Russian territory.

trade unions and NGOs – were only marginal actors in the democratization of post-Soviet regimes. He explains, for example, that the privileged links between government and former Soviet trade unions made free trade unions weak. He also affirms that, despite the role played by NGOs during the coloured revolutions, when social inputs were mobilized by reformist élite, they are not really relevant actors in defining domestic political dynamics, as most of them survive and work thanks to external support and cannot rely on the domestic support of a broad civil society. Wheatley [this volume] shares this position affirming that even if it is true that at certain critical junctures – as the Rose Revolution in Georgia in 2003 – society appears to mobilize, it is unable to do so autonomously, as NGOs represent a narrow élite and have few links with society at large. He adds [this volume] that the success of the Rose Revolution was not so much the result of a successful mobilization from below, but was instead the outcome of a carefully orchestrated mobilization from above by the most powerful dissident faction of the erstwhile political élite, that of the former justice minister Saakashvili.

The existence of independent media is a fundamental condition to define a political regime as democratic [see for example the minimum definition of democracy given by Morlino, 2003], and the presence of not independent media strongly limits democratic developments. Among European post-Soviet states, Belarus and Russia – which can both be defined as authoritarian regime – are the countries in which there is the strongest executive control on the media. In Russia, for example, pluralism in the media has dramatically fallen and it is now characterized by a *de facto* public control of the media (all television channels and almost all newspapers) [Baroncelli, this volume].

Not only these domestic actors – under the specific conditions indicated in Table 1 – but also some domestic factors or contexts – under certain specific conditions – can challenge the process of democratization. These domestic factors or contexts are: the political legacy, elections, corruption, the economy, religion, and ethnicity. Table 2 briefly indicates under what conditions these factors can pose a threat to a successful democratization.

Table 2. Obstacles to a successful democratization of political regimes
– domestic factors

Domestic factors	Obstacles
Political legacy	Authoritarian tradition and/or lack of pre-existing democratic culture
Elections	Not regularly held, and not free from excessive fraud
Corruption	Significant levels
Economy	Low or lack of economic development
	Country's mineral wealth/presence of energy routes
Politicization of Religion	Influence of religion over government decisions
Politicization of Ethnicity	Presence of ethno-political conflict

The first domestic context – the political legacy of the country [see Herz, 1982; Morlino, 2003; Grilli di Cortona, 2009; Bunce and Wolchik, this volume] – refers to the previous type of political regime, and the institutional structures and relationships it had created with its citizens. On the type of the previous authoritarian regime, and the consequences it has for the new regime, it has been noted that: (1) military regimes are more fragile, which means that the fall of this type of regime usually results in a democracy, even if it may not last; (2) hegemonic party regimes are more robust as when they cannot maintain their monopoly on power they prefer to be replaced by a democracy (rather than being replaced by an opposing authoritarian regime which is likely to exclude them) as they have a good change of continuing to be part of the political game and sometimes they initiate a new hegemonic party regime; (3) regimes in which power has been personalized under one individual are more likely to be replaced by a new dictatorship than by a democracy [see Geddes, 2007: 334]. Differently a previous experience of democratization or mass politics [see Huntington, 1991; Morlino, 2003; Grilli di Cortona, 2009] – especially when it is long-lasting and intense in terms of the structures and relationships established – seems to favour the consolidation of the new democratic regime. According to Baroncelli [this volume] the subsequent evolution of Russia from hybridism to a more consolidated form of authoritarianism is linked to elements of continuity in the long-seated tradition of *etatcratisme* and to the absence of a pre-existing democratic culture (in terms of absence of a pre-existing tradition in horizontal inter-institutional accountability) even in Russian pre-totalitarian years. In particular, Baroncelli [this volume] identifies the tradition of Russian self-redistributive authoritarianism as a key long-term element that contributed to orient élite's management of power in the 90s, their response to the financial crisis of 1998, and the ensuing deterioration of the prospects for Russian democratization.

Elections are obviously of critical importance for political regime change, and in particular democratic elections (free and fair elections regularly held) can be schools for democracy [Bunce and Wolchik, this volume] because authoritarians can either be defeated or persuaded to embrace more democratic priorities. In his contribution to this volume, Wheatley explains that elections are not truly competitive in Georgia as their purpose is not to give voters the opportunity to replace their government, but to confer legitimacy on the incumbent regime, as it is normally able to draw on the resources of the state to ensure victory. However, it should be recalled that even free and fair democratic elections can be a step towards authoritarianism, as happened, for example, with the 1994 elections in Belarus won by Lukashenko [see Figure 1; and Obydenkova, this volume].

Then, on corruption, it is usually believed that a high level of perceived corruption reduces the opportunities for democratization, as (1) it results in the enrichment of a few people (as the oligarchs in Russia and Ukraine) to the expenses of pensioners, workers and the professional middle class that are the main supporters of democracy; and (2) it creates a negative context for the attraction of foreign investments and thus for economic development which should favour democratic developments (for example Russia which has a very high level of perceived corruption, has also one among the worst investment climates in the world [World Bank, 2009]).

On the relationship between the economic domestic context and democratization the following two aspects should be underlined. First, as argued by Lipset in 1959 it can be expected that the richer the country, the greater the chance that it would sustain democracy [see also Boix and Stokes, 2003; Geddes, 2007: 317], as when people's lives are transformed by economic development, they increasingly espouse democratic values [see also Inkeles and Smith, 1974].[10] Indeed, it has been observed that in a number of countries, the success of authoritarian regimes in producing economic development raised levels of personal income, education, and thus awareness of the world in ways that jumpstarted democratization [see Diamond, 2008: 98]. All this seems valid even if economic development is not a sufficient and necessary condition for democratization, as today it can be observed that a surprising number of poor countries have adopted democratic systems.[11] The following figure shows data for our case study countries on Gross Domestic Product (GDP) per capita in purchasing power parity (PPP)[12] for the period 1989-2008. It can be observed that all economies have started to grow in the second half of the 90s and that this growth has been more pronounced for Russia and Belarus. It is not possible to say what will be the effect of this growth on the political regime, even if we should expect that, in the long-term, it favour the consolidation of democracy. However, for the time being, in Russia and Belarus economic development has been associated with a worsening of the democratic and human rights situation (see Figure 3).

---

[10] Inglehart and Welzel [2005] have predicted that "... China and Vietnam, with their booming economic growth, will experience transitions to democracy within twenty years".

[11] On this point Przeworski and his co-authors [1997; 2000] have argued that economic development rather than causing democratization, it reduces the likelihood of democratic breakdown. Thus, economic development increases the number of rich democratic countries even if it has no causal effect on transitions to democracy.

[12] PPP conversion factors take into account differences in the relative prices of goods and services – particularly non-tradable – and therefore provide a better overall measure of the real value of output produced by an economy compared to other economies.

Figure 3. Economic growth in our case study countries (1989-2008)

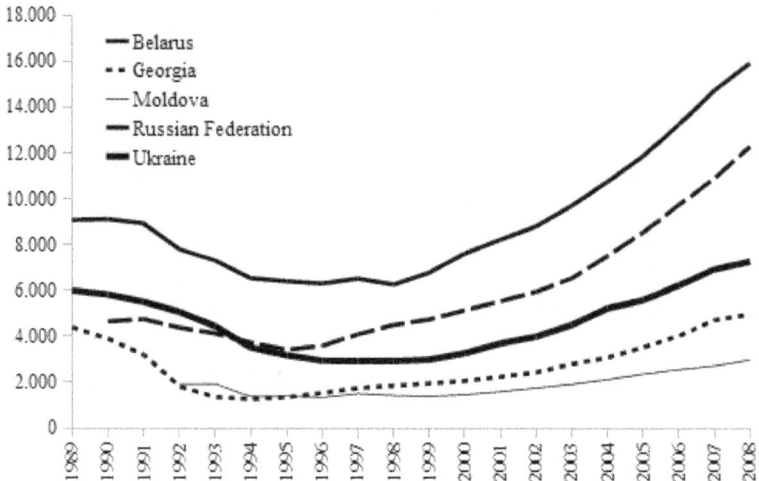

Source: World Bank, *Series on GDP per capita, PPP (current international $)*

Second, it has been noticed that when a country is rich in oil, gas or other mineral exports, this reduces the likelihood of democracy [Barro, 1996; Ross, 2001; Fish, 2002]. This happens for two main reasons. First, the so called "rentier states" use their rents from the sale of natural resources to distribute subsidies to large parts of the population and thus to maintain popular compliance with the regime [Anderson, 1987; Crystal, 1995]. Second, these countries are less vulnerable to external pressures for democratization, as they don't need external economic assistance. For example, in the case of Russia,[13] its economic recovery, thanks to the dramatic increase in gas and oil prices, freed Russia from the need for financial help, thus making external leverage for democratization ineffective.

Religion, when politicized, can represent another obstacle to democratization. With the expression "politicization of religion" I refer to those domestic contexts in which there is not separation

---

[13] Russia is the leading gas producer and the second largest oil exporter in the world.

between politics and religion. An extreme example of this situation is represented by an Islamic state, as the Islamic Republic of Iran. However, this context does not seem to be relevant to understand the evolution of the political regime in our case study countries.

The ethnic composition of society is another factor that can negatively affect democratization. When the society is deeply divided, with the presence of different ethnic groups, it is easier for an authoritarian regime to contain their political aspirations and make them coexist, while with the transition to democracy these groups start their political mobilization, which can also lead to the outbreak of ethnic violence. These ethno-political conflicts, if not solved, make more difficult for the state to define its boundaries, as argued by Bunce and Wolchik [this volume], and thus they can represent a further obstacle to democratization [see also Grilli di Cortona, 2009: 74]. In his contribution to this volume Wheatley explains that the SU managed the problem of ethnicity through the principle of ethno-federalism, which implied that the USSR was divided territorially into a hierarchical system of administrative units composed of union republics, autonomous republics, autonomous *oblast*, and national *okrug* (in descending order of autonomy). Autonomous republics, autonomous *oblast*, and national *okrug* were smaller regions deemed to belong to a particular nationality or ethnic group. Georgia, for example, contained in its territorial structure two autonomous republics (Abkhazia and Adjara) and one autonomous *oblast* (South Ossetia). With the collapse of the SU, at the beginning of the 90s, interethnic tensions both in Georgia and Moldova escalated into armed conflicts which led to the creation of *de facto* autonomous political entities in Abkhazia, South Ossetia, and Transnistria. The settlement of these ethno-political conflicts has been further hampered by the involvement of Russia. Therefore these conflicts, even if usually defined as "frozen", have not been solved, and this means that they might escalate again in the future, as happened in August 2008 in South Ossetia. This poses a further obstacle to these countries' process of state-building and democratization.

The academic literature seems to agree on the fact that democracy has increasingly become an international norm [Diamond, 2008: 136], and that democracy promotion has become a norm of practice within the international system [Gershman and Allen, 2006: 36]. However, obstacles to a successful democratization of a political regime can also emerge from the international system and in particular from its actors, with which the country interacts, especially when they do not recognize and promote democracy and when they do not exert a strong democratic anchoring (see Table 3).

Table 3. Obstacles to a successful democratization of political regimes
– external actors

External actors	Obstacles
Powerful states	Democracy is not an important domestic norm
	Lack of or low democratic leverage (pressure)
	Lack of coordination among democratic powerful states
	Lack of or low of democratic anchoring, i.e. political, economic, social and cultural linkages with democratic (powerful) states
	Dependence on or strong authoritarian anchoring with authoritarian (powerful) states
Regional and international organizations	Democracy is not an important norm
	Mismatch between democratic rhetoric and reality
	Lack of or low democratic leverage
	Lack or not sufficient incentives for democratization (or lack or low democratic anchoring)
	Lack of coordination

Even if obstacles to democratization derive mainly from the relations a country has with one or more non democratic powerful states, especially when it is dependent or strongly anchored to them (which means having strong political, economic, social and cultural linkages [Levitsky and Way, 2005, 2006, 2007]), obstacles to democratization can also originate from the relations a country has with one or more democratic powerful states, especially when (1) these actors don't exert democratic leverage on it, (2) there is not coordination among them, and (3) there is not democratic anchoring (which means that a country has not strong linkages with these democratic actors).

All countries considered in this volume are strongly linked and dependant, at least, on the economic relations (primarily the energetic sector) with Russia, whose sovereign democracy model [see Morini, this volume] allows us to define its anchoring on post-Soviet states as authoritarian, and which uses its economic strengths as a political weapon. Indeed, Moscow applies differential oil and gas tariffs to the former Soviet countries, which are inspired by political reasons. Among the countries analyzed in this volume, Belarus is the one to have the strongest linkages with Russia, not only economic, but also political and military [see Morini and Obydenkova, this volume]. This authoritarian anchoring seems to have played a key role in the establishment and survival of Lukashenko's authoritarian regime. For example, during the presidential elections of March 2006, Russia's decision to freeze natural gas prices for Belarus allowed Lukashenko to maintain impressive rates of economic growth as promised during the electoral campaign. Another example of the negative influence of authoritarian anchoring on democratization comes from Ukraine, when Moscow decided to withdraw its gas supplies to Kiev to curb the pro-European policies of the country after the Orange revolution.[14]

When considering external actors, it is also relevant to examine the role played by international and more notably regional organizations, as "with rising frequency and vigor, groupings of states have embraced democracy as an important regional norm … and have created mechanisms and taken actions to advance it" [Diamond, 2008: 136]. Among regional organizations, Diamond [2008: 136] observes that the EU has been the first regional body to take democracy seriously, and that no regional organization

---

[14] However, the economic (energy) relations between Ukraine and Russia is more complex, as on the one hand Ukraine is dependent on Turkmen gas supplies provided by Gazprom, but on the other hand Russia is dependent on Ukraine for the transit of the four-fifths of Gazprom's export to Europe (whereas in Belarus Gazprom bought 50% of the pipeline company in 2007, Ukraine refused to contemplate even a partial Gazprom ownership). However, once transit diversification projects are completed, the Ukrainian pipelines will be less important to Russia [for more details see Morini, this volume].

has had a more powerful impact on democratization than the EU (making reference to its model of democracy promotion through political integration).[15] However, obstacles to democratization can originate also from the regional level as when: (1) the organization, of which the state is part or wishes to join it, does not recognize democracy as an important norm (and consequently it does not pursue any democracy promotion activity); (2) when there is a mismatch between the regional organization rhetoric, in the field of democracy promotion, and its practice (as it won't exert any real democratic leverage/pressure on the target country); (3) when the regional organization does not offer worthwhile incentives in change for the respect of its democratic conditions (lack of democratic anchoring), or when these incentives are not perceived by the domestic leaders of the target country as sufficient in order to engage in the process of democratization; (4) when there are more regional organizations engaged in the field of democracy promotion which do not coordinate their pro-democracy activities in the target country.

An example of "soft" or lack of democratic leverage and its impact on the political regime is offered by the relations between Georgia and western organizations, such as the EU and NATO. Wheatley [this volume] explains that Georgia should be more vulnerable to pressures from western organizations than other post-Soviet states because of its self-proclamation as a European nation and its desire to integrate into Euro-Atlantic structures. But these organizations don't exert enough democratic leverage on the country, as EU democratic priorities listed in the European Neighbourhood Action Plan are jointly drafted [see Baracani, this volume] and in the case of NATO there was no meaningful democratic conditionality attached to a Membership Action Plan [see Wheatley, this volume]. Therefore, western regional organizations seem to contribute to the maintenance of Georgia's hybrid status rather than promoting democratization.

---

[15] Other regional organizations engaged in the field of democracy promotion are the Organization of American States and the African Union, while the Arab League and the Association of Southeast Asian Nations constitute notable exceptions to this regional trend.

A "soft" democratic anchoring exerted by a regional organization can be another obstacle to democratization. For example, Stanciulescu in her contribution [this volume] argues that a stronger hand on the EU's side in its monitoring of Moldova's fulfilment of its obligations as well as closer contacts between the European Parliament and Moldovan opposition, could help push through democratization, even in the absence of an accession perspective.

Table 4 suggests that obstacles to a successful democratization of political regimes can also emerge from the regional and international political and economic contexts in which the political regime operates. For example, a regional political context characterized by the absence of successful examples of democratization does not seem to favour democratization.[16] In addition, as shown by Di Quirico [this volume] international economic factors – as the 1998 international financial crisis which affected Russia – can also negatively influence democratization. For example, in this case the international financial crisis changed the socio-political equilibrium in Russia by destabilizing the role of oligarchs in restraining state power and thus contributed to clear the way for Putin's accession to power and the recovery of state supremacy in the economic field. In a similar way, on the influence of external economic shocks on domestic political dynamics, Baroncelli [this volume] argues that even if in Russia the introduction of competition in both the political and economic arenas will first depend on the will of political élite, much of these choices will be influenced by trends in economic cycles as oil prices and the current global crisis.

---

[16] The opposite is also true, as it is usually held that a region characterized by the presence of successful examples of democratization favours the spread or diffusion of democratic principles and practices in that area. According to Somaini [2009: 76] this dynamic of democratic diffusion explains the phenomenon of democratic concentration in continuous areas.

Table 4. Obstacles to a successful democratization of political regimes – external factors

External factors	Obstacles
Regional and world political and economic context	Lack of successful examples of democratic transition and consolidation
	Presence of successful examples of authoritarian transition and consolidation
	Regional/international financial crises

The following table provides some examples of the interactions that could occur among DEAFs and the likely results of these interactions on the political regime. One of the most important interactions is the one between the presence in the country of mineral wealth – as gas in the case of Russia – and external positive trends in oil prices. This interaction in Russia has led to an increase of Russian rents which allowed Putin domestically to buy popular consensus and externally not to be vulnerable to external pressures for democratization, and thus to consolidate the authoritarian traits of his regime. This example confirms the hypothesis made at the beginning of this Introduction that most important interactions, in terms of reinforcing or weakening democratization, are those combining the domestic and external levels of analysis.

Table 5. Interactions among DEAFs – some examples

Domestic actors and factors	External actors and factors	Likely results of interaction
The incumbents, and the opposition	External actors strategies of democracy promotion	The incumbents and the opposition may be strengthened or weakened by the external actors strategies of democracy promotion
Elections	External electoral assistance	The external presence should increase the correctness of elections
Country's mineral wealth	Positive trends in oil prices	No vulnerability to external leverage for democratization and consolidation of authoritarian traits
...	...	...

Part I

Definitions and Frameworks of Analysis

1

ARE THERE HYBRID REGIMES?
OR ARE THEY JUST AN OPTICAL ILLUSION?

Leonardo Morlino

The diffusion of democratization and the enormous development of related research in different areas of the world [Morlino, 2008] have recently aroused great interest in the more specific theme of the spread of hybrid regimes. As a consequence, the view of Croissant and Merkel [2004: 1] that "... the conceptual issues of diminished sub-type of democracy ... have begun the new predominant trend in democratic theory and democratization studies" comes as no surprise. Nor is the assertion by Epstein and colleagues [2006: 556 and 564-5] that "partial democracies" "account for an increasing portion of current regimes and the lion's share of regime transitions", adding however, that there is little available information about "what prevents full democracies from sliding back to partial democracies or autocracies, and what prevents partial democracies from sliding back to autocracy" and that "the determinants of the behaviour of the partial democracies elude our understanding". Nor, finally, is it surprising that a variety of labels have been coined for these regimes by different authors: "façade democracies" and "quasi-democracies" [Finer, 1970], *dictablandas* and *democraduras* [Rouquié, 1975; O'Donnell and Schmitter, 1986], "exclusionary democracy" [Remmer, 1985-86], "semi-democracies" [Diamond, Linz and Lipset, 1989], "electoral democracies" [Diamond, 1999 and Freedom House], "illiberal democracies" [Zakaria, 1997], "competitive authoritarianisms" [Letvitsky and Way, 2002], "semi-authoritarianisms" [Ottaway, 2003], "defective democracies" [Merkel, 2004]; "partial democracies" [Epstein *et al.*, 2006], "mixed regimes" [Bunce and Wolchik, 2008], to mention just some of the expressions and some of the scholars who have investigated what is denoted here by the broader term of *hybrid regimes* [see, in particular, Karl, 1995; Diamond, 2002; Wigell, 2008].[1]

In trying to gain a better understanding of the reasons for such attention it is worth bearing in mind that complex phenomena such as democratization are never linear, and cases of a return to more ambiguous situations have by no means been exceptions to the rule in recent years. Moreover, cases of democracies, even if minimal, going "all" the way back to stable authoritarian regimes have been much less frequent:[2] it is more difficult, though not impossible, to recreate conditions of stable coercion once the majority of a given society has been involved and become politically active in the course of transition. If nothing else, as Dahl noted many years ago [1971], greater coercive resources would be required. Furthermore, in periods of democratization, even if only as a result of an imitation effect, authoritarian crises and the resulting initial phases of change should be more frequent. Consequently, there are several reasons for the greater frequency of regimes characterized by uncertainty and transition. Moreover, if the ultimate goal is to examine and explain how regimes move towards democracy, it is fully justified, indeed opportune, to focus on those phases of uncertainty and change. But here we have a relevant aspect that – this time surprisingly – the literature has failed to address and solve: when considering those phases of uncertainty and ambiguity, are we dealing with an institutional arrangement with some, perhaps minimal, degree of stabilization, namely a regime in a proper sense; or are we actually analysing transitional phases from some kind of authoritarianism (or traditional regime) to democracy, or vice versa?

In addressing this key issue, this chapter will pinpoint the pertinent analytic dimensions, starting with definitions of the terms "regime", "authoritarianism" and "democracy"; discuss and clarify the reasons for the proposed definition of hybrid regime;

---

[1] See also Collier and Levitsky [1997: 440], where there is an exhaustive list of all "diminished subtypes", i.e. hybrid regimes, that are present in the literature on the topic.
[2] See below for more on the meaning of the terms as used here.

try to answer the key question posed in the title, which, as will become clear, is closely bound up with the prospects for change in the nations that have such ambiguous forms of political organization and, more in general, with the spread of democratization; propose a typology of hybrid regimes; and, in the last section, will reach a number of salient conclusions.

1 - A Widespread Phenomenon?

The simplest and most immediate way of understanding the nature of the phenomenon under scrutiny is to refer to the principal sets of macro-political data that exist in literature. Data has been gathered by international bodies like the World Bank, the OECD and the United Nations; by private foundations, such as the IDEA and Bertelsmann Stiftung; by individual scholars or research groups, like Polity IV, originally conceived by Ted Gurr, or the project on human rights protection undertaken by Todd Landman [2005], who formulated indicators of democracy and good governance, and also produced an effective survey [2003] of various initiatives in this field; and even by prominent magazines like the *Economist*, whose Intelligence Unit has drawn up a well-designed index of democracy. But it is not necessary to survey these here. Despite all the limitations and problems, which have been widely discussed,[3] for the purposes of this article the data provided by *Freedom House* have the insuperable advantage of enabling a longitudinal analysis. In fact, they have been collected since the beginning of the 1970s and regularly updated on an annual basis. These data can, therefore, be used to gain a better grasp of the phenomenon.[4]

---

[3] The main criticisms regarded the right-wing liberal bias of the Institute itself and consequently the compiling of unfair ratings for the assessed countries. Although basically appropriate at the beginning, these criticisms have been overcome and neutralized by the subsequent developments characterized by more reliable empirical results. This relevant conclusion is strongly supported by the high number of quotations and attention that Freedom House data have received in recent years. Even a quick look on the Internet will vividly show all this.

[4] Even some of the most interesting data, such as those of the *Index of failed states* (see www.foreignpolicy.com) or of *Polity IV* (see www.systemicpeace.org) were

In 2008 the Freedom House data feature 60 out of 193 formally independent countries (in 2007 there were 58), which have 30% of the world's population and are political arrangements that can be defined as partially free, the concrete term closest to the notion of hybrid regimes.[5] "Partially free" regimes have an overall rating ranging from 3 to 5.[6] They are present in every continent: 5 in Europe (4 of which are in the Balkans); 24 in Africa; 18 in Asia (6 are in the Middle East), 9 in the Americas (5 in South America and 4 in Central America) and 4 in Oceania. There are also 43 non-free regimes, which might be defined as stable authoritarianisms and correspond to 23% of the population,[7] and 90 democracies, amounting to 47% of the world's population. Overall, then, the partially free regimes exceed the non-free ones both in number and in terms of percentage of population. One further observation is that, with a few exceptions like Turkey,[8] most of the nations that fall within the "partially free" category are medium-small or small. Finally, from a European point of view, despite the intense efforts of the European Union, other international organizations and specific European governments, almost none of the Balkan nations have embraced democracy: apart from Slovenia and Croatia, Serbia is on the borderline while Albania, Bosnia-Herzegovina, Macedonia (which has even applied to join the European Union) and Montenegro are partially free regimes. The other European nation in the same situation is

---

discarded in favour of *Freedom House* data for the reasons mentioned in the text.

[5] See below for a necessary and more specific definition.

[6] It should be remembered that Freedom House adopts a reverse points system: a score of 1 corresponds to the greatest degree of democracy in terms of political rights and civil liberties, while 7 corresponds to the most repressive forms of authoritarianism as regards rights and freedom. The electoral democracies need to be distinguished amongst these. Formore on the definition thereof, see below.

[7] As is known, about half of this population lives in a single nation, China.

[8] The inclusion of Turkey in this group of countries has already prompted debate, and other analysts, especially Turkish scholars, place it amongst the minimal democracies, stressing the great and now long-standing fairness of the electoral procedure, for which Freedom House does not award the maximum rating.

Moldova, which borders onto Romania and Ukraine. However, before proceeding any further with the empirical analysis, it is necessary to define some terms, which will hopefully help to give greater precision to the current rather fuzzy terminology.

2 - Definition and Analytic Dimensions

Before proceeding with our analysis, it is worth stating that we prefer the term "hybrid regime" to all the others present in the literature (see above) as this, relatively speaking, is the broadest notion, whereas most of the others (e.g. "exclusionary democracy", "partial democracies", "electoral democracies", "illiberal democracies", "competitive authoritarianisms", "defective democracies", "semi-authoritarianisms") seem to refer to more specific models, mainly diminished forms of democracy. And it seems appropriate to come up with a precise definition of the broadest notion before going ahead and mapping out the diversified realities inside it.[9] In short, we are looking here for the "*genus*" that comes before the "*species*".

Moreover, an adequate conceptualization of the "hybrid regime" must start with a definition of both the noun and the adjective "trapped" between a non-democratic (above all, traditional, authoritarian and post-totalitarian) and a democratic set-up. As regards the term "regime", consideration will be given here to "the set of government institutions and of norms that are either formalized or are informally recognized as existing in a given territory and with respect to a given population."[10] Emphasis will be placed on the institutions, even if they are not formal, that exist in a

---

[9] Other terms, such as "mixed regimes", are also very broad, but ultimately "hybrid" was preferred to "mixed" as the former term gives more precisely the gist of the phenomenon where new and old aspects change each other , that is, it is not just a problem of "mixing" (see below for the definition and classification).

[10] A more complex definition is offered by O'Donnell [2004: 15], who suggests considering the patterns, explicit or otherwise, that determine the channels of access to the main government positions, the characteristics of the actors who are admitted or excluded from such access, and the resources or strategies that they can use to gain access. An empirically simpler line is adopted here, which is based on the old definition by Easton [1965]. But see also Fishman [1990].

given moment in a given nation. While they no longer configure some form of non-democracy and do not yet configure a complete democracy, such institutions still bear traces of the previous political reality. In addition, in order to have something that may be labelled as a regime we need an at least minimal stabilization. Fishman [1990, 428] recalls that regimes "are more permanent forms of political organization".[11] Otherwise, we "pick up fireflies for lanterns" by confusing a temporary changing situation with a more stabilized one, whatever the reasons might be. Obviously, the consequences of making such a distinction are very significant. In any case, we will totally misunderstand the entire situation if we fail to assess if there is or has been stabilization or not. This will be a key element of our definition, one that differentiates it from those existing in the literature, even the most prominent ones (see above).

The second point that can be stressed, then, is that a regime does not fulfil the minimum requirements of a democracy, in other words it does not meet all the more immediately controllable and empirically essential conditions that make it possible to establish a *threshold* below which a regime cannot be considered democratic. In this perspective for a minimal definition of democracy, we need at the same time: *a)* universal suffrage, both male and female; *b)* free, competitive, recurrent and fair elections; *c)* more than one party; *d)* different and alternative media sources. To better understand this definition, it is worth stressing that a regime of this kind must provide real guarantees of civil and political rights that enable the actual implementation of those four aspects. That is, such rights are assumed to exist if there is authentic universal suffrage, the supreme expression of political rights, that is the whole adult *demos* has the right to vote; if, there are free, fair and recurrent elections as an expression of the effective existence of freedom of speech and thought as well; if there is more than one effectively competing party, demonstrating the existence of genuine and practiced rights of assembly and association; and if there are

---

[11] He also adds that a state is a "more permanent structure of domination and coordination" than a regime [Fishman 1990: 428]. But on this see below.

different media sources belonging to different proprietors, proof of the existence of the liberties of expression and thought. One important aspect of this definition is that in the absence of just one of these requirements, or if at some point one of them is no longer met, there is no longer a democratic regime, but some other political and institutional set-up, possibly an intermediate one marked by varying degrees of uncertainty and ambiguity.

Finally, it is worth stressing that this minimal definition focuses on the institutions that characterize democracy: elections, competing parties (at least potentially so), and media pluralism. It can be added that it is also important, according to Schmitter and Karl [1993: 45-46], that these institutions and rights should not be subject to, or conditioned by, "non-elected actors" or exponents of other external regimes. The former refers to the armed forces, religious hierarchies, economic oligarchies, a hegemonic party or even a monarch with pretensions to influencing decision-making processes or at any rate the overall functioning of a democracy; in the second case, a regime might be conditioned by an external power that deprives the democracy in question of its independence and sovereignty by pursuing non-democratic policies.

To avoid terminological confusion it should be pointed out that the "electoral democracies" defined by Diamond [1999: 10] solely with regard to "constitutional systems in which parliament and executive are the result of regular, competitive, multi-party elections with universal suffrage" are not minimal liberal democracies, in which additionally there is no room for "reserved domains" of actors who are not electorally responsible, directly or indirectly, there is inter-institutional accountability, that is the responsibility of one organ towards another as laid down by the constitution, and finally, there are effectively applied norms to sustain and preserve pluralism and individual and group freedoms [Diamond, 1999: 10-11].[12] The term "electoral democracies" is also used by Freedom House with a similar meaning: an electoral democracy is understood as a multi-party, competitive system

[12] The other specific components of liberal democracies are delineated by Diamond [1999: 11-12].

with universal suffrage, fair and competitive elections with the guarantee of a secret ballot and voter safety, access to the media on the part of the principal parties and open electoral campaigns. In the application of the term by Freedom House, all democracies are "electoral democracies" but not all are liberal. Therefore, even those regimes that do not have a maximum score in the indicators for elections continue to be considered electoral democracies. More specifically, a score equal to or above 7, out of a maximum of 12, is sufficient for partially free nations to be classified as electoral democracies.[13] Thus, in both uses of the term, an "electoral democracy" could only be a specific model of a hybrid regime, but not a minimal democracy.

As regards the definition of non-democratic regimes, reference must be made at least to traditional and authoritarian regimes. The former are "based on the personal power of the sovereign, who binds his underlings in a relationship of fear and reward; they are typically *legibus soluti* regimes, where the sovereign's arbitrary decisions are not limited by norms and do not need to be justified ideologically. Power is thus used in particularistic forms and for essentially private ends. In these regimes, the armed forces and police play a central role, while there is an evident lack of any form of developed ideology and any structure of mass mobilization, as a single party usually is. Basically, then, the political set-up is dominated by traditional élite and institutions" [Morlino, 2003: 80].

As for the authoritarian regimes, the definition advanced by Linz [1964: 255] is still the most useful one: a "political system with limited, non-responsible political pluralism; without an elaborated and guiding ideology, but with distinctive mentalities; without either extensive or intense political mobilization, except at some points in their development, and in which a leader, or, occasionally, a small group, exercises power from within formally ill-defined, but actually quite predictable, limits". However, with respect to such a definition,

---

[13] The three indicators pertaining to the electoral process are: 1. head of government and principal posts elected with free and fair elections; 2. parliaments elected with free and fair elections; 3. electoral laws and other significant norms, applied correctly (see the site of Freedom House).

which identifies five significant dimensions, i.e. limited pluralism, distinctive values,[14] low political mobilization, a small leading group, ill-defined, but predictable limits to citizens' rights, for our purpose we need to stress the constraints imposed on political pluralism within a society that has no recognized autonomy or independence as well as no effective political participation of the people, with the consequent exercise of various forms of state suppression. A further, neglected, but nonetheless important dimension should also be added – the *institutions* that characterize authoritarian regimes, which are invariably of marked importance in many transitional cases. Once created and having become stabilized over a certain number of years, institutions often leave a significant legacy for a new regime, even when it has become firmly democratic.

In addition to Morlino [2003], other authors stress this aspect. For example, it is worth recalling the whole debate on "electoral authoritarianisms" [Schedler, 2006]. In fact, with this term Schedler [2006: 5] refers to specific models of authoritarianism – not to a hybrid regime – specifically characterized by electoral institutions and practices; in this instance, hybrid regimes are the result of changes that begin within these types of authoritarianism. Moreover, the attention given to authoritarian institutions is relevant for other important reasons. Firstly, the existence of efficient repressive apparatuses capable of implementing the above-mentioned demobilization policies, for instance security services, which may be autonomous or part of the military structure. Secondly, the partial weakness or the absence of mobilization structures, such as the single party or unions which may be vertical ones admitting both workers and employers, or other similar state institutions, that is, structures capable of simultaneously generating and controlling participation. There

---

[14] These values include notions like homeland, nation, order, hierarchy, authority and such like, where both traditional and modernizing positions can, and sometimes have, found common ground. In any case, the regime is not supported by any complex, articulated ideological elaboration. In other regimes, like the traditional ones, the only effective justification of the regime is personal in nature, that is, to serve a certain leader, who may, in the case of a monarch who has acceded to power on a hereditary basis, be backed by tradition.

could be distinct forms of parliamentary assembly, possibly based on the functional and corporative representation of interests (see below); distinctive electoral systems; military juntas; ad hoc constitutional organs; or other specific organs different from those that existed in the previous regime.[15] Obviously, there is also another implicit aspect that it is worth stressing: the absence of real guarantees regarding the various political and civil rights.

Limited, non-responsible pluralism, which may range from monism to a certain number of important and active actors in the regime, is a key aspect to recall. For every non-democratic regime, then, it is important above all to pinpoint the significant actors, for whom a distinction can be made between institutional actors and politically active social actors. Examples of the former are the army, the bureaucratic system or a part thereof and, where applicable, a single party; the latter include the Church, industrial or financial groups, landowners, and in some cases even unions or transnational economic structures with major interests in the nation concerned. Such actors are not politically responsible according to the typical mechanism of liberal democracies, that is, through free, competitive and fair elections. If there is "responsibility", it is exercised at the level of "invisible politics" in the real relations between, for instance, military leaders and economic groups or landowners. Furthermore, elections or the other forms of electoral participation that may exist, for instance direct consultations through plebiscites, have no democratic significance and, above all, are not the expression of rights, freedom and the genuine competition to be found in democratic regimes. They have a mainly symbolic, legitimating significance, an expression of consensus and support for the regime on the part of a controlled, non-autonomous civil society.

Having proposed definitions for minimal democracy, traditional regime and authoritarianism, it is now possible to start delineating *hybrid regimes*. They are more than just "mixed regimes", which, as defined by Bunce and Wolchik [this

---

[15] For another more recent analysis of non-democratic regimes, especially authoritarian ones, see Brooker [2000].

volume], "fall in the sprawling middle of a political continuum anchored by democracy on one end ... and dictatorship on the other end". As suggested by Karl [1995: 80] in relation to some Latin American countries, they may be characterized by "uneven acquisition of procedural requisites of democracy", without a "civilian control over the military", with sectors of the population that "remain politically and economically disenfranchised" and with a "weak judiciary". But again this definition only refers to authoritarianisms that partially lose some of their key characteristics, retain some authoritarian or traditional features and at the same time acquire some of the characteristic institutions and procedures of democracy, but not others. A hybrid regime, on the other hand, may also have a set of institutions where, going down the inverse path, some key elements of democracy have been lost and authoritarian characteristics acquired. Thus, it has to be adequately completed, for example, by including some of the aspects mentioned by Levitsky and Way [2002: 52-58] in their analysis of a specific model of hybrid regime (competitive authoritarianism), such as the existence of "incumbents [who] routinely abuse state resources, deny the opposition adequate media coverage, harass opposition candidates and their supporters, and in some case manipulate electoral results".

This discussion, however, prompts reflection about two elements. First, a hybrid regime is always a set of ambiguous institutions that maintain aspects of the past. In other words, and this is the second point, it is a "corruption" of the preceding regime, lacking as it does one or more essential characteristics of that regime but also failing to acquire other characteristics that would make it fully democratic or authoritarian (see definitions above). Consequently, to define hybrid regimes more precisely it seems appropriate to take a different line from the one suggested in the literature and to explicitly include the past of such regimes in the definition itself. The term "hybrid" can thus be applied to all those regimes preceded by a period of authoritarian or traditional rule, followed by the beginnings of greater tolerance, liberalization and a partial relaxation of the restrictions on pluralism; or, all those regimes which, following a period of minimal democracy in the sense indicated above, are subject to the intervention of non-elected bodies – the military, above all – that place restrictions on competitive pluralism without, however, creating a more or less stable authoritarian regime. There are, then, three possible hypotheses behind a definition taking account of the context of origin, which can be better explicated as follows: the regime arises out of one of the different types of authoritarianism that have existed in recent decades, or even earlier; the regime arises out of a traditional regime, a monarchy or sultanism; or the regime arises out of the crisis of a previous democracy. To these must be added a fourth, which is an important specification of the second: the regime is the result of decolonialization that has never been followed by either authoritarian or democratic stabilization.

If, to gain a closer empirical understanding of a hybrid regime, one develops at least the first and second of these hypotheses a little further – though the majority of cases in recent decades would seem to fall into the first category – it can be seen that alongside the old actors of the previous authoritarian or traditional regime, a number of opposition groups have clearly taken root, thanks also to some partial, relative respect of civil rights. These groups are allowed to participate in the political process, but have little substantial possibility of governing. There are, then, a number of parties, of which one may remain hegemonic-dominant in semi-competitive elections; at the same time there is already some form of real competition amongst the candidates of that party. The other parties are fairly unorganized, of recent creation or re-creation, and have only a small following. There is some degree of real participation, but it is minimal and usually limited to the election period. Often, a powerfully distorting electoral system allows the hegemonic-dominant party to maintain an enormous advantage in the distribution of seats; in many cases the party in question is a bureaucratic structure rife with patronage favours and intent on surviving the on-going transformation. This means that there is no longer any justification for the regime, not even merely on the basis of all-encompassing and ambiguous values. Other forms of participation during the authoritarian period, if there have ever been any, are just a memory of the past. Evident forms of police repression are also absent, and so the role of the relative apparatuses is not prominent, while the position of the armed forces is even more low-key. Overall, there is little institutionalization and, above all, organization of the "State", if not a full-blown process of deinstitutionalization. The armed forces may, however, maintain an evident political role, though it is still less explicit and direct.[16]

Moreover, hybrid regimes often stem from the attempt, at least temporarily successful, by moderate governmental actors in the previous authoritarian or traditional regime to resist internal or external pressures on the dominant regime, to continue to maintain order and the previous distributive set-up and to partially satisfy – or at least appear to do so – the demand for greater democratization on the part of other actors, the participation of whom is also contained within limits. Consequently, there are potentially as many different variants of transitional regimes as there are types of authoritarian and traditional models. Many cases could be fitted into this model, which says a good deal about their potential significance.[17]

---

[16] Despite her empirical focus on Central America the analysis by Karl [1995] is also useful to better understand the conditions and perspectives of hybrid regimes in other areas.

[17] As mentioned above, many years ago Finer [1970: 441-531] seemed to have detected the existence of hybrid regimes when he analysed "façade democracies" and "quasi-democracies". Looking more closely at these two models, however, it is clear that the former can be tied in with the category of traditional regimes, while the latter falls within the broader authoritarian *genus*. In fact, typical examples of "quasi-democracies" are considered to be Mexico, obviously prior to 1976, and certain African nations with a one-party system. A third notion, that of the "pseudo-democracy", refers not to a hybrid regime, but to instances of authoritarian regimes with certain exterior forms of the democratic regime, such as constitutions claiming to guarantee rights and free elections but which do not reflect an even partially democratic state of affairs. There is, then, no genuine respect for civil and political rights, and consequently no form of political competition either.

In disentangling empirical realities that fit the previously formulated definition of the hybrid regime from different transitional situations, we should add that there has been some sort of stabilization or duration, at least – we submit – for a decade, of those ambiguous uncertain institutional set-ups. Consequently, to avoid a misleading analysis of democratization processes we can define a hybrid regime as *a set of institutions that have been persistent, be they stable or unstable, for about a decade, have been preceded by an authoritarianism, a traditional regime (possibly with colonial characteristics), or even a minimal democracy and are characterized by the break-up of limited pluralism and forms of independent, autonomous participation, but the absence of at least one of the four aspects of a minimal democracy.*

As a way of stressing the differences with the existing literature (see above) and of making sense of the definition above, it is useful to emphasize the reasons that justify it: to better understand what hybrid regimes are, it is necessary to disentangle cases of transitional phases from hybrid regimes *stricto sensu*, where the extent of achieved stabilization has to be taken into account. At the same time it is important to grasp the ambiguities and the fuzziness of regimes in which features of both democracy and authoritarianism coexist, and in this vein, to consider the institutional past that is so important to them. But if this is the case, two key questions need to be addressed: 1. Are there actually cases of hybrid regimes, or does reality just throw up transitional cases, as might sound more reasonable?; 2. If there actually are hybrid regimes and transitional phases as well, what characterizes one and the other?; in other words, is it possible to elaborate a good typology of hybrid regimes and single out the recurrent characteristics of transitional phases? The remaining sections of the chapter will be devoted to answering these questions.

3 - Empirical Cases of Hybrid Regimes, or Sheer Fantasy?

A key element that runs against the effective existence of hybrid regime, that is, institutional set-ups that are neither democracy, nor authoritarianism, nor traditionalism is the expected low probability of duration. In fact, once some degree of freedom and competition exists and is implemented in various ways, it seems inevitable that the process will continue, even though the direction it will actually take is unknown. It might lead to the establishment of a democracy, but it could also move backwards, with the restoration of the previous authoritarian or other type of regime, or the establishment of a different authoritarian or non-democratic regime. Is this constitutive short duration or high instability confirmed by the Freedom House data?

Table 6. Transitional cases: towards democracy, authoritarianism, or uncertainty (1989-2007)

Transitions to democracy	Transition to authoritarianism	Uncertainty in a democratic context	Uncertainty in an authoritarian context
Brazil (9)	Afghanistan (3)	Bolivia (5)	Burundi (5)
Croatia (9)	Algeria (3)	Ecuador (8)	Congo (Brazzav.)
Domin. Rep. (5)	Azerbaijan (6)	East Timor (9)	(6+6)
El Salvador (8)	Bahrain (6)	Honduras (9)	Cote d'Ivoire (4+3)
Ghana (8)	Belarus (6)	Malawi (9)	Djibouti (9)
Guyana (4)	Bhutan (3)	Papua N. Guinea	Gambia (7)
India (7)	Egypt (4)	(5+5)	Haiti (6+2)
Indonesia (7)	Eritrea (4)	Philippines (6+3)	Kenya (6)
Romania (5)	Kazakhstan (3)	Solomon Islands	Kyrgyzstan (9+3)
South Africa (5)	Swaziland (4)	(8)	Lebanon (4+3)
Taiwan (7)	Thailand (7+1)	Venezuela (4+9)	Liberia (5+4)
	Togo (3)		Mauritania (3)
	Tunisia (4)		Niger (5+9)
			Yemen (4+5)

Note: The number in parenthesis refers to the years the country was assessed as partially free (PF). When there is a plus (+), it means an interruption in the continuity of assessment.

Source: Freedom House, *Freedom in the World. Country Ratings* 1972- 2007, www.freedomhouse.org.

If we assume that we are facing a transitional period when the "partially free" assessment is assigned for more than two years but less than a decade and there is a regime in the proper sense when the same/similar political set-up has been lasted for 10 years or more, and we consider all countries that were "partially free" between 1989-2007, we can immediately detect and differentiate the 46 cases of transition from the hybrid regimes.

Among the transitional cases (see Table 6), we can find four different situations. There are: (1) countries that after years of uncertainty became democracies, such as Brazil, Croatia and El Salvador, which had long transitional periods, and countries with shorter transitions, such as Guyana, Romania and South Africa; (2) countries where transition led to authoritarian regimes, such as Algeria, Belarus, Thailand; (3) countries where there is great uncertainty because a decade has not yet elapsed, but which have a democratic legacy, such as Bolivia, Ecuador and Venezuela; (4) countries where there was also non-stabilization, but which have an authoritarian past.

Table 7 surprisingly confirms that not only can hybrid regimes stabilize as such, but they are half (45) of the entire group (91). Here, if we distinguish between more stabilized hybrid regimes, that is regimes that have been "partially free" for 15 years or more, we have 26 cases where at least there has been a continual stand-off between veto players and democratic élite resulting in a stalemate, where all the main actors, especially the élite, might even find satisfactory solutions for their concerns, perhaps not ideal but nonetheless viewed pragmatically as the best ones currently available; or because a dominant power or even a coalition keeps the regime in a intermediate limbo; or, finally, due to the lack of any central, governing institution. Moreover, we can immediately distinguish a second category of 9 slightly less stabilized countries, at least in terms of duration until 2007. But we also have two smaller categories of hybrid regimes on the grounds of our assumptions: regimes that after a long period became democracies, such as Mexico or Peru, and regimes that became authoritarianisms, like Russia or Zimbabwe.

Table 7. Hybrid regimes (1989-2007)

More persisting hybrid regimes	Less persisting hybrid regimes	Hybrid regime + transition to democracy	Hybrid regime + transition to authoritarianism
Albania (17)	Bosnia-	Antigua &	Pakistan (10)
Armenia (17)	Herzegovina (12)	Barbuda (13)	Russia (13)
Bangladesh (15)	Central Afr. Rep	Lesotho (11)	Zimbabwe (12)
Burkina Faso (16)	(12+3)	Mexico (11)	
Colombia (19)	Ethiopia (12)	Peru (12)	
Comoros (18)	Mozambique (14)	Senegal (13)	
Fiji (18)	Nepal (12+2)	Suriname (11)	
Gabon (18)	Nigeria (4+10)	Ukraine (14)	
Georgia (16)	Sierra Leone (10)		
Guatemala (19)	Tanzania (13)		
Guinea-Bissau(17)	Uganda (14)		
Jordan (19)			
Kuwait (16)			
Macedonia (16)			
Madagascar (19)			
Malaysia (19)			
Moldova (17)			
Morocco (19)			
Nicaragua (19)			
Paraguay (19)			
Seychelles (16)			
Singapore (19)			
Sri Lanka (19)			
Tonga (19)			
Turkey (19)			
Zambia (2+15)			

Note: See Table 6.

Source: Freedom House, *Freedom in the World. Country Ratings* 1972-2007, www.freedomhouse.org.

Let's, however, consider the possibility that our assumptions (less than 10 years is to be considered a transitional phase; a decade or more to be regarded as a hybrid regime and more than 15 years as a more stabilized hybrid), as reasonable or practical as they might sound, are not accepted: Is one year's difference (from 9 to 10) enough to call the first one a case of transition and the second one a hybrid regime?[18] However, even if we do not make those assumptions, two basic findings have to be accepted and are worth singling out and emphasizing strongly: (1) hybrid regimes do exist, as the first column of Table 7 shows beyond any doubt; (2) the cases of hybrid regimes (according to our definition) that turn into democracies or authoritarianisms are very few vis-à-vis the other ones: 10 out of 45. In other words, at least the traditional, recurrent hypothesis that once some seed of competition is installed then it is difficult to stop it and some sort of democratic arrangement will come out is heavily undermined. On the contrary, uncertainty and constraints on competition (and rights) can last for decades: in the first column of Table 7 there 14 cases out of 26 where the hybrid regime has been in place for almost two decades. At this point, to try to understand the reasons that might explain all this, we need to look more closely at those regimes. The first important step in this direction is to develop a classification of the 35 regimes present in the first two columns of Table 6.

4 - What Kind of Classification?

On the basis of the previous definition, then, a crucial aspect of hybrid regimes is the break-up of the limited pluralism or the introduction of limitations on an open, competitive pluralism where previously there had been at least a minimal democracy; or the prolonging of a situation of uncertainty when the country in question gains independence but does not have, or is unable to establish, its own autonomous institutions (authoritarian or democratic), and cannot revert to traditional institutions, which have either disappeared or have been completely delegitimated. In all these hypotheses there may be (or there may emerge) veto players, that is, individual or collective actors who are influential or decisive in maintaining the regime in its characteristic state of ambiguity and uncertainty. These actors may be: an external foreign power that interferes in the politics of the nation; a monarch or authoritarian ruler who has come to

---

[18] On the whole, we still think that those hypotheses are reasonable and practical for our purposes. Above all, they are obligatory when trying to make better sense of the set of cases with which we are dealing.

power with more or less violent means; the armed forces; a hegemonic party run by a small group or a single leader; religious hierarchies; economic oligarchies; other powerful groups, or a mixture of such actors, who, however, are either unable or unwilling to eliminate other pro-democratic actors, assuming that in the majority of current hybrid regimes the alternative is between democracy and non-democracy.[19]

In the face of this variety in the origin and ambiguity of internal structures, four possible directions can be taken to understand what effectively distinguishes these regimes: the drawing up of a classification based on the legacy of the previous regime; scrutiny of the processes of change undergone by the nations in question and the consequences for the institutional set-up that emerges; a third line which, rather more "simply", considers the result, that is, the distinguishing characteristics at a given point in time – for example, in 2007 – of those nations that fall within the genus of hybrid regimes; and a fourth possibility, where the key classificatory criterion is given by the constraints that prevented a country from becoming at least a minimal democracy. The objectives of the first possible classification would be more explicitly explanatory, focusing on the resistance of institutions to change; the second, though this too would have explicative ends, would be more attentive to how modes of change themselves help to define what kind of hybrid regime one is up against; the third would be chiefly descriptive, and would start from the results, that is, from the characteristic traits of the regime; the fourth, which has explicative goals, would focus on the reasons that prevent the transformation toward a democracy. But before going any further, it is essential to consider how the issue has been tackled by other authors in the past.

Without making any claim to being exhaustive, one might start by citing the simplest solution, proposed by Freedom House, which took the third approach mentioned above. Using its own data, it broke down the ensemble of nations defined as "partially

---

[19] For a more in-depth discussion of veto players in hybrid regimes and in the democratization process, see Morlino and Magen [2009a and 2009b].

free" into semi-consolidated democracies, transitional or hybrid
regimes in the strict sense, and semi-consolidated authoritarian
regimes. The first type comprises regimes with an average rating
between 3.00 and 3.99, the second has an average total between
4.00 and 4.99 while the third is between 5.00 and 5.99 (see Table
6). Merkel [2004] also proposes an interesting classification of
"defective democracies". This category can be divided into
"exclusive democracies", which offer only limited guarantees with
regard to political rights; "domain democracies", in which
powerful groups condition and limit the autonomy of elected
leaders; and "illiberal democracies", which only provide partial
civil rights guarantees. Finally, Diamond [2002], who starts from
the more general notion of the hybrid regime as has been done
here,[20] proposes four categories on the basis of the degree of
existing competition: hegemonic electoral authoritarian,
competitive authoritarian, electoral democracy [see above] and a
residual category of ambiguous regimes. The regimes in three out
of these four categories fail to provide the minimum guarantee of
civil rights that would qualify them to be classified as an electoral
democracy.[21] Starting from the elementary fact that hybrid regimes
no longer have some of the essential aspects of the non-democratic
genus, but still do not have all the characteristics required to meet
the minimum definition of democracy, Morlino [2003: 45]
formulated another classification of hybrid regimes. First and
foremost, if limits are placed by specific actors on people's
effective freedom to vote or even on the admission of dissent and
opposition, and on the correct handling of the elections themselves,
one can talk of a protected democracy. By this term it is

---

[20] Such a regime combines "democratic and authoritarian elements" [Diamond, 2002: 23].
[21] It should be noted that Diamond uses the term "electoral democracy" with a different meaning to that of Freedom House, as has already been clarified above. For Diamond "electoral democracy" and "liberal democracy" are two different categories, while for Freedom House all liberal democracies are also electoral, but not vice versa. So, for example, according to Freedom House a nation like the United Kingdom is a liberal democracy, but is also electoral, while for Diamond it is not.

understood that inside the regime being analysed – defined by Merkel [2004: 49] as a "domain democracy" – there are powerful veto players, such as the army, strong economic oligarchies, traditional powers like the monarch, or even forces external to the country, which heavily condition the regime. Moreover, there is a limited democracy when there is universal suffrage, a formally correct electoral procedure, elective posts occupied on the basis of elections and a multi-party system, but civil rights are constrained by the police or other effective forms of suppression. Consequently, there is no effective political opposition and, above all, the media are compromised by a situation of monopoly to the point that part of the population is effectively prevented from exercising their rights. The notion of the "illiberal democracy" advanced by Merkel [2000] coincides with that of the limited democracy as presented here. The notion of "limited democracy" is also well developed by Wigell [2008] within a typology which still includes the "electoral democracy" and the "constitutional democracy" as sub-types of democracy, complemented by the "liberal democracy" as the type of fully fledged democratic set-up.[22] The main difference between the different proposals lies in the fact that, while also having explanatory objectives, the authors

---

[22] To build his typology Wigell [2008] develops the two well-known Dahlian criteria [participation and competition/opposition] [Dahl, 1971] into the notions of "electoralism" and "constitutionalism" seen at a limited and at effective stages. If there is a limited development then there are minimal electoral conditions, such as free, fair, competitive, inclusive elections; and/or minimal constitutional conditions, such as freedom of organization, expression, alternative information, and freedom from discrimination. If there is more effective development, then there are additional electoral conditions, such as electoral empowerment, electoral integrity, electoral sovereignty, electoral irreversibility, and/or additional constitutional conditions, such as executive accountability, legal accountability, bureaucratic integrity, local government accountability. The result is a four-cell matrix with liberal democracy in the case of effective electoralism and effective constitutionalism; limited democracy in the case of limited, minimal electoralism and limited, minimal constitutionalism; electoral democracy in the case of minimal constitutionalism and effective electoralism; and constitutional democracy in the case of limited electoralism and limited constitutionalism.

point to different factors as the crucial elements for explaining the real nature of these regimes.

Without going on to review the literature in detail, it is better to stop here and to take stock of the more convincing solutions. In this perspective a combination of the first direction, i.e. focussing on the legacy of the previous regime, and the fourth one, i.e. constraints that restrained a country from becoming or being a minimal democracy, seems to provide a more effective typology. Thus, if the criterion of classification concerns the reasons that prevent the transformation toward a democracy and the first hypothesis of institutional inertia is assumed in its entirety, what was sustained above can be reformulated more clearly: the types of hybrid regimes that might come into being depend directly on the typologies of authoritarian regimes and democracies that have already been established by focusing on the factors that prevent democratic change. As evidenced in Figure 4, the core assumption of this possible typology is that traditional and democratic regimes can, by virtue of their characteristics, give rise to different results, while it is more likely that the survival of authoritarian veto players points towards a single solution, that of protected democracies. In any case, the elaboration of this classification or typology leads us to propose three possible classes: the *protected democracy* and the *limited democracy*, which have already been described above; and a third, logically necessary one in which it is hypothesized that there are no relevant legacies or powerful veto players, nor are there any forms of state suppression or non guarantee of rights, but simply a situation of widespread illegality in which the state is incapable of performing properly due to poorly functioning institutions. This third class can be defined as "democracy without law" or rather, "*democracy without state*", as the state can be conceived as a "government based on the primacy of the law".

The second perspective, i.e. the focus on processes of change undergone by a country and the consequences for the institutional set-up that emerges, may be complementary to the first one. If the context is one of regime change and there is a hybrid resulting from a process of transition during which the characteristics of the previous regime have disappeared (as mentioned above), starting with the break-up of limited pluralism (the hypothesis here is obviously that of a transition from authoritarianism) – it is necessary to see what process of change has started and how, in order to assess and predict its future course. The advantage of this classificatory perspective is that, given that the regimes in question are undergoing transformation, the direction and possible outcomes of such change can be seen more clearly. So, if there is *liberalization*, without or with little resort to violence, that is, a process of granting more political and civil rights from above, never very extensive or complete, but so as to enable the controlled organization of society at both the élite and mass level, what one has is an institutional hybrid that should permit an "opening up" of the authoritarian regime, extending the social support base and at the same time saving the governing groups or leaders already in power. The most probable result, then, would be a hybrid that can be defined as a protected democracy, capable, moreover, of lasting for a considerable or very long time. In order to have some probability of persistence, such a political hybrid must be able to rely not only on the support of the institutional élite, both political and social, but also on the maintenance of a limited mass participation (in other words, on the governing élite's capacity to repress or dissuade participation) and on the limited attraction of the democratic model in the political culture of the country, especially amongst the élite. Another possibility is the occurrence of a rupture of authoritarianism as a result of a grassroots mobilization of groups in society or of the armed forces, or due to foreign intervention. If it proves impossible to move towards a democratic situation, even if only slowly, due to the presence of antidemocratic veto players, then a more or less enduring situation characterized by a lack of the guarantees regarding order and basic rights to be found in a limited democracy becomes a concrete outcome. In this dynamic perspective, the third solution, that of the *democracy without state*, does not even entail liberalization or the break-up of limited pluralism as such, in that there is no previously existing stable regime or working state institutions.

Figure 4. What kind of hybrid regime?

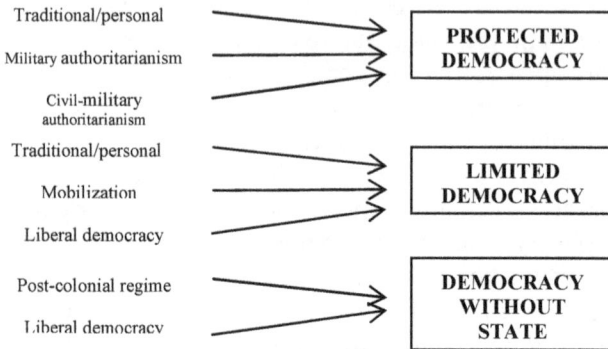

Traditional/personal	
Military authoritarianism	**PROTECTED DEMOCRACY**
Civil-military authoritarianism	
Traditional/personal	
Mobilization	**LIMITED DEMOCRACY**
Liberal democracy	
Post-colonial regime	**DEMOCRACY WITHOUT STATE**
Liberal democracy	

However, these modes of classification are *a priori* and do not include an empirical survey of the countries defined as hybrid regimes. In this respect they still fail to carry out one of the principal tasks of any good classification, which is to examine all the empirical phenomena associated with hybrid regimes and then arrive at some form of simplification that makes it possible to grasp the phenomenon as a whole as well as its internal differences. So do the three classificatory types outlined above hold up when empirical cases are considered? Looking at the *Freedom House* data and assuming that the regimes regarded as "partially free" coincide with the notion of the hybrid regime developed here, there seems to be a need for some revision and integration. Above all, it is worth examining in greater detail the ratings of the countries belonging to the category of hybrid regimes (Table 6) on the set of indicators relating to seven ambits that are important when analysing any political regime, democratic or otherwise: rule of law, electoral process, functioning of government, political pluralism and participation, freedom of expression and beliefs, freedom of association and organization, personal autonomy and individual freedom.[23] If

---

[23] The macroindicators for each ambit are, for the rule of law: 1. independent judiciary; 2. application of civil and penal law and civilian control of the police;

those ambits are matched with the elements that appear in the definition of the hybrid regime suggested above, the connections can be immediately grasped: all aspects of minimal democracy as well as the elements that are present in the definition of authoritarianism, such as limited pluralism and participation (to mention just the most salient ones), are *prima facie* closely related to all seven ambits. In his discussion of how to map political regimes, Wigell [2008: 237-41] also refers to the same or similar aspects.[24] Levitsky and Way [2002: 54-58] prefer to

---

3. protection of personal freedom, including that of opponents, and absence of wars and revolts [civil order]; 4. law equal for everyone, including the application thereof; for the electoral process: 1. head of government and principal posts elected with free and fair elections; 2. parliaments elected with free and fair elections; 3. existence of electoral laws and other significant norms, applied correctly; for government functioning: 1. government policies decided by the head of the government and elected parliamentarians; 2. government free from widespread corruption; 3. responsible government that acts openly; for political pluralism and participation: 1. right to organize different parties and the existence of a competitive party system; 2. existence of an opposition and of the concrete possibility for the opposition to build support and win power through elections; 3. freedom from the influence of the armed forces, foreign powers, totalitarian parties, religious hierarchies, economic oligarchies or other powerful groups; 4. protection of cultural, ethnic, religious and other minorities; for freedom of expression and beliefs: 1. free media and freedom of other forms of expression; 2. religious freedom; 3. freedom to teach and an educational system free from widespread indoctrination; 4. freedom of speech; for the freedom of association and organization: 1. guarantee of the rights of free speech, assembly and demonstration; 2. freedom for non-governmental organizations; 3. freedom to form unions, conduct collective bargaining and form professional bodies; for personal autonomy and individual freedoms: 1. absence of state control on travel, residence, occupation and higher education; 2. right to own property and freedom to establish businesses without improper conditioning by the government, security forces, parties, criminal organizations; 3. social freedom, such as gender equality, freedom to marry and freedom regarding family size (government control of births); 4. freedom of opportunity and absence of economic exploitation (see the web site of Freedom House). It should be borne in mind that the rating system here is the "obvious" one, i.e. a higher score corresponds to the higher presence of the aspect in question, up to 4 points per general indicator. The maximum score for the rule of law is 16, while for electoral process it is 12, and so on.

[24] More precisely, Wigell [2008: 237-241] includes in his list the minimal electoral conditions (free, fair, competitive, inclusive elections), minimal

group the aspects around four arenas of contestation (electoral arena, legislative arena, judicial arena, media). This, in fact, is correct, as research on democratic transition has shown that these four arenas frequently prove to be the most important ones.[25] However, a more detailed and precise set of indicators, as those suggested by Freedom House, seems in this case to be more appropriate for analysing the various key aspects of hybrid regimes, where the opposite process (from democracy toward authoritarianism) has to be included, whether or not there is the stabilization stressed above.

On the basis of the profiles for the 35 cases of hybrid regimes, a great variety of situations emerge. Thus, when a first implementation of a fuzzy set analysis is applied, that is a QCA method as elaborated by Ragin [2000 and 2008: esp. Chapter 4], the reduction of the truth table, built up from the seven different variables, leads to 17 different possible categories, with some of them including just one case. In other words, there are too many classes containing too few cases for meaningful classification.[26] One way of reducing the number of categories is to see if, when applied to the cases underneath the seven groups of indicators, some key conceptual elements emerge from the seven original variables. A factor analysis may help in singling out those elements. In fact, when applied to our 35 cases the result is very revealing. As displayed in Table 8, three components emerge with great clarity: a first component where electoral process, political pluralism and participation, freedom of expression and

---

constitutional conditions (freedom of organization, expression, right to alternative information and freedom from discrimination), additional electoral conditions (electoral empowerment, integrity, sovereignty, irreversibility) additional constitutional conditions (executive, legal, local government accountabilities, bureaucratic integrity). But here, in the perspective of hybrid regimes only the minimal electoral and constitutional conditions are relevant.

[25] For example, as regards the salience of the judicial arena, see Morlino and Magen [2009b].

[26] Please note that while the main purpose of such a method is explanatory, it is used here to provide a better classification of my cases. It is worth recalling, however, the existing connection between explanation and a good classification, although this cannot be discussed here.

beliefs, freedom of association and organization are grouped together closely; a second component where rule of law and personal autonomy and individual freedoms are also strongly connected; and a third component, conceptually close to the second one, where state functioning stands alone. When considered in its entirety, the lack or the high weakness of the first component can be considered a key aspect of *limited democracies* while the lack of weakness of the second component can be regarded as a key element of *democracies without law* and the lack or weakness of the third component the result of inefficient democracy.[27] If we consider that the second and third components are conceptually contiguous (see above), we can group them in just one category that could be labelled as *democracies without state*. But whether this is a good step to take or not must be decided by the empirical control.

Table 8. The three components of hybrid regimes

Variable	Components		
	1	2	3
Rule of law		0.856	
Electoral process	0.835		
Government functioning			0.818
Pluralism and participation	0.862		
Freedom of expression & beliefs	0.713		
Freedom of association & organization	0.865		
Personal autonomy and individual freedom		0.858	

Notes: Percentage of explained variance: 80.623%; Method of Extraction: Principal Component Analysis; Method of rotation: Varimax with Kaiser normalization. Only factor loadings > 0.5 represented.

With these fairly precise indications we can go back to the QCA method. In particular, profiting from the strong correlations that emerged from our previous principal component analysis, we can build a truth table where: (1) the lack or high weakness (0) of a new component with the four sets of indicators, that is absence/weakness of electoral process and/or political pluralism and participation and/or freedom of expression and beliefs and/or

---

[27] For details of the indicators see above, ftn. 23.

freedom of association and organization, shape a *limited democracy*; (2) the lack or high weakness (0) of a new component with the two sets of indicators, that is absence/weakness of rule of law and/or personal autonomy and individual freedoms, depicts a *democracy without law*; (3) the lack or high weakness (0) of a component with one set of indicators, that is absence/weakness of state functioning, depicts an *inefficient democracy*.[28] When the related truth table is applied,[29] the results are very meaningful and empirically relevant (see Table 9).

Table 9. Classification and cases of hybrid regimes (2007)

Categories	Quasi- democracies	Limited democracies	Democracies without state
Countries	Albania Bosnia Herzegovina Colombia Georgia Macedonia Madagascar Malaysia Moldova Mozambique Seychelles Singapore Sri Lanka Tanzania Turkey Zambia	Bangladesh Comoros Fiji Guatemala Guinea-Bissau Jordan Nicaragua Paraguay Sierra Leone Tonga	Armenia Burkina Faso Central African Rep. Ethiopia Gabon Kuwait Morocco Nepal Nigeria Uganda

First of all, there are several cases with at least a weak presence of all three components or characteristics. Evidently, in the light of these new results a new category or class is required, which can be labelled *quasi-democracies*. Out of the 15 cases of quasi-

---

[28] All the truth tables are available upon request.

[29] Please note that because of the strong correlations the specific group of variables (i.e. 1. electoral process + political pluralism and participation + freedom of expression and beliefs + freedom of association and organization; 2. rule of law and personal autonomy and individual freedoms) have been combined on the basis of the rule of sufficiency, that is, the existence of one component is sufficient to represent the class.

democracies, 6 are European, 5 African and only 3 Asian, with one additional case in Latin America (Colombia). There is also a sizeable group of *limited democracies*, as expected, and half of them are African. Third, because of the conceptual contiguity and limited presence of real cases (only Armenia and Morocco), the class of inefficient democracies can be merged with the democracy without law into a new more effective *democracies without state* with 10 cases; most of these (7) are from Africa.

5 - Concluding Remarks

In general, the analysis above has ended up moving in a different direction to the one considered in recent literature, a direction that is more consistent with that taken in an older, more traditional literature that appeared in the 1950s where the stress was on instability. The debate on democratization has led to neglect of this aspect, even though it is highly evident at an empirical level: the most significant problem in terms of specific cases is to ensure the existence of institutions more or less capable of performing their functions; one of the most relevant results of our analysis is that there are countries where a strengthening of the state and an effective guarantee of rights would transform several regimes into democracies. As far as the problem of state functioning and the rule of law are concerned, this theme has already been discussed by other authors, for instance Fukuyama [2004], and is still a central issue that deserves attention.

Moreover, there are a number of more specific conclusions. First, although literature to date has failed to be precise on this and there are only a few case studies, some comparative analyses and good insights, on the grounds of our analysis we can conclude that hybrid regimes are a substantial reality and can be considered an autonomous model of regime vis-à-vis democracy, authoritarianism and the traditional regime. Second, a good adequate definition of that regime was still required. In the proposal made in this article, the semantic field, that is the notions of democracy, authoritarianism and traditional regime, was fully considered and the relevant analytic dimensions emerged clearly. Third, in view of the absence of a good adequate definition of that regime, we made a proposal which takes account of the semantic field, that is the notions of democracy, authoritarianism and the traditional regime, and we hope it will be widely accepted. Third, once we went from an *a priori* classification, grounded on the criterion of the constraints to an effective minimal democracy, to an empirical one, a few changes and adaptations proved necessary. On the whole, even if different trajectories are theoretically relevant (see also Figure 4), all the cases that might be considered as hybrid regimes have either an authoritarian past or a traditional one. In other words, although they should by no means be discarded theoretically, the possibility of democracies reverting to some form of hybridism is not empirically supported by the existing cases.

For obvious reasons, i.e. the sort of data we had, the class of *protected democracies* did not emerge. However, for example, in cases such as Jordan and Morocco, which we would have unquestionably labelled as such because of the strong political role of a traditional power like that of the monarchy, our empirical analysis suggests that the inefficiency of the state (Morocco) or the limited guarantee of rights (Jordan) is more relevant. As regards this, the data and a different theoretical emphasis account for an unexpected result. However, the data clearly suggest that what counts in hybrid regimes is not so much the existence of a legacy or of veto players, but a lack of state or the effective guarantee of basic rights in the case of a working non-democratic state.

The *quasi-democracies* are a more relevant class than expected, with 15 cases, and this is perhaps grounds for optimism in terms of the future possibility of change towards democracy. In particular, in an international context characterized by cooperation rather than high conflict, a stronger role of international actors or of democratic governments is possible and seems to have some chance of success in a democratic perspective.[30]

---

[30] On this point, see also the results of research on the role of international actors in the democratization processes of a number of Europe"s neighbour nations [Morlino and Magen, 2009b].

Limited democracies and *democracies without state* are confirmed as empirically relevant classes for which different, contrasting elements need to be stressed: on the one hand, the lack of an effective guarantee of rights despite the presence of state institutions and, on the other hand, the lack of the rule of law and of a functioning state, with laws that are not applied because the judiciary has no effective independence, there is widespread corruption and the bureaucracy is flawed and inefficient. In these cases too, governments and international organizations have a potentially strong role to play in helping to strengthen the respect of rights and building state institutions, prior even to establishing democracies, in countries that have manifested a strong incapacity in this respect over the years.

As a final remark, the present analysis suggests that the proposed classification has some explicative potential and in this perspective seem more meaningful. However, as usually happens in this field of studies, in order to pursue this line of research, we need to return to the analysis of specific cases, either in the form of single case studies or a small-n comparative strategy.

2

MIXED REGIMES IN POST-COMMUNIST EURASIA: TIPPING DEMOCRATIC AND TIPPING AUTHORITARIAN

Valerie Bunce and Sharon Wolchik

> *"One of the most striking features*
> *of the 'late period' of the third wave*
> *has been the unprecedented growth*
> *in the number of regimes that are neither*
> *clearly democratic nor conventionally*
> *authoritarian"* [Diamond, 2002: 25]

1 - Introduction

During the Cold War, the eastern half of Europe was composed of nine communist states that featured nearly identical political and economic systems. With the dissolution of communism, the Soviet bloc, and the Soviet, Yugoslav and Czechoslovak states from 1989-1992, however, the region underwent a dramatic differentiation [Bunce, 1999a; 1999b]. The number of states in the area multiplied from nine in 1991 to twenty-seven by 1993 (with the addition to two more from 2006 to 2008), and the types of regimes multiplied as well [see Bunce, 1999a, 1999b, 2006, 2008; McFaul, 2002]. In particular, three types of political-economic systems emerged from the wreckage of the communist experiment. In a minority of cases, such as Uzbekistan and Turkmenistan, communism was succeeded by new, but still fully authoritarian regimes that maintained for the most part the economic structure of the communist era. At the other extreme and also in a minority of cases, communism was replaced by its "other"; that is, fully democratic polities that were quick to build liberal economic systems. This was the pathway followed by the eight countries that joined the European Union (EU) in 2004. However, the most common type of political and economic regime to emerge after the collapse of regimes and states was a mixed system that combined elements of dictatorship and democracy and that featured partial economic reforms that also straddled the liberal-illiberal divide [see, especially, Bunce, 1994; 1999a, 2004, 2006; Hellman, 1998]. Such mixed political economies formed in particular in Albania, Armenia, Azerbaijan, Belarus, Croatia, Kazakhstan, Kyrgyzstan, Macedonia, Moldova, Romania, Russia, Serbia, and Ukraine during the early years of the transition.

What explains the rise of mixed regimes? What has happened to these regimes over the course of the transition, and how can we account for their divergent evolution? The purpose of this chapter is to provide answers to these questions by comparing regime developments over time in four post-Soviet successor states: Belarus, Moldova, Russia and Ukraine. These four countries are of interest for several reasons. One is that they share a number of similarities. They are all new states that were once republics within the Soviet Union (SU); they all began the transition as mixed regimes; and they have become what two analysts have termed the "new outsiders" in post-communist Eurasia as a result of bordering the enlarged EU [see White and McAllister, 2007; and, for the European Neighbourhood Policy, see Fischer, 2005; Kelley, 2006; Beichelt, 2007; Schimmelfennig and Scholtz, 2007]. These four states also exhibit some continuity with the Soviet past. In contrast to much of east-central Europe, the communist parties in these four countries maintained their names and lacked strong reformist wings. At the same time, they managed to maintain an important political role after the "fall of communism". Moreover, the economies of Moldova and especially Ukraine and Belarus are closely tied to the Russian economy. Finally, just as all four states have a long history of authoritarian politics that predate the Soviet period, so they have been the targets of considerable support for democratic development on the part of both the EU and the United States (US) government, along with a variety of private foundations based in specific countries in the West [see, especially, Finkel, et.al., 2006; Fischer, 2005; Beichelt, 2007; Green, 2007; Van Wertsch and de Zeeuv, 2005].

These similarities, however, are joined with some differences – which make these four countries ideal for comparative purposes. Perhaps the most important difference – and one of the puzzles addressed in this chapter – is the variation in regime trajectories since mixed regimes formed in all four states at the beginning of the transition. While Belarus and Russia, like most of the mixed regimes in the post-Soviet space, have become increasingly authoritarian over time, both Moldova and Ukraine have bucked the post-Soviet trend by successfully resisting major authoritarian challenges and, in the Ukrainian case in particular, by making significant democratic progress in the aftermath of the "Orange Revolution" in 2004 [see, for example, Bunce and Wolchik, 2008; McFaul, 2004a, 2007; Åslund and McFaul, 2006; Kuzio, 2005, 2006]. These developments notwithstanding, unlike the mixed regimes of east-central Europe, which have all become demonstrably more democratic over time, whether through a more gradual process (as in Albania, the Baltic countries, Macedonia and Romania) or a more dramatic break with post-communist authoritarianism (as in Bosnia, Croatia, and Serbia), the successor regimes in Moldova and Ukraine have nonetheless remained mixed polities falling short of full-scale democratic standards. In this sense, while democratic progress in these two countries has been disappointing from the vantage point of the transition experiences of mixed regimes in east-central Europe, such as Slovakia and Romania, it is impressive from the political perspective of the twelve successor states (minus the Baltic countries) that make up the core of the former SU.

The analysis is divided into three parts. We begin by defining mixed regimes and highlighting some of their key characteristics. As we will discover, mixed regimes have a number of common characteristics, and these characteristics are well-represented in our four post-communist cases. We then address the question of why mixed regimes form – in general and in the cases of Belarus, Moldova, Russia and Ukraine. This discussion reminds us, once again, of the typicality of the post-communist region, while helping us define the point of political and economic departure for subsequent regime developments in our four countries. In the final section of the chapter, we trace and explain the contrasting political trajectories of Belarus, Moldova, Russia and Ukraine since the early 1990s. What is striking in this discussion is that, while all four of these regimes were tilting in a more authoritarian direction by the beginning of the twenty-first century, key elections in Ukraine in 2004 and in Moldova in 2005 moved these two countries away from authoritarian consolidation. Behind these elections, we argue, were some important factors that differentiated Ukraine and Moldova from Russia and Belarus – in particular, the design of political institutions in the early stages of the transition, subsequent patterns of political competition and turnover, and the role of international influences on regime developments.

2 - Mixed Regimes: Definitions and Generalizations

By mixed regimes, we refer to regimes that combine elements of dictatorship and democracy. Thus, mixed regimes fall in the sprawling middle of a political continuum anchored by democracy on one end – that is, a type of regime where elections are regular, free, fair and competitive, where political institutions are representative, and where there are significant civil liberties and political rights guaranteed by law – and dictatorship on the other end – or a regime where government lacks accountability to its citizenry as a result of the absence of competition, widespread rights, rule of law, and representative institutions. While mixed regimes usually share the commonality of having an authoritarian leader in office who governs within the context of at least formally democratic institutions, and while all such regimes feature degrees of political competition that give oppositions some opportunity to win power, they nonetheless diverge from one another and over time with respect to *where* they are located along the continuum running from dictatorship to democracy. Thus, some mixed regimes are more competitive than others; the independence of the media and the courts varies; legislatures can be relatively powerful or relatively weak; and laws can be more or less consistent across time, space and circumstances. At the same time, a given mixed regime can limit civil liberties more in one period than another; elections can be rigged in one round and more open in another; and the powers of representative institutions can also change over time. It is precisely because of such variations within and across such regimes and the importance of agency, as well as structures in shaping these differences across country and over time that we prefer the looser category, mixed regimes, to the more precise (but ultimately misleadingly precise) designations of illiberal democracies, electoral democracies, semi-authoritarianism, or competitive authoritarianism [see, for example, Ottaway, 2003; Levitsky and Way, 2002; Diamond, 2002; Zakaria, 2005; Carothers, 2002; and Bunce and Wolchik, 2008: Chapter Two].

There are several useful generalizations we can draw about mixed regimes that will help frame the discussion that follows. One is that authoritarian rule is rarely followed by the rise of full-scale democratic orders. Just as a long-term and global perspective on regime transitions suggests that authoritarian regimes in fact usually succeed authoritarianism [Hadenius and Teorell, 2007], so the experience of the third wave of democratization in particular suggests that the most common successor to authoritarianism has been in fact mixed regimes, rather than full-scale democracies [Diamond, 2002; Carothers, 2002, 2007a, 2007b; Roessler and Howard, 2007]. When judged from these comparative vantage points, the regime transitions that have taken place in post-communist Europe and Eurasia have been typical, rather than unusual. Thus, a "jump" to democracy, when authoritarian regimes weaken, has been both the regional and the global exception, not the norm.

Mixed regimes, moreover, tend to be unusually unstable – in several ways [see Goldstone, et.al., 2000; Epstein, et.al., 2006; Roessler and Howard, 2007]. One is that they have a pronounced tendency of moving back and forth along the continuum defined by the extremes of dictatorship and democracy, with the latter two types of regimes far more "sticky" over time than regimes that fall in between these two poles. The other is that such regimes, again in comparison with dictatorships and democracy, tend to stand out with respect to their political deficits – in particular, the weakness of their states, their lacklustre economic performance, and their unusually high levels of political disorder. For example, in one study it was found that mixed regimes were seven times as likely to become failed states as either fully democratic or fully autocratic regimes [Goldstone, *et.al.*, 2000]. What these difficulties suggest is that mixed regimes are distinctive in their failure to achieve a political equilibrium – which is another reason why we are uncomfortable with exercises that try to draw refined distinctions among types of mixed regimes. Because of their fluidity, they are less "regime-ish" than most regimes, and their fluid structure means that specific events, such as elections, and the role of agency, such as the goals and calculations of individual leaders, can play an unusually important role in shaping regime developments over time.

Once again, the post-communist experience seems to be relatively typical of global patterns with respect to these indicators of problematic political and economic performance. For example, the worst-performing economies in the post-communist region have been mixed regimes [see, for example, Bunce, 1999a; Frye, 2002]. Poor economic performance was certainly typical, moreover, of three of the countries of interest in this chapter, with Belarus the one exception. Indeed, together with Serbia and Georgia, Ukraine, Russia and Moldova exhibit the worst economic performance in the entire region.

Moreover, most of the mixed regimes in the region have confronted the problem of fluid state borders. This is because their leaders tried to expand the size of the state as the larger state within which they were encased began to crumble (Croatia, Serbia, and Armenia); neighbouring countries have challenged existing borders (Azerbaijan and Macedonia); regional leaders within the state have tried to continue the processes of state dissolution by pursuing secessionist political agendas (Bosnia, Georgia, Moldova, Russia, and Ukraine); or because it is in the interest of leaders to encourage tensions between the state and troublesome regions in order to consolidate political power and divert attention from policy failures [which was the story of Russian Presidents Yeltsin and Putin in Chechnya and is the current situation with respect to relations between the Georgian President Mikheil Saakashvili and Abkhazia and Southern Ossetia [see Bunce and Watts, 2005; Bunce, 2006; Protsyk, 2006]. While taking place in every case early in the processes of regime and state transition, many of these challenges to the integrity of the state – with the recent exception of Kosovo – have congealed into "frozen conflicts" that continue to this day to block solidification of state boundaries.

A final generalization about mixed regimes is that they are more likely than authoritarian regimes to give way to fully democratic polities [Hadenius and Teorell, 2007; Teorell and Hadenius, 2007]. This is not surprising, if we understand mixed regimes to be in effect a "halfway house" to democracy – in contrast to their fully authoritarian counterparts. Moreover, mixed regimes provide opportunities for democratic change, because they feature representative institutions; they hold regular and at least semi-competitive elections; their very absence of structure means that they resist attempts by authoritarians to institutionalize their powers; and they have often been the focus of considerable external democracy promotion efforts [see Bunce and Wolchik, 2006; Finkel, et.al., 2006; Schedler, 2006; Schedler, 2007; Hale, 2005, 2006; Levitsky and Way, 2007].

However, there are, nonetheless, sizeable constraints on democratization in mixed regime settings – constraints that have been underplayed, especially in studies of democratization in east-central Europe, and that appear quite applicable to the experiences of Moldova, Russia and Ukraine in particular [see, especially, Bunce and Wolchik, 2008: Chapter 2]. At the most general level, as Steven Levitsky and Lucan Way [2007: 28] have argued, such regimes "…vary considerably in their ability to control civil society, co-opt or divide oppositions, repress protest, and steal elections". On a more specific level, the mixed character of these regimes, in combination with the resources enjoyed by authoritarian leaders, often translate into the construction of a powerful political apparatus supporting authoritarian rule and quite fragmented oppositions unable to make strong bids for political power [see, especially, Way, 2005;

Way, 2005, 2008; Hale, 2005, 2006; Silitski, 2005]. In addition, authoritarian leaders in such regimes are in a good position, because of these assets, to control the media, rig elections, and demobilize their opponents. It is also the case, but often ignored, that such leaders can be popular or at least more popular than oppositions that in many countries are widely viewed by the citizenry as divided, corrupt and incompetent. Indeed, it is easy for citizens to argue that, while both authoritarians and democrats are corrupt, at least authoritarians know how to coalesce and make durable governments.

There is also a more general constraint on political change. Mixed regimes, we must remember, are often mixed for some very good reasons. The combination of dictatorial and democratic features often speaks to the existence of important and durable divisions within the citizenry regarding national identities and regime-type preferences and, at the same time, the value of forming various external alliances that would push such regimes in a more democratic or a more authoritarian direction [see, for example, White and McAllister, 2007 on Ukraine, Belarus and Russia]. Such cleavages, moreover, play out in the party system, with the common effect of producing the multiplication of parties and their resistance to forming broad coalitions willing and able to challenge authoritarian incumbents. At the same time, most mixed regimes have a long history of authoritarian politics that has made its mark on the political culture, the ways political institutions operate, and the size, goals, and organization of the opposition.

Challenging the power of authoritarian leaders in mixed regimes, therefore, is difficult. This has certainly been the case in all four of our countries, especially in Belarus and Russia, where incumbent élite, such as Lukashenko and Putin, have had the "double" advantages of building strong institutions to back their power and significant personal popularity. However, while the first could be said to also apply to Ukraine under Kuchma, the second was not, and this provided an opportunity for Yushchenko to challenge the power of his former patron. This opportunity, however, was "earned" by Yushchenko and his allies in a hard political struggle for power in 2004. Here, Larry Diamond's observation [2002: 24] is a telling one, whether we focus on Ukraine or on Belarus and Russia. The defeat of authoritarian leaders in mixed regimes "... requires a level of opposition mobilization, unity, skill and heroism for beyond what would normally be required for victory in a democracy".

However, perhaps the biggest problem for democratic development in mixed regimes – and one that is particularly relevant to the four cases analyzed in this chapter – is one that Dankwart Rustow [1970] noted thirty-eight years ago. Sustained democratic development is unlikely in the absence of a viable state and a popular consensus around the definition and the geographical reach of the nation, as well as the rights associated with membership in national communities [Bunce, 2005a, 2005b, 2006; Bunce and Watts, 2005]. If nation and state issues are not settled, politics can become extraordinarily divisive; liberal constituencies can be divided and therefore ineffective; and the state can become too weak to provide a minimal level of political order [see, especially, Gagnon, 2004; Bunce, 1999b, 2005a, 2005b]. This is a story, in a nutshell, of all of the countries of interest in this study, along with Georgia, Macedonia, and Serbia in particular. This is hardly surprising, since the countries of interest here are new states with diverse populations that tend to be geographically concentrated and that tend to lack as well a history of stateness.

It is also important to recognize that debates about the nation are costly in terms of both political stability and democratic development, because such discussions are invariably exclusionary [see Marx, 2003]. In practice, this means that such debates create security dilemmas for minorities, especially in the post-communist context where many minorities had earlier been protected, if not courted by the larger state that dissolved. This was precisely what happened, for example, in the cases of Transnistria in Moldova and Crimea in Ukraine. Such debates, moreover, have a pronounced tendency of privileging illiberal nationalist discourse in the struggles for political power that are unleashed by state disintegration and regime and state formation.

3 - Origins of Mixed Regimes

One puzzle in the study of democratization is explaining the rise of so many mixed regimes – in the third wave in general and in the particular case of the post-communist region. There are four lines of argument that we can propose, with each of them, it is important to emphasize, quite applicable to the formation of mixed regimes in the early years of the transition in Belarus, Moldova, Russia and Ukraine. One explanation focuses on historical legacies. Most mixed regimes in the world, including the four of interest in this chapter, have a long history of authoritarianism, whereas the most successful cases of democratization during the third wave have often involved re-democratization. This contrast is one reason, for instance, why mixed regimes are so much more prevalent in Sub-Saharan Africa and the post-communist region than in Latin America. Long experience with authoritarian rule can compromise subsequent democratic development by bequeathing a weak tradition in rule of law, an independent media, well-defined political parties anchored in socio-economic cleavages, robust civil society, and strong political institutions; a mass political culture that can embrace democracy in surprisingly rapid fashion, but nonetheless exhibit some ambivalence about liberal values; and an opposition that is weak, divided and often politically compromised [see, especially, Howard, 2002; Gelman, 2005; Stoner-Weiss, 2001; Rose, 2000; Gibson, 2001a, 2001b; Hale, 2005b]. In addition, many authoritarian regimes stayed in power by building institutions that divided publics in general and the opposition in particular and that played groups off against one another. As the war in Iraq, for example, reminds us, with liberalization of politics, especially in the absence of strong institutions, the short-term result can be heightened conflicts among citizens, as well as between the government and various groups. Such conflicts are all the more likely when there is a widespread perception that short-term bargaining outcomes will have powerful and lasting effects on the future character of the regime and the power and resources of individuals and groups in the state and the economy.

Mixed regimes also tend to form in contexts, common in much of Sub-Saharan Africa and post-Soviet Eurasia and the Balkans, where there are severe difficulties involved in defining the nation and solidifying the boundaries of the state. While these difficulties, as already noted, undermine democratic development, they also work against the consolidation of dictatorship – largely because continuing contestation over the nation and the state weaken the ability of authoritarian leaders to consolidate their powers as a result of contentious politics at home, fragmented states, and threats to state sovereignty abroad. Thus, mixed regimes represent a compromise between the limitations of both democracy and dictatorship in a transitional context where there has developed: 1) an explosion of rival definitions of the nation; 2) weakened and often brand new states that have little historical precedent and that are composed of multiple national communities with very different experiences during authoritarian rule; 3) increasingly assertive majorities committed to "nation-building," which in practice usually meant homogenization of the nation in their own image; 4) increasingly nervous minorities that are usually geographically concentrated, live on the perimeters of the state, have a recent history of privileged status under the old regime and state, and that often serve as majorities in neighbouring states. These dynamics in turn lead to other outcomes associated with mixed regimes, as noted earlier; that is, the syndrome of weak states, secessionist regions, failing economies, and unstable governments and more generally politics.

While severe in all four of our cases, the problems with nation and state formation nonetheless varied [Way, 2005a]. In Belarus, a state tradition was lacking, and ethnic diversity combined with both a strong connection to the Russian state and Russian identity (especially in terms of language and culture). With independence, therefore, Belarusian identity was weak [Marples, 1999]. However, unlike the other three countries, Belarus did not face secessionist pressures or economic collapse. Put simply: it had a state because of its republican status and the dissolution of the SU, but a limited sense of the community in whose name the state existed [Ioffe, 2004; Silitski, 2007b; Kunker, 2000].

In the Moldovan transition, a complex political struggle unfolded that included minorities seeking independence or in some cases a return to the Russian state and a majority that was also divided in this case over the question of whether to embrace a distinctive Moldovan identity and an independent state or merge with Romania [King, 2000; Cashu, 2005; March and Herb, 2006; Mungiu-Pippidi, 2007]. In this sense, Moldova featured virtually every alternative available with respect to policies addressing the definition of the nation and the state.

In Ukraine, the Russian/Ukrainian divide (which was complicated, as in Belarus, by overlapping use of the Russian language and identification with Russian culture and the Soviet state) combined with three other divides, making the national [and linguistic and religious] distinction quite potent in politics [Kubicek, 2000; Way, 2005a, 2005b]. One divide was geography, with western and north-western Ukraine counter-posed to the east and south. Another was economic interests, with the corridor abutting Russia an area of heavy industry that was tightly integrated with the Russian economy versus the rest of Ukraine. Finally, there were significant differences in historical experiences. Western Ukraine had been part of the Habsburg, not Russian empire; it was added to the SU during World War II; and Crimea, a largely Russian area in the far south, was in turn added to Ukraine in a capricious decision by Nikita Khrushchev in the 1950s. Like Moldova and the Transnistria issue, moreover, there were secessionist pressures on the new Ukrainian state – in this instance, from Crimea (with such demands also appearing, more generally, in eastern Ukraine in response to the Orange Revolution in 2004).

Finally, although the Russian federation was far more homogeneous in ethnic terms (though more heterogeneous along religious lines) than the other three countries, it faced nonetheless considerable secessionist pressures from Chechnya, as well as Tatarstan – with the former leading to two unusually violent wars and the latter leading to the establishment, thanks to the clever actions of Shamiev, of significant local autonomy [Bunce, 2004b]. In addition, Russian identity was closely tied to Soviet identity, the role of the SU as a super power, and, more generally, the communist experiment.

This leads to a third explanation for the rise of mixed regimes: the impact of international factors. As Steve Levitsky and Lucan Way [2007, 2006] have argued, sustainable and full-scale democracies are more likely to succeed authoritarian politics where countries are located close to well-established democratic polities – what they term linkage – and where democratic change is in the clear interest of the West – what they term leverage. Just as linkage speaks to high levels of interaction between the two sets of countries as a result of shared borders and commonalities in history, culture and institutional forms, so leverage is an important contributor to democratic change because of the incentives and resources made available to leaders and citizens in strategically-located countries. Such incentives and resources, moreover, can tip the balance of domestic politics in countries in transition in the direction of empowering supporters of democratic change against their opponents [see, especially, Vachudova, 2005; Kubicek, 2005; Linden, 2002; Pevehouse, 2005; Youngs, 2004].

This line of analysis, it can be noted, explains the striking contrast in the post-communist region, whether focusing on the early years of the transition or later, between political developments in east-central Europe, on the one hand, and the former SU, on the other. In contrast with new democracies, mixed regimes, it can be argued, are less affected by linkage – since they tend to be more geographically removed from the Western core – and leverage – because their political trajectories tend to be either irrelevant to the West or what one might call "too relevant" in the sense that Western leaders value oil, tight alliances, and political stability too much to press for anything other than relatively cosmetic democratic reforms. This is the story in part of Western relations with Russia, as well as Azerbaijan and Kazakhstan.

It is fair to argue, therefore, that the mixed regimes in the post-communist region, with the four countries of interest in this chapter providing particularly good examples, occupy the borderlands between east and west. This means far fewer linkages to the West than in, say, Poland, but more than in, say, the Caucasus or Central

Asia. This also means more divided political cultures (with each "camp" often occupying different geographical locales as well), and heightened competition among external players providing resources and making threats for the purpose of influencing regime developments, whether in a democratic or a dictatorial direction [see, especially, White and McAllister, 2007].

The international context of democratization and its consequences for the formation of mixed regimes can also be analyzed with respect to democratic norms. Because of the rise of democracy as a global value and the widespread belief among citizens around the world (as public opinion surveys repeatedly show in the post-communist region as elsewhere) that legitimate regimes are those that can claim to be democratic by, for example, having liberal constitutions and holding competitive elections, authoritarian leaders have been under growing pressure to add some democratic "decorations" to the way they conduct politics. Such "decorations" also have a practical side. Even rigged elections can reveal the distribution of public sentiments to authoritarians and help them fine-tune patronage networks [Lust-Okar, 2004, 2007]. In addition, since the second half of the 1980s, we have seen the proliferation of non-governmental organizations that increasingly serve as the core distributors of external economic assistance and that also serve as major proponents of democratic improvements [Mendelson and Glenn, 2002; but see Gershman and Allen, 2006]. During the same period, we have also seen a change in the international financial community. Questioning the effectiveness of both defining development in purely economic terms and making direct transfers to governments, International Financial Institutions have increasingly defined their mission as one of linking development assistance to the expansion of social capital and civil society and to demonstration on the part of the recipient regime that it has made strides in improving democratic performance [see, for example, Knack, 2004]. While these policy changes can have some negative consequences, such as strengthening the power of illiberal groups, creating a fragile and dependent civil society, and weakening the state by forcing political leaders to hide their coercive tendencies by "farming out" responsibilities for repression to allies outside the state and then losing control of the privatization of violence [see Jamal, 2008 and Roessler, 2005], the message of such actions is nonetheless clear. Mixing democracy with dictatorship can be beneficial for regime survival. As a result (and with a certain amount of irony), it can be argued that rational authoritarians can prolong their rule by adding some democratic features to their regimes – to divide the opposition while courting external funding. In this sense, mixed regimes are an "efficient" response to the demands of the international system – as leaders in Belarus, Moldova, Russia and Ukraine quickly recognized early in the transition.

Finally, a number of scholars have drawn on the focus in early third wave studies of democratization as a bargaining outcome and argued that mixed regimes reflect a specific set of bargaining processes and consequences that take place once authoritarian regimes weaken [Bunce, 1999a; McFaul, 2002]. In particular, in the post-communist region, mixed regimes have tended to form under one of two conditions. The first is a balance between weak and divided oppositions versus weak and divided authoritarians – which describes quite well what happened in Russia and Moldova throughout the 1990s and Belarus in the first half of that decade. The other is a balance between the same two groups, but in conditions where both are relatively strong. This describes the politics of Ukraine throughout the 1990s. Thus, mixed regimes are testimony to the failure of either of the two key players in the transition to establish an overwhelming political advantage.

Indeed, the outcomes of the first competitive elections in the post-communist world as a whole provide strong evidence of the importance of these considerations. Just as the countries that were quick to establish fully democratic polities all featured decisive victories of the opposition in the first competitive elections (with the communists at times defecting in effect to the liberal project, as in Hungary and Slovenia in particular), so the authoritarian countries in the region feature one of two scenarios. One was a decisive victory of the communists coupled with limited support, especially outside of major cities, of the opposition, and the other is an equally decisive victory by an illiberal opposition (as in Croatia and Georgia in particular). In the latter cases, the common story was that the communists had lost support from key players because they were associated with repressing nationalist mobilizations during communism. As a result, once the regime and state began to disintegrate, the struggle for political power shifted to struggles within the opposition, which the nationalist agenda had divided into liberal and illiberal groups. The illiberal flank won, among other reasons, because it was able to demobilize the liberal opposition, and it could lay claim to being long at the forefront of the struggle for the nation and statehood against communism and the larger state.

Finally, with respect to mixed regimes, we see in the post-communist region what can be termed ambiguous electoral outcomes [also see Fish, 1998; Frye, 2002]. For example, in Ukraine and Russia, the first elections allowed the opposition to establish a clear presence in the legislature, though communists or former communists won the Presidency; in Moldova, the liberal opposition won with a weak mandate and then divided over the question of Moldova's relationship to Romania; and in Belarus, while the opposition was weak, the communists were quite divided. A rough balance between contending political forces, therefore, led to compromise with respect to both democratic development and economic reform, with the result that both dynamics had the effect of generating in regional terms unusually unstable politics and either limited economic reforms (as in Belarus and Ukraine) or stop and start economic reforms (as in Russia and Moldova). The failure to reach closure on both democratization and economic reform, therefore, as a result of important divisions in society as a whole, the communist party, and the opposition created not just mixed regimes, but also unstable politics and unusually poor economic performance. Also common in these scenarios was considerable corruption, reflecting the partial character of economic reforms and the continuing power of rent-seekers to capitalize on the gaps created by occupying a halfway house between socialism and capitalism [Hellman, 1998].

4 - Points of Departure: Belarus and Russia

This discussion of the origins of mixed regimes leads to a clear conclusion. When all is said and done, the key point is that such regimes – in contrast to transitions from authoritarian rule that lead either to democracy or dictatorship – reflect *continuing* contestation among élite and among publics over the regime, the state and the economy. They occupy, in short, what Thomas Carothers [2002] has termed the grey zone, but with the additional meaning that this zone is at once political, economic, cultural and historical.

What did this mean in practice? On Table 10, we have provided a snapshot of our four regimes in the early years of the transition. As this table suggests, all four regimes were mixed – though Russia and Moldova, interestingly enough, tilted more in a democratic direction than Belarus and Ukraine.

Table 10. Freedom House scores: point of departure

Country	1993	1994
Belarus	5/4	4/4
Moldova	5/5	4/4
Russia	3/4	3/4
Ukraine	4/4	3/4
Albania	2/4	3/4
Bulgaria	2/2	2/2
Romania	4/4	4/3

Source: Freedom House, *Comparative Scores for All Countries from 1973 to 2006*

Table 11. Freedom House scores over time

Country	1993	1996	1999	2003	2007
Belarus	5/4	6/6	6/6	6/6	7/6
Moldova	5/5	3/4	2/4	3/4	3/4
Russia	3/4	3/4	4/5	5/5	6/5
Ukraine	4/4	3/4	3/4	4/4	3/2

Source: Freedom House, *Comparative Scores for All Countries from 1973 to 2006*, and Freedom House, *Freedom in the World 2008*

However, as Table 11 indicates, once we take a longer-term view of the transition, we find significant changes in these regimes over time. To put the matter simply and to echo an earlier point: these mixed regimes were far from frozen in their political attributes.

We now turn to a brief overview of our four regime trajectories. We begin with a synopsis of what transpired in Russia and Belarus: the two countries that became more authoritarian over time.

In Belarus, the key development was the election of Aleksander Lukashenko to the Presidency in 1994. While a longstanding member of the communist party, Lukashenko was very low in the hierarchy of the Belorussian Communist Party, and he came in effect out of nowhere to win the Presidency. Once in office, Lukashenko committed himself to weeding out non-supporters in the party and building a strong political machine and a strong state – in direct contrast, for example, to what transpired during communist rule in Ukraine and Moldova [see Way, 2005; Silitski, 2005a, 2005b, 2006, 2007a, 2007b]. Over the course of his time in office, Lukashenko has avoided economic reforms; formed a close alliance with Russia (which has been quite frayed in the past two years); and built a full-scale authoritarian system based upon state control over the media, the courts and the legislature. He has also done a thorough-going job of rigging local and national rigged elections; harassing the opposition; and supporting a quite corrupt system that uses economic benefits to pay off supporters. He is a very popular leader, in part because of personal charisma and in part because of the striking economic stability of Belarus over the course of the transition, and he was very successful at limiting the ability of the opposition to make effective challenges to his powers in both the 2001 and 2006 presidential elections. This is because Lukashenko has been unusually attentive to any potential threats to his power. For example, just as he was a careful student of what happened to Milosevic in Serbia in 2000, so he followed developments in Georgia in 2003 and Ukraine in 2004, when democratic oppositions coalesced to oust Shevardnadze in the first case and when they managed in the second to defeat Kuchma's designated successor. For example, when participants in Georgia's Rose Revolution in 2003 entered Belarus to help the opposition prepare for the 2006 presidential elections, Lukashenko was quick to throw them in jail.

The Russian road to authoritarianism began later, but it was also a function of the work of one leader who also benefited from strong economic performance; that is, Vladimir Putin, who was chosen by Boris Yeltsin to succeed him in late 1999 and who was elected in landslide presidential elections in 2000 and again in 2004 [see, especially, Knight, 2008; Fish, 2005; Lyall, 2006; Stoner-Weiss, 2007; Wilson, 2005; Wilson, 2006; Kamhi, 2006; Krastev, 2005, 2006; Hale, 2006; Dimitrov, 2008]. Moreover, while having to step down as President because of the two-term limit specified in the Russian constitution and choosing a close ally, Dmitry Medvedev, to succeed him, Putin has nonetheless succeeded in maintaining his powerful position in Russian politics by agreeing to become the Prime Minister under President Medvedev. Here, it is striking to note, first, that Medvedev has been rumoured to have headed the failed Russian attempt to influence the outcome of the 2004 Ukrainian elections by supporting Viktor Yanukovytch – who lost to Viktor Yuskchenko. At the same time, a March, 2008 poll in Russia showed that sixty-six percent of Russians assumed that a vote for Medvedev for President would necessarily lead, in contrast to the time Putin was President, to a shift in power in the direct of the office of the Prime Minister [Knight, 2008]. Put simply: Russians assumed that Putin would remain in charge. With United Russia, headed by Putin, dominating the legislature, it is unlikely that Medvedev will be able to carve out an independent political position – though his background, unlike much of the rest of the Russian political élite, is not in the security services.

Like Lukashenko, Putin has been committed to building a strong state by constructing an authoritarian regime, using many of the same mechanisms, such as control over the media and elections, harassment of the opposition, the use of nationalism to promote public support, and widespread corruption. To provide two telling examples: in 2008 eight journalists have been killed in Russia, and Transparency International ranks Russia 123 out of 175 (with Moldova 111; Ukraine 118; and Belarus 150).

These similarities recognized, there are nonetheless some contrasts between Putin and Lukashenko with respect to how they have consolidated their power and their approach to de-democratization [and see Hassner, 2008]. In Putin's case, the regime is dominated by the "siloviki;" that is, members of the security police (currently termed the FSB) and the Foreign Intelligence Service. Moreover, unlike Belarus, the Russian state was very weak at the time of Putin's rise to power, given difficulties the Russian state had with respect to maintaining its borders, collecting taxes, imposing a common legal framework on the regions, and providing political order. At the same time, the Russian economy, again in contrast to Belarus, was in shambles. Putin responded to these problems by "winning" the second war in Chechnya (which in practice unleashed terrible devastation and widespread violations of human rights) and introducing a series of institutional reforms that strengthened the presidency, while weakening parliament, the courts, and local governments (which were consolidated into much larger units and then denied institutional opportunities for separate political voices through changes in parliament and voting procedures). He has also made it far harder for the opposition to contest, let alone win power at the local or national levels, and to organize large scale and effective political protests [Benardo and Neier, 2006; Robertson, 2008].

For example, it has become very hard, given the huge number of signatures required for candidates to run for office, the absence of transparency in electoral commissions, and the high thresholds for representation in parliament after the elections, for the opposition to run for and take office. Moreover, United Russia currently controls seventy percent of the seats in the Russian parliament. As a result, the Russian opposition has decided that electoral politics are no longer a meaningful route to popular influence, and their leaders have focused instead on two kinds of activities: popular demonstrations and the slow formation of a nation-wide, Solidarity-like political movement [see Lyall, 2006]. Both actions have also been embraced by the Belorussian opposition. These reactions, ironically, signify a return to the communist past, where mobilization outside formal political institutions constituted the only effectively available approach to challenging dictatorial power. At the same time, Putin has reasserted state control over the energy sector, and he has benefited from a return of the Russian economy to growth, largely as a result of buoyant energy prices. As Putin has boasted, Russian incomes are two and one-half the size of what they were when he came into office, and the Gross Domestic Product is seventy per cent larger [see Knight, 2008].

There is little doubt, therefore, that Russia has de-democratized under Putin. A recent strategy paper by the European Commission has provided an apt summary of Putin's – and Medvedev's – Russia at this time: "Russia is characterized by a powerful bureaucracy, increasingly dominated by the Kremlin and widely seen as highly corrupt, a legal system described by some as politically-biased, powerful and repressive law enforcement agencies, and a relatively weak civil society" [EU Country Strategy Paper, 2007: 14-15].

5 - Resisting Authoritarianism: Moldova and Ukraine

As Lucan Way [2002, 2003, 2005a] has argued, Moldova during the 1990s was a good example of "pluralism by default" [also see Mungiu-Pippidi, 2007; Quinlan, 2007]. During this period, while the Moldovan economy imploded and the issue of either an independent Transnistria or its reincorporation into the state continued to fester, Moldova nonetheless maintained a relatively democratic polity, especially with respect to such standards as extensive civil liberties and regular, free and fair elections (though the communist party was banned from 1991-1994). However, there were many problems besetting Moldova throughout the 1990s. For example, the Gross National Product in 2000 was approximately thirty percent of the size it was in 1990; there was a huge emigration of the working age population in response to constricted economic opportunities at home; and the ruling opposition was plagued by divisions, political paralysis, and very high rates of turnover in office. Not surprisingly (though the results took most observers by surprise, much like the 1994 election in Belarus), the opposition lost power in the 2001 parliamentary elections to the communists, who won a strong political mandate in elections that were, it is important to note, fully free and fair. The communists, who had not reformed themselves in either name or ideology, ran on a platform that combined economic populism with closer relations with Russia – a platform that was similar to the one that was embraced by Lukashenko in his elections, beginning in the 1994 and continuing thereafter [but see Liakhovich, 2007].

From 2001 to late 2004, it appeared that Moldova under the leadership of its new President, Vladimir Voronin, would go the way of Belarus and Russia. For example, like Lukashenko, Voronin sought closer economic and political relations with Russia, and, like both Putin and Lukashenko, Voronin intimidated the opposition; packed the judiciary; revised the constitution; attacked the media; returned the structure of local government to its design during communism; and held rigged local elections [Barbarosie, 2001; Cashu, 2005; Fenger, 2008; Quinlan, 2007]. However, the media managed to stay relatively independent and active, as did the opposition, which began a cycle of protests in 2002, and Russia overplayed its hand with respect to both its interventions in Transnistria (where Russian troops were still stationed) and the prices charged Moldova for Russian energy products. As a result of these factors, along with large-scale political protests, declining public support for the communists, and the precedent of the Orange Revolution next door (which in the short-term had led Voronin to push through a bill prohibiting students from participation in demonstrations), Voronin reconsidered his approach to governing by the end of 2004 in anticipation of the upcoming parliamentary elections in 2005. Stealing the thunder of the opposition, he embraced a return to Europe and with that moved away from his authoritarian political practices. He was re-elected, helped in part by a relatively successful economic record, and he has come to resemble in his rhetoric and policies the reform communists that, for example, came back to power in Hungary in 1994. To draw on an observation by Alina Mungiu-Pippidi [2007]: if the choice for Moldova was between Romania and Belarus, Moldova, as of this writing, has opted for the former over the latter.

In the case of Ukraine, a similar choice was confronted during the second and final term of President Leonid Kuchma, a communist like earlier leaders of independent Ukraine, who was, in contrast to his predecessor, a very close ally of Russia (and Putin) and a leader with strong support in both the Russian-speaking, heavy industrial belt of Ukraine that borders Russia, along with the Crimea. Like Russia and Moldova, the Ukrainian economy was in a freefall throughout the 1990s, with Ukrainian economic performance, not surprisingly, moving in tandem with its neighbour and closest trade partner, Russia. During that period, there was a two-way competition for power – between the communists and the opposition, with the opposition well-represented in the parliament, and, especially with respect to the office of the presidency, within the communist party as well, which was divided with respect to its geographical and economic bases of power, along with its commitments to economic and political reform [see Way, 2005a, 2005b; McFaul, 2004a, 2007; Åslund and McFaul, 2006].

Over the course of Kuchma's second term in office (with Ukraine, like Russia, having a two-term limit for presidents), politics in Ukraine became far more violent and authoritarian. For example, Kuchma cracked down on the media, going so far as to kill a journalist. However, there was resistance to his policies – as revealed, for example, in popular protests and in the local elections in 2002, where the opposition came together and won a number of elections. In early 2004, Kuchma selected his prime minister, Viktor Yanukovytch, to be his successor in the presidential elections that were to take place late in the fall of that year. Kuchma's former Finance Minister, Viktor Yushchenko, also decided to run and built a large and powerful coalition of opposition groups along with other groups in Ukrainian society, including important members of the economic élite. Thanks to Western assistance for free and fair elections and an empowered civil society, rapid critiques of electoral procedures on the part of the US and the Europeans (with the Polish President, Aleksander Kwasniewski playing a key role, along with the Lithuanian President), massive protests in Kyiv and throughout Ukraine, the breakdown of the regime's control over the media and the police, and key decisions by the Ukrainian Supreme Court and, at the same time, despite rigged elections, the poisoning of Yushchenko, and substantial Russian support, the electoral battle between the "two Viktors" in the fall and winter of 2004 finally led, after the election was held again, to the defeat of Yanukovytch and the victory of Yushchenko [See Åslund and McFaul, 2006; Bunce and Wolchik, 2006, 2008: Chapter 5].

While Yushchenko has faced enormous difficulties since the Orange Revolution in creating a stable and effective government, given the divisions of the Ukrainian opposition, the continuing impact of political, economic and geographical divisions in Ukraine, and subsequent electoral pressures to name his former opponent, Yanukovytch as Prime Minister, Ukraine has nonetheless made significant progress in democratization since Kuchma was in power. Put succinctly, while turbulent, the Ukrainian political scene is a good deal more democratic than it has ever been, especially with respect to civil liberties and political rights, the independence of the media, the powers of the legislature, rule of law, and the existence of free and fair elections.

While different in many ways, political changes in Ukraine and Moldova are similar in three key respects. In both countries, there was a serious brush with authoritarianism, beginning a decade or so after the transition from communism began. At the same time, in both countries, elections have played a key role – first in moving these mixed regimes in a more authoritarian direction and then in returning both countries to a far more democratic path. It is also striking that both countries are currently ruled by presidents with a similar profile of being communists who embraced a reformist position; who won power in part by supporting more ties with Europe, while distancing themselves from Russia; who sit on top of a quite factionalized coalition of supporters; and who are associated in the public mind with improved economic performance.

6 - Explaining Divergent Trajectories

The four synopses of regime developments presented above suggest a more muddied contrast than one of, say, two mixed regimes becoming increasingly authoritarian over time, on the one hand, and, on the other, two mixed regimes moving into the democratic column. Instead, what we found was that, while both Belarus and Russia slid in a consistent way into authoritarian politics since the transition began, with Belarus starting its journey earlier than Russia, Moldova and Ukraine, also confronting the threat of de-democratization, succeeded in returning to the democratic path, but in a manner lacking the democratic guarantees built into stable and full-scale democratic polities. In this sense, while Russia and Belarus have become authoritarian orders, both Moldova and Ukraine were able to remain mixed regimes – albeit ones where the future of democracy, especially in Ukraine, is far better than in the past. The question then becomes: what explains this contrast between what could be termed, alternatively, authoritarian versus mixed polities, or successful versus failed authoritarianism?

We can begin to answer this question by noting some factors that fail to differentiate well among our two sets of cases. Economic performance, for example, does not account for the contrast. The Ukrainian economy was in fact on the upswing the last years of the Kuchma regime – a trend that also applies to the Russian economy prior to Putin's attack on democracy and the Moldovan economy during the first term of Voronin. At the same time, it is striking that neither cultural heterogeneity nor the presence of secessionist pressures on the state explains the contrast between Belarus and Russia, on the one hand, and Moldova and Ukraine, on the other. Third, it is notable that *all* the leaders who played key roles in either building authoritarian orders or deconstructing them were tied to the communists, rather than being political outsiders whose entire career was associated with the liberal opposition. Moreover, external factors have not played a consistent role. Both the US and the EU have devoted substantial resources to the promotion of democracy in all four of these countries – though far less so in Russia and especially Belarus in recent years, given concerted actions by Lukashenko to block foreign democratic assistance [and see Gershman and Allen, 2006; Bunce and Wolchik, 2008; Finkel, *et al.*, 2006;

Green, 2007; Spector and Krickovic, 2007; The Role, 2006; USAID, 2005]. Finally, it is important to note that the two countries closest to Russia in economic terms and with respect to the location of Russian pipelines – that is, Belarus and Ukraine – have moved in different political directions [see Yasmann, 2008].

There are, nonetheless, three factors that stand out as playing critical roles in these "showdowns" with authoritarianism. One grows out of contrasts in the outcome of the first competitive elections and their consequences in turn for the selection of political institutions at the beginning of the transition (see Table 12).

Table 12. Nations in Transit scores for 1997 and 2007

Indicator	Year	Belarus	Moldova	Russia	Ukraine
Electoral Process	1997	6	3.25	3.50	3.25
	2007	7	3.75	6.50	3.00
Civil Society	1997	5.25	3.75	3.75	4.00
	2007	6.50	3.75	5.25	2.75
Independent Media	1997	6.25	4.00	3.75	4.50
	2007	6.75	5.25	6.25	3.75
Judicial Framework and Independence	1997	6.00	N/A	4.00	3.75
	2007	6.75	4.50	5.25	4.50
Governance*	1997	6.00	4.25	4.00	4.50
	2007	7/6.50	5.75/5.75	6/5.75	4.75/5.25
Democracy Score	1997	5.90	3.81	3.80	4.00
	2007	6.68	4.96	5.86	4.25

Source: Freedom House, *Nations in Transit* (2007, 1997)

In Moldova, the first competitive election led to a victory of the opposition, whereas in Ukraine the first election led to the victory of the communists in the presidential election, but sizeable representation of the opposition in parliament. As a result, in both Moldova and Ukraine, the combination of divided, but nonetheless sizeable oppositions facing divided and far from hegemonic communists led to a decision to adopt in the Moldovan case a parliamentary system, where the president is elected by parliament, and in the Ukrainian case, a mixed presidential-parliamentary system, where the parliament has significant powers. Because of the investment in strong legislatures, therefore, it was far harder in both of these countries for communist presidents to build durable coalitions and ambitious political machines that supported their power and that allowed them to centralize and abuse the powers of the presidency. As Steven Fish [2004, 2006: 5] has summarized his study with Matthew Kroenig of legislatures around the world: "...the presence of a powerful legislature is an unmixed blessing for democratization". We might also add here that of the fifteen successor states that arose from the dissolution of the SU, only four were parliamentary: the three Baltic states, together with Moldova. These were also the only successor states where the opposition won the first competitive election – a pattern that we also see in east-central Europe.

By contrast and far more typical of the post-Soviet space, both Russia (albeit with a more divided electoral outcome) and Belarus opted for more powerful presidencies and weaker legislatures – with the latter becoming even weaker over time as presidents in both of these countries consolidated their powers. What this meant is that presidents, such as Putin and Lukashenko, bent on limiting civil liberties and political rights, rigging elections, preventing the opposition from competing for power, exerting control over key economic sectors and the media, harassing and sometimes murdering journalists, and redrawing the structure of local governments and even parliaments and their rules for operation in favour of limiting political competition and independence, were in a position to use the presidential office as a platform to carry out these actions and expand their powers [and see McFaul and Stoner-Weiss, 2008]. It is also telling that, while the courts in Russia and Belarus were silenced, they played a more active role in Moldova and especially Ukraine in limiting what presidents and their anointed successors could do to amass political and economic resources. While it is hard to disentangle electoral outcomes from institutional selection (especially given the Russian case), since they correlate with one another, the key point remains that weaker presidential offices are associated with greater resistance to authoritarian challenges in the mixed regimes of interest in this chapter.

A second factor that differentiates between the two cases is political mobilization and competition. Here, we refer to all types of political actions, ranging from protests and public engagement in local politics to competition for national office and turnover in governments. While political protests have been relatively constant in Moldova and have played a key role in Ukraine, especially from 2002 to 2004, they have been far less evident in either Russia or Belarus [Lyall, 2006; Barbarosie, 2001; Cashu, 2005; Mendelson and Gerber, 2005; Robertson, 2008]. While repression increasingly explains the contrast, it is striking that neither Putin nor Lukashenko was challenged in their early years of their rule by political protests; that is, before their political agenda became evidence and before they consolidated their powers. By contrast, both Ukrainians and Moldovans were quick to challenge signs of growing authoritarianism.

At the same time, local elections in both Moldova and Ukraine, especially during the period of growing authoritarianism, have functioned as constraints on the centre (as they also did in Serbia and Georgia, which also experienced pivotal elections), whereas they have failed to do so in Belarus and Russia. This contrast leads in turn to a more general point. The overall level of competition and turnover of officials in Belarus and Russia has been lower than in Ukraine and Moldova. Over the course of the transition, the latter two countries have more often been the sites of divided and changing governments, ample representation of the opposition in parliaments and in Moldova in the Presidential office as well. This has meant in turn considerably more turnover in governing officials. This is in sharp contrast to the relative continuity in electoral coalitions in Russia and especially Belarus.

This leads to a final consideration, which applies to three of the four countries: the role of Russia. It is fair to argue that Voronin (in his first term), Kuchma (in his two terms in office), and Lukashenko all built very close ties to Russia, while rejecting linkages to Europe. However, the Russian state has engaged in a series of policies that alienated publics in both Ukraine and Moldova − for example, interfering in the 2004 Ukrainian elections to the point where Putin congratulated Yanukovytch on his victory even before the votes were counted, pushing a radical decentralization plan for Transnistria which undermined opportunities for a political compromise, and raising energy prices by substantial amounts. Moreover, Russia has taken a similar tack in Belarus over the past two years, pushing Lukashenko towards a more conciliatory policy with the West (though less so over the past year). The key point here is that, while Russia does indeed have both strong historical and economic connections with Moldova and especially Belarus and Ukraine, it has pursued at times policies that, counter to its interests, have encouraged Moldova and Ukraine to turn to the West. Thus, it can be suggested that, while a number of criticisms have been levelled at Western policies towards Belarus, Ukraine and Moldova, these concerns about the limits and the costs of democracy promotion must be placed alongside the surprisingly inept policies of Russia in all three countries. While Russia under Putin has become more assertive in international affairs, especially in countries that were once part of the SU, it has done so with rather mixed results. In this sense, if the West has been clumsy at times with respect to promoting democracy abroad, so has Russia with its support of "managed democracy."

7 - Conclusions

The purpose of this chapter has been to use the cases of Belarus, Moldova, Russia and Ukraine to address two questions. One is: why do mixed regimes form? Second, what explains variations over time in the weight of democratic versus authoritarian elements in mixed regimes? Our answer to the first question emphasized a variety of factors, including contestation over the nation and the state along with a rough balance at the time of the transition between authoritarians and democrats. With regards to the second question, we argued that three factors seemed to have played a key role in how mixed regimes evolved: institutional selection in the early years of the transition, the degree of political competition and contestation during the transition, and international influences on the transition, such as the role of Russia in the particular cases of Moldova, Belarus and Ukraine.

Embedded in these arguments, however, is a larger generalization that our comparison has highlighted. The formation and evolution of our four mixed regimes points to the important role of elections. A number of analysts of both democratization and international democracy assistance have rightly argued that perhaps too much emphasis has been placed on elections – as an indicator of overall democratic performance and as a "producer" of political change. However, it is nonetheless striking in this study that elections feature quite prominently in our story of both why mixed regimes form and why they move in either an authoritarian or a democratic direction. It is not just that founding elections carry implications for institutional choice, or that specific elections can function as turning points. It is also that a pattern of vibrant competitive politics and high rates of turnover in governing parties and public officials – a pattern that, we must remember, also characterized those post-communist countries that have joined the EU – seems to contribute to democratic development. They do so for a variety of reasons – because elections themselves can be schools for democracy; because authoritarians can either be defeated (as in Ukraine in 2004) or persuaded to embrace more democratic priorities (as in Moldova in 2005), and because democrats replace dictators. Elections, therefore, are critical to democratic and authoritarian change, because of both their dynamics and their outcomes [and see Bunce and Wolchik, 2008; Forbrig and Demes, 2007].

3

EXTERNAL ECONOMIC CONSTRAINTS AND DEMOCRATIZATION

Roberto Di Quirico

1 - Introduction

During the last fifteen years, attention has been devoted to the topic of the diffusion of democracy and the role of international actors in supporting this process. Before the 1990s and the fall of the Communist Bloc, scholars considered internal actors and processes to be the crucial elements in explaining democratization. However, events in Eastern Europe led them to reconsider this view. In particular, literature has insisted on the role of international organizations and the main international political actors (European Union, United States) in inducing democracy in post-communist countries.[1]

Transformations in the post-communist era have been concerned not only with the political field. Transformations in the economy and the advent of a free market economy also characterized those years. The political and economic transformations were two sides of the wider process of liberalization that followed the end of the communist system and which took place thanks to international support. Besides, the two processes interacted extensively and conditioned each other's outcomes.

If external political pressures depend mainly on the coordinated and planned actions of external actors, economic pressures don't. In fact, the international economic structure is largely the result of colliding preferences and strategies of states and international actors, sometimes correctly perceived or planned, sometimes not. So, external economic constraints on countries during the

---

[1] About this topic see Whitehead, 1996; Pridham, Herring, and Sanford 1997; Burnell, 2000; Pevehouse, 2005; Schimmelfenning, 2007.

democratization or democratic consolidation phases may be erratic and unmanageable.

In this chapter I will analyze how external economic constraints affect democratization in EU post-Soviet neighbours, and how their impact on the national economy and society influences the internal dynamics.[2] Moreover, I will study the role of external economic constraints in the rise of different regimes in these countries. This analysis points to some general conclusions that could be useful for democratization theory in general.

2 - Different Types of External Economic Constraints that Influence Democratization

All countries face external constraints, in particular economic constraints. This happens because they are not insulated from the rest of the world nor from the international economy. External constraints limit the economic and political independence of a country and its ability to implement policies. In fact, the existence of external constraints reduces the working space of governments and their freedom to define their policies by limiting the number of choices they have. Usually external constraints and the limits they impose escape the control of the particular governments that face them. These governments have a poor influence on the dimension and essence of external constraints and they can only adapt their choices to the limits imposed by external constraints. Constraints may result from deliberate policies of foreign countries or international institutions as well as from mechanisms of the international economy and politics that single states cannot manage. Usually these constraints work independently of the political regime of the countries they affect. However, their impact may be different depending on the internal actors and dynamics affected. Therefore, interactions between external constraints and internal processes are crucial elements for the analysis of changes in post-Soviet regimes.

---

[2] The term EU post-Soviet neighbours indicate those former Soviet countries now neighbours of the European Union. They are Belarus, Russia, Moldova and Ukraine.

This chapter deals only with economic constraints. This doesn't mean that political constraints are not relevant; on the contrary, they are – and as such they are widely discussed in other chapters of this book. On the other hand, we must remember that political constraints also influence the effects of economic constraints. In fact, changes in the political structure, normative environment and rule of law effectiveness in hybrid regimes determined by external pressures may have a relevant impact on the effects and transmission channels of external economic constraints. So, political constraints able to influence these internal elements will also have relevant effects on the impact of external economic constraints.[3]

The existence of specific relationships between external economic constraints and internal dynamics is obvious for European post-Soviet countries. In fact, these countries faced, and in certain cases continue to face, a double transformation in the political and economic field: democracy building and market building (marketization). This dramatically enlarges the influence of external economic constraints because their influence on internal marketization reverberates on democratization through the interactions between the two internal processes.

External economic constraints can be divided into two macro categories: constraints planned and imposed directly by external institutions such as IMF and EU, and constraints which arise indirectly from certain aspects of the international context such as international economy and political geography. The latter are usually unmanageable and unpredictable in term of outcomes and timing. I will refer to them as erratic constraints. Also, while the government may negotiate with international actors the strictness of external constraints the latter impose, this is impossible in the case of erratic constraints.[4] However, planned constraints may

---

[3] The most evident example of this relationship is conditionality for EU membership.

[4] We need to distinguish among states, regional organization and international institutions. We define regional organization bodies like the European Union that are neither states nor institutions. Instead, for international institutions we mean those bodies like the International Monetary Fund or the World Bank that have specific functions worldwide.

also produce erratic and unplanned outcomes. On the other hand, erratic constraints may induce states to negotiate an international coordinated action to manage the effects of those constraints.

To analyze the impact of external economic constraints we need to identify their transmission mechanisms inside the country. Also, it is crucial to understand who are the main external and internal actors involved in this transmission, who among them are the main receptors of the external constraints, how they react to this impact and what kind of outcomes are produced. To do this we need to define a typology of external economic constraints which serves the purposes of this chapter, that is, the study of the transmission and impact of external constraints. The main criteria I employ here are the predictability of external constraints, the origin and nature of the inputs, and the main internal receptors of these inputs. The importance of these criteria depends on the theoretical assumptions we use to analyze democratization in EU post-Soviet neighbours. In this chapter, the transformation approach is preferred to the more traditional transitological approach.[5] In other words, I assume that if the preconditions for democratization are present, this doesn't mean that democratization will necessarily be successful. Instead, a complex process of interaction of various factors shapes a country's transformation and the final result may be democratization, a return to authoritarianism or permanent hybridization [Morlino, 2008; Morlino, forthcoming].This kind of approach is based on the analysis of actors' interactions and of the processes they enact. Therefore, to understand the impact of external economic constraints, it is crucial to consider who the main actors are (internal and external), what they do (actions of external actors and reactions of internal actors as receivers of the input) and how the actors interact. For an analysis of the internal actors' reactions, it is also important to know if the external constraints are planned or unplanned (erratic) and if the internal actors have any room for manoeuvring over the size and timing of the external constraints.

---

[5] On the debate about transition and transformation approaches for post-Soviet democratization see Schmitter and Karl, 1994; Bunce, 1995; Gans-Morse, 2004; Carothers, 2002.

The literature doesn't offer a classification of external constraints useful for the purposes of this chapter. Therefore, I will advance a new classification starting from the main criteria illustrated above. By grouping actors according to similarities in their nature and actions, and to the targets of their actions (main receptors of external inputs), I propose a classification comprising four categories of external economic constraints, as follows: institutional, structural, international, and geo-economic constraints. Institutional and structural constraints are planned constraints because governments have the possibility of managing their effects or of negotiating the timing and size of their impact. This is not possible for the remaining two categories (international and geo-economics) because of their erratic nature. Each category of constraints has a different influence on the process of democratization in hybrid regimes; each has a specific influence on the internal actors and processes.

By the term 'institutional constraints' I mean those conditions imposed by international institutions (for example the International Monetary Fund). The fulfilment of these conditions is indispensable to accede to financial aid or for being admitted into international organizations such as the World Trade Organization or the European Union. Part of these conditions may be of an economic nature, such as creating a market economy, liberalizing economic activities and prices, or adopting laws to regulate economic activity. Until the 1990s, in the EU post-Soviet neighbours, the institutional constraints set up by the IMF were effective because of these countries' need for loans to pay for economic reconstruction. Institutional constraints do not only affect the economic sphere. International institutions may also use their economic power to impel political transformations such as democratization, the respect of human rights or the rule of law. On the other hand, political conditionality may reinforce economic transformations supported by international organizations. In fact, democracy and rule of law are important conditions for effective economic reforms.

Structural constraints are those limits imposed on a country by the influence of international economic structure on the internal economy. They are predictable because internal actors know the main features of the international economy and the way in which it interacts with a country's internal economic structure. These external economic constraints may influence democratization, addressing economic and political élite to move towards or away from external political models, as democracy does. Western democracies are among the richest economies of the world. Therefore the attraction they exert is not only limited to their economy. Economic interaction with Western democracies implies a diffusion of their values and rules. It means that, if the internal economic structure of a hybrid regime is dependent for its growth on economic interactions (goods and financial markets) with democratic countries, an effective incentive to democratization will also arise. Otherwise, if the economic links are prevalently with other hybrid or authoritarian regimes, democratization will be difficult. The internal economic structure also shapes the élite' and social groups' preferences of the economic policies the government has to adopt. In certain cases, there are economic and political groups in need of external finance and markets. In other cases, these groups need rules which are specific to democratic regimes. This will impel these groups to make pressures for political and normative changes inspired by the Western democratic model. However, their interests may collide with those of other groups that reject the same external political models. This in turn creates tensions but also favours pluralism and opposition to the government by those groups who are unsatisfied with its policies.

International constraints rise from the impact of unpredictable international economy dynamics on the economy and politics of the country. They are usually defined as the result of the interdependence between national economies.[6] International

---

[6] During the last twenty years economic interdependence had been included in the wider contest of globalization. However, since the 1950s, some scholars have emphasized asymmetries in interdependence that create a form of dependence of certain countries on others. These theories known as "dependencia" are applied in particular to the dependency of Latin American states on the US.

constraints are different from structural constraints and the impact of structural constraints does not only depend on the internal structure. Decisions and strategies adopted by the political and economic groups also matter. They may change the internal structure in order to fit with the international economy or to limit its influence on the country economy. Instead, the impact of international economy dynamics (exogenous shocks) can be erratic and unplanned. The way in which the international economy works does not only depend on the internal politics of the different countries or on their agreements. It mainly depends on interactions that no single country may decide. So, the international economy influences by default the internal situation of all countries despite their being democratic, authoritarian or hybrid regimes. This influence may create incentives for political transformation and help or hinder democratization by suddenly changing the internal equilibria and empowering or weakening the democracy-oriented groups. A wider definition of structural constraints or of international constraints could permit them to be united under a single category of external constraints. However, historical experiences and recent events that affect EU post-Soviet neighbours suggest that the two categories should remain separate.

Finally, geo-economic constraints depend on a country's geographical position and its role in the regional economy. In the EU post-Soviet neighbour's case, the routes of transport lines and gas and oil pipelines make them strategic for Western Europe. This induces the European Union and Russia to put pressure on these countries by using economic tools and economic constraints in the form of sanctions and aids. These constraints may change internal attitudes towards democracy.

The following table suggests some examples of the internal impact of external economic constraints and how they may affect democratization in post-Soviet hybrid regimes. A detailed discussion of these dynamics will follow in section 4.

Table 13. Classification of external economic constraints and their impact mechanism

	External economic constraint	Input from	Action	Main receptor	Positive reaction	Potential results
Planned	Institutional	International and regional institutions	Prescription of rules	Government	Adoption of rules	Democracy and free market
Planned	Structural	External economic structure	Definition of preferences	Economic élite	Pressures on the government	Imitation/adaptation to external political models
Erratic	International	Exogenous shocks	Impact on internal economic structure	Economic élite	Adaptation	Balance of power's redefinition
Erratic	Geo-economic	Foreign states	Foreign policy	Government	Negotiation	External policies

3 - External Economic Constraints and Democratization: Some Examples from Case Studies

Post-Soviet transition offers various interesting case studies to analyze. These cases may help us understand the mechanisms connecting external constraints and internal economic and political dynamics in hybrid regimes.

On the following pages I discuss some examples of the impact of external economic constraints. These examples may help to clarify how each constraint works.

3.1 – The International Monetary Fund's Financial Assistance and Democratization in Russia

The case of IMF conditionality for loans is a perfect example of institutional external economic constraint.[1] After the fall of the Soviet Union, Russia, as well as the other post-Soviet countries, was in need of external financial aid. Output collapse, state budget crises and the problems of transition demanded international loans. These loans were available either from the IMF or others investors under the patronage of the IMF. So, the IMF was able to impose on Russia a set of rules aimed at introducing the country to the free market and democracy. These rules arose from the so-called Washington consensus that inspired the IMF's policy throughout the 1990s.[2] Apparently, the IMF's policy aimed at the contemporary introduction of democracy and the free market. In reality, the free market was a priority in the IMF's view in which democracy was considered a logical result of marketization. In other words, democracy follows marketization.

The way in which the free market emerged in Russia was inspired by the ideology of the IMF and the work of external advisers who suggested the so-called shock therapy strategy. This

---

[1] See also Moschella, this volume.

[2] The Washington consensus is a set of rules and policies that some international institutions centred in Washington (International Monetary Fund, World Bank) have indicated as the 'good ones' for countries aiming to reach financial stability. The Washington consensus shaped for years the policy aims imposed by IMF to countries in transition such as the post-Soviet ones.

strategy implied a sudden liberalization of prices and privatization of state-owned firms [Åslund, 2007; *idem*, 2002; Lavigne, 1999; Stiglitz, 2002]. The expected results were a short period of output collapse followed by a rapid recover of the economy and consolidation of the free market. This strategy had worked well in Poland and advisers believed it was the solution for Russian transition. Unfortunately, they did not consider the dramatic social impact the strategy had. Besides, shock therapy failed to create a "democratic" free market [Reddaway and Glinski, 2001]. Corruption and the rise of criminality and mafias resulted in the enrichment of a few people (who afterwards were called oligarchs) and criminals and in a dramatic impoverishment of pensioners, workers and professional middle-class, precisely some of the social classes usually considered as the main supporters of democracy and democratization. They associated free market and its disasters with democracy and this explains why democracy soon became unpopular.

The IMF and other international institutions and actors (mainly US and Western European countries) soon realized that reforms in Russia depended on Yeltsin's ability to remain in power. So, keeping him in power became a priority for international institutions such as the IMF, despite the fact that he was discredited as a democrat after the parliament's bombing in 1993 and the support granted to oligarchs. The best way to help him was by continuing to finance the Russian government, despite the widespread corruption and the oligarchs-prone policy of the Russian president. When the rise of post-communist parties threatened Yeltsin's re-election, only financial support by oligarchs and IMF allowed the Russian president to stay in power. In that case, the external economic constraints imposed by international institutions became a trap for the institutions themselves. They had to help a president and to accept a situation that hindered and discredited democratization in Russia [Stiglitz, 2002].

3.2 – Economic Interdependence and the Influence of External Political Models

The interdependence between the internal economic structure of a country and external markets is an example of structural constraint. In fact, this interdependence may shape a hybrid regime's propensity to democratic or non-democratic evolution through isomorphism of political regimes. Strong interdependence with an economic area characterized by democracy and a specific set of democratic rules creates pressures for adapting the norms and practices in the economic field to the external model. These norms imply a democratic context. So, their adoption helps the transition to democracy. On the other hand, interdependence with a non-democratic economic area hinders democratization not only for adverse isomorphism, but also because democratization becomes unnecessary. The Ukraine and Belarus provide two opposite examples of this connection between structural economic constraints and democratization. Both the Ukraine and Belarus depend on Russia for oil and gas supplies. However, the Ukraine also depends on the EU economic area for exports and aims to gain access to European financial markets and pay lower interest rates. This made the Ukraine sensible to EU pressures for reforms in economic regulation, transparency and the rule of law. All these elements, if carried out, support the transition to democracy. Besides, the need for cheap money from EU's financial market induces many entrepreneurs to ask for reforms that enable them to gain foreign funds. In particular, small and middle industrialists in need of finance to enlarge their plants and business see the EU not only as a financial market but also as a political model able to help economic growth. In this way, internal support for democratization grows.

Of course, also Belarus may gain by external funding for its internal industrial investments. However, access to the Russian market and government control on production and the financial system have helped Lukashenko's regime to resist external pressures and avoid internal ones in favour of economic reforms which might endanger the regime's stability. In this case, economic interdependence with a non-democratic area like Russia has today become an advantage for authoritarian regimes and may push hybrid regimes towards authoritarian evolution.

3.3 – The 1998 Financial Crisis and the Balance of Power Transformation in Russian Politics

The 1998 financial crisis is an example of how the erratic impact of the international economy may influence democratization. In fact, the crisis changed the socio-political equilibrium in Russia by destabilizing the role of oligarchs in restraining state power and, as a result, its ability to curb pluralism and impose an authoritarian regime.

Russia in the 1990s was not a democracy. The efforts of Western politicians and IMF officers to legitimate the democratic image of the Yeltsin's regime were ridiculous. At best, it was a hybrid regime of that type Morlino [this volume] calls "democracy without law". However, some conditions useful for democratic transition existed. One of them was the need of oligarchs to legitimize themselves. After having collected enormous richness, they needed a more stable regime able to guarantee they kept the money gained in suspicious ways. After the introduction of the rule of law, the regime and oligarchs overtime could accept and support the consolidation of democratic regime. The oligarchs were able to fund opposition parties and movements to defend their interests and support pluralism, which led to the rise of a so-called competitive authoritarianism, that is, a hybrid democracy-oriented regime [Way, 2005].

After the 1998 international financial crisis, democratic transition in Russia worsened. The Asian financial crisis also had an impact on the fragile Russian financial structure. The outflow of capital combined with the structural budget deficit led the Russian government to default in debt service and the collapse of the rouble. This ruined many banks in Russia, in particular those owned by oligarchs who lost part of their influence on the government and became dependent on its help [Åslund, 2007]. The disastrous impact of the 1998 crisis cleared the way for

Putin's accession to power and, more generally, the recovery of state supremacy in the economic field. This allowed the imposition of taxes that oligarchs had never previously paid by forcing them to return properties to the State.[3] Sometimes local governors were granted by central government the power to manage these renationalized firms. Governors then had the opportunity to use their position to enrich themselves and their families. This, and the decision that governors should no longer be elected but would instead be designated by the president, were important elements in consolidating Putin's regime[4] which became a hybrid regime that was more and more authoritarian-oriented. In fact, local governors had to preserve the president's trust to keep office and gain enrichment opportunities instead of electoral consensus. So, democracy was firstly derailed at a local level and then at a national level [Fish, 2005]. Meanwhile, some oligarchs had been ruined or escaped abroad or were imprisoned. The others accepted surrendering political influence in exchange for an undisturbed business life.

3.4 – Belarus, the Ukraine and Pipelines

The problem of pipelines and, more generally, energy and transport networks connecting EU and Russia create external economic constraints for the countries crossed by these networks. This is an example of geo-economics constraint. Strategically the needs of the EU and Russia have induced both to develop specific foreign policies towards the countries crossed by the networks. This influences political dynamics in those countries and has had an impact on regimes' evolution. In fact, the needs of international actors became predominant in their aims for political transformation in these regimes. So, the existence of geo-economic constraints can change the essence and the impact of other external constraints, in particular the institutional and structural ones. For example, it may be that a democratic area renounces making pressures for democratization or makes easy

---

[3] *Idem.*
[4] *Idem.*

the access of a hybrid regime's goods to its market, although the regime does not move to democratization. In this way internal mechanisms for democratization stop. On the other hand democracy may become the ideological weapon in a wider conflict which has arisen for economic and strategic reasons. In these cases economic sanctions may become artificial external economic constraints against democratization. Examples are the Russian embargo for Moldovan and Georgian wines, and the withdrawal of gas supplies by Russia to curb the pro-European policies of the Ukraine after the so-called Orange revolution. However, external economic and technical support for pro-democratic groups and NGOs or in support of democratic governance may counterbalance the effects of antidemocratic external constraints.

4 - How External Economic Constraints Influence Democratization in Hybrid Regimes

The different types of external economic constraints we propose, and the examples analyzed above, suggest specific dynamics connecting external economic constraints and democratization in post-Soviet hybrid regimes. Table 13 (above) and Figure 5 (below) show how these dynamics work.

Table 13 shows the transmission chain of external economic constraints' effects. Each group of constraints results from the input of specific actors or events that create constraints which shape preferences or the working margins of internal actors. The type of constraint depends on the action performed by the external actor that provided the input. These actions may be planned actions such as prescribing rules, ineluctable impacts of exogenous shocks or orientation of preferences for internal economic and foreign policy. The actions resulting from the inputs of external agents influence the behaviour of those internal agents heavily touched by these actions and the external constraints they create. These internal agents are the main receptors of the external pressures. In certain cases external pressures are deliberately addressed to these specific internal actors as for prescription of rules by the IMF to national governments. In other cases these internal agents are the "victims" who suffer more from the economic effects of external actions and the reduction of windows of opportunity they have in defining their choices. These receptors react to external pressures and the limits imposed by external constraints putting in place action or policies like the adoption or rejection of rules or negotiations with other actors inside or outside the national arena. Because of this transmission chain, different outcomes will result. In Table 13 we only show those reactions and outcomes favourable to democratization. However, reactions and outcomes may be unfavourable to democratic transition, as shown in Figure 5.

The transmission chain is different for each group of external constraints. Institutional constraints created by international institutions by prescription of rules may induce the governments to adopt the rules. In this case, these rules may help democratization and market building. International constraints, carried by exogenous shocks to national economic élite by their impact on national economic structure, impel élite to face this impact and may change the internal balance of power between economic and political élite. Instead, structural constraints, rose by the interdependence of national economy with the international economic system, shape the preferences of economic élite that make pressures on the governments and may result in the adoption of external economic and political models. Finally, geo-economics constraints created by external actors shape the foreign policy of the governments and their attitude in negotiating with neighbour countries, including democratic reforms.

The dynamics pictured in Table 13 are not automatic and neither are they unidirectional. In fact, the impact of the same external economic constraint may help or hinder democratization in hybrid regimes as EU post-Soviet neighbours are. The divergent cases of the Ukraine and Moldova on the one hand, and Russia and Belarus on the other prove the existence of divergent outcomes of the impact of external constraints.

Figure 5 represents the effects of the dynamics represented in Table 13 and the potential divergent outcomes. The model represented in the graph implies two main channels for the transmission of external constraints and two main agents. The channels are political and economic. Pressures by international institutions and external actors directly on the government represent the political channel while the impact of their pressures and of exogenous shocks on the internal economy represents the economic channel. The government and élite are the main receptors of external pressures and the main internal actors and agents of change. Sometimes, élite may be not only the economic ones but also the political élite that control the government, in particular political parties. In fact, the impact of external pressures may influence voters' attitudes towards certain parties and these parties react by exerting pressures on the governments. Pressures on the government may be direct or indirect. Specifically, élite may use direct connections to address government policies or use indirect form of pressures by media they own or funding parties to push or stop reforms in a democratic or authoritarian direction. Both élite and government are not homogeneous entities. Instead, there are internal contrasts and competition between different groups with divergent interest. Some of these groups may support democratic changes but other may be against and democrats may lose. This is the reason why the outcomes of external constraint on hybrid regimes may be divergent, addressing pro-democratic or pro-authoritarian evolutions.

Also, main receptors may be hostile to the transformations planned by external actors, which may induce to insulation by external contest and pressures. In this case external constraints planned to support democratization may fail their mission, creating the conditions for pro-authoritarian evolutions as with Putin's Russia. Also, erratic external constraints may undermine democratic reforms and create an environment more favourable for the concentration of power in a few strong hands[5].

---

[5] There are well known historical examples of the strict relations between economic crises, market collapse and authoritarian consolidation.

Figure 5. Dynamics of external influence on internal politics in former Soviet hybrid regimes

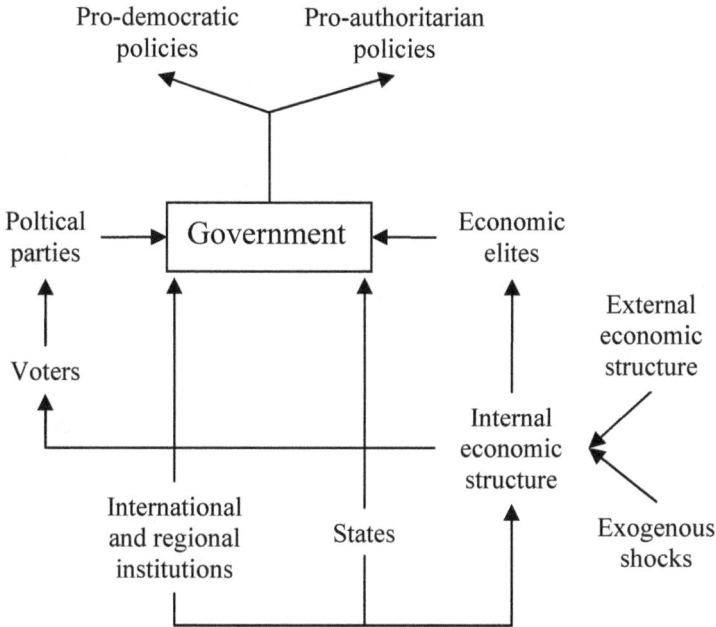

The model represented in Figure 5 has specific implications for post-Soviet democratization theory. However, while these implications may work in EU post-Soviet neighbours, the results may be misleading for other hybrid regimes elsewhere in the world. Among these implications is that certain interest groups such as trade unions and the so-called civil society are marginal actors in the democratization of post-Soviet hybrid regimes. In fact, they do not appear among main receptors and the internal actors considered relevant for transforming external pressures in effective internal democratization. This seems a hazardous hypothesis because of the role of NGOs in the so-called coloured revolutions in the Ukraine and Georgia and, more generally, in civil society mobilization in Moldova, Russia and Belarus. Besides, one of the main targets of international economic support for democratization in post-Soviet countries is NGOs. External actors rely on NGOs and civil society for democratization and pressures on the governments for democratic reforms. The same governments of authoritarian and hybrid regimes fear the effects of NGOs' activities in their countries [March, and Herd, 2006]. So, considering the role of NGOs to be marginal means denying the effectiveness of NGO-oriented policies developed by the EU and USA. Furthermore, excluding trade unions from the list of the main actors of democratization seems to be in contrast with traditional democratization theory.

Various studies on trade unions, NGOs and coloured revolutions in EU post-Soviet neighbours support the idea of their marginality in democratizing their countries. Trade unions paid the cost for their role during the Soviet period. In fact, Soviet trade unions acted as kinds of welfare institutions rather than associations devoted to defending workers' interests. So, the large membership in Soviet trade unions is mainly due to the benefits delivered to their members (sea holidays, cultural events, health relief). After the collapse of the Soviet Union, old trade unions changed their names and statutes but preserved their proprieties. This put them in an advantageous position against the free trade unions that appeared after 1990 because the latter were unable to offer the same services to their members. However, former Soviet trade unions became hostages to the governments that had the power to deprive them of their proprieties. Also, members of these trade unions were both workers and managers, which reduced their capacity to assume roles similar to their Western counterparts [Kubicek, 2000; idem, 2002]. Apathy by workers towards former Soviet trade unions has resulted in the fact that few participate in the rare strikes they organize. On the other hand, limited resources and the privileged links between government and former Soviet trade unions have made free trade unions weak. Finally, workers in troubled sectors are much too poor and firms are much too fragile to allow strikes. Therefore, trade unions in the EU's former Soviet neighbours are unable to play a determining role in internal politics.[6] Furthermore, NGOs are not so relevant in settling internal political dynamics. Despite their role in the so-called "coloured revolutions" some of them survive and work thanks to external support and cannot rely on the support of a diffuse civil society. Besides, some authors suggest that the success of coloured revolutions depends mainly on the so-called "lame duck" situation.[7] In fact, successful revolutions happened in countries where the president in command who granted the equilibrium among the oligarchic group in power was close to being removed from power [Hale, 2006; Tudoroiu, 2007]. The fight for succession induced members of the oligarchy to abandon it and become competitors [Way, 2004; idem. 2005]. Finally, governments contrasted NGOs activity in hybrid and authoritarian regimes both with repression and hostile laws as in Belarus and Russia and with political tactics addressed to include NGOs proposals in the governments programme.[8]

Instead economic élite with political power seem to be the pivotal element for democratization in European post-Soviet hybrid regimes. In particular oligarchs are powerful actors in supporting the democratization of hybrid regimes or at least containing their transformation in fully authoritarian regimes. In fact, oligarchs aim to free themselves from strict state control. As a result they may oppose efficaciously authoritarian involutions using their economic and influential resources. Besides, oligarchs and big industrialists have strong ties with the government and usually set up corporative relations with political power. Therefore, their problem has become that they risk losing their

---

[6] The soviet-style regime of Belarus explains the incapacity of trade union and other interest groups to foster political changes. In Moldova the government recently induced the two main trade unions to unite as a single one, giving predominance to the less independent of the two.
[7] A "lame duck" situation exists when a president or someone who maintains political equilibrium is close to finish his mandate and cannot be re-elected.
[8] This is the case with Moldova where the Voronin government adopted Europeanist attitudes, using a very powerful argument on NGOs that had generally been used by the opposition [see March and Herd, 2006].

power and wealth if the balance of power changes and the winners gain unlimited power [Way, 2005; Puglisi, 2003].

5 - Why External Economic Constrains Have Different Impact on Different Countries?

The case studies drawn above suggest the impact of external economic constraints on hybrid regimes changes depending on different variables. In other words, certain external constraints affect the internal dynamics of hybrid regimes more than others. Besides, the impact of the same external constraint may be more or less relevant depending on specific conditions.

One of the main variables able to explain the different impact of different constraints is time. Specifically, the period in which a specific external constraint influences the internal dynamics of a hybrid regime, settles the intensity of the constraint's influence. In fact, the internal conditions that make the external constraint severe in a certain period may disappear or change in the following period after which the impact of the external constraint decreases. This is the case with institutional constraints in Russia. The country was in dramatic need of financial help during the 1990s, which enabled international institutions to put strong pressure on it. Thus, the impact of institutional constraints became relevant. Later Russia's economic recovery and the dramatic increase in gas and oil prices freed Russia from the need for financial help, making institutional constraint ineffective.

Another variable to consider is the internal social structure of the hybrid regime. If there is a mixed social structure including big industrialists (or oligarchs), as well as small entrepreneurs and shopkeepers who may mobilize to defend their interests, the impact of external economic constraints will be deeper, as happened in the Ukraine and, in a pro-authoritarian sense, in Russia. This is because external constraints will touch a large number of people, mainly those who have the economic resources to lobby the government or to mobilize for protest. In hybrid regimes without wide social differentiation, such as Belarus where there are no oligarchs and a large part of the economic system is under government control, the impact of external economic constraints will be softer and democratization will not be influenced.

In addition, economic structure matters. External economic constraints have a different impact on industrial or agrarian countries. Usually industrial countries are more influenced by international economy and finance than the agrarian ones. This is the case with Moldova, where the economic attractiveness of EU and Russia is limited to remittances of emigrants (in a large part illegal immigrants) or their markets for Moldovan wines. Of course Moldova may welcome investments or economic aids, but the economic structure and the laws of the country make investments not attractive. Furthermore, the international economy impact is poor. Post-Soviet agrarian countries react slowly to changes in international economy because of their scarce involvement in it. As a result external economic pressures do not activate the mechanism of transmission described below and the potential democratizing effect they have.

Finally, external pressures and external constraints may be exerted by actors with different attitudes towards democracy. The EU, the US and the IMF had different views of democracy and the best way to induce it in post-Soviet countries. Russia has an unenthusiastic attitude to Western interference with former Soviet countries and their political regimes. Instead Russia proposes a semi-authoritarian political model and uses its economic potential to contrast pro-Western attitudes in its neighbours. We must remember that external constraints interact. So the impact of divergent external constraints' may reinforce or reduce the outcomes of each of them and orient internal political change towards or against democratization.

There are also many internal elements that help to explain differences in the evolution of hybrid regimes in post-Soviet Europe. The political regime of each post-Soviet country we have analyzed has resulted in reverting to a pre-existing hybrid regime. After the collapse of the Soviet Union Belarus moved quickly towards dictatorship while Russia seemed on the road to becoming a democracy but finally became an authoritarian regime. The Ukraine started as a hybrid regime with an authoritarian attitude and moved towards more democratic standards after 2003. Moldova from the early 1990s until today remains a hybrid regime with an unstable democratic trend.

The internal social structure is another element that explains different evolutions in EU post-Soviet neighbours. The different impacts of the 1998 financial crises on Russia and the Ukraine explain in part the different role of oligarchs in those countries today. Besides, it helps us to understand the divergent path towards democracy taken by the two countries because of the impact of the 1998 crises on the socio-economic structure of the Ukraine and Russia. Also, the transition policies adopted by different countries in accord or in contrast with IMF pressures, explain the rise of different internal balance of powers between the old political élite and the new economic élite. Despite this balance of power being an internal element, it was influenced by external constraints. So, external constraints shaped an important internal element whose dynamics explain the different trajectories of the transformation of hybrid regimes in the EU's post-Soviet neighbours.

In other cases the same external constraints that shaped the evolution of certain hybrid regimes had no effect on other countries. That was the case with the effect of the 1998 financial crisis on Moldova. In fact, the country has no oligarchs and does not attract huge investments and capital flows from abroad. Also geo-economics constraints arising from issues of energy that are relevant to the Ukraine or Georgia, do not affect Moldova which is out of gas pipelines routes.

In conclusion, external economic constraints matter, but are neither the only nor the most important element that influence democratization in EU post-Soviet neighbours. Internal elements shape the impact of external constraints and determine their effectiveness. They rose through years of transformations and through the heritage of the authoritarian past. So, internal elements are difficult to change in the short term and create a predisposition to amplify or limit the impact of external constraints on the internal regime. Different predispositions explain the different outcomes of external constraints in different countries.

Part II

International Anchors

4

EUROPEAN UNION DEMOCRATIC ANCHORING

Elena Baracani

1 - Introduction

The main objective of this chapter is to provide a comparative description of the EU's democratic anchoring on European post-Soviet countries (Belarus, Georgia, Moldova, Russia, and Ukraine) to evaluate the Union's potential and main limits in promoting democratization in this area. This is motivated by the fact that in order to exploit the EU's potential and limits in democracy promotion, it is not enough to consider only those specific activities aiming at democracy promotion; it is necessary also to examine what the EU offers the target countries in exchange for the respect for its democratic conditions. Indeed, these incentives are the main instruments which can favour, in the short or medium-term, a convergence with the EU's democratic principles and practices, and in the long-term the internalization of these norms.

As previously said [see the Introduction to this volume], in the only systematic analysis of the impact of the EU's anchoring on democratic reforms of different countries at the Union's borders, external anchoring has been defined as a process in which national political regimes are subject to variably dense external linkages, pressures and stimuli influencing the conditions of democracy [Magen and Morlino, 2008: 28]. Here, I propose to define external anchoring as a process in which an external actor keeps a target country close to itself by offering some incentives. The anchoring exercised by the EU can be defined as democratic as these linkages – mainly institutional links (which refer to the current status and final objectives of bilateral relations), economic assistance, and trade with its member states –

conditioned to the respect for democracy, can favour, at least potentially, domestic pro-democracy dynamics.[1]

All the incentives offered by the EU – institutional links, economic assistance, and trade – and its pro-democracy activity can be defined as EU structural foreign policy instruments [see Keukeleire and MacNaughtan, 2008: 19 and 25], which allow the EU to influence the behaviour of third countries.

2 – An Historical Perspective on EU Democracy Promotion

If we compare the EU's history of democracy promotion with that of the US it can be fairly argued that the EU has a shorter history which dates back to the end of the Cold War [see Baracani, 2010] and that it has become a democracy promoter more by accident, than by design, as a result of its enlargement [see Bunce and Wolchik, 2008].

Indeed, in the original founding treaties of the EU there was no mention of "democracy."[2] It was only in January 1962, when the European Parliament approved the Birkelbach report, that, for the first time, the necessary political conditions were established for membership and also association status of the European Community (EC) (see Table 14). On this basis, the February 1962 application by Franco's Spain for association status with the EC was dropped for political reasons, and after the 1967 Colonels' coup in Greece the EC decided to freeze its association with this country.

The last years of the 1970s and the first part of the 1980s were characterized by the Declaration on Democracy at the Copenhagen summit in April 1978 (see Table 14), and by the accession processes of Greece, Spain and Portugal. In this enlargement, the EC membership, conditional on the existence of

---

[1] Obviously these incentives have to be perceived by the target country as relevant in order to engage in the process of domestic political reforms.

[2] The 1951 Treaty of Paris was more concerned with preventing the reoccurrence of war. However, the Rome Treaty of 1957 noted in the preamble that member states "resolved by thus pooling their resources to preserve and strengthen peace and liberty and calling upon the other peoples of Europe who share their ideal to join their efforts" [Pridham, 2005: 30].

a democratic form of government, helped the applicants, which had just emerged from a period of dictatorship, to consolidate their new democratic regimes. Indeed, the existing member states (MSs) accepted their applications to ensure political stability on the southern periphery of Western Europe, and they established the precedent for the acceptance of applications for geo-strategic and political reasons, even where the economic conditions are not ideal. However, the way in which this enlargement was handled shows the reason why I affirmed at the beginning of this chapter that the EU has become a democracy promoter more by accident than by design as a result of enlargement [quoting Bunce and Wolchik, 2008]. Indeed, Pridham [2005: 35] explains that the EC's strategy of democracy promotion in this period "was marked by a distinct lack of procedure and its operation by *ad hoc* approaches and a continuing tendency to react to events rather than trying to determine their outcome".

In the 1990s, with the creation of the EU at Maastricht in 1992, the "development and consolidation of democracy" became one of the objectives of its Common Foreign and Security Policy (CFSP), and the EU started to exert a more structured influence on the democratization process of accession candidate countries from Central and Eastern Europe. The key developments in the EU relationship with Central and Eastern European applicants, which allowed the Union to exert a more structured influence on their domestic dynamics, were the 1993 Copenhagen European Council, and the 1997 Luxemburg European Council. In 1993 the heads of state and government of the EU agreed that those associated countries of Central and Eastern Europe desiring membership could become members of the EU, even though, for the first time, the promise of membership was accompanied by a statement of formal membership conditions, among which was "democracy" (see Table 14). Then, in 1997, the Luxemburg European Council launched the enhanced pre-accession strategy to be applied to all Central and Eastern European applicants, which made possible for the EU to implement its general political conditionality into the request of specific democratic reforms for each accession candidate, and thus to play a more structured influence on the process of democratization. This is, first of all, because the Copenhagen political conditions started to be translated by the EU (in the Accession Partnerships) into the demand for specific political reforms from each candidate. Moreover, the progress of each candidate in complying with these demands began to be monitored annually by the European Commission in specific reports. Third, the EU started to grant its economic assistance in order to achieve the reforms indicated in the Accession Partnerships.

At the beginning of the XXIst century, the EU would like to replicate this successful strategy of "democracy promotion through integration" [Dimitrova and Pridham, 2004], not only with the current candidate countries (Turkey, Croatia and the Former Yugoslav Republic of Macedonia), and with the remaining potential candidate countries of the western Balkans (Albania, Bosnia-Herzegovina, Serbia, Montenegro, and Kosovo), but also with its neighbours, as European post-Soviet states, which do not have the prospect of membership of the Union. Therefore the challenge for the EU towards these countries is whether it will be able to favour domestic dynamics in ways that are conducive to more democratization, without offering the incentive of full political integration. Will the other incentives – see the following section – be enough in favouring the adoption and implementation of democratic reforms?

The Lisbon Treaty does not add much to what already established. However, if we look at art. 49 of the TEU (see Table 14), it can be observed that, first, two new democratic values – human dignity and equality – have been added to those already established by the 2003 Copenhagen European Council and by the Amsterdam Treaty, and second, that any European state wishing to apply to become a member of the EU should not only respect its democratic values but also "be committed to promoting them". This is innovative, as for the first time it is established that democracy promotion should be a practice not only for the EU, but also for its future members.

Table 14. Turning points in EU democracy promotion

1962 Birkelbach Report	"only states which guarantee on their territories *truly democratic practices and respect for fundamental rights and freedoms* can become members of the Community"
1978 Declaration on Democracy	It states that respect for and maintenance of parliamentary democracy and human rights in all member states are "*essential elements of their membership* in the EC [European Community]"
1981 and 1986 Mediterranean Enlargement	Membership helps the applicants to consolidate their new democracies
1992 Maastricht Treaty	The "development and consolidation of *democracy, the rule of law, and respect for human rights and fundamental freedoms*" becomes one of the objectives of the CFSP
1993 Copenhagen European Council	"Membership requires that the candidate country has achieved *stability of institutions guaranteeing democracy, the rule of law, human rights and respect for and protection of minorities* ..."
1997 Luxembourg European Council	The enhanced pre-accession strategy allows the EU to play a more structured influence on democratization
1997 Amsterdam Treaty	"Any European State *which respects the principles set out in Article 6(1)* [liberty, democracy, respect for human rights and fundamental freedoms, and the rule of law] may apply to become a member of the Union" (art. 49 TEU)
2003 European Security Strategy	"[o]ur task is to promote a ring of *well-governed countries* to the East of the European Union and on the borders of the Mediterranean"
2004 and 2007 Eastern Enlargement	Successful strategy of "democracy promotion through integration"
2007 Lisbon Treaty	"Any European State which respects the values referred to in Article 2 [*human dignity*, freedom, democracy, *equality*, the rule of law and respect for human rights, including the *rights of persons belonging to minorities*] *and is committed to promoting them* may apply to become a member of the Union" (art. 49 TEU) "The Union's action on the international scene shall be guided by the principles which have inspired its own creation ... and which it seeks to advance in the wider world: democracy, the rule of law, the universality and indivisibility of human rights and fundamental freedoms, respect for human dignity, the principles of equality and solidarity, and respect for the principles of the United Nations Charter and international law. ... The Union shall define and pursue common policies and actions ... in order to: ... (b) consolidate and support democracy, the rule of law, human rights and the principles of international law" (art. 21 TEU)

3 – EU's Anchoring: Main Structural Foreign Policy Tools
As previously said, the main structural foreign policy instruments used by the EU to anchor European post-Soviet countries are institutional links, economic assistance, and trade with its member states.[3]

By the expression "institutional links" I am referring primarily to the current status and the final objectives of bilateral relations between the target country and the EU. In terms of institutional links, the strongest incentive that a third country can be offered by the Union is membership, but all former Soviet republics are not offered this incentive. Differently from Russia and Belarus, Moldova, Ukraine and Georgia would seek EU membership. However, there is a clear majority among the member states against acknowledging them as potential candidates in the foreseeable future.

There are also other "institutional" incentives that the Union can offer to third countries in the framework of different contractual relations (cooperation, partnership, association, common spaces etc.) as preferential trading arrangements, liberalization of the movement of persons, partial inclusion in EU policies (as the free trade area, the customs union, the single market and the Schengen

---

[3] In addition to the structural foreign policy tools presented in this section, the EU made also use of conventional foreign policy tools (its second pillar instruments, traditional tools as diplomacy included), which contributed to anchor European post-Soviet states to the EU. For example, after the 1999 CFSP Common Strategies on respectively Russia and Ukraine, which were not extended beyond their expiry date as they did not offer any added value, in 2003 the first EU Special Representative (SP) for Southern Caucasus was appointed, in 2005 the EU launched its border assistance mission for Moldova and Ukraine, in 2007 the first EUSR for Moldova was appointed, and after the escalation of the South Ossetia conflict in 2008, EU diplomacy played an important role (French President Nicholas Sarkozy mediated, on behalf of the EU, the peace plan) and a few days after the escalation of the conflict, the EU decided to dispatch a European Security and Defence Policy (ESDP) civilian monitoring mission and to appoint an EUSR for the crisis in Georgia.

regime), participation in EU programmes, association with EU agencies, and at least some political dialogue.[4]

In terms of bilateral relations, all former Soviet republics negotiated in the late 90s bilateral Partnership and Cooperation Agreements (PCAs),[5] and all of them (with the exception of Russia and Central Asian former Soviet republics[6]) are partners of the European Neighbourhood Policy (ENP)[7], and of the Eastern Partnership (EaP).

PCAs, which constitute the legal basis for bilateral relations with the EU, were concluded for a period of ten years, and aimed at providing a framework for structured political dialogue, supporting the country's efforts to consolidate democracy and to complete the transition into a market economy, promoting trade, and providing a basis for legislative, economic, social, financial, civil, scientific, technological and cultural cooperation. The PCAs with Russia, Ukraine and Moldova were more extensive than the PCA with Georgia (and the PCAs with the other southern Caucasus and central Asian countries), as only the former included the prospect of a free trade agreement [Vahl, 2007: 126].

In 2003 the PCAs were complemented by a new external policy, the European Neighbourhood Policy (ENP), to enhance stability and security at the borders of the EU by promoting political and economic development and regional cooperation among its neighbours of the southern Mediterranean, Eastern

---

[4] Political dialogue represents the minimal form of institutional links, as it can be developed even without contractual relations. It refers to all bilateral political contacts between the EU and a third country, and varies in quantity and quality according to the frequency of these contacts and the topics discussed.

[5] The PCA with Russia was signed in 1994 and entered into force in 1997 (the EU and Russia are currently negotiating a new agreement, replacing the 10-year old PCA), the PCAs with Moldova and Ukraine were signed in 1994 and entered into force in 1998, and the PCA with Georgia and EU was signed in 1996 and entered into force in 1999. The PCA with Belarus was negotiated in 1995, but it never came into force, as the EU refused to ratify it because of Lukashenko's moves towards authoritarian rule.

[6] Kazakhstan, Kyrgyzstan, Uzbekistan, Tajikistan and Turkmenistan.

[7] Belarus is included in the ENP, but it has not been granted the full benefits of this policy because of its authoritarian regime.

Europe and the Southern Caucasus [European Commission, 2003: 3]. Differently from accession candidate countries and potential candidate countries, ENP partners are not offered the incentive of membership. In the short-term, they are offered the Union's support to meet European norms and standards, some of the Union's internal policies and programmes, and ultimately the possibility to be integrated in the EU single market. However, in exchange for the above mentioned offer, the EU asks neighbours for their commitment to the Union's common values, as democracy, the rule of law, respect for human rights, including minority rights, the promotion of good neighbourly relations, the principles of market economy and sustainable development. The positive conditionality attached to shared values has been made explicit: increased security as well as political, economic and cultural cooperation is offered in return for political and economic reform [European Commission, 2003a: 16]. The ENP is based on three components that are very similar to the ones identified for the pre-accession strategy, with a few key differences. These components are Action Plans incorporating a set of priorities for partner countries in such areas as political dialogue, trade, justice and home affairs, energy, and social policy; the monitoring of progress in meeting the priorities listed in the Action Plans; and assistance programmed to help partners satisfy the priorities listed in the Action Plans [European Commission, 2004: 3]. Action Plans for ENP partners are similar to Accession Partnerships for candidate countries, as they both list a set of priorities, which, if fulfilled, bring them closer to the EU. However, differently from the Accession Partnerships, Action Plans are not unilateral acts by the Council but have to be jointly agreed upon with the partner and approved by the respective Cooperation or Association Council. This means that if a certain ENP partner does not want some priorities to be included in the Action Plan, the Commission and the Council cannot oblige the partner to add them. As in the case of accession candidate countries, the progress of ENP partners will be monitored by the bodies established by the PCAs (or Association Agreements for the southern neighbours) and the Commission reports yearly on the progress made. Finally, as in the case of Accession Partnerships, Actions Plans provide a reference for the programming of assistance to the ENP partners. Among our case study countries, ENP Action Plans have been adopted for Ukraine, Moldova, and Georgia, while Belarus has been excluded because of its authoritarian regime.[8]

As previously said, Russia was also offered by the EU the possibility to be part of the ENP, but it refused as it didn't want to be treated as just another neighbour and considered the ENP conditionality unacceptable. This is the reason why in 2003 the EU and Russia decided to develop a strategic partnership and centre their cooperation on the long-term creation of four jointly agreed Common Spaces, in the framework of the PCA: a Common economic space (CES), a Common space of freedom, security and justice, a Common space of external security, and a Common space of research, education and cultural aspects.

Among these four common spaces, the central one is the CES. Vinokurov [2007] explains that the idea of a CES was introduced, during the EU-Russia summit in May 2001, by Romano Prodi in discussions with Vladimir Putin, and then the concept was elaborated by a joint high level group co-chaired by Russian Deputy Prime Minister Khristenko and EU Commissioner Chris Patten. The CES concept was agreed upon by the parties in 2003 and it involves "an open and integrated market between the EU and Russia, based on the implementation of common or compatible rules and regulations, including compatible administrative practices", which "shall ultimately cover substantially all sectors of the economy" [Joint Statement, 2003, Annex 1: art. 12]. However, according to Vinokurov [2007: 228] the CES "integrated market" should imply no more than a free

---

[8] The EU-Ukraine Action Plan was approved in February 2005; the EU-Moldova ENP Action Plan was approved in February 2005 and extended by mutual agreement from February 2008 onwards; the EU-Georgia ENP Action Plan was approved in November 2006 for a period of five years.

trade area supplemented by a deeper degree of integration in individual sectors, as energy and transport.

In April 2004 the European Commission submitted to its Russian counterparts a proposal for an Action Plan specifying more concrete objectives and measures to realize the Common Spaces. The Commission wanted to couple the four spaces together in order not to create discontinuity of advancements in matters that are linked to each other. But Russia insisted on having four separate Road Maps, and thus decoupling various issues. The four Road Maps were agreed in 2005. The one on the CES is the longest one, and reiterates that the goal of the CES is to create an "open and integrated market between the EU and Russia" (Joint Statement, 2005, Annex I: 1). Vahl [2007, 130] compares these Road Maps with ENP Action Plans and argue that "the Road Maps are less ambitious, less easily translated into concrete action, with fewer conditions attached to further cooperation ... In short, the Road Maps for the four common spaces are indeed a 'weaker and fuzzier' derivative of the ENP Action Plans".

On the implementation of these common spaces and in particular of the CES, Vinokurov [2007: 229 and 233] rightly observes that the policy-taker problem[9] is extremely hard to avoid, and that it might represent a serious hurdle to EU-Russian relations in the years to come, as "[w]hile Russia is willing to adjust its legislation in accordance with its pragmatic commercial interests [WTO accession], it will try by all means to avoid the situation of being dictated from Brussels".

Recently the EU has launched a new policy framework for relations with its six eastern ENP partners (Ukraine, Moldova, Armenia, Azerbaijan, Georgia, and Belarus[10]), the Eastern Partnership (EaP). According to the Joint Declaration on the EaP of May 2009 [Council of the European Union, 2009] the aim of the EaP is to create a "more ambitious partnership between the

---

[9] The problem arises when states are obliged to follow the changes in EU legislation while possessing only limited leverage on EU's internal affairs.

[10] As for the ENP, Belarus participation is conditional upon an improved human rights record and moves towards democracy.

EU and the partner countries". It is specified that it is "complementary to existing bilateral contractual relations", and that it should be considered as the "specific Eastern dimension of the ENP". Therefore, it represents the evolution of the ENP for Eastern partners. It is also underlined that the EaP "will be developed without prejudice to individual partner countries' aspirations for their future relationship with the EU" [Council of the European Union, 2009: 5], which is important as it does not preclude future membership.

According to the Joint Declaration [Council of the European Union, 2009], the guiding principles of the EaP are: (1) differentiation; (2) conditionality, and (3) joint ownership – the same guiding principles of the ENP – and it is specified that: (1) the intensification of bilateral relations will take into account "the specific situation and ambition of each partner country"; (2) the EaP is based on mutual "commitments to the principles of international law and to fundamental values, including democracy, the rule of law and the respect for human rights and fundamental freedoms, as well as to, market economy, sustainable development and good governance"; (3) the EaP "will be developed jointly, in a fully transparent manner".

This new policy framework has both a bilateral and a multilateral dimension. The bilateral dimension of the EaP offers partner countries the possibility to sign "New Association Agreements (AA)", superseding the PCAs, that "will provide for the establishment or the objective of establishing deep and comprehensive free trade areas [DCFTA], where the positive effects of trade and investment liberalization will be strengthened by regulatory approximation leading to convergence with EU laws and standards". In addition, the EaP "will promote mobility of citizens of the partner countries through visa facilitation and readmission agreements" (having full visa liberalisation as a long term goal for individual partner countries on a case-by-case basis provided that conditions for well-managed and secure mobility are in place).

The multilateral dimension of the EaP aims at fostering links among partner countries themselves, providing for cooperation activities and a forum to share information and experience on the partner countries' steps towards reform and to discuss further developments of the EaP. This dimension should focus on four thematic platforms: (1) democracy, good governance and stability, (2) economic integration and convergence with EU sectoral policies, (3) energy security, and (4) contacts between people; and it should be organized at four levels: (1) the level of meetings of the heads of state or government of the EaP every two years, (2) the level of meetings of the ministers of foreign affairs once every year; (3) the level of meetings of senior officials engaged in reform work in the four thematic platforms at least twice a year;[11] (4) the level of panels to support the work of the thematic platforms in specific areas.

On funding of this new policy framework, the Joint Declaration affirms that "increased EU financial support will be provided serving the goals of the EaP and taking into consideration progress made by individual partner countries" [Council of the European Union, 2009: 10]. Then, in addition to Community grant assistance (and national co-financing), other donors – the international financial institutions and the private sector – are called to provide additional financing in support of reforms. The European Commission [2009: 3] has specified that € 600 million have been earmarked for the period 2010-13 to address the new needs specifically linked to the EaP, and that they are part of the European Neighbourhood and Partnership Instrument (ENPI).[12] In particular, these resources will be used for the following purposes: (1) comprehensive institution building (CIB) programmes aiming to support the process of reform within the partner countries' institutions in order to implement AAs (approximately € 175 million)[13]; (2) pilot regional development

---

[11] They should adopt a set of core objectives, updated periodically, with a corresponding work programme, and should review the progress achieved.

[12] These funds constitute about a quarter of the total funding that will be made available to East partners over the period 2010-13.

[13] According to the European Commission [2009: 4] twinning should be at the core of the implementation of CIBs, while other measures could include high-level advice, training and exchanges, professional placements and internships, secondment of personnel to sister-institutions in interested member states, scholarships for professional training, etc.

programmes aiming to address challenges stemming from sharp economic and social disparities between partner countries' regions and population groups (approximately € 75 million)[14]; (3) implementation of the EaP multilateral dimension – EaP Civil Society Forum[15] and flagship initiatives[16] included (approximately € 350 million) [see European Commission, 2009: 3].

Most important developments in terms of the implementation of this new policy framework are that the EU is currently negotiating AAs with Ukraine,[17] Moldova and Georgia.

Table 15. All donors, EC, US, EUMSs, and EC+EUMSs ODA to Belarus, Georgia, Moldova, and Ukraine, 1991-2008, (2008 US$ millions)

	Belarus	Georgia	Moldova	Ukraine
All Donors	363.43	5,976.96	2,216.75	2,108.66
US	23.75	1,647.97	420.80	436.65
EC	51.30	785.36	335.02	639.64
EUMSs	150.60	1,193.43	470.15	533.36
EC+EUMSs	201.90	1,978.79	805.17	1,173.00

Note: Net disbursements (actual expenditures). Data on Russia are not available.

Source: IDS Online-DAC Database – Destination of Official Development Assistance and Official Aid – OECD.Stat

---

[14] These programmes should address local needs for infrastructure, human capital, and small and medium sized enterprises (SMEs), modelled on EU cohesion policy [European Commission, 2009: 4].

[15] It has been launched on 16-17 November 2009 in Brussels to promote contacts among civil society organizations and facilitate their dialogue with public authorities [see European Commission, 2008: 12].

[16] According to the European Commission [2008: 12] these initiatives should seek to mobilise multi-donor support, funding from different international financial institutions and investment from the private sector.

[17] In November 2009 the EU and Ukraine adopted the Association Agenda, an instrument to help prepare for the entry into force of the EU-Ukraine AA including a DCFTA. This document lists priorities for 2010 in the following fields: political dialogue; combating corruption; foreign and security policy; cooperation on justice, freedom and security issue; trade and trade related matters, energy cooperation including nuclear issues, and other cooperation issues.

Table 16. European post-Soviet countries' trade with the EU and Russia in current US$ millions (1994-2009)

		1994	1997	1999	2003	2005	2008	2009
BELARUS	Imports from EU	756	2,184	1,827	2,527	3,606	8,543	6,550
	Imports from Russia	1,874	4,632	3,767	7,601	10,118	23,507	16,717
	Exports to EU	581	1,115	1,353	3,622	7,130	14,169	9,289
	Exports to Russia	1,157	4,626	3,222	4,880	5,716	10,552	6,714
GEORGIA	Imports from EU	19	288	330	461	784	1,757	1,333
	Imports from Russia	26	125	63	161	384	426	350
	Exports to EU	3	31	111	83	217	335	454
	Exports to Russia	52	69	45	84	154	30	18
MOLDOVA	Imports from EU	142	442	284	633	1,039	2,765	1,893
	Imports from Russia	309	333	139	183	268	1,258	557
	Exports to EU	147	186	177	307	408	1,002	651
	Exports to Russia	289	509	191	308	347	591	307
RUSSIA	Imports from EU	19,165	24,318	13,055	26,228	43,898	116,329	77,226
	Exports to EU	30,002	41,562	34,922	69,006	138,678	26,3594	134,754
UKRAINE	Imports from EU	1,512	5,245	3,453	7,865	12,192	28,871	15,395
	Imports from Russia	5,998	7,838	5,592	8,645	12,842	16,838	13,236
	Exports to EU	1,829	3,488	3,658	8,702	10,238	18,131	9,510
	Exports to Russia	3,837	3,723	2,396	4,311	7,490	15,763	8,459

Source: IMF, Direction of Trade Statistics (DoTS), online database

Economic assistance is another main benefit that European post-Soviet countries are offered by the EU. In order to evaluate the country's susceptibility to democratic leverage, it is necessary to assess whether the EU (which means in this case European Commission plus EUMSs) is its principal donor of economic assistance. The following table presents data on official development assistance (ODA)[18] to our case study countries in the period 1991-2008, and it can be observed that for all our countries the EU has been the main donor of economic assistance.

Trade with its MSs is another important dimension of the EU's anchoring on European post-Soviet states, as it increases their economic dependence on the EU. The following table shows that after the Eastern enlargement (2004 and 2007) trade between European post-Soviet countries and EUMSs has strongly increased. For example, even if Russia is still the main import partner of Belarus, after the 2004 enlargement the EU has become its first export partner. In the case of Georgia, after the 2004 enlargement the EU has become its first import and export partner. For Moldova the EU was already its first import partner in the second half of the 90s, while it has become its first export partner after the 2004 enlargement. In the case of Ukraine the EU was already its first export partner at the end of the 90s and after the 2007 enlargement it has become also its first import partner. Russia, after 2004 and 2007 has experienced a relevant increase in trade with EUMSs. It can be concluded that the EU has become, at present, the main trade partner for European post-Soviet countries, with the only exception of Belarus.[19]

4 – Pro-Democracy Activity

According to the European Commission "[t]he EU draws on a wide-range of tools to promote human rights and democratization objectives in its external relations. Some of these tools are instruments of traditional diplomacy and foreign policy ... In addition, the EU promotes human rights and democratization through various cooperation and assistance programmes it implements with third countries and through the political dialogues that it conducts with them. In doing so it uses a specific legal basis: a 'human rights clause' that is incorporated in nearly

---

[18] This indicator allows a comparison of the total economic assistance provided by different external actors.
[19] The main trade partner of Belarus is still Russia. However, while Russia is still Belarus major import partner, the EU has become, after 2004, its first export partner.

all EU agreements with third countries, as an essential element" [European Commission, 2007: 7].

Trying to propose a systematic way to analyse EU tools to promote democracy, Figure 6 indicates all the peaceful instruments of democracy promotion (diplomacy, assistance, political dialogue, positive conditionality, and sanctions) used by the EU, with some variation and differences among the case study countries.[20]

Diplomacy usually takes the form of declarations, *demarches*, resolutions and interventions within international *fora*, whose function is to inform the target country of the EU's view on recent democratic shortcomings in a third country. An example of how the EU's diplomatic activity can favour democratization is offered by Ukraine during the Orange revolution, when the EU's constant scrutiny of the events seems to have contributed to the peaceful nature of this revolution.[21]

Democracy assistance comprises "all aid for which the primary purpose, not the secondary or indirect purpose, is to foster democracy in the recipient country" [Carothers, 2000: 187-188], and it can be both economic and technical: "[t]he provision of advice and instruction, training programmes, equipment and other forms of material support to institutional capacity building are typical examples, as are financial subventions to pro-democracy bodies and subsides to cover the costs of certain democratizing processes" [Burnell, 2000: 9].

---

[20] Figure 6 also has two extreme poles. At one there is no active external leverage, but what has been called diffusion, contagion, or example, to describe a situation in which ideas and models of democratic change come from outside, but without any direct activity by external actors. The other pole represents the ending of peaceful forms of pressure, democratization by force, military intervention, or what has been called control, to describe a situation in which an external actor promotes democracy through the use or threat of force.

[21] The way in which the EU handled this revolution has been defined as one of the Union's main diplomatic successes [Karatnycky, 2005].

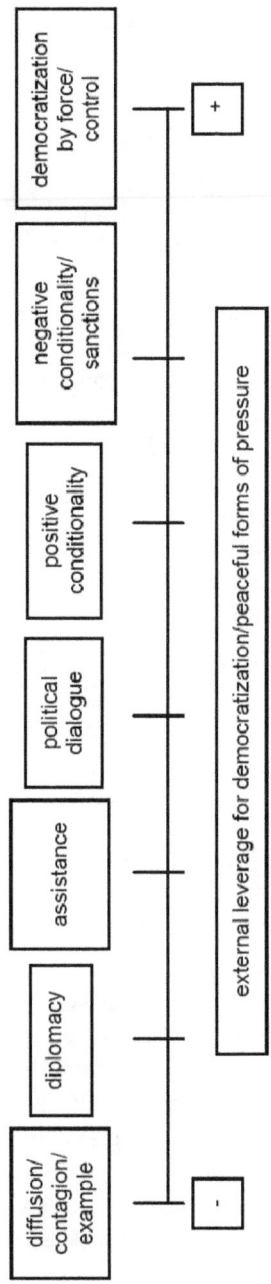

Figure 6. Degrees of external leverage for democratization

128

The EU provides its economic democracy assistance mainly through its geographical assistance programmes, which aim also at democracy assistance (as for example TACIS[1], which has been replaced by ENPI in 2007), as well as through the European Instrument/Initiative for Democracy and Human Rights (EIDHR). The advantage of using geographical assistance programmes is that they include considerable funding for democracy assistance in comparison with EIDHR allocations. For example, Ukraine was allocated in the period 2002-05 an average annually of about 27 million euro of TACIS assistance for "institutional, legal and administrative reform" [Baracani, 2008: 65], while in the period 2000-06 it was allocated only a total of about 7 million euro under the EIDHR budget line for macro projects (see also Table 17 for the percentage of democracy assistance of ENPI allocations).

Table 17. ENPI allocations for country programmes (2007-10)

	total allocations (million €)	% of democracy assistance
Belarus	30	30
Georgia	120	26
Moldova	209	25-35
Ukraine	494	30
Russia	120	0

Source: ENPI, National Indicative Programmes (2007-10)

However, the disadvantage of using geographical assistance programmes to grant democracy assistance is that third country's governments must consent to these programmes [Keukeleire and MacNaughtan, 2008: 226], and that the beneficiaries of these programmes are usually state actors (mainly ministries).

The EIDHR is an *ad hoc* programme, created in 1994 on the European Parliament's initiative, to support worldwide the activities of local civil society organizations working in the field of human rights and democracy (micro-projects), and of regional and

---

[1] TACIS national programme has been the first source of EC assistance towards former Soviet Republics. It aimed to support institutional, legal and administrative reform and to address the social consequences of transition.

129

international organizations as the Council of Europe, the Organization for Security and Cooperation in Europe, and some UN agencies (macro-projects). At the beginning of 2007, a new Regulation for the EIDHR entered into force, and introduced the important principle of the independence of action, allowing for the delivery of assistance without the need for government consent [European Commission, 2007: 19]. However, in the framework of this budget line, the EU supports only apolitical NGOs, and thus denies its assistance to NGOs and opposition groups that adopt a too confrontational approach [Keukeleire and MacNaughtan, 2008: 227].

Data on the percentage of EIDHR assistance for micro projects allocated in the period 2002-06 [European Commission, 2007] show that Russia was allocated 5.5 per cent (€5,8m) of total allocations, Ukraine 3.5 per cent (€3,6m), Georgia 3.3 per cent (€3,5m), and Belarus 0.7 per cent (€0,8m) [European Commission 2007: 17].[2] Data on EIDHR total allocations for country projects (macro-projects) in the period 2000-06 [see ENPI National Indicative Programmes; EIDHR, 2009] show that, among our case study countries, Russia and Georgia were allocated a relatively high amount of assistance for democracy and human rights projects (about €13m each), followed by Ukraine (about €7m), Belarus (€5m), and Moldova (about €1m).

As underlined by Burnell [2000: 9] democracy assistance can have both an economic and a technical nature. An example of EU technical assistance for democracy is the first civilian ESDP mission, in the form of rule of law mission, EUJUST Themis, which the EU decided to deploy in Georgia, in 2004, following the request of Georgian authorities. This mission terminated one year later and it accomplished its mandate of assisting a high-level working group in the development of a strategy for reforming Georgian criminal legislation.[3]

---

[2] Moldova was no allocated EIDHR assistance for micro projects in this period [European Commission, 2007].
[3] Other examples of EU technical assistance which contributes to democratization are twinning programmes and TAIEX (Technical Assistance and Information Exchange), originally designed to help accession candidate

"Political dialogue" refers to the possibility the EU has to discuss the democracy and human rights situation of the country concerned during summits at the highest political level, or, more likely, in the framework of the bilateral and/or multilateral institutions established with the partner countries.[4] For example, each PCA establishes three institutions for political dialogue: a Cooperation Council – composed of members of the EU Council and of the European Commission, and of members of the government of the post-Soviet country – that usually meets once a year; a Cooperation Committee – composed of members of the EU Council and of the European Commission, and of members of the government of the third country at senior civil servants level – that usually meets more regularly; and a Parliamentary Cooperation Committee – composed of members of the Parliament of the post-Soviet country and of the European Parliament – that meets once a year. In the case of Russia, the institutional framework with the EU has been reinforced in 2003 with the conversion of the Cooperation Council into a Permanent Partnership Council. Therefore, at present, the EU-Russia institutional framework consists of: (1) summit meetings twice a year – Russia is the only country with which the EU has regular biannual meetings, Ukraine has yearly summits, while the other post-Soviet states do not meet with the EU at the highest political level; (2) a Permanent Partnership Council which meets at ministerial level – it is the first in EU external relations which can meet in different formations as for the EU Council of Ministers; (3) a Cooperation Committee which meets at senior officials' level; (4) sub-committees on technical issues; and (5) a Joint

---

countries acquire the necessary skills and experience to adopt, implement and enforce EU legislation, and lately extended to ENP partners.

[4] The European Commission [2007: 11] explains that the main objectives of political dialogue on human rights are: (1) seeking information about the human rights situation in the country concerned; (2) expressing EU concerns about aspects of the country's human rights record; (3) identifying practical steps to improve the human rights situation on the ground, in particular through the setting up of cooperation projects; (4) discussing questions of mutual interest and enhancing cooperation on human rights; and (5) exposing governments to international human rights standards and EU practices.

Parliamentary Committee. In addition to all these bilateral institutions in which the EU could address democratic and human rights issues, the EaP has added, as previously said, a multilateral dimension for political dialogue on "democracy, good governance and stability" at four levels: the level of meetings of the heads of state or government of the EaP every two years, the level of meetings of the ministers of foreign affairs once every year, the level of meetings of senior officials engaged in reform work, and the level of specific panels. All this shows that – with the exception of Belarus[5] – the EU has many opportunities to address democracy and human rights issues with its Eastern partners and to socialize their political élite with its democratic principles and practices.

"Positive conditionality" refers to the situation in which the target country has to satisfy the democratic conditions required by the EU in order to be granted additional benefits or "carrots" [Carothers, 2000: 187], while negative conditionality (or sanctions) involves that an international actor may penalize or sanction a country that does not respect the required democratic conditions by suspending, for example, economic assistance, or freezing their bilateral relations.

Until the introduction of the ENP, the EU conditionality towards post-Soviet countries was mainly negative. It can be recalled, for example, that EU refused to ratify the PCA with Belarus because of Lukashenko's moves towards authoritarian rule, and in the case of Russia, the ratification of the PCA was temporarily delayed and TACIS funding was put on hold because of Russia's Chechnya policy. Indeed, PCAs established that respect for democracy, principles of international law and human rights constitute essential elements of the Agreement, and that a violation of these essential elements can lead the EU to take appropriate measures. In addition, according to article 16 of TACIS regulation "[w]hen an essential element for the continuation of cooperation through assistance is missing, in

---

[5] The EU and Belarus held the first round of human rights dialogue in June 2009.

particular in cases of violation of democratic principles and human rights, the Council may, on a proposal from the Commission, acting by a qualified majority, decide upon appropriate measures concerning assistance to a partner State" [Council of the European Union, 1999].

EU negative conditionality continues to exist in the framework of the ENP, for example Belarus has not been granted the full benefits of this policy because of its authoritarian regime,[6] and an "appropriate measure" clause is present in the 2006 ENPI Regulation.[7] However, the ENP is important in terms of its conditionality, because it contains a strong emphasis on positive conditionality, reiterated by the EaP, which, if implemented, could encourage reform-willing states to further pursue their reform agenda. However, this positive conditionality is not quite the same conditionality the EU uses in the case of accession and potential candidate countries. First, the benefits offered by the EU are different as shown in the previous section. Therefore, the so-called strategy of "democracy promotion through [political] integration" [Dimitrova and Pridham, 2004] cannot be applied to ENP partners. The second difference is that, while in the case of countries that have a prospect of membership, it is the EU to indicate the specific political conditions each of them has to satisfy, in the case of ENP partners, the specific political conditions are decided jointly by the ENP partner and the EU.

---

[6] Other examples of negative conditionality on Belarus are the EU Council decisions that contacts with Belarus will be established solely through the Presidency, Secretary General/High Representative, the Commission and the Troika; that Community and MSs' assistance programmes will support only the needs of the population and democratization; and on restrictive measures against some Belarusian officials, President Lukashenko included, responsible for the violations of international human rights law.

[7] Indeed, according to this clause "where a partner country fails to observe the principles referred to in Article 1 [liberty, democracy, respect for human rights and fundamental freedoms and the rule of law], the Council, acting by a qualified majority on a proposal from the Commission, may take appropriate steps in respect of any Community assistance granted to the partner country under this Regulation" [Council of the European Union and European Parliament, 2006: article 28].

This means that if a certain ENP partner does not want some priorities to be included in the Action Plan, the EU cannot oblige the partner to add them. Therefore, the EU can promote democratization – through the ENP instruments – only towards those partners that are willing to engage in this process.

5 – Conclusions

Does the EU's anchoring provide sufficient incentives to European post-Soviet countries in order to encourage their convergence towards a full democratization? Is the EU pro-democracy activity useful in favouring democratization in these countries?

It can be argued that the EU's anchoring should provide enough incentives for two main reasons. First, European post-Soviet countries are offered very strong economic ties with the EU, which is their first donor of economic assistance,[8] their first trade partner,[9] and it is offering them the possibility to establish a free trade area. In addition, these countries are offered visa facilitation with the aim of visa liberalization in the long-term, participation in EU programmes, and the Union's support to meet European norms. Of particular importance is the offer of a free trade area with the EU, as they would be given access to a huge market of more than 500 million consumers, where they could sell their products whilst enjoying a certain advantage in labour costs. A privileged market access has always been very attractive to third countries, and it seems the most important structural foreign policy instruments – after membership – the EU has at its disposal to influence internal dynamics of third countries. Second, for those countries wishing to join the EU – Georgia, Moldova and Ukraine – the EU is not precluding this option in the future, and this might be a further incentive for committing themselves to adopt and implement democratic reforms.

However, these anchors should be more strongly conditioned to the respect for democracy and human rights. In the case of EaP partners, additional incentives should be granted only in

---

[8] Even if data on Russia were not available in the OECD statistics database on ODA.
[9] As previously said, with the exception of Belarus.

exchange for real democratic progress (i.e. implementation rather than adoption of democratic reforms). In addition, in order to enhance the EU's impartiality, and thus its credibility, independent experts from the academic community and the international NGOs' sector, rather than European Commission officials, should report on democratic progress accomplished by EaP partners. In the case of Russia, the EU does not adopt the same standards of EaP partners. Indeed, the Union's policy towards Russia lacks any democratic conditionality, as the MSs prioritize their energy security over democracy promotion. Therefore, the EU should seek to decrease its energy dependence on Russia in order to prioritize its values-driven goals also in the relations with this actor, and thus ending the use of different standards in the relations with European post-Soviet states.

5

UNITED STATES DEMOCRATIC ANCHORING

Alessandra Pinna

1 - Introduction

Since the end of the Cold War, democracy promotion has been a very important aspect of the United States (US) foreign policy in the independent countries of the former Soviet Union (SU). But how can the US help these states in proceeding along the path toward becoming stable and pluralistic? This chapter analyzes the different strategies implemented by the US in order to encourage democratic reforms in Belarus, Georgia, Moldova and Ukraine.

My analysis is based on the concept of *democratic anchoring* [see the Introduction to this volume; and Baracani, this volume], namely its main empirical analysis dimensions (*institutional links* and *economic assistance*) and mechanisms (*conditionality* and *socialization*), which explain the impact of external actors on the democratization process in target countries. I investigate the US democracy promotion in our case studies on the basis of these dimensions and mechanisms, identifying similarities and differences between both the external democracy promotion strategies and the cases. My hypothesis is that in the particular instances analyzed in the chapter, the pro-democratic anchors and mechanisms have different strategic influence, and the most effective ones are economic assistance and socialization. The US is, in fact, geographically distant from the countries of the former SU, and unlike the European Union (EU), the US cannot submit democratic conditionality to the membership of an international political institution where a state, becoming its member, can participate in the decision-making process and can benefit from the redistributive policies.

The analysis begins with a description of the institutional links that tie the US to Belarus, Georgia, Moldova and Ukraine. I delineate the closeness of these bilateral relations and examine the political agreements that define them, especially on the issue of "strengthening democracy". The second section investigates the US economic assistance in our case studies in order to evaluate the importance of the US as a foreign donor, the relevance of the pro-democratic aid compared to the assistance to other sectors, and the main programs and actors involved in it. Next, I analyze the US use of conditionality, both negative and positive, and its repercussions on democracy promotion in the case studies where this mechanism is playing a role. Finally, the chapter examines the US democratic socialization that emerges from democracy assistance actions. In the conclusion, in order to test my hypothesis, I evaluate the impact of the US democratic anchoring by discussing the implications of data emerging from the comparative empirical analysis of the case studies.

2 - Institutional Links

The expression *institutional links* refers to the status of contractual relations between the external actor promoting democracy and the democratizing countries [Baracani, 2008: 47].

In our empirical study this anchor plays a role in democracy promotion if the US has activated contractual relations with Belarus, Georgia, Moldova and Ukraine.

The disintegration of the SU in December 1991 entailed the end of the Cold War and marked the opportunity for the US to develop bilateral relations with the new states that had made up the former SU, as they activated political and economic transformations. Between 1991 and 1992, the US recognized the independence of all the countries analyzed in this chapter, established diplomatic relations with them and opened an American embassy in their capitals. Despite this common starting point, in the following years the US relation with these four countries became more and more diversified. Currently, the US has a very close relationship with Ukraine and Georgia, and Washington concluded strategic partnership treaties with these countries in December 2008 and January 2009, respectively. Previously, the US had signed only specific cooperative agreements with these two former SU states. Its connection with Georgia was almost entirely on security, while with Ukraine was broader. Since 2000 the US and Ukraine began to organize annual conferences in order to improve cooperation between private sectors and governments of their respective countries on matters of mutual benefits: trade and investments, security and policy decisions. These conferences have improved cooperation between the governments of Ukraine and the US and have also sped up business-to-business contacts, thus increasing trade and investments.[1] The US institutional links with Moldova are limited to economic agreements without any political accords, and the Belarusian-American relations are undergoing a difficult and ambiguous period because of the negative conditions imposed in 2006 by the US on some Belarusian officials for human rights abuses and electoral fraud.[2]

As mentioned above, the US recently concluded an important agreement, called Charter on Strategic Partnership, with both Ukraine and Georgia.[3] These treaties are very similar and differ only in some details. The partnership establishes political cooperation between the US and the two Eurasian countries in four fields: security, energy, economy and democracy. For the first time the US relationship with Ukraine and Georgia is based on the concept of reciprocity, and the treaties set down a mutual political commitment over a broad spectrum of common priorities.

---

[1] For more information on the US-Ukrainian annual conferences, see the link: http://usukrainianrelations.org/index.php?option=com_content&task=view&id=14 &Itemid=39 (accessed 1 August 2009).

[2] Both the US Department of State and the Ministry of Foreign Affairs of the Republic of Belarus recognize the drastic deterioration of the bilateral cooperation between the two countries, certainly their motivations for such a cold relationship defend their own government positions. In order to have an idea of the different standings of these ministries, see two official documents publicized in their web sites: "Belarus: U.S. Relations" in www.state.gov and "Bilateral Cooperation: United States" in www.mfa.gov.

[3] The texts of the United States-Ukraine Charter on Strategic Partnership and of the the United States-Georgia Charter on Strategic Partnership are available at http://merln.ndu.edu.

Democracy represents the real pillar of these two agreements for at least three reasons. First, democracy is mentioned as a principle part of the core beliefs shared by the contracting parties, and is defined as "the chief basis for political legitimacy, and therefore, stability" and "the real guarantor of security, prosperity and freedom" (section I). Moreover, on one hand the charters assert that increasingly democratic Ukraine and Georgia can produce positive effects throughout the whole Eurasian region, and on the other the documents state that cooperation between democracies in the fields of defence and security is essential to respond effectively to threats to peace. All partnership countries consider democracy a fundamental principle, which acts as a contagious element for their authoritarian neighbours, as well as a defensive factor for allied democratic states.

Second, both the charters identify strengthening democracy in Ukraine and Georgia as one of the main interests and aims of the contracting parties. Cooperation between the US and the two Eurasian countries differs because with regard to democracy Ukraine and Georgia present different domestic situations; therefore, the sectors where collaboration has to work are different. The combined efforts of the Ukrainian government and the US are designed to bolster the rule of law and good governance by increasing professionalism, transparency and independence in the judicial system, and combating corruption and heightening accountability through citizen and media access to the legislative process. Instead, Georgian and American authorities plan to work together to strengthen the capacity of civil society, foster independent media freedom and increase political pluralism. Moreover, the two countries cooperate to promote the rule of law by reinforcing judicial independence, and reinforce good governance by increasing the accountability of the executive and legislative branches.

Finally, democracy represents an implicit basic requirement in order to achieve US cooperation with Georgia and Ukraine in the fields of trade and energy; this kind of collaboration is founded on a liberal market economy, an essential prerequisite of democracy. In accordance with the partnerships, the US endeavours to facilitate the integration of the two Eurasian countries into the global economy and the market-oriented energy sector by pursuing bilateral treaties and expanding their accession to the appropriate international organizations.

Unlike US relations with Ukraine and Georgia, the institutional links between the US and Moldova have never assumed the form of a political partnership; moreover, these two countries have not renewed their cooperation treaties for many years. Their formal accords date back to the early 90s and their contents concern only economic topics. The US established some agreements with Moldova mainly involving a mutual most-favoured-nation tariff treatment and encouraging reciprocal private investments. These bilateral treaties do not openly support democracy, because they only create commercial opportunities for emerging Moldovan enterprises and enhance favourable circumstances for US business, without specifying any political requirements. However, these agreements indirectly affect the Moldovan democratization process by promoting the development of its open market system, since a free competitive liberal economy is one of the main elements of every democracy.

Institutional links thus constitute an important democratic anchor only in the case of Georgia and Ukraine, because the US has established a pro-democratic contractual relation, through a bilateral political commitment, exclusively with these two countries, even if the effective relevance of this anchor can be evaluated only in the coming years by analyzing the implementation of the partnership by both Georgia and Ukraine. This anchor, however, is quite weak in Moldova as its contractual cooperation with the US is limited to the economic field; moreover, this collaboration has not been re-affirmed during the last fifteen years. Political dialogue between these two countries is absent and their institutional links have only indirectly influenced Moldovan democratization. Finally, the relationship between the US and Belarus is restricted to the diplomatic level. Until now these two states have never signed a political or economical bilateral agreement, and therefore in this specific case the democratic anchor of institutional links is completely lacking.

3 - Economic Assistance

According to the concept of anchoring given in the Introduction to this volume, *economic assistance* is the other main benefit that international donors, namely governmental agencies and multilateral institutions, offer target countries in order to develop, directly or indirectly, their democracy. In this section, I analyze US economic assistance to Belarus, Georgia, Moldova and Ukraine throughout the last two decades. First, I compare the US economic aid provided to these countries with the support granted by other important donors. Second, I look at the annual change in the total US government funds disbursed to our empirical cases and I describe the main US economic assistance programs earmarked to Eurasia. Finally, I analyze American economic assistance in each case study, focusing on two crucial points: first, the distribution of US aid to five different sectors, namely social reform, economic reform, security and law enforcement, democratic reform and humanitarian assistance; and second, the allocation of US funds disbursed for democracy assistance programs and public diplomacy actions.

3.1 – The Economic Assistance Provided by the US and Other Important Donors

Every year, the Organization for Economic Co-operation and Development (OECD) compiles a statistical analysis on international support to developing countries based on the Official Development Aid (ODA) index. This coefficient is defined as those "flows of official financing administrated with the promotion of the economic development and welfare of developing countries as the main objectives, and which are concessional in character with a grant element of at least 25 percent" [OECD, 2007].

Examining ODA disbursed in our case studies during the years 2006-2007, a considerable difference emerges between the countries (see Table 18). In fact Ukraine and Georgia appear to be the top recipients of the total development aid, gathering respectively, and on average in the period 2006-07, 483 and 441 million US$, followed by Moldova with 269 million US$ and

Belarus with only 86 million US$. However, the data interpretation changes if we consider the international economic assistance per capita. Indeed, Georgia turns out to be the largest beneficiary of total aid per capita amounting to 100 US$, followed by Moldova with 71 US$. Ukraine, in contrast, receives only 10 US$ per unit of population, just a little more than Belarus, which gets less than 9 US$.[4]

Table 18. Top ten donors of Official Development Assistance, gross disbursements, in 2007 US$ millions (2006-07 average)

Donor	Belarus		Georgia		Moldova		Ukraine	
	Total	86.15	Total	440.71	Total	269.15	Total	482.79
1st	Germany	18.3	US	97.5	IMF[b]	51.09	EU	125.7
2nd	EU	12.0	Germany	46.2	EU	47.7	US	122.0
3rd	Poland	11.4	EU	44.8	IDA[a]	36.8	Germany	67.8
4th	US	10.0	IMF[b]	43.6	US	24.0	Global Fund	27.2
5th	Sweden	9.6	IDA[a]	36.8	Sweden	15.2	Sweden	21.4
6th	Global Fund	4.2	Austria	28.1	Germany	9.9	Canada	16.6
7th	France	3.4	Sweden	10.7	Turkey	8.8	France	11.7
8th	Switzerland	2.9	Netherlands	10.0	Netherlands	7.8	Turkey	11.1
9th	CR[c]	1.7	Turkey	10.0	France	7.3	UK[d]	10.6
10th	Norway	1.4	Japan	9.2	Japan	5.8	Poland	10.4

Notes: [a]: International Development Association; [b]: International Monetary Fund; [c]: Czech Republic; [d]: United Kingdom.

Source: IDS Online-DAC Database – Destination of Official Development Assistance and Official Aid, OECD.Stat

In each case study, the US is one of the principal donors, but its weight changes depending on the recipient country. ODA data for 2006-07 makes clear the different roles that the US plays as a donor. Among the case studies, Ukraine received the highest US development aid, amounting to 122 million US$, equivalent to 25% of the total ODA. In this country, US economic assistance was second only to the EU by a mere 3.7 million US$. On the

---

[4] The total aid per capita data are based on the ODA data (Table 9) and the population data of the case studied [World Bank, 2007].

other hand, the US was the largest donor in Georgia, followed by Germany, the EU and the International Monetary Fund (IMF). During the years 2006-07, Washington disbursed 97.5 million US$ to Tbilisi, equivalent to 22% of the total ODA. Unlike Ukraine and Georgia, the US was the fourth largest donor in both Moldova and Belarus. In the first case, the IMF, the EU and the International Development Association (IDA) earmarked higher disbursements then the US, which expended 24 million US$, less than 9% of the total ODA. In Belarus, the first three donors before the US were Germany, the EU and Poland. US development aid amounted to 10 million US$, almost 12% of the total ODA.

3.2 – US Economic Assistance in the Last Two Decades

Total US Government funds disbursed to our empirical cases has changed during the last two decades, and a comparison between the annual US expenditures in our four countries highlights the oscillating trend in US disbursements (see Table 19).

Belarus is the country that underwent the largest decrease in US economic assistance. During the 90s, Minsk received 41 million US$ on average per year, but this amount fell down to 11 million US$ throughout the period 2001-07. In contrast, the US annual disbursement for Georgia has increased considerably in recent years, averaging 79 million US$ until 2000 and then rising to 138 million US$ in the following seven years. Annual average US economic assistance swelled in Moldova as well, but only slightly: from 44 million US$ during 1992-2000 to 49 million US$ in 2001-07. However, it is important to mention that since 2002, aid to Moldova has gradually decreased: in 2002 Moldova got 107 million US$ and in 2007 only 27 million US$. Finally, the benefit that Ukraine is getting from the US is falling: from 1992 to 2000, the country received on average 243 million US$, but during the period 2001-07 this amount decreased to 205 million US$. Additionally, a detailed analysis of the annual change in US funds disbursed to Ukraine shows that US aid has gradually fallen: in 2001 it was 250 million US$ and after a gradual decline in 2007 it reached only 177 million US$.

Table 19. Total US Government funds disbursed in current millions US$
(1992-2007)

	1992-2000	2001	2002	2003	2004	2005	2006	2007	2001-2007	TOT.
Belarus	368	6	15	10	10	8	15	13	77	445
Georgia	708	114	172	134	136	123	160	124	963	1,671
Moldova	394	49	107	50	44	36	28	27	341	735
Ukraine	2,191	250	224	235	190	172	184	177	1,432	3,623

Notes: The data of this table and the following ones are not in constant US$ because the US Government Fiscal Years always present data in current million US$.

Source: FY 2000-2007 U. S. Government Assistance to and Cooperative Activities with Eurasia, Bureau of European and Eurasia Affairs

Table 20. Total US funds disbursed for democracy promotion and the
main implementation actors in current millions US$ (2001-07)

	USAID		DEPARTMENT OF STATE		NED		TOTAL
Belarus	40.79	57%	25.50	35%	5.59	8%	71.88
Georgia	83.36	72%	30.64	26%	2.01	2%	116.01
Moldova	32.26	66%	15.89	32%	0.77	2%	48.92
Ukraine	181	63%	97.48	34%	10.22	3%	288.70

Source: FY 2001-2007 U. S. Government Assistance to and Cooperative Activities with Eurasia, Bureau of European and Eurasia Affairs

In our case studies, US economic assistance is based on specific programs, some of them exclusively addressed to the states of the former SU and others generically directed to developing countries. The US actors involved in the implementation of these programs are the US Agency for International Development (USAID), the Department of State and the National Endowment for Democracy (NED) (see Table 20).

The most important Eurasian program is the Freedom Support Act (FSA).[5] It passed in the US Congress in 1992 with the purpose of providing the post-communist states with funds to support the free market and democracy through demilitarization and humanitarian and technical assistance. Looking at the Table 21, the relevance of

---

[5] For an exhaustive description of the Freedom Support Act, see the *Freedom Support Act of 1992 Fact Sheet* [White House, 1992].

the FSA is evident: in Ukraine, Moldova and Georgia, FSA funds exceed the economic support of all the other assistance programs; only in Belarus FSA aid is less than half of non-FSA benefits. The Freedom Support Act has several objectives, but the two main ones are the promotion of democratic institutions to facilitate democratization and the development of the private sector to strengthen free market economies. Analyzing total US government funds disbursed between 1992 and 2007, it emerges that in all case studies FSA aid represents 99% of US assistance aimed at economic reforms for a free market economy and approximately 90% of the US endowment to democratization.[6]

In Belarus, Georgia and Moldova, FSA funds comprise half of all US support in the humanitarian field. The rest is provided by the Public Law 480 Food Aid Program (PL 480). This bill offers agricultural assistance to developing countries that have demonstrated the potential to become commercial markets, are undertaking measures to improve their food security and agricultural development, and exhibit a great need for food. Only in Ukraine FSA funds constitute 80% of the US humanitarian assistance, while PL 480 aid amounts to merely 20%.

Table 21. Total US Government funds spent by programs in current millions US$ (1992-2007)

	FSA	NON-FSA	TOTAL
Belarus	123	322	445
Georgia	895	776	1,671
Moldova	444	291	735
Ukraine	2,378	1,245	3,623

Source: FY 2000-2007 U. S. Government Assistance to and Cooperative Activities with Eurasia, Bureau of European and Eurasia Affairs

[6] The percentages of the Unites States Government funds disbursed during the period 1992-2007 by programs mentioned in this paragraph are calculated on the data of the *Fiscal Years 2000-2007 U.S. Government Assistance to and Cooperative Activities with Eurasia*; the distribution of the US aid in sectors (social reform, economic reform, security and law enforcement, democratic reform and humanitarian assistance) is based on the parameters of the classification illustrated in *Fiscal Year 2004 U.S. Government Assistance to and Cooperative Activities with Eurasia*.

The FSA also provides funding for social and security sectors. In Georgia, Moldova and Ukraine, this program contributed to US economic assistance with 60% to social reforms and 30% to security and law enforcement. In Belarus, in contrast, FSA aid represents only 2% in both categories. In the social sector, FSA aid is supplemented by the Peace Corps Program, which organizes volunteers in developing countries working with local community members in areas like education, community development, environment and information technology. In the security sector, the FSA supplies funds for nuclear non-proliferation programs, as well as for the dismantlement and destruction of biological, chemical and conventional weapons. However, there are other US assistance programs that play an important role in the security sphere as well. The most relevant one is the Cooperative Threat Reduction Program, which started in 1993 and provides funds to facilitate the elimination of nuclear weapons in the former SU and to prevent the proliferation of weapons of mass destruction. Funds from this program represent a large part of US security assistance in our case studies: 90% in Belarus, 55% in Ukraine, 38% in Moldova and 28% in Georgia. Moreover, in 1996 the Warsaw Initiative Program was approved in order to advance closer military relations between NATO and countries committed to democratic principles. This endowment amounts to 10% of US security aid in Moldova, 5% in Georgia and 2% in Ukraine. This program is not operating in Belarus. Finally, the Bureau of Political Military Affairs of the U.S. Department of State administrates three security assistance programs: the Foreign Military Financing Program, the International Military Education and Training Program and the Non-Proliferation, Anti-terrorism, Demining, and Related Programs.[7] Funds from these projects comprise 33% of total US security assistance in Georgia and 25% in Moldova, but only 8% in Ukraine and 1% in Belarus.

---

7 For an exhaustive description of the Security Assistance Funds administrated by the Bureau of Political-Military Affairs, see the website of the U.S. Department of State at the link http://www.state.gov.

3.3 – The Effective Distribution of US Economic Assistance

In order to evaluate the relevance of US economic assistance in democracy promotion, it is important to analyze the effective distribution of US aid to different sectors. From the US economic assistance classification published in fiscal year 2004, titled *U.S. Government Assistance to and Cooperative Activities with Eurasia*, I have identified five main sectors and their respective programs: social reform, economic reform, security and law enforcement, democratic reform and humanitarian assistance.

Table 22. Main sectors of US Government funds disbursed in Belarus, Georgia, Moldova and Ukraine in current millions US$ (1992-2007)

	Belarus		Georgia		Moldova		Ukraine	
	1992-2000	2001-2007	1992-2000	2001-2007	1992-2000	1901-2007	1992 20-00	2001-2007
Social reform	10	0	12	64	21	42	113	121
Economic reform	14	29	81	228	111	147	611	333
Security and law enforcement	79	3	38	346	54	51	741	529
Democratic reform	30	66	53	114	25	48	275	282
Humanitarian assistance	393	25	857	204	302	56	792	51

Source: FY 2000-2007 U. S. Government Assistance to and Cooperative Activities with Eurasia, Bureau of European and Eurasia Affairs

The effective US aid allocation considerably changed throughout the period 1992-2007 and to analyze this shift, it is useful to divide the US assistance period into two phases: the first spans from 1992 to 2000, the second from 2001 to 2007[8] (Table 22).

---

[8] In order to conduct a rigorous comparison, the two phases should embrace the same time-frame, instead in this study the first period lasts eight years and the second one six years. This choice is justified by three motivations: 1) the analysis has the goal to examine the US assistance in the four case studies since the beginning, that is 1992; 2) data referring to the years 1992-2000 are indivisible per years, because the *Fiscal Years 2000 U.S. Government Assistance to and Cooperative Activities with Eurasia* reports only aggregate data for the period 1992-2000; 3) data on the United States Government funds disbursed in 2008 and 2009 are currently not available.

In Belarus, US assistance was drastically reduced after 2001 and the sectors mainly affected were humanitarian assistance and security and law enforcement. Analyzing the annual changes in the second phase, it is evident that US economic assistance decreased so radically that it nearly ceased in all sectors with the exception of democratic reform. Indeed, in the last years US aid to Belarus has been earmarked exclusively for democracy promotion.

A comparison of US economic support in Georgia between the first and second phase highlights the fact that only the humanitarian sector was considerably downsized in this period, and in 2007 amounted only to 1.76 million US$. All other forms of assistance increased, especially security reinforcement, rising by 800% with two peaks in 2002 and 2006. In fact, since 2005 this sector has received the most absolute support from the US. In contrast, during the period 2001-2007, economic reform assistance decreased, democracy aid was quite invariable and only the social reform sector had a positive trend with the exception of the 2004 decline.

In Moldova as well, the most important difference between the two phases is the level of economic aid earmarked for humanitarian assistance: it drastically decreased in the second period. US support for the security sector, in contrast, was almost the same, and social, economic and democratic reform aid increased. Examining the annual data for 2001-2007, we see a sharp rise in 2002, with US aid increasing for all sectors with the exception of humanitarian assistance. However, from 2003 until 2007 this positive trend reversed: only democracy aid kept increasing.

Comparing US economic help in Ukraine over the two phases, we can make three observations: during the period 2001-2007 humanitarian assistance radically decreased, economic reform and security were much less supported and aid to democratic and social reform barely increased. Looking at yearly US assistance during the second phase, democracy aid is the only kind of assistance with a constant positive trend. Indeed, although the security sector received higher US support, its trend was negative, and US economic reform aid declined with the exception of the increasing funds earmarked in 2004 and 2007.

From this analysis of the effective distribution of the US economic assistance, democratic reform emerges as one of the most financed sectors. In 2007, it was the first target in Belarus and Moldova, the second after economic reform in Ukraine and the third following security and law enforcement and economic reform in Georgia. All sectors in different proportion, contribute to create and strengthen a democracy founded on a market economy and pluralistic and healthy society, but democratic reform is undoubtedly the form of aid most focused on this goal. This sector includes all the "voluntary activities adopted, supported, and (directly or indirectly) implemented by (public or private) foreign actors explicitly designed to contribute to the political liberalization of autocratic regimes, democratization of autocratic regimes, or consolidation of democracy in specific recipient countries" [Schmitter and Brouwer, 1999: 12]. These copious activities can be divided into two different classes, namely democracy assistance and public diplomacy actions. The former corresponds to actions that openly develop the different dimensions of democracy, through specific programs addressed to domestic actors in recipient countries.[9] Public diplomacy, in contrast, "seeks to influence opinions and mobilize publics in ways that support specific US interests and policies" [Peterson, 2002: 84]. Democracy promotion has always been one of the most important American interests especially after the end of the Cold War and even more after September 11th [Cox, Ikenberry and Inoguchi, 2000; Risse, Magen and McFaul, 2009]. The US government has operated public diplomacy programs creating its own radio and television broadcasting systems to transmit democratic messages around the world, and supporting local pro-democratic independent media through specific democracy assistance projects.

Table 23 calculates US democratic reform aid to our case study countries during the period 1992-2007, specifying the funds disbursed for democracy assistance activities and public diplomacy programs. Ukraine clearly received the most copious US support, amounting to 557 million US$, while the second largest target state, Georgia,

---

[9] The main dimensions of democracy identified by Diamond and Morlino [2005] are: the rule of law, participation, competition, accountability, freedom, equality and responsiveness. The development degree of each dimension defines the quality of democracy.

obtained only 167 million US$. Belarus got 96 million US$, more than Moldova which was given only 73 million US$. However, taking into account the international economic assistance per capita, the analysis drastically changes. Indeed, it turns out that US aid for democratization in the Ukraine is lower than in some of the other countries: from 1992 to 2007 it obtained 11.83 US$ per unit of population, only slightly more than Belarus, which received 9.81 US$. On the other hand, Georgia emerges as the most supported state, with 37.14 US$ per person, followed by Moldova with 17.42 US$. These data should be examined very carefully, because they could be misleading. On the one hand, the size of the population cannot be considered a principal factor inducing international actors to promote democracy in a country, while geopolitical position and nuclear weapons possession are definitely more influential; on the other hand, the goal of democracy assistance is a political transition which does not depend on the size of the population, but on the type of non-democratic regime, presence of pro-democratic parties, proliferation of social pluralism, previous democratic experience and so on.

Table 23. The US funds disbursed for democracy assistance and public diplomacy in current millions US$ (1992-2007)

	DEMOCRACY ASSISTANCE		PUBLIC DIPLOMACY		TOTAL	PER CAPITA TOTAL
Belarus	62.99	65%	33.23	35%	96.22	9.81
Georgia	122.95	74%	44.21	26%	167.16	37.14
Moldova	43.08	59%	30.12	41%	73.20	17.42
Ukraine	376.79	68%	180.47	32%	557.26	11.83

Note: The per capita total values are expressed in current US$.

Source: FY 1992-2007 U.S. Government Assistance to and Cooperative Activities with Eurasia, Bureau of European and Eurasia Affairs and World Development Indicators (my compilation).

Looking at Table 23, in each case study democracy assistance activities received more funding than public diplomacy programs. Percentages of the two kinds of aid are closest in Moldova, 59% versus 41%, and Georgia is the case with the greatest discrepancy, 74% versus 26%. Although in the period 1992-2007 public diplomacy funds were much less than democracy assistance ones, their amount was quite high if we consider that public diplomacy programs are directed to the only activity of democratic propaganda through US mass media, while democracy assistance consists of several different projects supporting various domestic actors, from public institutions to civil society, in a plurality of democratic topics.

4 - Conditionality

Conditionality is a mechanism that explains the way through which domestic actors comply, in the short term, with the democratic demands established by the external actors. Conditionality works through the threat or imposition of sanctions and/or through the promise or grant of rewards. Therefore there are two different kinds of conditionality, a negative and a positive one. The former refers to non-military, coercive political, diplomatic and economic measures used to induce a democratic policy change in another state, while the latter involves a democratic reinforcement by reward, namely material and symbolic goods are provided only after that a target government complies with the democratic conditions required [Magen and Morlino, 2008: 40]. The US has used both forms of conditionality in our Eurasian case studies. The US has, in fact, exercised the negative one against Belarus and the positive one towards Georgia, Moldova and Ukraine, implementing the Millennium Challenge Corporation initiative.

In June 2006 the US Government, in concert with the EU, imposed travel restrictions and financial sanctions against members of the Lukashenko's Belarusian government. These measures were addressed to officials implicated in human rights abuses, election frauds and corruption, because with their political attitude they were impeding the transition to democracy in Belarus. Moreover, the economic sanctions prohibited US entrepreneurs from engaging in financial transactions with specific Belarusian persons. During 2007, these measures became more restrictive: six other executive officers were forbidden to entry into the US and assets of Belneftekhim, Belarusian state-controlled oil-processing and chemical company, were frozen by the US Treasury Department, and finally American companies were barred from doing business with this firm. In the beginning, Belarus reacted by stiffening its position and expelled ten diplomats from the US Embassy in Minsk, in May 2008. After only three months, Belarusian government released some political prisoners. This decision, combined with other positive steps on human rights, improved its relation with the US, so that Washington partially suspended sanctions for six months.[10]

The US has resorted to positive conditionality in order to grant Millennium Challenge Corporation (MCC) aid. This specific project was established in 2004 and its mission is to reduce global poverty through the promotion of sustainable economic growth. A country's eligibility for receiving assistance depends on its performance on a set of 17 independent and transparent indicators designed to measure a country's effectiveness in ruling justly, investing in people and fostering entrepreneurship. All these indicators are processed by qualified ranking actors, such as the World Bank Institute, World Health Organization, Freedom House and others. There are six democratic political criteria, labelled under the ruling justly category: civil liberties, political rights, voice and accountability, government effectiveness, rule of law, control of corruption.

Currently, eighteen states have been made eligible for receiving MCC economic assistance. This aid is granted through Compact Program Assistance (CPA), which is a multi-year agreement between MCC and target countries which regulates funding of specific projects directed to reduce poverty, stimulate economic growth and improve good governance. CPA must be developed in consultation with local citizens and implemented, managed and maintained by the developing states. In the course of time, if a recipient country fails to perform on indicators, it will lose its status, according to the main principles of positive conditionality. This occurred twice: Gambia was suspended from eligibility for

---

[10] In order to reconstruct the US use of negative conditionality in Belarus and the Belarusian reaction, I have referred to the US Department of State and US Government web sites.

152

its deterioration in eight of 17 criteria and Fiji was no longer eligible due to its military coup.[11] Countries that have demonstrated significant improvement in policy indicators, but do not qualify for a CPA, are eligible for Threshold Program Assistance (TPA). This kind of aid is a small endowment designed to assist a country close to meeting account suitability to become eligible for CPA.

In our case studies, Georgia is the only country that signed the CPA with the US. The agreement came into force in April 2006 and established a 295.3 million US$ grant to implement a five year program. In 2008, a US amendment allocated an additional 100 million US$ to Georgian CPA. American and Georgian MCC officials identified two different obstacles to poverty reduction and economic growth in the region outside of Tbilisi: a lack of reliable infrastructure and the slow development of business. In order to overcome these impediments, the Georgian CPA is working to achieve two main goals: first, the creation of key regional infrastructures, thus improving transportation for regional trade, ensuring a reliable supply of energy and municipal service delivery; and second, the development of regional enterprises by funding investment and technical assistance and increasing productivity, especially in farms and agro-businesses. All CPA activities are currently underway and monitoring has been assigned to a non-governmental organization called Economic Policy Research Centre.[12]

In 2006, Moldova and Ukraine received TPA status. In both countries, the aid program is focused on reducing corruption in the public sector because this phenomenon strongly undermines their democratic performance, one of the three pillars of the CPA. The strategy adopted in these target states is almost the same. Both programs aim to fight bribery by bolstering the capacity of

---

[11] For more information about these two cases, see the following documents: *Board Meeting Summery, June 16, 2006*, http://www.mcc.gov; and *Congressional Notification Transmittal Sheet, August 24, 2007*, http://www.mcc.gov.

[12] For more information on the MCC Compact assistance to Georgia, see "MCC – Georgia: An Overview", http://www.mcc.gov.

the judiciary, strengthening the monitoring capability of civil society and mass media, and fulfilling ethical and administrative standards. The US budgeted 24.7 million US$ for Moldova and 45 million US$ for Ukraine in order to help these countries to combat the problem of corruption, which more than the others prevents them from enjoying the benefits of the CPA.[13]

5 - Socialization

Magen and Morlino define *international democratic socialization* as a "process of inducting individuals and states into the democratic norms and rules of a given regional, international and transnational community" [Magen and Morlino, 2008: 44]. This mechanism fosters the internalization of democratic values and interests through the creation of linkages between democratizing actors and domestic pro-democratic change agents[14].

The most perceptible linkage is the relation between the internal and external actors established by the implementation of the international economic assistance programs, especially the ones involved directly with democracy support. External aid in this specific field is generally undertaken through training and advice projects led by international staff addressed to people of a target country who, over time, should be socialized to democratic principles and practices. These activities are particularly relevant for democratic socialization because they are based on the mechanism of persuasion: the international actors strive to activate democratic political changes in other states through a free transfer of democratic ideas, values and practices. The goal is that political and social actors in countries in transition will internalize democratic norms because attracted and induced through their interactions with external democratic trainers and advisors.

---

[13] For more information on Threshold Program Assistance in Moldova and Ukraine, see "MCC – Moldova: An Overview", http://www.mcc.gov; and "MCC – Ukraine: An Overview", http://www.mcc.gov.

[14] Change agents are norm entrepreneurs who "mobilize in the domestic context and persuade others to redefine their interests and identities" [Börzel and Risse, 2000: 2].

According to the *Congressional Budget Justification for the Foreign Operations*, fiscal year 2008 and 2009, US democracy assistance in our case studies is usually directed at four different kinds of actors: governmental establishment, judicial system, political parties and civil society. The analysis of each case shows that the US pays more attention to some kinds of recipients than others, and moreover, that the amount of support differs depending on the domestic context of the target country (see Table 24).

Table 24. Governing Justly & Democratically Program by elements in current millions US$ (2006-2009)

	GOOD GOVERNANCE		JUSTICE SECTOR		POLITICAL PARTIES		CIVIL SOCIETY	
Belarus	-	-	-	-	6,802	19%	29,337	81%
Georgia	19,465	34%	12,619	22%	7,275	13%	17,433	31%
Moldova	6,459	20%	6,235	19%	5,373	17%	14,004	44%
Ukraine	30,957	34%	17,538	19%	7,015	8%	35,843	39%

Note: 2009 fiscal data are request funds, 2008 fiscal data are estimate obligations and 2006-07 fiscal data are actual funds.

Source: Congressional Budget Justification for Foreign Operations, Fiscal Year 2008 and 2009, U. S. Department of State

Ukraine and Georgia present a similar situation, and in both countries the US directs 34% of its democracy assistance actions to the governmental establishment and about 20% to the judicial system. Despite the similar percentages, the US projects in these two countries do not have exactly the same priorities. In Ukraine, US support for good governance reinforces local government and strengthens the legislative function. On the first point, the US helps the Association of Ukrainian Cities by offering professional training to municipal officials. In addition, the US supports with its technical assistance a legislative reform in order to bolster local government fiscal and political autonomy. On the second point, American actors are particularly involved in pushing for drafting compliance directed at Ukraine's admittance to Euro-Atlantic institutions. In Georgia, the US first of all enhances efficiency, effectiveness and accountability of the executive by assisting reforms, encouraging inter-ministerial coordination and promoting cooperation among think tanks, civil society organizations and public institutions in policy analysis. Second, as in Ukraine, US assistance supports decentralization legislation. US aid to the judicial sector, in Ukraine, is oriented to reducing corruption through educational and information campaigns, staff training, and by improving procedures for selecting and appointing judges and promoting reforms in order to increase transparency of court management. In Georgia, in contrast, US programs are focused on increasing judicial independence, developing new procedures on the enforcement of civil judgments and assisting legal education reforms.

Moldova, compared with the two previous cases, receives a quite different percentage for US assistance to good governance (20%), and a similar one for aid to justice sector (19%). On the first point, as in Ukraine, the US is intensely focused on assisting democratic local government and decentralization by providing training for municipal officials, increasing transparency, enhancing local financial management and developing the quality of local services. In order to support the judicial sector, US programs organize advocacy training and technical assistance in human rights, legal association building and institutional capacity building.

Belarus is the only country in our case studies where the US is not addressing assistance to the governmental establishment or judicial system. US aid is directed mostly to civil society (81%), with only 19% reserved for democratic parties. In the latter sector, the US supports political forces striving for democratic reforms by providing training in political party building, planning and management of election campaigns and media relations. The US programs designed to strengthen civil society focus on building the capacity of non-governmental organizations through training in governance, volunteer recruitment, fundraising and public advocacy. Furthermore, the US supports independent media with grants and technical assistance in order to improve professional standards in providing objective and quality information.

Also in Moldova, the US directs the majority of its support to civil society; however the percentage is much lower than in Belarus at 44%. This assistance mainly supports non-governmental organizations and civic groups in order to develop campaigns and projects on community needs to engage citizens to political sphere and to make them capable of demanding transparency and accountability from their institutions, especially at the local level. The US is also aiding Moldovan democratic political parties (19%). The programs aimed at this kind of assistance have three main goals: to empower political activists and persuade them to be organized in political structures; to develop democratic initiatives from the bottom up; and to increase political party transparency and organizational structure at the national level.

In our case studies, Ukraine and Georgia are the countries where civil society and democratic political parties receive the lowest assistance from the US. In Ukraine, the percentage of US aid to civic groups is 39%, and 8% to political parties. The American programs strengthening civil society support non-governmental advocacy activities and public debates conducted by think tanks in order to turn the third sector into an integrated and permanent part of Ukrainian society. To assist parties and establish multiparty competition, the US organizes training for political activists on action planning and structural organization, provides grants and advice courses on platform-building, and helps to increase participation by women in politics. Finally, the US directs to Georgian civil society and democratic political parties respectively only 31% and 13% of its endowments. In both fields, the US projects are particularly focused on young people and women, promoting their participation in politics and civic activities by training them to run for political office and project management. Moreover, the US provides support for countrywide polling to help democratic parties to be responsive to constituents' needs and to organize get-out-the-vote campaigns and voter education. Lastly, the US projects assist schools in promotion of civic education and the dissemination of democratic values.

6- Conclusion

This chapter has pointed out that the US is an important pro-democratic actor in our four cases, namely Belarus, Georgia, Moldova and Ukraine. The study has also indicated that US strategy is based on two anchors, institutional links and economic assistance that try to hook these target countries up to democracy through two mechanisms, conditionality and socialization. Finally, the empirical analysis has confirmed the research hypothesis on the predominant influence and effectiveness of economic assistance for anchoring the socialization mechanism. The existing difference between adoption and performance of the anchors and mechanisms can be explained by taking into account two main points. First, the US, unlike the EU, cannot assert a strong incentive, such as the promise of membership, in order to encourage a democratic compliance through institutional links and conditionality. Furthermore the US could not claim a common history, tradition and culture with these countries in order to promote an emulation of its own democratic institutions. Second, the diversified democratic status of the countries causes some anchors and mechanisms not to operate or to operate differently. Belarus, an entirely authoritarian regime, is definitely the most deviant case, and in comparison with the others, this state presents numerous dissimilarities in relation to US democratic anchoring. According to Freedom House and Polity IV data, all the other cases are hybrid regimes which lost the main authoritarian characters without assuming all the basic democratic aspects. In each of these countries, especially in Georgia and Ukraine, US anchoring works in a similar way.

The section on economic assistance has shown that the US pays particular attention to the countries analyzed in this chapter for at least two reasons. First, the US is one of the main donors in our four cases, especially in Ukraine and Georgia where its contribution is about 25% of the total international endowment, but also in Moldova and Belarus it is quite significant, around 10%. Second, the US supports these states, particularly in the area of democratic and economic reform, not only through general US aid programs for developing countries, but mostly by means of specific assistance programs exclusively addressed to the area of the former SU. Although since the end of the Cold War, US economic aid has always been quite high in our cases, its amount has changed over time in both quantity and quality terms. On the first point, the analysis of the yearly US funds disbursed in our four states during the period 1992-2007 shows that the US assistance has a positive trend only in Georgia, in fact in Ukraine and Moldova it is progressively decreasing, while in Belarus it has drastically diminished. It is plausible to consider this change in the US attitude as a consequence of the World Trade Centre attack which shifted the United States political and economical resources from the Eastern Europe to Middle East, the new crucial area in the international system. On the second point, the study of the effective distribution by sectors of the US aid points out that the financing changed throughout the time. Humanitarian assistance has been generally subjected to a drastic reduction, and the aid for a free market economic reform decreased as well, but not in the same negative proportion of the previous topic. Similarly, US funds for security and law enforcement have diminished in all cases with the exception of Georgia; in order to better understand this unexpected data, it is important to take into account the South Ossetia War between Georgia and Russia that took place in August 2008. Conversely, the US assistance for a democratic reform enhanced in all countries, mainly in Belarus and Moldova where this sector has become the most financed one by the US. In Georgia, the US pro-democratic aid in the last years doubled in comparison with the previous period, although this area is still in third place for US funding, after security and law enforcement and economic reform. Finally, in Ukraine the US endowment for democratic reform is constant, but for the decreasing aid to other sectors, this one is second only to economic reform.

The section on democratic socialization has shown that the US is inducing the four countries to democratic norms and rules pre-eminently through the implementation of democracy aid programs. Therefore, the spread of this mechanism depends on the development of a specific anchor, namely the economic assistance to democracy. Nevertheless, socialization represents a crucial mechanism because it carries out the very important function of transferring democratic ideas and values to domestic change agents who will spread them at both institutional and social levels. In all case studies the US accomplishes democratic socialization through training and advice programs, but their achievement varies according to the political regimes where they are implemented. In Belarus, the only one of the four countries with an authoritarian regime, democracy assistance is wholly directed to social actors, namely democratic political parties and civil society. The explanation is that all institutional potential recipients are completely unreliable, because they are entirely implicated in the authoritarian regime that the US democracy promotion tries to undermine. As collaboration with political and judicial institutions is impossible, the US seeks a proactive dialogue exclusively with the social actors already involved in a democratic opposition to the Belarus political system. On the other hand, all the other three countries are hybrid regimes; therefore they make overtures to democracy. Given that context, the US directs its attention to both institutional and social levels, looking for actors implicated in pro-democratic activities to address its democracy assistance programs. In all these cases, the US has never chosen the institutional subjects as preferential interlocutors. Its strategy has always been directed to both actors, namely institutional and social ones, with the purpose of promoting democracy in both top-down way and bottom-up direction, without excluding any opportunity.

The analysis of the US institutional links and conditionality has shown that in our case studies this anchor and mechanism are the weakest ones, especially for two reasons: they are not implemented in either country, and their effectiveness in producing democratic changes is quite limited. The US has established a political and diplomatic pro-democratic relation only with Georgia and Ukraine and their partnership explicitly recognizes the importance of democracy and sets up the collaboration between the parts in order to encourage the Georgian and Ukrainian democratization, without fully providing the instruments to achieve this goal. The risk is that these agreements would be only declarations of intent, unless the parties sign specific operative treaties. As for the mechanism of democratic conditionality, it has been used by the US only in specific circumstances, situations that are too exclusive to produce positive systemic consequences. The US imposition of negative conditionality has been limited to Belarus. At the moment the sanctions have been suspended, but their effects have been limited to the release of some political prisoners, that can be considered important as such, but it is quite irrelevant for the entire democratization process. Instead, the US has used positive conditionality in order to allocate Millennium Challenge Corporation funds through CPA and TPA, hence in this specific case the mechanism of conditionality is connected with the economic assistance anchor. In our case studies, Georgia has been the only country to comply with all criteria required, therefore this state has qualified for the CPA, while Ukraine and Moldova complied only partially with the conditions, and consequently received the smaller endowments guaranteed by the TPA. The main problem with this use of conditionality is that the reward does not have many important political implications, such as the EU membership, because it is only an economic aid which is not always helping the democratization of the recipient state, as has been happening in Georgia where CPA is working on regional infrastructures and regional enterprises. Despite the limits of the US institutional links and conditionality in our four cases, the most recent US pro-democracy activities reveal that during the last years the US has been trying to emulate the most successful European democratizing anchoring, namely political dialogue through partnerships and imposition of democratic conditions for reward. Finally, it is important to recognize that the US is not simply using the typical European democratic anchoring, but is also adapting it both to its own capabilities and the context where it is working.

6

RUSSIA ANCHORING ON BELARUS, GEORGIA, MOLDOVA AND UKRAINE

Mara Morini

1 - Introduction

In the comparative literature, the scientific debate on the process of democratization in the post-Soviet space has recently acquired a strong relevance and become a matter of high priority, due to the economic and political effects that the path towards democracy might have both in the region and in the relationship with other political actors in the world. Existing studies on external influences on domestic democratic reform processes have paid much more attention to Western actors that were able either to encourage and strengthen or weaken democratic anchoring in the Central Eastern European Countries (CEECs) at the beginning of the 21st century [Levitsky and Way, 2006; Carothers, 2006]. The evidence of such an approach comes from the enlargement-democratization nexus [Magen and Morlino 2008] by which the European Union (EU) has attempted to use "reinforcement by reward" type conditionality measures [Schimmelfennig, Engert and Knobel, 2003: 496] in the political and economic spheres of the "candidate countries", in order to improve their chances of becoming effective members and, consequently, to guarantee their path towards democratic consolidation. On the other hand, the same scientific relevance has not addressed other regime type interventions which try to influence domestic change in their neighbouring countries. This is particularly so in the case of Russia, where, largely for historical and cultural reasons, the interaction with the Former Soviet Republics has been characterized by complex political-economic issues and mutual interests. Russian foreign policy towards the Commonwealth of Independent States (CIS) still faces particular challenges and stages which reflect domestic factors and external pressures related to the state of Russia's relations with the West, the kind of political developments in the Newly Independent States (NIS), and the unresolved identity question [Bertil, 2008]. Such a lack of interest and deeper research might be explained by the fact that Russia is defined as a hybrid regime and, consequently, it is taken for granted that its economic, historical and political legacies negatively influence the path towards democracy and also reduce any possibility of democratic consolidation. The case studies of Belarus, Georgia, Ukraine and Moldova considered in this book describe the domestic process of democratization in an attempt to explain the main factors that influenced the path towards the hybrid regimes or more authoritarian perspectives in this geopolitical area. Using such theoretical framework, the quality of the relationship between Russia and its "Slavic Brothers" can be analyzed in terms of the dynamics of political change, also taking into account the external pressure of both the EU and United States (US) in the democracy anchoring of these countries, which are located in an area of real priorities, such as energy and transport networks, investments and capital flows, consolidation of the market economy and the rule of law in the field of the economic regulation, financial stability, repayment of external debts and military alliances. Adopting the hypothesis that "it is external-internal interactions, rather than external factors *per se*, which are more accurately said to shape domestic outcomes" [Magen and Morlino, 2008: 29], this chapter will analyze the role played by the Russian government in shaping the institutional, economic and social settings of these four countries and the extent of the impact of external pressures on the post-Soviet regimes, offering some insights into the main factors which can exert some constraints on their internal dynamics.

Russia has a huge influence in the domestic politics of these neighbouring countries – either by supporting ethnic minorities who aspire to be separated from their country (Georgia and Moldova) or pro-Russian political forces as in the Ukrainian elections of 2004 – but, in particular, they strongly depend on the economic relations with Russia, primarily the energetic sector and the import/export exchange rate [Pirchner, 2005]. Political and economic external constraints are the crucial elements to better understanding the kind of interaction between external pressures and internal processes in the particular geographical position and international situation of the CIS, i.e. the "new outsiders" of post-communist Eurasia, where the legacies of the Soviet past are still strong and can lead to the implementation of the Russian sovereign democracy model *versus* attraction towards the alternative institutional model of the EU and its economic opportunities [Grabbe, 2006]. These two geopolitical areas and institutional models have characterized the regime change, the institutional setting and the economic development in the transition process, which makes it more difficult to split the analysis of economic conditionalities from the political factors in the study of democratizations [Pop-Eleches, 2007]. So, within their own geopolitical sphere, these countries deserve much more study than has been the case to date, focusing on Russian conditionalities, and on external influences in post-communist democratization.

2 - The Political Anchoring Ties

After the collapse of the USSR the dispute within the Russian élite about the country's identity, place in the world and the paradigm of foreign policy clearly emerged and paved the way to three traditional concepts, all rooted in the 17th century: Atlanticism (*zapadnichestvo*), Eurasianism (*evrasiystvo*) and anti-Westernism. As far as contemporary Atlanticism is concerned, the former Minister of Foreign Affairs, Andrey Kozyrev, regarded the countries of Western Europe "as natural allies of the new Russia" and believed that the "establishment of qualitatively new relations with them is the single priority of foreign policy" [Kozyrev, 1992: 288]. On the other hand, the anti-Western approach (neo-imperialism) is based on notions of a conspiracy against Russia and is intended to create a new counterweight to the US, to lead the opposition of the Third World to the West. Finally, the traditional concept of *evrasiystvo* implies that Russia should play the role of an intermediary actor, a bridge between East and West, or even isolate itself in order to concentrate exclusively on domestic development.

In Russian political discourses the West had "dismembered" (*raschlenen*) the USSR and, consequently, Russia stopped being considered a giant actor in the international setting. Thus, the main geo-strategic task of the new deal in the "foreign doctrine" was to preserve the geopolitical nature of the historical Russian state area, putting up barriers to the fundamentally dangerous re-orientation of the new states towards non-friendly partners. In this scenario, Ukraine, Moldova and Georgia represented the states on the line of unprecedented pressure from the West upon historical Russian borders. As a reaction, during the first term of President Putin the "zero point" of the Russian foreign policy towards the CIS started and was followed by the December 2003 elections in Georgia, which symbolized the beginning of élite generation changes in the NIS, as well as the Ukrainian elections a year later and the so-called "Kozak" plan for Transnistria and Moldova [Way, 2005]. These political events made Russia start to think about new forms of commonwealth with Former Soviet Republics. In 2002, President Putin proposed that Belarus joined Russia, and tried to establish contacts with Kuchma's successors in Ukraine; the crisis with Georgia reached its highest negative point and, finally, the "intractable" problem of Chechnya and the kind of special status for non-recognized territories, "the post-Soviet orphans" – Abkhazia, Transnistria, Nagorno-Karabakh and Chechnya – emerged. The Ukrainian case and the "Rose Revolution" in Georgia represented a trend in Russian foreign policy and reflected the main changes in that policy, such as the diminishing role of legislative bodies and the concentration of vertical power in the presidential administration, making Russian foreign policy more managerial and technological. In 2003 Russia also tried to institutionalize cooperation with the CIS through various structures – the Eurasian Economic Community (EurAsEC) and the Single Economic Space – while old ones (the Collective Security Treaty Organization) were strengthened. In the economic sector, Russia's Gazprom and Unified Energy

System (UES) were effective levers in Moscow's political and economic disputes with Minsk, Kiev and even Tbilisi over further integration and the privatization project in the CIS. Given this political background, Russian politics has been often characterized by political phases which have had a great impact on the transition process. It can be argued that the most important political event has to be the change which occurred in 1999, with the end of Boris Yeltsin's era and the birth of a new one with Vladimir Putin's election some months later.

During the last few years a "realistic foreign policy" emerged among élite and was based on Russian need and priority to concentrate on problems of national development, avoiding isolationism and confrontation in international relations. This is particularly evident in the publication of the new official documents: "The foreign policy concept of the Russian Federation" (*kontseptsiya vneshnei* 2000), "The military doctrine" (*voennaya doktrina* 2000), "The national security concept" (*kontseptsiya natsionallnoi* 2000) and "The sea doctrine of the Russian Federation in the period until 2020" (*morskaya doktrina* 2001).[1] The main aim of such documents is to integrate Russia into the world economy as deeply as the competitiveness of the national economy allows, and to use new opportunities to attract foreign investments, stimulate economic growth, and to provide optimal conditions for the development of the national economy. Since the first months of his presidency, Putin has clearly expressed his intention to make Russia stronger and stable in order to open a new Russia's era. So, since 2000 the political strategy adopted by the Kremlin has changed significantly towards a more hegemonic role of Russia around the world [Carnaghan, 2007]. Moreover, the second Putin presidential legislature witnessed a significant political and economic change which has given rise to different attitudes and policies towards the West; the Fifth European Enlargement has undoubtedly had an impact on this new perception of Russian foreign policy and it seems, especially in recent years, to have worsened the dialogue

---

[1] All documents are available on the website of the Russian Foreign Ministry: http://www.mid.ru.

between the EU and Russia [Averre, 2007]. Consequently, the Russian foreign attitude towards the West is somewhat ambiguous. On the one hand, Russia wants to be integrated into the main international organizations in order to have the same influence; on the other it must counterbalance the enlargement of the EU and NATO in the former Soviet countries, which has been considered an attempt to isolate Russia from Europe. So it is obvious that Russia is worried about the external conditionality of the EU and its capacity to attract former Soviet countries as is shown by the number of quotations in official documents, speaking of different values and perspectives as the result of globalization.

As described by the political analyst Bogaturov [2007], the first doctrine of the foreign policy of the Russian Federation is also clearly expressed in official statements, such as Putin's speech in Munich in June 2006 and the report on foreign policy, published by the Ministry of Foreign Affairs in March 2007, where the new priorities of Russia in the worldwide were announced. Consequently, the need to implement a more effective influence can be the real expression of the economic power of the country: Russia must give its own contribution to the economic and social development in the world in relation to its position and potential. From a geopolitical perspective, this statement expresses the building of a recognized sphere of influence in the international setting, especially in the economic field, thanks to the energetic sector, which has become the real tool of domestic and foreign policies at both regional and global levels. Taking advantage of its energetic role and flows, the Russian government aims to acquire a more effective position in the world through the creation of a multi-polar axis in which Russia, as an economic superpower, can also have a stronger role at a political level. Russia's economic power has grown under Putin, with the primary hard currency earners being exports of natural gas and oil, as well as military and nuclear energy equipment, but both Putin and his predecessor, President Boris Yeltsin (1991-1999), also implemented several regional economic integration agreements that give Russia a dominant position among the post-Soviet states.

In addition, in the opinion of the Foreign Minister, Sergei Lavrov, the Russian government in foreign policy "works for the country and the protection of national interests" in order to preserve historical and spiritual heritage, geography, economic interdependence and cultural/civilization communality. In contrast with the idea of a multi-polar scheme in international relations, the underlying principle of President Putin's foreign policy [Polikanov and Timmins, 2004] appears to be unilateral action in pursuit of Russia's national interest. It has been argued that for Russia to achieve Primakovian multi-polarity it needs first of all to consolidate the CIS space, in order to become the centre of gravity in that area, and also to establish regional hegemony. Russia remains unattractive, especially for those CIS countries that look to the West, but in Central Asia its policies have been more successful. Russia's national interest lies in creating a power block in the CIS area, where it is the dominant country, but at the same time, it needs an arena in which to hold bilateral talks with those CIS countries which are not so willing to integrate with Russia. In contrast to the "Primakov School", which regarded the international setting as an interaction between "centres of power", President Putin developed a more complex and realistic idea, both pragmatic and aggressive (see Table 25). The rhetoric and attendant policy that saw Russia as a unique Eurasianist power with the right and authority to control its neighbouring states also continued with Vladimir Putin (2000-2004, 2004-2008), who assumed control and retained Russia's interest in playing the role of a great state, including regional economic and military integration, and adding a multi-vector approach that enabled Russia to ally with any state that would aid its economy, and more broadly, its world position.

So it is against this political and economic background that one must analyze the kind of relationship between Russian élite and those of the former Soviet countries in the NIS. One of the clearest examples of the good relationship between Russia and the former Soviet countries is the case of Belarus, which is considered the continent's last dictatorship established by the country's President Lukashenko and supported by the Russian Federation in the political, economic and diplomatic spheres.

Table 25. Russian foreign "schools"

	"The Primakov School"	**Vladimir Putin**
Conceptualization of Russia	A great power, one of the centres of the "multi-polar world"	A European country and equal member of the Western community of nations
Basic world trend	Two antagonist trends: the formation of a "multi-polar world" and the U.S. attempt to dominate global politics	Internationalism and globalization. Competition for markets and investment. A rise in extremism and terrorism
Key threats to Russia	The formation of a "unipolar world". The American policy of global domination	Terrorism, extremism, WMD proliferation. Transnational organized crime
Russia's key strategic policies	A "Strategic Partnership" with China, India, and the "quickly integrating" Europe on an anti-American basis. Anticipation of the disintegration of NATO	A "Strategic Partnership" with the United States, NATO, and EU; normal relations with China

Source: Smith, 2005: 17.

The kind of relationship between the two parties can be described as an alliance dominated by ideological rather than pragmatic reasons [Sannikov, 2002]. In 1995 the Friendship and Cooperation Treaty was signed, which allowed Russia to retain its military presence in Belarus until 2010 and secure free-of-charge use of air defence facilities. Moreover, a customs union was established and the north-western frontier of Belarus was to be *de-facto* transferred to the military and customs border of the Russian Federation. Belarus offered Russia a corridor to the Baltic enclave of Kaliningrad, while it abstained from levying fees on the transit of Russian goods, oil, and gas. Belarus also emerged as an active arms trader, and while most of the arms it sold were produced in Russia (and often modernized in Belarus), some of the sales were apparently conducted to countries with which Russia preferred not to deal, in order to avoid blemishing its international image. In 1996 Belarus and Russia initiated a process of integration, signing an association treaty based on economic and military cooperation, as well as political convergence. Yeltsin and Lukashenko made agreements on the formation of a political union in 1997 and on a common united state in 1999. These attempts to consolidate a stronger union through formal documents and institutional acts show that the Belarus-Russia union has served the Kremlin under both Boris Yeltsin and Vladimir Putin, and the official Minsk government throughout the last decade. On the one hand, Lukashenko tried to influence Russian domestic politics through communist and ultranationalist forces directly connected with Russian political parties and setting himself up as Russia's best friend in the near abroad, in order to secure enormous economic benefits that enhanced the stability of his rule. On the other hand, this question changed Lukashenko's image to one of an "integrator" while he decided to implement a policy of domestic autarky making a distinction between the Belarusian model, and the West and Russia. The second stage of the Belarus-Russia relationship lasted from Putin's accession to power in 2000 until the end of 2004.[2] In this period the Orange Revolution took place and the Belarusian constitutional referendum gave Lukashenko the chance to be re-elected an unlimited number of times. Russian economic and political ties played a key role in the establishment and survival of Lukashenko's autocratic regime. In March 2006, during the presidential elections, the Russian government decided to freeze natural gas prices for Belarus, allowing Lukashenko to achieve the "economic miracle", in order to maintain impressive rates of economic growth as promised in the election campaign. This subsidy could also be considered a signal to the less compliant regimes, particularly in Ukraine, Moldova and Georgia. Nevertheless, relations between the two brotherly Slavic

---

[2] Russia and Belarus are also working together to create a unified information space, broadcasting an hour-long discussion of issues of Russian-Belarusian integration, and cooperating through the Information Agency of Belarus and Russia (http://www.soyuzinfo.ru). This agency provides news about Belarus to regional newspapers in Russia and vice-versa.

nations worsened during the second term of Putin's presidency to the extent that Lukashenko expressed the idea of developing as much cooperation with Europe as necessary to ensure the country's energy security [Silitsky, 2005]. In comparison with the first period of democratization in Belarus, Russia's pre-emptive assistance to Lukashenko may turn into the long-term factor impeding its democratization, enhancing its international isolation, minimizing the impact of external efforts to promote democracy, and permanently threatening its status as an independent state. As a reaction, Belarusian foreign policy is trying to diversify its contacts beyond the "Russia-West" axis, promoting relations with Venezuela, Iran, China, and other Latin American and Arab countries. Recently, Belarus has been actively promoting relations with Ukraine, Azerbaijan and Kazakhstan, clearly seeking ways to diversify energy imports. These contacts cannot rid Belarus of its critical economic dependence on Russia, but they can bring temporary relief, provide some financial assistance and, in particular, indirectly affect the behaviour of Moscow, which will have to take into account the possibility of Minsk strengthening the positions of Russia's opponents in the post-Soviet space.

As far as the diplomatic relations between Georgia and Russia are concerned, the historical debate, used as a tool for political competition in the Caucasus area, has stressed that Russia's great historical contribution to the survival of the Georgian nation is witnessed by the Russian soldiers who died for the return of autochthonous Georgian territories. According to members of the Historical Legacy NGO in Tbilisi, which spread throughout the country and among young generations "the objective research on the most important periods of Georgian history", the "cleansing of the historical memory" has provoked bloody conflicts between the brotherly peoples to solve geopolitical issues. In the Caucasus region Russia still plays an important role concerning the area of "frozen conflicts" which have recently taken place over ethnic and nationalistic issues in Abkhazia and Southern Ossetia, parts of the Georgian territory. Russia is still present in the area as a peacekeeper within the framework of the United Nations (UN) action. Russia has always formally declared that its main goal is to control and preserve the integrity of those areas. Even during the Yeltsin's presidency, a Joint Control Commission (JCC) was created, consisting of Russia, Georgia, Abkhazia and Ossetia, in order to control the peacekeeping in that region. Officially Russia has acknowledged Georgian integrity but *de facto* has supported regions which aimed to be independent and did not recognize international borders. Until August 2008 the Russian government neglected the aspirations of Abkhazia and Ossetia, even though sometimes, in the 1990s, Russian leaders gave positive consideration to joining Ossetia to Russia. As far as Abkhazia is concerned, Russia offered to the UN to be guarantee of peace. In January 1996 the CIS decided to impose economic sanctions on Abkhazia; in this agreement it was stipulated that all countries must not support independent regimes, neither political, economic or whatever relationship, neither economically, financially, military or whatsoever and not establish political and economic relations. It also condemned the political behaviour of the leadership of Abkhazia and underlined the necessity of the return of the Georgian refugees who had been obliged to leave the territories. The agreement coincided with the period of the First Chechen War, so there was quite evident Russian hostility towards those regions which wanted to become independent. Moreover, Abkhazia has always had economic and political relations with Russia, which invests a large amount of money in the region. The first sign of a good relationship with these areas came in 2000, when Russia required visas of citizens from Georgia (not necessary for those coming from the CIS) in order to create an obstacle towards Chechen terrorists who, according to the Russian leadership, were located in Georgia, apart from citizens living in Abkhazia and Southern Ossetia. After the implementation of a law on visa requirements in 2002, the number of Russian passport holders living in Georgia was 98% of the population. This provoked a bad reaction in Tbilisi, because people from Abkhazia and Ossetia were able to move and work in Russia, while

Georgians faced passport difficulties and were not able to receive, for instance, pension, unlike their neighbours.[3] Other matters of concern were the enlargement of NATO to include Georgia and the recognition of the independence of Kosovo. Both Putin and Medvedev have stressed the fact that the situation in Ossetia and Abkhazia can be compared to the Kosovo situation. There was therefore no need to accuse Russia over its support for the independence of these territories, taking into consideration that there are not important pipelines of oil and gas and, consequently it cannot be argued in the international setting that there is a direct correlation between the Russian military attack and energy supplies. If, generally, Russia encourages ethnic separatism in former Soviet states and uses energy supplies as a political weapon, the Georgian conflict is much more related to political issues, such as the geopolitical strategy of NATO, the EU and the US in this area.[4] Turning to domestic politics, Georgia's élite is more interested in modernizing the country than democratizing it [see Wheatley this volume]. This is not surprising if we consider the President's ambitions to be cited by historians as the one who made Georgia a modern state, supported by the Georgian élite, who want to achieve societal transformation, territorial restoration, and economic prosperity.

On the other hand, the case of Ukraine represents one of the most important political and economic issues for the Russian government, as well as cultural relevance in public opinion because it is widely considered the cradle of Russian civilization. Nevertheless, the Russia-Ukraine gas dispute has dominated their dialogue, influenced by economic conditions, such as the financial crisis and falling oil prices, although it is possible to trace the origins of this gas war back to 1991, because of the Soviet-era infrastructure legacy. The relevance of this issue is mainly due to the fact that four-fifths of Gazprom's exports to

---

[3] Abkhazia is also considered a tourist place by Russians who have continued to spend their holidays there since the USSR, and the rouble is used as currency.

[4] "For example, NATO's decision in Bucharest not to offer Georgia and Ukraine membership Action Plans contributed neither to appeasement of Russia nor to further democratization of Georgia.

Europe go through Ukraine's pipelines, while all Ukrainian industries mainly depend on Turkmen supplies provided (through Rosukrenergo, an intermediary company used by Gazprom to transport and/or resell Central Asian gas to Ukraine) by Gazprom [Kuzio, 2005]. Whereas in Belarus Gazprom bought 50% of the pipeline company in 2007, Ukraine has refused to contemplate even partial Gazprom ownership. Consequently, the conflict between the two parties arose as soon as Yula Timoshenko, the multi-millionaire former gas trader, returned to the Ukrainian Prime Minister's office in December 2007 and expressed her desire to remove Rosukrenergo. It was in October 2008 that the relationship worsened, because Ukraine did not clear its debts promptly and because the two sides failed to agree on how exactly European netback prices should be arrived at.[5] In January 2009 Timoshenko and Yuschenko united in proposing $201/mcm and increasing the use of tuff for transporting Russian gas to Europe; the dispute came to an end with the separation of the agreement on gas supplies to Ukraine from the one on gas transit. Meanwhile Gazprom managers wanted to press ahead with projects, such as the North Stream and South Stream pipelines, in order to reduce transit dependence on Ukraine; once transit diversification projects are completed, the Ukrainian pipelines will be less important to Russia and less of a bargaining chip for Ukraine. The energy war is the result of Ukraine's difficulty in driving a distinct national interest separate from Russia's and of the Kuchma-era corruption, under whose leadership the energy business continued to be a prime area of corruption and competition between "clans". Deep conflict and lack of clearly divided spheres of competence between President and Prime Minister contributed to the crisis. The strongly worded statement of the Russian President Dmitry Medvedev on 11 August 2009 criticized the Ukrainian President for his anti-Russian policy and announced that the new Russian envoy to Ukraine would remain

---

[5] Economic factors: oil prices plunged after the Wall Street financial meltdown. The subsequent recession made the IMF provide a record-breaking $16.5 billion loan to Ukraine. The price of steel, Ukraine's main export, has sunk.

in Moscow for the time being. The same attitude is observed towards another country within the post-Soviet space: Georgia. The two countries broke off diplomatic relations after the five-day war last year while Ukraine and Russia do still have diplomatic relations, which are at the moment in their worst state since the collapse of the USSR. These countries are certainly a long way from a peaceful coexistence based on mutual respect and political equality.

The frozen conflict of Transnistria on Moldovan territory bordering Ukraine is another hotbed of tension [Hamilton and Mangott, 2007]. By late 1992, forces of the Russian 14th Army had enabled the Russian minority to consolidate control over most of the Dnestr region. Russia's actions chilled its relations with the newly independent Moldova, whose legislature had not ratified the 1991 CIS agreement. The pressure of a Russian trade blockade contributed to the victory of anti-communist candidates in Moldova's legislative elections in February 1994 and the new legislature ratified Moldova's membership of the CIS, bringing the last of the non-Baltic Soviet Republics into the organization. In October 1994, Russia and Moldova agreed on the withdrawal of the 14th Army, pending settlement of the political status of Transnistria. The agreement was jeopardized immediately, however, when Russia unexpectedly declared that the State Duma had to ratify the agreement, which it had not done by mid-1996. The split between the Transnistrian and Moldovan populations was created by the political élite after the independence of Moldova in 1991 and the presence of multiple cultural identities within the country. When the Soviet Union broke up in 1991, some of the political leaders in the Transnistria region, a long strip of territory on Moldova's eastern border with Ukraine – some 500,000 people – fearing that Moldova would be reintegrated with Romania, declared Transnistria a separate state. The demand for independence led to a civil war in 1992, which ended with the entry of Russian "peacekeeping" troops, which are still there. The separation of Transnistria has further weakened the Moldovan economy as a whole, though Transnistria has become the home of a prosperous underworld economy in the sale of weapons, drugs and people trafficking. It would be in the socio-economic interest of most people to have Transnistria re-integrated into Moldova. This situation creates a cleavage within Moldovan society, as Transnistrians accept Russia as their regional leader, while Moldova faces westward towards the EU. Proposals for such integration have been made by the Organization for Security and Cooperation in Europe (OSCE), Ukraine and Russia, but to date, there has not been the political will for the necessary political and economic compromises. The ties that Moldova has with the Russian Federation, still connecting the two countries, are the legacy of the older communist model that constrains the future development of Moldova. As a historical and regional hegemon, Russia still indirectly imposes its policies on the neighbouring states, as it has heavy-handed politics stretching from its past experience as leader of the SU [Lynch, 2001]. The position that Moldova occupies geographically is highly strategic because of its location on the periphery of Europe, Eurasia, the Middle East and Asia. Consequently, Moldova plays an important role in different spheres in international affairs, ranging from military to cultural and economic. The relationship between Moldova and Russia provides the fundamental flow in the autonomous development of the Republic of Moldova. Russia supplies Moldova with oil, natural gas, foodstuffs and other essential resources for development and sustainability. Russia's interference in the area is very strong both in the economic sphere and in the cultural, ethnic and linguistic, while it still lacks international economic support outside the Russian sphere of influence. Thus, Moldova is in a political and economic dilemma: to pursue autonomy away from Russia and face possible negative effects on economic and political policies or embrace westernization and globalization or remain on the periphery of Moscow politics. The most recent parliamentary elections held in Moldova in April 2009 gave the ruling Party of Communists a majority in the Parliament. The current President, Vladimir Voronin, first elected in 2001 and again in 2005, has reached his two-term constitutional limit and thus will be replaced, most likely by someone else from the Party. There is speculation that, inspired by the Russian example of Vladimir Putin, Voronin will be elected Chairman of the Parliament, and there will be a shift in decision-making from the Presidency to Parliament. Although election observers from the OSCE reported that the elections were generally "free and fair", some protesters demonstrated in the streets of the Moldovan capital Chisinau, arguing that the elections were rigged and that ballot-box stuffing had produced the majority.[6] The protesters demanded new elections or a recount. Some demanded the departure of Voronin; others that Moldova be reunited with Romania. The violence and the fires attracted international attention to Moldova – rarely a headline country. It is too early to say whether the demonstrations are the start of a process which will lead to a change of government or whether they will serve as a warning sign to the government that a process of reform and socio-economic development is needed. But, arguably, the demonstrations will be the start of both a necessary governmental reform process and regional socio-economic development in which Romania, Ukraine and Russia can play a positive role.

3 - The Economic Anchoring

In the comparative literature, transition countries have been a laboratory for the investigation of the relationship between the politics and economics of reforms [Coricelli, 2007]. The interplay between these two analytical dimensions has theoretically and empirically enriched the scientific debate on the effects that economic reforms in particular might have in the process of democratization in most countries of the Former Soviet Union, characterized by neither a well-functioning market economy nor a democratic and free society [Lipset, 1959]. So, assuming that a market economy is a necessary but not sufficient condition for democracy, this section will describe the extent to which economic

---

[6] Moldova, then known as Bessarabia, had been part of Romania until 1940, when Bessarabia was incorporated by Soviet troops into the USSR, becoming the Moldova SSR. There have always been people in both Romania and Moldova who would like to see Moldova and its 4 million people integrated into Romania.

cooperation between Russia and these countries has influenced the kind of political relationship and the overall process of democratization. In the 1990s, Russia faced difficult periods of political and economic uncertainty due to the complex transition after the collapse of the USSR. The need to improve the development of its economy and to find its place in a new international setting paved the way to a new strategy in political economy which relied, and still does, on energetic resources, such as gas and oil, in order to take its role as an "energetic power" in the world. It is well known that after Saudi Arabia, Russia is the second largest oil exporter in the world and the leading gas producer (it has been estimated that more than ¼ of the world's gas resources are in Russia). Consequently, many countries around the world, especially in the EU, depend on Russian gas.

The "energetic issue" has also been used by the Russian leadership as a means of political influence and struggle, especially with Ukraine and Georgia, reaching the highest level of conflict in the past two years. This situation has its origin in the unresolved question of the political borders and the consequences of the dissolution of the Soviet system. It is worth pointing out that, after Russia,[7] Ukraine is the second largest consumer of natural gas in the CIS area. It imports more than two-thirds of the gas it needs (according to the International Energy Agency, in 2007 Ukraine consumed about 70 bcm of which 50 were imported), all of which comes from or via Russia. Moreover, Ukraine is the most important Russian gas transit corridor, because 65% of all gas from Russia and small quantities from Central Asia to the EU passes through its territory feeding Western Central and Southern Europe via the Young Europe and Blue Stream pipelines. The energy crisis started in 1993, when Ukraine did not pay Gazprom and, consequently, Moscow stopped the flow; negotiations in the following years led to a discussion of the prices to be paid by the Ukrainian government. In June 2000, President Leonid Kuchma admitted that Ukraine had stolen 13 billion cubic meters of gas

---

[7] Russia has the world's largest known natural gas reserves and its oil and gas deliveries represent more than 25% of the EU's consumption.

flowing to the east. Since then a conflict has dominated the dialogue between the two parties. On the one hand, Ukraine has threatened the Russian government with the closure of the flow westwards, while Russia wants to reduce the level of flow towards Ukraine permanently. In January 2009 the gas conflict reached the most critical moment in the long history of relations between Russia and Ukraine. In addition, the domestic political scene and rising divisions between the Ukrainian President and the Prime Minister have made the conflict more difficult to solve. So the current situation is one of a never-ending gas dispute, influenced by the wider context of bilateral political relations which have been deteriorating since the Ukraine's Orange Revolution and Yuschenko's presidency. Ukraine is historically a volatile part of a geopolitically critical region between East and West, between Europe and Eurasia; consequently Moscow is against Ukrainian rapprochement with the EU and NATO and it is trying to develop the gas dispute in order to avoid a political and real change on its borders [Schmidtke and Yekelchyk, 2008]. However, Ukraine thinks that Moscow is trying to repeat the Georgian scenario, claiming that the gas conflict was an attempt to gain control not only over the whole energy sector but also over the country's economy and sovereignty. Putin's will is that Ukraine remained in Russia's orbit and hence the gas disputes between Russia and Ukraine have been as much about money as politics. The energy crisis has become a political one which also involves the EU, considering that most of the European countries need gas from Ukrainian pipelines (about 25%). On the European side, Relations between the EU and Ukraine are based on misunderstanding while on the Russian side, Medvedev has accused Ukraine of having helped and sold arms to the Georgian army in the attack in Tbilisi against Southern Ossetia and to have implemented some decisions which are openly anti-Russia and against positive cooperation between the two countries. Medvedev is waiting for a change in the political orientation in Ukraine after the elections, so that a new dialogue can start with a new president orientated towards Russia and not the EU or NATO.

As far as Georgia is concerned, this territory has also a geopolitically strategic role in the dialogue over the energetic flow of gas and oil which transit from the Caspian Sea to the EU. Consequently, Russia has substantially invested in the building of pipelines in that area, starting in 2003 when President Shevardnadze, due to the bad condition of the network of distribution of Georgian gas, decided to initiate negotiations with the Russian Gazprom, in order to create a new and modern infrastructure in the area and improve the quantity of exportation of Russian gas to Armenia and Turkey. An agreement was reached, based on the control of Georgian gas by Gazprom and a reduction in gas prices offered to Georgia. The agreement provoked reactions by the US, which considered it an obstacle to the development of the Azeri deposit – Shah Deniz – without the participation of Russian companies and of the Baku-Tbilisi-Erzurum pipeline (the South Caucasus pipeline), which would have allowed the transit from the Caspian Sea to the EU bypass Russian pipelines. This agreement was frozen until 2005, when the new President Saakashvili declared his intention to sell its resources to Russia.[8] Since 2005 economic relations between Georgia and Russia have been at an all-time low, due to the following events: 1) because of the violation of photo-sanitary norms, the export of vegetable products from Georgia to Russia was banned; 2) the import of Georgian wine, wine material, brandy and sparkling wine and mineral water were also banned; and 3) the only legal check-point on the Georgian-Russian border – "Kazbegi-Zemo Larsi" – was closed for reconstruction works.

As far as Belarus is concerned, economic relations have qualitatively changed since Russia's decisions to raise the price that Belarus pays for natural gas and to impose a duty on oil exports to Belarus, together with the brief oil war that followed those decisions. Since 1st January 2009, the price of gas has risen from $47 per thousand cubic metres to $100, Gazprom's aim

---

[8] The Ministry of Energy said that it would have been better first to find the money to start the restructuring rather than to sell to Russia. Funds were raised thanks to the assistance of $295 million from the American project called USAID, "Millennium Challenge Compact" to be distributed during 2005-2010.

being to increase price annually so as to reach European levels by 2011. Russian oil companies, which previously exported oil to Belarus duty-free, will now pay $53 per ton. Furthermore, the tax on refined oil products collected in Belarus should now be returned to Russia, whose share is supposed to increase from 70% in 2007 to 85% in 2009. In exchange for gradual rises in prices, Belarus has agreed to sell 50% of its national pipeline network to Gazprom for $2.5 billion. If these plans materialize, the leverage Minsk can be assumed to exert against Moscow in future political developments between the two will diminish. The construction of a by-pass pipeline to Primorsk (Koivisto), announced by Russian Transneft in early February, would have an even stronger impact. Nowadays the most important pipelines are those that transit in Belarus and Ukraine reaching Eastern Europe. However, their prospects are weak because of the unstable relationship between the suppliers and the countries where these resources transit, which have been transformed into dangerous political and economic threats. Russian gas which flows through Ukraine "Soyuz" and Belarus "Yamal" is more expensive than that in Algeria and in Norway, due to the liberalization of the European market as regards common rules for gas, which started with the directives 98/30/CE and 2003/55/CE. The sole exception to the exclusive Russian position is the new pipeline BTC (Baku-Tiblisi-Cheyan) installed between Azerbaijan, Georgia and Turkey with the support of the US, interested in weakening Russian influence in the area, designed to lessen American dependence on the Middle East.

Finally, in August 1991, the Republic of Moldova declared independence and started a complex stage of transition to market economy, marked by a significant economic recession which lasted for 10 years (from 1990 to 1999). In 2000 the economy underwent a steady recovery of its production output, the GDP increased significantly, and the country achieved macroeconomic stability. Moldova largely depends on Russia and other CIS countries, both for energy imports and export markets, although it is trying to diversify its services of energy supplies. Economic growth unfortunately depends on industry, electricity and generating plants located in the secessionist Transnistria.

Moldova's economic weakness is also the result of the doubling of the price of the natural gas imports from Russia and by the Russian ban on the importation of Moldovan wine since the end of March 2006. Moldova, the poorest country in Europe, is the second smallest of the former Soviet Republics and the most densely populated. The most prosperous aspect of the Moldovan economy is the emigration of people. Some 25% of the active population work outside the country, about half in the EU, mostly Western Europe and half in Russia and Ukraine. Remittances from citizens working abroad is the most dynamic part of the economy but the loss of regular employment in Western Europe limits the remittances sent to Moldova. Some efforts to develop the economy have taken place since the mid-1990s.

Table 26. Exports to/Imports from Russia

		1995	2000	2002	2003	2004	2005	2006	2007
EXP.	Belarus	2,965	5,568	5,922	7,602	11,219	10,118	13,099	17,187
	Georgia	48.9	42.3	91.4	153	230	353	570	586
	Moldova	413	210	269	306	372	448	664	870
	Ukraine	7,149	5,024	5,885	7,595	10,770	12,402	14,983	16,323
IMP.	Belarus	2,185	3,710	3,977	4,880	6,485	5,716	6,845	8,887
	Georgia	57.9	76.6	69.0	84.2	107	158	70.8	61.1
	Moldova	636	325	281	403	496	548	323	490
	Ukraine	6,617	3,651	3,230	4,437	6,100	7,819	9,238	13,323

Source: Foreign commerce of the Russian Federation, 2008 (www.economy.gov.ru)

In 1997, Moldova was the sponsor of an Economic Cooperative Organization of some former Soviet Republics seeking cooperation outside direct Russian influence: Ukraine, Moldova, Georgia, Azerbaijan and Uzbekistan. The Moldovan economy depends on cooperation with Ukraine and Russia on one side, with Romania and the EU on the other. Since March 1993 a program has privatized 80% of all housing units and nearly 2,000 small, medium, and large enterprises. Other successes include the privatization of nearly all Moldova's state-controlled agricultural land, as a result of an American assistance program – "Pamint" ("land") – completed in 2000. Moldova's proximity to the Black Sea makes the area ideal for agriculture, which accounts for about 40% of the country's GDP. Its best-known product comes from its extensive and well-developed vineyards concentrated in the central and southern regions. When the Moldova government was in good terms with the Russians, the GDP increased by and over from 2000 to 2005, thus enhancing the economy, despite the economic problems caused by the presence of a separate regime in the region of Transnistria.

Both Russia and the CIS have a mutual interest in developing and extending economic interaction. As far as the ranking of investments in the Russian economy is concerned, both Ukraine and Belarus show a positive trend, with an average of about 20% of dollars invested in the Russian economy (see Table 27). On the eastern side, Kazakhstan is again the country which has invested more than 30% of dollars between 2005 and 2007, while its neighbours show lower levels, due essentially to difficulties in the face of globalization.

Table 26 shows the trend in exports and imports between Russia and the Former Soviet Republics. Apart from Moldova, where the level of imports has decreased to that of the first years of the transition process, the trend seems to be positive and increasing in all countries. However, there are some significant differences which underline a better Russian attitude towards those countries located on the western side of the Russian Federation. Both Belarus and Ukraine have a much higher level of exports and imports with Russia in comparison with Moldova and Georgia, while on the eastern side the only economically reliable partner is Kazakhstan.

Table 27. Investment of the CIS countries in the Russian economy in total US$ (%)

	2002		2005		2006		2007	
Azerbaijan	831	3.7	54,983	3.3	72,400	2.4	95,165	2.0
Armenia	5	0.0	4,541	0.3	2,034	0.1	24,482	0.5
Kazakhstan	5,632	25.2	732,788	44.0	1,116,111	36.8	1,468,720	31.4
Kirghizstan	839	3.8	140,168	8.4	451,836	14.9	534,177	11.4
Tajikistan	27	0.1	13,843	0.8	17,704	0.6	30,672	0.7
Turkmenistan	1,024	4.6	2,288	0.1	678	0.0	2,198	0.1
Uzbekistan	2,738	12.2	10,639	0.6	20,301	0.7	60,498	0.3
Belarus	1,007	4.5	447,135	26.9	623,723	20.6	955,772	20.5
Georgia	207	0.9	7,902	0.5	4,551	0.1	9,275	0.2
Moldova	1,069	4.8	18,100	1.1	17,805	0,6	21,416	0.5
Ukraine	8,996	40.2	232,870	14.0	704,952	23.2	1,468,975	31.4

Source: Federal Statistics Office, 2008 (www.gks.ru)

183

The largest amount of Russian investments (see Table 28) are again into Belarus and Ukraine (and also Kazakhstan), showing the high degree of economic interaction which characterizes the long-lasting relationship among these countries and influences on the domestic and external political dynamics since the transition process which started at the beginning of the 1990s.

Table 28. Investment of the Russian Federation in the CIS economy in total US$ (%)

	2002		2005		2006		2007	
Azerbaijan	26	0.0	6,734	1.1	6,661	0.2	8,994	0.3
Armenia	5	0.0	138,185	22.3	3,168	0.1	3,907	0.1
Kazakhstan	3,453	2.6	204,314	32.9	189,231	4.6	445,068	16.5
Kirghizstan	7	0.0	1,247	0.2	112,094	2.7	207,718	7.7
Tajikistan	-	-	496	0.1	22,315	0.5	105,683	3.9
Turkmenistan	2,934	2.3	-	-	-	-	0.4	0.0
Uzbekistan	929	0.7	6,968	1.1	176,174	4.3	93,040	3.6
Belarus	77,238	59	102,438	16.5	572,329	13.8	1,314,092	48.7
Georgia	133	0.1	60	0.0	328	0.0	433	0.0
Moldova	31,224	23.8	4,904	0.8	44,131	1.1	4,248	0.2
Ukraine	15,032	11.5	155,176	25.0	3,001,326	72.7	513,580	19.0

Source: Federal Statistics Office, 2008 (www.gks.ru)

4 - The Civil Society Anchoring

As Samuel P. Huntington argued, "Russia has been a torn country since Peter the Great, divided over the issue whether it is part of Western civilization or is at the core of distinct Eurasian Orthodox civilization" [1997: 138]. The issue of Russian identity has always dominated the political and cultural debate for nearly three centuries within and outside Russia, but it is especially in recent years that such a debate has acquired further importance, as post-Soviet Russia is faced with the task of defining its place in the present international arena. The conflictual nature of Russia's relations with the West can be explained from different perspectives (geopolitical, geo-economic and geo-cultural), all of which underline the civilizational differences neatly represented in Russia's state emblem: the two-headed Russian eagle, looking in both directions – East and West. Russia's problematic identity is uncontested and has its origin in the middle of the 19th century, when the Westernizer-Slavophile debate spread throughout the country. On the one hand, the Slavophiles were opposed to the political and economic reforms of Peter the Great and his successors (Westernizers and pro-Europe) and influenced the birth of the *"narodnic* movement", which preached agrarian socialism on peasant communes. Moreover, they opposed the Slavish imitation of the West and supported a triumphant assertion of the ability of Russia to think in her own right. From this perspective, studies of the Russian élite's attitudes to foreign policy have consistently found contrasting views of the world [Zimmerman 2002; 2005: 196]. After Gorbachev's "Glasnost" this issue was once again discussed and linked to the larger debate about foreign policy orientation, which can be summarized as two options: European and Eurasian. As we have already argued, the former are represented by the Atlanticists or Liberal Internationalists (Westernizers), whose advocate was the Foreign Minister Andrei Kozyrev, who believed that Russia's culture and identity have been deeply influenced by both Europe and Asia. He implemented a pro-Western foreign policy but neglected relations with the CIS, China and the Islamic States. Starting from the replacement of Kozyrev by Evegenii Primakov as Foreign Minister in January 1996, Russian diplomacy shifted from a Western-oriented to a Eurasian-oriented foreign policy, with its geographical location facilitating regular contact with many of the eastern civilizations – even if, as Peter Chadaeev[9] argued, in terms of religion, language, and aspects of culture, Russia also has affinity with European civilization. So it is quite evident that in the post-Soviet era the new leadership initially tried to integrate Russia into the Western political economy and security system, while the New Eurasianism was considered more geopolitical than a cultural or philosophical ideology, intended to justify Russia's continuing significance and role in Asia and to

[9] Chadaeev debated Russia's position in human history and initially believed that Russia belonged neither to the East nor to the West. Subsequently, he admitted that Russians are situated to the East of Europe i.e. it does not mean that they have ever been a part of the East.

reassert its status as a Great Power.[10] Historical and cultural differences between the Russian élite about where the country's future lies can also be identified by examining what exactly the Russian public thinks about this issue, using data from surveys published recently and discussed in Rose and Munro [2008]. This can provide a general overview of the gap between Russian policymaking in foreign relations and Russian citizen's perception of the "near abroad".

Although Russian foreign policy is not a matter of interest for most Russians [White, 2006], some issues do affect the general public and thus can potentially mobilize them to support or oppose government policy in relation to the conflict between Westernizers and those rejecting the West. In 2005 more than two thirds saw the country's future with the CIS because of traditional identities and national pride, while less than one third saw it with Europe, thanks to cosmopolitan contacts of individuals with the West. Those who support closer relations with the West believe that emulating European customs and habits was the best method of promoting economic, political and cultural progress during the transition process. These people usually know a European language or have contacts with Europeans, are younger and see the country's future as linked with Western Europe rather than with the CIS. Insofar as freedom and democracy are identified as Western rather than traditional Russian values, then those who appreciate freedom and democracy tend to see Russia's future linked with Western Europe. On the other hand, respondents who have a positive attitude towards the East favoured the supremacy of the Slavic culture, the Orthodox Church and traditional political and social institutions. They usually had relatives or friends who lived or had lived in the near abroad.

Two other important issues deserve mention. On the one hand, the effects of the use of the Russian language, which distinguishes between being citizens of the Federation

---

[10] As a matter of fact Russia's perception of Asia was shaped by the dominant European discourse on the East, which was portrayed as the inferior "other" in order to justify the occupation of the countries labelled "Oriental".

(*rossiiskii or rossiiskaya*) and ethnically Russian (*russkii/russkaya*), can influence the "pro" attitude towards neighbouring countries. On the other, the influence of age on Russians' views of the world can play an important role only through a gradual turnover of generations, with younger Russians leading a gradual reorientation of the majority of Russians from the near abroad to Western Europe. Indeed, as Mishler and Rose stress, an analysis of NRB surveys from 1992 reveals that all generations change their opinions as a reaction to national economic conditions and the political performance of the government. In economic terms it is also possible to distinguish two approaches: that of the more educated and cosmopolitan, who wish to reach European living standards and, consequently, think that only economic integration with the EU can provide it; and "older Russians", who were socialized to consider territories of the NIS as part of the former Soviet Union, and who may therefore give priority to the near abroad. The preference that Russians have for the CIS is consistent with official statistics: there are an estimated 25 million people of Russian nationality living in other successor states to the Soviet Union. The most salient aspect from these data is the influence and role of Russian culture and identity – which represents the unresolved civilizational debate on Russia between "West" and "East" – in defining the image of the EU in Putin's Russia.

Looking at the Russian political discussion of the last decade, there is a striking presence of prejudices used to substantiate anti-Russian or anti-European (anti-Western) policy. It is easy to find examples of "Russian imperialism syndrome", "pan-Slavonic solidarity" or "organic hostility to the West" in Russian history and use them to explain contemporary Russia. By contrast, Russians "opinions about self-identity, other countries and international relations" go beyond the framework of ideological myths, and demonstrate that Russians themselves pay little attention to the situation abroad, because they are deeply preoccupied with domestic problems. As shown in Table 29, Russians were asked which country Russia should join with. A large number of the respondents chose Belarus (46%), Ukraine (37%) and Kazakhstan (30%), while 27% did not want any kind of Commonwealth and only 16% of the respondents would join with the EU. It seems that the closer the country to Russia, the greater the likelihood of a positive answer.

Table 29. In your opinion with which country Russia should join in the future?

	April 2006	October 2006	May 2007
Ukraine	37	39	36
Belarus	46	45	42
Kazakhstan	30	29	30
Azerbaijan	11	10	13
Uzbekistan	10	12	14
Kirghizstan	9	12	13
Tajikistan	8	10	12
Armenia	11	12	15
Georgia	7	8	11
Moldova	-	11	14
Turkey	3	2	4
EU	16	16	17
None	27	27	33
Hard to answer	8	8	9

Source: Russian Public Opinion Research Centre, 2007 (www.wciom.ru).

As far as the European issue is concerned, there is a clear distinction for Russians between the idea of being part of Europe, with some kind (especially economic) of cooperation, and the desire to join it, an attitude not so far from the Kremlin's policy, which can be summarized as "Russia – soul in Europe and body in Asia". So, if Russia is not Europe in the West-European sense of the term, neither is it Asia. "Russia is *another Europe*" where one of the most important shifts in Russian society is the emergence of a new type of personality, called by Kantor [1999] "modern Russian European" (*russky evropeets*). Although these people often cannot themselves define their European identity, their behaviour patterns are quite European. Their guidelines are Western standards of living, which means good household conditions, a car, electronic and other modern household appliances, good quality education for their children, holidays and other kinds of active leisure. People with this value system do not rely upon the state but rather upon themselves. They appreciate the emerging possibilities of choosing their sphere of activity and ways to earn money, and they are ready to work hard to provide a high standard of living for themselves and for their families. Based on this system of values, a civil consciousness and political positions have begun to be formed. It is impossible to estimate the number of such "Russian Europeans" in the total population of the country, but undoubtedly there are many. They have not yet become a moving force for further economic and political reforms, but their influence on the political process is increasing steadily.

Russia is *another Europe*. While nobody questions the European nature of such countries as Greece, Poland or Slovenia, equally nobody can deny the huge differences between them and France, Germany or the United Kingdom. Today the boundary of Europe is moving eastward, but it is not a boundary between European and non-European societies. Rather, it is separating those who have already reformed themselves, and adopted new economic and political cultures, and those who are still in transition. If these data provide some information about Russian attitudes towards neighbouring countries, a recent public survey by the Ukrainian FOM allows a better understanding of the issues concerning the attitude of the Ukrainians towards Russia and President Medvedev in the different regions of the country. Table 30 gives an overview of the Ukrainians' responses - 41% of the respondents expressed their trust in the President of the Russian Federation, against 31% of those who distrusted him and 28% who were unable to answer the question. The level of trust changes in the western part of the Ukraine, where trust in Medvedev decreases (58% of respondents declares that they do not trust him), 33% in the central area, 20% in the southern and 8% in the eastern.

Conversely, those who express more trust are concentrated in the eastern part of the country (60%), followed by the southern (47%), the central (35%) and only 14% in the western area, as shown in Table 31. So it can be argued that borders matter, to the extent that the closer Ukrainians are to Russian culture and heritage, the more they trust the President.

Table 30. Trust in the President of the Russian Federation

Trust	41 %
Distrust	31 %
Hard to answer	28 %

Source: Ukrainian FOM, 2009 (www.fom.ru)

Table 31. Trust in the different regions

Trust	Western	14%
	Central	35%
	Southern	47%
	Eastern	60%
Distrust	Western	58%
	Central	33%
	Southern	20 %
	Eastern	8%

Source: Ukrainian FOM, 2009 (www.fom.ru)

This distribution reflects shared opinions among citizens about their political orientation and perception of the future of their country in a Western direction, as opposed to a return to past Soviet dependence. In general, the respondents had a positive attitude towards Russia (68%), in contrast with 9% of those who were against it, while 21% had neither a positive nor a negative view. It is important to underline that in this situation, too, geographical distribution matters, because in the western region about 92% speak Ukrainian, while exactly the same percentage speak Russian in the eastern. This can be confirmed if we take into consideration what the Ukrainians think about the rulers' political orientation. Those respondents who live in the southern part of Ukraine think that their leaders should get in touch with Russia (40%), Russia and the West (38%), and only with the West 14%. Another important point is their attitude towards NATO enlargement: 57% of respondents do not agree with this process, 21% agree, about 14% think that it is hard to answer and only 9% would not vote in a referendum on this political issue.

As far as Belarus is concerned, respondents were asked for their perception of the relationship between Russia and their country. In this case the majority of those interviewed (39%) admitted that it was hard to answer, 35% said that relations were bad and only 26% good. Nevertheless, 61% of respondents thought that Russia was trying to get closer to Belarus. On the question whether Belarus should implement a foreign policy which is strictly connected with the Russian one, 40% of respondents agreed, while 28% said it was hard to answer and 32% expressed a negative opinion. On the quality of such relations, 54% thought that relations were good and only 18% regarded them as bad (last October 2008).

The relationship between Georgia and Russia can be best assessed by looking at the trend of Georgian respondents' attitudes from 2002 to 2008. Seven years ago 17% of Georgian respondents thought that there were positive elements in the politics of these countries. This rose to a peak of 31% in 2004, but fell to 7% in 2008; on the other hand, the 58% who were negative in 2002 became 28% in 2004, and rose to 68% in 2008. The answers "hard to answer" were much more frequent in 2004 (40%), but fell to 25% in 2002 and 2008. Among those (43%) who thought that the relationship had definitely worsened, 24% thought that there were no changes and 26% said it was hard to answer. The main reason for this change is policies implemented by Georgia which are much more hostile to Russia and pro-Western, especially the US.

Table 32. Assessment of the present relationship between the Republic of Moldova and the selected states

Country	Very Bad	Bad	Good	Very good
Russia	0.3	7.8	66.3	14.7
Ukraine	1.4	19.7	59.2	0.5
EU	2.5	17.2	50.6	2.1
US	1.7	14.2	44.8	1.7
Romania	10.1	48.4	23.7	0.5

Source: Institul de Politici Publice/Gallup, 2009

New data from the "Barometer of Public Opinion" in Moldova, conducted by Gallup in July 2009 with the financial support of Soros

Foundation provide an interesting insight into Moldovan foreign relations. Table 32 summarizes responses to the question concerning respondents' assessment of the present relationship between Moldova and other states. As far as Russia is concerned, about 66.3% of Moldovans thought that relations were good (14.7% said "very good") and only 7.8% expressed a negative view. The second country is Ukraine, for which 12% of respondents had a positive feeling (59.2%) and 9.7% a negative one, while the EU is in third position (with 50.6% of people thinking that relations were good and 17.2% bad), followed by the US (44.8%) and Romania (23.7%).

Looking at the stratification of the sample, among those who thought relations with Russia were good/very good there was no significant difference concerning gender and age, although the percentage of these respondents in low socio-economic strata and with low education levels was about 6% less than the average for the population. Much more support came from Russians (85.8%), Ukrainians (91.8%), and those who live in the urban area. On the issue of the most strategic partner for Moldova, 51.8% of respondents chose Russia, only 26.2% the EU and 10.8% Romania. This positive perception of the strategic role played by Russia is most commonly expressed by those who are 45 years old and over, are Russian or Ukrainian, have a low/average level of education and belong to a low socio-economic class. When asked "if a referendum on the accession of the Republic of Moldova to the EU was held next Sunday, would you vote for or against it?" about 66.5% of respondents would vote for, 16.7% against and 12.9% had not decided yet. Among those who do not support the accession of Moldova were the older, Russian and Ukrainian nationalities, and individuals with low level of both education and socio-economic status. A similar question, but concerning possible accession to NATO, elicited only a 20.7% positive response and 46.6% against, while 57.5% thought that the best solution for ensuring the security of the country was to be neutral.

General public support for democracy as the best form of government encompasses an absolute majority of citizens in Georgia, Ukraine, Moldova, and Belarus, as well as a relative majority of Russian citizens. Political support for the current regimes declined between 1992 and 2002 and collapsed in Georgia, Ukraine and Moldova, contributing to the "revolutions" in Georgia and Ukraine. Trust in governmental institutions and support for the current regime is at very similar levels in Russia, Belarus, and Moldova. The main explanation for differences between these CIS countries relates to widespread disaffection with the current political regime as the cause for an increase in the number of "democrats" and a strong resulting pressure for structural democratic change. One of the critical reasons for the Rose Revolution in Georgia was that only 4% supported the old regime of President Shevardnadze, while 81% supported democracy as a form of government at the pre-revolutionary stage. The Orange Revolution in Ukraine was preceded by there being only 11% in support of President Kuchma in comparison with 67% supporting a normative concept of democracy. The increase of the share of democrats in Ukraine over time can be explained by the corresponding decrease of popular support for the old regime before the Orange Revolution. Support for a new market economy in these former centrally planned command economies appears to be another strong precondition of becoming a democratic citizen in Russia and the CIS.

5 - Conclusion

Since the Soviet collapse, much scholarly attention has been devoted to the process of democratization in the post-Soviet area, trying to point out the main analytical dimensions which can better explain the limits and/or advantages of specific institutional, economic and cultural settings in shaping a positive regime change [O'Donnell, Schmitter and Whitehead, 1986; Whitehead, 1996]. Recently the democratization literature has also begun to focus on the interaction between external conditionalities and domestic factors in the development of the process towards the implementation of a more democratic political system [Schimmelfennig and Sedelmeier, 2005; Magen and Morlino, 2008]. This study has attempted to address new questions in democratization studies: the dynamics of endurance and change of hybrid regimes, focusing on the role played by an external actor –

Russia – which differs from others due to an important missing key dimension of analysis: the rule of law. Being so far from a definition of substantive democracy, it is expected that Russia will avoid promoting accountability, responsiveness, equality, and freedom, i.e. crucial elements of the rule of law as a reaction to interference from the West or from other international actors. Indeed, attempts to explain exogenous influence by Western actors such as the EU, NATO, the World Bank and OSCE have underlined the extent of their conditionality of democracy promotion in CEECs. When it comes to Russia, both theoretical and empirical patterns of external-internal interactions require radical adjustment. Firstly, the external agent is also a case of hybrid regime. Consequently Russia faces, at the same time, domestic problems of democratic consolidation and attempts forcefully interaction with its neighbouring countries, slowing down their path to political and economic development. Secondly, Russia is an eastern foreign country which shares the same traditions, culture, history and legacies of the past, making their influence in domestic dynamics stronger than those based on western criteria and living standards. Thirdly, Georgia, Belarus, Ukraine and Moldova are non-enlargement countries, i.e. there are different levels of formal and informal agreement with the EU which could have a softer impact in domestic change, in comparison with those countries whose *status* of *candidate countries* has positively affected democracy anchoring. Applying this model to the Russian case, it can be argued that the legacy of the Soviet past is far from being forgiven in the Former Soviet Republics, not only because of cultural aspects which have strengthened social and political ties among populations and rulers. The analysis of the importance of economic conditionalities in the area has clearly shown the higher degree of dependence of the market system in the CIS on the Russian economic giant. Energetic resources and the path towards a market economy have been used as a tool of foreign policy, a sort of "blackmail" to orientate political and economic development in those countries which are at the crossroads in the process of structural reforms. The study of Russian foreign policy has underlined its need to assert its international power, to represent the country which protects its Slavic brothers from the Western attempt to be part of a dangerous sphere of influence which cannot guarantee the same benefits as Russia and the Former Soviet Union have always provided in the past. So Russian foreign policy reflects both the return to the idea of the "Empire", the "Great Power" of which to be proud and, at the same time, takes into consideration the political threats coming from the Fifth European Enlargement and the joining of NATO. Looking at the attempts to overcome the ruling autocratic élite in Ukraine, Georgia and Moldova in order to promote democratic consolidation, it seems that the "European option" has been failing due to a cautious and ambivalent European foreign policy able to support such political efforts in these countries and the recent military escalation between Georgia and Russia over South Ossetia, and the unilateral recognition of South Ossetia and Abkhazia by Russia. From this perspective, Russian political behaviour has become more aggressive at the beginning of the new century since President Putin started the implementation of his political program, which aimed to improve the quality of international relations, making Russia the main actor, the "protector" state in such a challenge. Russia is still able to influence international politics through economic tools, such as exports, mining, transit and management of oil and gas, due to three main energetic factors: the use of the energetic sector as a political tool; the use of transit-flow of energy as a tool of foreign policy; and the search for different entries into the export market. Being marked by a strong interaction between politics and the economy, Russia wants to control the energetic companies, which leads to the presence of forms a corporative system of interests where the economic élite are related to the bureaucratic apparatus, guaranteeing for the Russian leadership the establishment of a monopoly state through Gazprom and Lukoil.[11] Thanks to its strategic position in the energetic flows coming from Central Asia

---

[11] Their downstream activities are spread from the Black Sea to Croatia, attracted by the process of privatization of local enterprises sponsored by Brussels.

(Kazakhstan, Turkmenistan and Uzbekistan) to the European markets, Russia has more chances to influence the political events in the "near abroad", as the Ukrainian case clearly shows. According to the process of diversification (*diversifikatsja*) the flow coming from Ukraine and Belarus towards Europe must be modified through the creation of new directories. Thus, the Balkans could represent an interesting area of energetic flows for Central Asia and Russia. Moreover, Russia wants to maintain its control both in the Balkans and in the Caucasus because they are considered spheres of influence for economic and political-military reasons. The "North Stream" in the Baltic Sea could ensure direct access to the German, British and Dutch markets while the South Stream pipeline could reach Bulgaria, Greece, Italy, Serbia, Hungary and Austria. Since the 1990s, it can be argued that bilateral relations have made little progress in terms of political integration, while trade relations between the countries have expanded rapidly, establishing some interregional ties in order to improve the exchange rates and the quantity of goods between Russia and its "near abroad".

In an attempt to summarize and highlight the main insights and differences among our case studies, it can be argued that Belarus and Georgia represent the opposite position in the quality of the relationship with Russia. On the one hand, Belarus is more closely intertwined with Russia than with any other state in the Former Soviet Union, and economic and political ties played a key role in the establishment and survival of Lukashenko's autocratic regime. As long as Russia continues to support his regime economically, Lukashenko does not seem to be worried about his isolation in the international setting. On the other hand, Russian-Georgian relations have deteriorated to the point that some Russian officials are seriously weighing up a military operation, which they hope will produce a military defeat for Georgia and topple President Saakashivili. Russia has been irritated by the Georgian government because they are applying to join NATO, have threatened to raise objections to Russia's membership of the World Trade Organization, and broke diplomatic relations after the five-day war last year. Ukrainian-

Russian relations are closer to the Georgian case, even if for historical and cultural reasons these two countries should be more closely tied. Ukraine and Russia still have diplomatic relations but they are in their worst state since the dissolution of the USSR. The matter of the political conflict is connected with the fact that President Medvedev accused the Ukrainian leader of imposing NATO membership upon a reluctant population.[12] Moreover, the repression of the use of the Russian language and the attempt to eliminate its widespread use in the country where more than 1,400 schools in Ukraine teach in Russian or teach Russian language and literature.[13] So, on the Russian side, there is no solution to these issues in the context of bilateral Russia-Ukrainian relations, or even multilateral Russian-Ukrainian-European relations, other than changing the whole current paradigm of Russian foreign policy. Finally, bilateral relations between Moldova and Russia can be considered better than Georgia and Ukraine but not as good as with Belarus. Moldova[14] is still trying to rebuild itself and successfully advance in its political and economic objectives. Although there has been some noticeable progress, Moldova still has a long way to go to be accepted by the international community as a country able to overcome its communist past. While many countries were trying to separate from Russia and create their own ethnic identity, Moldovans were embracing their past by introducing Romanian as their language and establishing the Latin alphabet as the official script [King, 2000]. The initial desire of the Moldovan population and politicians to unify with Romania diminished after Russian minority revolted against unification, and Moldova remained an independent state with its own Moldovan culture and its own Moldovan language [Trombitcaia, 1998; Sunley, 1994]. However, without Russian economic involvement, which creates

---

[12] For the Russian ruling elite it is impossible to see NATO troops on the Dnepr River.

[13] On the other hand, there is no Ukrainian school in Russia, despite the presence of more than 12 million ethnic Ukrainians in the Russian Federation.

[14] In post-World War II Soviet economic planning, Moldova was to be an "orchard" for the USSR. In return, the Moscow central government provided funds for education, health, pensions and other social welfare measures.

dependency and prevents Moldova from developing an independent economic system, it has little chance of developing its independent and autonomous politics and economics oriented toward the West, as it still lacks international economic support outside of the Russian sphere of influence [Jeffries, 2004: 365]. In conclusion, Tandemocracy[15] wants to prevent former Soviet countries from sliding towards the West and internationally by reclaiming its great power status, taking advantages of economic conditionalities, cultural legacies, political patterns of behaviour among élite, as well as the geographic and psychological proximity of Slavic brothers.

---

[15] This term firstly appeared in the Russian newspaper "Kommersant" in 2008 to describe Russian diarchy or bicefalism in government [see Ryabov, 2008: 2-6].

7

INTERNATIONAL MONETARY FUND AND DEMOCRATIC ANCHORING. FOSTERING ECONOMIC GROWTH AND INSTITUTIONAL STRENGTHENING

Manuela Moschella

1 - Introduction

Among the problems that the international community has faced over the past twenty years, helping the transition of the planned economies to a market economy has certainly been one of the most challenging. Although there were large differences from country to country, after decades of central planning the countries of the former Soviet Union (FSU) were characterized by common and serious problems. Indeed, the disintegration of the old structures of planning and control created the conditions of economic and political crisis in virtually all new independent states. Economic activity declined sharply, prices spiked up and with the decreased revenues governments found it increasingly difficult to govern the domestic economy. Furthermore, all transition economies confronted the problem of creating new currencies and institutions that were unknown in the planned economic system, such as independent central banks and Treasuries.

From such starting conditions, the transition to a market economy was an extraordinary process that required the cooperation among a multitude of domestic and international actors, including the International Monetary Fund (IMF) and other international financial institutions, such as the World Bank (WB) and the European Bank for Reconstruction and Development (EBRD). Although the activities of these financial actors has sometimes been criticized [Stiglitz, 2002], it would be difficult to deny the contribution that their advice and financial assistance gave to what is widely regarded as a successful transition in most of the countries of the FSU [see, for instance, Åslund, 2007].

This chapter focuses on the role of the IMF in helping the transition. Specifically, it investigates the potential anchoring effects that IMF assistance had in fostering democratization processes in two of the countries of the FSU, which can be considered as hybrid regimes: Georgia and Moldova. Building on the literature on the role of external actors in domestic democratization processes [Magen and Morlino, 2008], the objective of this paper is that of identifying the activities carried out by the IMF that may serve as an anchor to democratic processes.

It is worth stressing at the outset that, contrary to most of the international actors analyzed in this book, the IMF has no responsibility over democratization processes. The Fund's main goal is that of helping countries to identify and adopt the macroeconomic policies that would help them to achieve and maintain high levels of employment and income. Hence, it is not a goal of the IMF to foster democracy, the rule of law or the protection of political rights in its member countries. Rather, the technical character of the Fund action has always been considered as a crucial element for the effectiveness of the Fund's action [Barnett and Finnemore, 2004: Chapter 3; Swedberg, 1986]. In this connection, the conditionality of IMF assistance is not based upon political achievements or democratic credentials but on the assessment of quantitative economic benchmarks. This does not mean that political considerations never make their way into the decisions taken by the organization. Rather, several scholars have found that IMF assistance is politically biased [Broz and Hawes, 2006; Momani, 2004; Thacker, 1998] and it often provides political cover for governments that want to reform their economies but face opposition at home [Haggard and Kaufman, 1995; Vreeland, 2003]. However, stressing the technical, as opposed to political, nature of the Fund is meant to draw attention to the fact that the IMF has not been directly involved in shaping members' democratic trajectories.

In spite of its legal mandate, there are various reasons that may help explain why the IMF can nonetheless be considered a relevant actor to the purposes of this book. To start with, the IMF is one of the most prominent international actors involved in the ex-Soviet area and an actor with a long-stand relationship with the countries born from the break-up of the Soviet Union. Indeed, in the early 1990s, the international community, and especially the G7, decided to grant the IMF the primary role in dealing with the new countries. That is to say, the IMF was put front and centre in the transition process [Boughton, 2000]. According to the then IMF Managing Director Michel Camdessus [1994], "helping these countries to reorient their economies toward market-based systems and to integrate themselves into the global market economy has been one of the Fund's greatest challenges in its 50-year history."

Furthermore, the activity of the IMF is relevant to purposes of investigating the democratic anchoring potential of international actors because of the evolution of the IMF strategy in the FSU countries over time. Indeed, whereas the Fund initially focused on issues of economic stabilization, at the end of the 1990s, it redressed its strategy to incorporate governance-related issues. That is to say, the Fund has increasingly supported measures that are closely related to democratization processes such as strengthening institutional capacity and enforcing the rule of law.

If we accept the substantive point that, in spite of its mandate, the IMF is nonetheless a relevant external actor to the democratic trajectory of the countries analyzed in this book, the question to address becomes primarily methodological. How can we assess the Fund's role in the democratization processes in Georgia and Moldova? What are the relevant actions and strategies that need to be analyzed? What are the anchors that the IMF offers to democratization?

In answering these questions, I build on the literature on the economic determinants of democracy in order to derive some propositions about the Fund's democratic anchors. In particular, I build on two broad findings in the literature. The first is that there is a strong correlation between economic growth and democracy.[1] Although the arrows of causation between economic growth and democracy are still the object of intense scholarly debate as will be discussed below, the assumption here is that economic growth supports democratization processes. Hence, the hypothesis is that the IMF offers an anchor to democratization to the extent that it helps triggering and sustaining economic growth. The second finding of the literature that is used as a starting point in this chapter is that inequality and institutional weaknesses may hamper democratic developments [Leblang, 1996]. Since institutional weaknesses may also slow down economic development [Burnside and Dollar, 1997; World Bank, 1998], the importance of sound domestic institutions appears as the most important to democracy. Drawing on these observations, the second hypothesis is that the IMF provides an anchor to democratization processes to the extent that it promotes institutional development, good governance and reduction of inequality.

In sum, the hypotheses that guide the empirical analyses will be that the IMF contributed to the democratic developments in Georgia and in Moldova by supporting economic growth and by strengthening domestic institutions, good governance, and by reducing inequalities. In what follow, I thereby read the history of the IMF-Georgia and IMF-Moldova relationship from the early 1990s to present through the lenses provided by the two anchors identified above. That is to say, I will bring to the surface the measures promoted by the IMF in the two countries in order to (1) promote growth; (2) strengthen institutions and good governance, and reduce inequality. As we are going to see, the emphasis placed on one anchor over the other has changed over time with the IMF emphasizing growth issues in the early 1990s and later shifting attention to good governance and fight against corruption.

Before proceeding, some clarifications are in order. First, it is necessary to clarify what this paper is not about. As already implicitly suggested, this chapter tackles the issue of anchoring from

---

[1] For an early statement of the relationship between economic growth and democracy see Lipset, 1959.

the perspective of the international actors (i.e. the IMF). In this connection, it is possible to say that the chapter focuses on issues of design and not implementation. That is to say, I do not investigate the domestic political economic variables and forces that led to certain outcomes over others.[2] Therefore, in carrying out the empirical analysis, the goal is not to isolate the impact of the IMF's activities on democratic developments from those of other domestic and international actors. More simply, the analysis is meant to start researching on the democratic anchors of an international actor, i.e. the IMF, whose activity has been traditionally associated with economic and not democratic developments.

Second, in order to bring to the surface the Fund's anchors, I will limit the analysis to the measures suggested by the IMF to Georgia and Moldova within the framework of IMF financial assistance programs. That is to say, the empirical analysis is based on IMF archival documents dealing with lending programs, including staff country reports, national authorities' letters of intents, staff memoranda, and Executive Board discussions. In contrast, I will not examine the IMF surveillance documents, such as Article IV reports, which nonetheless constitute one of the main activities carried out by the IMF along with that of financing.

Finally, but certainly not less important, it is necessary to clarify the criteria that lie behind the selection of the two case-studies. Bearing in mind the goal of the chapter, the countries have been selected based on some of their economic and political similarities so to assess whether there exists a pattern in IMF activity that can be associated with democratization processes. On the economic front, both Georgia and Moldova, are considered low-income countries of the Commonwealth of Independent States,[3] relatively poor of natural resources and

---

[2] In contrast, for an analysis that investigates the role of domestic actors and institutions on democratic developments see, among others, Vachudova, 2005; Magen and Morlino, 2008.

[3] Low-income countries of the Commonwealth of Independent States, referred throughout the paper as the CIS-7 countries, include Armenia, Azerbaijan, Georgia, the Kyrgyz Republic, Moldova, Tajikistan and Uzbekistan [Loukoianova and Unigovskaya, 2004].

agricultural dependent countries. Still, the two countries have also been selected on the type of relationship with the Fund. Indeed, both Georgia and Moldova received IMF traditional and concessional assistance. Moving from economic to political considerations, it is worth stressing that both Georgia and Moldova are conflict-ridden countries and are regarded as hybrid regimes [see Bunce and Wolchik, this volume].

This chapter is organized as follows. The next section introduces the reader to the activity of the IMF and develops the propositions about its potential democratic anchoring in the two selected countries. Section II and III provide the empirical evidence to the anchoring hypotheses. Specifically, reviewing IMF archival documents from 1993 to present, section II traces the IMF-sponsored measures to stabilize the domestic economies of Georgia and Moldova thereby promoting growth and contributing to democracy. Section III investigates IMF-sponsored measures in the area of institution building, good governance and inequality. The last section concludes.

2 - The IMF and its Anchors

Contrary to most of the international actors analyzed in this book, the IMF does not pursue the goal of democracy promotion. Created in the aftermath of the Second World War to help the establishment of a liberal economic order, the Fund presides over the stability of the international monetary and financial system.[4] Specifically, as its Articles of Agreement read, the organization is tasked with the responsibility of facilitating international trade, and thus fostering economic growth, by promoting exchange rate stability and an open system of international payments. In discharging its responsibilities, the Fund provides policy advice

---

[4] Created to preside over a fixed exchange rate system, and to provide financing to countries facing temporary current account deficits, the Fund has gradually taken on new responsibilities, developed new means to achieve its goals, and enlarged its membership. However, its task of contributing to international monetary and financial stability has remained intact. For an analysis of the evolution of the Fund's activities see, for instance, Boughton, 2001; James, 1995; Pauly, 1999.

to governments and central banks on macroeconomic policies and assesses member countries' domestic financial vulnerabilities. The IMF is also charged with the responsibility of lending members foreign exchange, on a temporary basis and under adequate safeguards, to help them address balance of payments problems that can arise as a consequence of trade openness. In sum, the Fund carries out two broad activities to attain the goals for which it has been created: it provides advice to member countries on what is appropriate set of macroeconomic policies (the so called Article IV reports) and provides loans to member countries to give them confidence had a crisis occur. In short, the IMF contributes to international economic and financial stability by carrying through its key activities: lending, and surveillance.

The activity of the Fund is carried out by its staff, primarily recruited from the economics profession.[5] Staff members operate under the guidance of a Managing Director who, in turn, is accountable to the Executive Board.[6] The Board is the Fund's core decision-making body. In particular, it is responsible for the adoption of both programmatic decisions (such as staff reports on members) and operational decisions (such as lending programs). The Board, which usually meets three times a week in full-day sessions, is made up of 24 Executive Directors.[7] Although the Executive Board enjoys large autonomy in the daily operation of the Fund, its

---

[5] On the influence of the economic culture of IMF staff on the policies of the organization see, for instance, Chwieroth, 2008; Momani, 2005.

[6] The informal convention is that the IMF Managing Director is selected by European member countries – completing the tradition that the US government selects the First Deputy Managing Director and the World Bank's Presidency. For an overview of the IMF decision making process see Van Houtven, 2002.

[7] The five members with the largest quotas – the United States, the United Kingdom, Germany, Japan, and France – along with China, Russia, and Saudi Arabia, appoint their own director. The other 16 Executive Directors are elected for two-year terms by groups of countries, known as constituencies. In order to select the ED, each group has its own rules. In some groups, representation rotates among members; in others, the name suggested by the most powerful member is consistently chosen as ED.

powers are delegated to it by the Board of Governors that has the responsibility of steering and presiding over the activity of the IMF.[8]

Although the Fund has neither the mandate nor the jurisdiction to promote democracy, it is possible to identify some of its activities that may bear upon democratic processes across its membership and in the transition economies in particular. Indeed, as the former IMF Managing Director Michel Camdessus [1995] put it "the Bretton Woods institutions were founded on two major principles: democracy and open markets. Nowhere has our work been guided more by these two beacons than in our efforts to promote the successful transformation of the former centrally planned economies."

Building on the literature on the economic determinants of democracy, it is possible to identify two activities that the IMF traditionally performs that have implications for democratic developments. These activities, which may well be regarded as anchors to democratization processes, relate to the relationship between economic growth and democracy, on the one hand, and institutional structure and democracy, on the other hand.

As far as concerns the relationship between economic growth and democracy, scholars have long debated the causal arrow between the two. On the one hand, there is a group of scholars that have investigated the effects of economic development on democracy [Huber et al., 1993; Li and Reuveny, 2003; Lipset, 1959; Papaioannou and Siourounis, 2008; Przeworski, 1991: Chapter 3]. Their main finding is that improvements in the standard of living – measured by GDP, health status, and education – raise the probability that political freedoms will grow, often via the creation of a middle class. Hence, by tracing the level of economic developments, it is possible to make predictions about which countries will become more or less democratic over time [Barro, 1996]. On the other hand, another group of scholars has examined

---

[8] The Board of Governors, which consists of one governor and one alternate governor for each member country, is advised by two ministerial committees: the International Monetary and Financial Committee (IMFC) and the Development Committee.

the impact of different institutional factors and types of governments, including democracies, on economic growth [Burkhart and Beck, 1994; Leblang, 1996; Przeworski and Limongi, 1993; Sirowy and Inkeles, 1990; Weede, 2007]. The literature, which has found that democracy has an indirect effect on growth through spending in education and investments, is not nonetheless unanimous. Rather, there are mixed results of the impact of democratization on growth [Leblang, 1997], usually linked to different stages of economic development [Muller, 1995].

Although a clear line of causation has not been established yet, what can nonetheless be concluded is that there is a two-way linkage between democracy and economic growth [Helliwell, 1994], which is all the more important to the purposes of this chapter. Indeed, considering the crucial role played by IMF in economic development, its activity can be regarded as a contribution, or an anchor, to democracy. In other words, if we accept the finding that economic development is associated with democratic forms of governments, the IMF offers an anchor to democracy by providing financial assistance and advice to its members. In particular, the IMF has focused on monetary and fiscal measures that help stabilize domestic economies, setting the foundations for economic growth.

Moving from the relationship between economic growth and democracy to the one between institutional structures and democracy, a crucial finding in the literature is that institutional weaknesses can hamper both economic and democratic developments. For instance, it has been found that improving domestic institutions (such as bureaucracy and property rights) facilitate economic growth [Burnside and Dollar, 1997; 1998; Chong and Calderón, 2000]. Likewise, there is evidence that political regimes committed to the protection of property rights positively influence economic growth [Leblang, 1996] and thereby democratic outcomes. Furthermore, a great impediment to democratic developments can be found in growing inequalities. As Muller [1995: 968] notes "while capitalist economic development increases the size and organizational power of subordinate classes with an interest in democracy, it generates greater inequality in the distribution of income". The conclusion that can be drawn from this literature is thereby that removing institutional weaknesses and inequalities is a contribution to the promotion of democracy. Hence, the IMF contributes to democracy, or is an anchor to democratization processes, by strengthening domestic institutions and promoting good governance.

Besides, the IMF's role in governance issues has taken on increasing importance in its traditional mandate of promoting economic stability in recent years. As numerous internal studies have shown that where governance is poor, domestic investment and growth suffer [Mauro, 1997], because of losses in government revenue and lower quality in public investment, the IMF has increasingly incorporated issues of transparency and good governance in its activities, primarily in its lending programs. In 1996, for instance, the Interim Committee of the Fund identified "promoting good governance in all its aspects, including ensuring the rule of law, improving the efficiency and accountability of the public sector, and tackling corruption" as an essential element of a framework within which economies can prosper [IMF, 1996]. Furthermore, there has been a growing consensus within the Fund that reducing inequality should be part of economic policy [IMF Fiscal Affairs Department, 1999].

While good governance commonly entails a broad range of practices, the Fund has attempted to specify the contours of good governance that is relevant to its activities. In particular, an attempt has been made to make the promotion of good governance as closely related as possible to the traditional areas of competence of the Fund. Indeed, as the 1997 Guidelines make clear, "the IMF should focus its policy advice and technical assistance on areas of the IMF's traditional purview and expertise" [IMF, 1997: 4]. In particular, the Fund contributes to good governance in "fighting against corruption and fostering good codes of conduct and promoting transparency, rule of law and accountability". The justification lies in the fact it is a purpose of the IMF to improve public resource management and financial sector soundness and strengthen countries' institutional capacity, including combating corruption.

In sum, the IMF anchors the democratization processes by providing financial assistance that help promote economic growth and strengthen the domestic institutional system by improving governance and fighting corruption. In what follows, I am going to map the Fund's democratizing anchoring by analyzing the documents that defined the relationship between the IMF and Georgia and between the IMF and Moldova from the early 1990s to present.

As already anticipated, the empirical analysis is solely based on IMF assistance-related documents. Indeed, lending is probably the most crucial activity for the relationship between the Fund and a member. Indeed, the Fund has an obligation to help member countries facing "a fundamental disequilibrium" in its balance of payments problems – that is, when the country cannot find sufficient financing to meet its net international payments. The IMF assists countries by providing money and helping national authorities to devise programs of corrective policies. Loans are provided under the approval of a formal agreement between the IMF and the member country that takes the form of a "Letter of Intent" addressed to the IMF Executive Board. Specifically, the "Letter", which is negotiated between national authorities and IMF staff members, details the economic programme and the conditions for Fund's disbursement. The Managing Director gives the final approval to the programme concerted, before submission to the Executive Board for the formal approval of the IMF-country agreement.[9] Once money has been lent, loans require to be repaid in time, so to assure that other members in need would be guaranteed the same treatment.

IMF financial assistance may take different forms and sizes according to the country's circumstance.[10] Over the years, the Fund has developed several instruments, or facilities, to lend to countries in need. Non-concessional facilities – loans are subject

---

[9] As the Articles of Agreement (Article XII, 5c) stipulates decisions, including lending decisions, require a simple majority of votes.

[10] The amount that a country can borrow from the Fund depends on the type of loan, but is typically dependent on the member's quota – even though exceptional access may be granted when the member's needs are very large, such as in capital account crises.

to the IMF's market-related interest rate, known as the rate of charge – include, Stand-By Arrangements (SBA), the Extended Fund Facility (EFF), the Supplemental Reserve Facility (SRF), and the Compensatory Financing Facility (CFF). An example of concessional facility is the Enhanced Structural Adjustment Facility (ESAF) later transformed into the Poverty Reduction and Growth Facility (PRGF) through which low-income countries may borrow at a concessional interest rate. Furthermore, a series of ad hoc facilities have been developed over the years, including the creation of the Systemic Transformation Facility (STF) tailored for the countries of the FSU.

In what follows, I therefore turn to the empirical analysis of the various lending programs negotiated between the IMF and Georgia and IMF and Moldova from the early 1990s to present. In doing so, the Chapter will attempt to bring to the surface the pro-growth and pro-good governance activities that the IMF performs and that may have a bearing on the democratic developments of Georgia and Moldova.

3 - Stabilization and Economic Growth

IMF lending assistance to Georgia and Moldova, and its associated advice on how to manage the domestic economy, dates back to 1993-94 when both countries were facing the difficulties deriving from the disintegration of the Soviet economic system. In particular, both Georgia and Moldova, like the other transition economies, started suffering from severe decline in output and growing inflation that undermined Governments' revenues and their capacity to govern the economy. The war in Abkhazia and Transnistria further complicated the economic management in the two countries. While conditions started improving in the late 1995, Georgia and Moldova faced major challenges in the aftermath of the 1998 Russian financial crisis that led to a renewed slowdown in economic activity.[11] As we are going to see in the next pages, the political and economic developments in

---

[11] As Russia recovered, stronger import-demand from Russia provided an impetus for recovery [Loukoianova and Unigovskaya, 2004: 11].

Georgia and Moldova have been accompanied by IMF financial assistance in promoting economic growth throughout the entire period since their independence.

3.1 – Georgia

The relationship between the IMF and Georgia stretches back to 1994 when the country first applied to the STF following the meeting between Shevardnadze (the Head of State) and the IMF Managing Director Michel Camdessus on March 8, 1994. Indeed, following Georgia's independence in 1991, the country faced severe disruptions in its trade relations and sharply increased energy import prices. In addition, the economy has suffered from civil conflicts, a war in Abkhazia and associated refugee problems. By 1994, economic activity had declined sharply, making it difficult for the Government to conduct economic policy [IMF Archives 1994c]. In particular, with the dramatic decline in revenues, the Government could not perform its most basic functions, such as paying wages and pensions. As output and revenues declined, the standard of living of the population declined sharply and the country became more and more dependent on external humanitarian aid.

Intervening under these circumstances, IMF programs were crucial to stabilize the economy and trigger economic growth. The IMF and Georgia negotiated several lending programs. After the already mentioned STF facility, Georgia obtained a one-year SBA in January 1995 and a three-year arrangement under the ESAF, which was approved on February 28, 1996. After having asked for an extension of IMF-supported program in 1999, since the end of the 1990s, the IMF-Georgia relationship has taken place within the framework of PRGF that were adopted in 2001 and in 2004. In September 2008, the IMF disbursed a new stand-by-arrangement for supporting the Georgian economy.

Under the lending programs, which were negotiated between Georgian authorities and IMF officials, the Fund initially encouraged Georgia to undertake a series of macroeconomic reforms that would have helped stalled the output decline that followed the break-up of the Soviet Union. IMF strategy, as evidenced from the analysis of the archival documents, aimed to increase Government revenues to finance domestic expenditure by reducing central financing of the fiscal deficit and the accumulation of domestic and external arrears. Tightening monetary policy to tame hyperinflation and allowing the introduction of a national currency was also part and parcel of the IMF strategy in Georgia and, as we are going to see later, in Moldova too. In general, on the stabilization side, IMF programs aimed to reduce inflation, strengthen the gross reserve position of the National Bank of Georgia (NBG), and arrest the decline in output.

Analyzing some specific characteristics of the IMF programs, we can distinguish between the fiscal and the monetary measures that the IMF suggested. On the fiscal front, IMF advice focused on tightening the fiscal position by reducing deficit and external debt. In order to that, the IMF encouraged spending cuts and reduction in public sector employees. A crucial part of the early programs was also the extension of the taxation base and the elimination of subsidies on bread, gas, and electricity to bring about a major improvement in public finances [IMF Archives, 1994a]. To this end, average domestic prices for gas and electricity were increased to reflect full import and distribution costs [IMF Archives, 1995d].

Along with measures to increase tax revenues, price liberalization also played a crucial part to further supplement the revenue base. For instance, the Government introduced VAT rates on flour, bread, and bread products, and VAT exemptions for road transport, casinos, some agricultural raw materials and precious metals were eliminated.

The effort to improve revenue performance was coupled with the attention paid to monitoring government expenditure commitments. The 1994 program, for instance, focused on the creation of a legal basis for a Treasury that would have enabled the authorities to make substantive progress in managing public expenditures [IMF Archives, 1994a]. Specifically, the Government adopted a system of strict expenditure management at the Republican Government level to control expenditure commitments. The Cabinet of Ministers had to authorize the

Minister of Finance to limit, monitor, and control all expenditure commitments at the level of the Republican Government. Still, IMF program aimed to adopt policies to ensure that bank financing of the operations of the General Government (Republican, Local, Extra budgetary Funds) stayed within negotiated limits. Finally, the 1995 program called for "a reduction of the fiscal deficit ... from nearly 17 percent of GDP in 1994 to 7 percent in 1995 and 6 percent in 1996, through a determined effort to improve revenue performance and continued implementation of a very tight expenditure program" [IMF Archives, 1995c].

On the November 1995 general elections, Shevardnadze was elected President by a sizeable margin, and the party that supported him – the Citizens' Union of Georgia – became the majority party in Parliament and engaging in new IMF-supported programs. Indeed, in February 1996, the IMF approved a three-year ESAF that contained important fiscal measures aimed at providing the basis for economic growth. Specifically, the program aimed to restore financial balance to the energy sector, by improving collections and restructuring the state gas and electricity companies. The Government also committed to refrain from providing budgetary assistance, subsidized credit, or guarantees to the energy sector [IMF Archives, 1996a].

In 1996, the word "growth" figured prominently in the new IMF-supported program. Indeed, the first-listed objective of the 1996 ESAF program was achieving an average annual growth rate of 8-10 percent per annum. The program also required continued implementation of tight financial policies, with special focus on strengthening public finances, progress in normalizing relations with Georgia's creditors.

Moving from the fiscal to the monetary front, the 1994 STF program already contained important measures. As clarified in the Statement of Economic Policies and Technical Memorandum submitted to the IMF Board in November 1994 [IMF Archives, 1994c], the program aimed "to halt hyperinflation at an early stage and to establish the necessary conditions for resumption of sustainable economic growth." Specifically, the program aimed to reduce monthly inflation to 1 percent by the end of 1995, to strengthen the gross reserve position of the Central Bank, and to limit domestic bank financing of the budget deficit. Still, the 1994 program provided for the cooperation between the NBG and the Government with the Fund staff on the timing and the procedures for the introduction of the national currency, the lari.

The 1995 program, which was discussed in Tbilisi during February 27-March 13, 1995, and May 4-19, 1995,[12] contained important measures to revitalize economic growth in the country. Indeed, the country was suffering a severe decline in output, very large financial imbalances leading to hyperinflation and massive currency substitution, a near collapse of the institutional capacity of the Government, and a disintegration of public infrastructure. Political and economic chaos in Georgia also complicated the situation in the country. In the program, monetary measures played a key role to the extent that they set the performance criteria against which to judge the Georgian government's economic conduct. In particular, it was provided that IMF disbursement would be interrupted had the limits on the net assets of the central bank and on net credit of the banking system to the government be exceeded.

Although the immediate focus of the early 1990s programs was macroeconomic stabilization, they also promoted some structural reforms that aimed at promoting economic growth while helping the creation of a middle class. Among these measures, the process of privatization of state-owned enterprises stands out. Since the 1994 program, indeed, the IMF supported the Georgian authorities to accelerate of privatization of state enterprises [IMF Archives, 1994a]. Still, in their assessment of Georgian policies in 1995, IMF staff members noted with satisfaction the progress made in privatizing the small-scale enterprises and the steps taken to privatize larger enterprises in 1996 [IMF Archives, 1995c].

---

[12] The Georgian representatives included Deputy Prime Minister Basilia, Finance Minister Iacobidze, Economy Minister Papava, NBG President Javakhishvili, and other senior officials of the Government and the NBG. On several occasions, the mission also met the Head of State, Shevardnadze, and Prime Minister Patsatsia.

In conclusion, what emerges from the analysis of first IMF-supported measures in Georgia is the focus on economic stabilization by taming inflation and expanding the government' revenues base. Although it is difficult to disentangle the impact of IMF actions on the political developments that Georgia undertook in the early years from its independence, including the establishment of free and fair election, what the analysis suggests here is that the IMF certainly helped setting the foundations for an orderly political development. By helping national authorities stabilize the economy and re-starting economic growth, the IMF indirectly contributed to the path that led Georgia to be considered today as a hybrid regime.

3.2 – Moldova

The relationship between the IMF and Republic of Moldova started in December 1993, when the Government requested a stand-by arrangement for a 15-month period and applied for the Systemic Transformation Facility. In spite of IMF early support, at the end of 1994, the decline in economic activity accelerated also because of a severe drought. As the IMF staff noted at the time, "the effects of these natural calamities are magnified by the importance of the agricultural sector, which, together with the agricultural processing industry, accounts for roughly 60 percent of GDP" [IMF Archives, 1994b: 3].

In light of these economic difficulties, on March 22, 1995, Moldova requested a stand-by arrangement for a 12-month period. At the end of 1995, although inflation remained high, output began to recover, and the domestic currency was stable. Fiscal performance started improving, with revenues up and expenditure down. Major sources of economic instability seemed to arise from the political situation in the country. Indeed, as the IMF staff report recorded, "political tensions increased during 1995, following President Snegur's decision in June to leave the ruling party .... Negotiations on the constitutional status of Transnistria stalled in the second half of 1995, as the Transnistrian leadership came under attack at home for making too many concessions, but resumed recently with an agreement on customs issues" [IMF Archives, 1996b: 2].

Against these political and economic developments, the IMF approved a three-year EFF arrangement for Moldova on May 20, 1996, an arrangement that was extended for a year by the IMF Board on January 4, 1999 at the time of the third review. On March 23, 1999, Moldova was made ESAF eligible and thereby started applying for concessional funding also because the economic situation remained difficult in 1999 and 2000. Since Moldova was hard hit by the Russian crisis of 1998, and a drought and rising energy prices affected output in 2000, Moldova requested a three-year arrangement under the IMF's Poverty Reduction and Growth Facility. Finally, in May 2006, the Executive Board of IMF approved a new three-year arrangement under the PRGF for Moldova.

As had been done in reviewing the IMF-Georgia relationship, it is possible to distinguish two broad categories of IMF-supported measures meant to stimulate economic growth and thereby setting the foundations for the country's democratic trajectory: fiscal and monetary measures.

On the fiscal front, an important part of the fiscal program was reducing and improving government spending. Specifically, the main objectives of the IMF-supported tax reform which began in late 1992 were to widen the tax base, simplify and modernize the tax system, and eliminate exemptions. In this connection, within the framework of IMF-supported programs, the Moldovan Government introduced the road tax, and extended VAT to non-CIS imports. Still, the Government committed to introducing a tax on the physical assets of enterprises, a major broadening of the present real estate tax, and a tax on natural resources.

Removing tax exemptions via liberalization and privatisation was also a crucial part of IMF-supported programs. Since the early 1990s, under the Fund suggestions, the Government started eliminating price controls at all levels (production, wholesale, retail, and trade), with a view to completing the liberalization of prices within the program period [IMF Archives, 1993; IMF Archives, 1995a]. The prices for bread and milk were increased. Transport fares and other administered prices were also increased. Subsidies on gas and coal for heating purposes were limited to those segments of the population that were most in need of them. Still, the 1996 program prescribed the rise of residential electricity and heating tariffs to rise by 50 percent immediately; all energy tariffs to rise to full cost recovery levels by end-1997 [IMF Archives, 1996b].

An important pillar of the policies meant to eliminate distortions in the economy was via privatization. Since large state-owned companied had long benefited from exemptions, the new goal became that of imposing financial constraints on public enterprises [IMF Archives, 1994b: 23]. Furthermore, as already pointed out for the economic programs in Georgia, privatization was a key measure for the creation of a new middle class. In Moldova, following the adoption of the 1993-1994 Privatization Program (PP), the Parliament set up the legal and institutional framework for privatization. The objective of the program was the sale of some 1,600 small, medium, and large-scale enterprises [IMF Archives, 1993]. In 1996, privatization entered an important new phase, the process was open to foreign investors allowing them to bid for majority stakes, including in important domestic sectors such as the tobacco industry [IMF Archives, 1996b].

The importance that the IMF attached to privatization as a mechanism to trigger economic development is also relevant from the Fund decision to interrupt the 1995 EFF program with Moldova. Indeed, in the spring of 2000, the fifth review under the EFF could not be completed "as parliament twice rejected legislation that would allow the privatization of the economically important wineries and tobacco companies" (a prior action for the completion of the review and also a condition for further World Bank disbursements) [IMF Archives, 2000a: 4]. Beyond the early years, privatization also figured prominently in the 2000 PRGF and its focus on poverty reduction. Indeed, the authorities pledged to extend large-scale privatization to strategic investors, especially in agro-processing, energy, and telecommunications. In this connection, the IMF encouraged the privatization of Moldtelecom in order to use the proceeds from its sale to service or retire Moldova's external debt [IMF Archives, 2000a; IMF Archives, 2000b].

218

On the monetary front, since the beginning the IMF suggested measures meant to reduce inflation also via granting independence to the central bank. In the 1993 Memorandum for Economic and Financial Policies, for instance, the Moldovan government committed to review the domestic banking law "in order to enhance the credibility of the NBM's (i.e. the central bank) monetary program" by providing its operational impendence? [IMF Archives, 1993: 3]. Taming domestic inflation was also one of the central concerns in the 1995 and 1996 programs, with a commitment in reducing annual inflation to about 10 percent and 15 percent respectively. In sum, monetary stability was conceived as a crucial goal. As the Moldovan authorities put it, "the attainment of (monetary stability) will provide a sound basis for the stability of the lieu and a revival of investment activities, including from foreign sources, thus laying a foundation for sustainable growth of the economy and an improvement in the standard of living of Moldovan people" [IMF Archives, 1995a: 40].

Although over time stabilization concerns receded in favour of new concerns such as poverty reduction and strengthening the investment climate, even in the most recent programs the IMF stressed the importance of a sound monetary and fiscal management. For instance, the PRGF adopted in 2006 provided "for further gradual disinflation" and the IMF welcomed "the authorities' decision to amend the National Bank law to establish price stability as its key objective" [IMF, 2006].

In sum, as has been the case with the IMF-Georgia relationship, in supporting the Moldovan authorities, the IMF fostered fiscal and monetary measures that would have provided the foundations for economic growth and, possibly, democracy too. While it is not a purpose of this study to investigate how and to what extent the IMF-suggested measures were actually implemented, it is worth noting that political economic factors may impede even the best-designed assistance programs. Indeed, the IMF lamented several times that the domestic political setting was an impediment to IMF programs because of recurrent periods of political uncertainty and a lack of cooperation between the presidency and parliament. As the IMF staff put it, "ownership of the Fund supported program was weak at the highest levels of government until early 1999" [IMF Archives, 2000a: 5]. A more reform-oriented government was later in power allowing the parliament approved two amendments to the constitution in July 2000: the first made Moldova a parliamentary republic; the second strengthened the powers of the government relative to both the presidency and parliament. As IMF staff commented, "this change should end the power struggle between the presidency and parliament, which at times has stood in the way of the reform process" [IMF Archives, 2000a: 6].

4 - Strengthening Domestic Institutions, Good Governance and Social Equality

The set of IMF-supported measures analyzed in this section ranges from the set up of ministries and bureaucracies to the creation of social safety nets. These measures became predominant in the late 1990s after economic stabilization was put firmly in place. They are closely associated with concessional assistance program such as ESAF and PRGF that formed the core of the IMF-Georgia and IMF-Moldova relationship in second half of the 1990s. The key characteristics of such concessional facilities is their focus on domestic institutions and poverty reduction as mechanisms to attain economic growth.

For instance, the documents prepared under the PRGF describe the country's poverty profile, review the policies implemented over the past years to strengthen the economy and reduce poverty, sets out the medium-term economic scenario on which the IMF-supported economic program is based, and indicates the key elements of a poverty reduction strategy. To strengthen its effectiveness, the strategy is prepared by the Government in close consultation with, and broad participation from, representatives of the Parliament, civil society, and the donor community.

In what follows, I thereby review the measures suggested to Georgia and Moldova with the aim of directly tackling domestic institutional weaknesses and reduce poverty. As we are going to see, issues of good governance and fight against corruption quickly became dominant in IMF-supported program in both countries.

4.1 – Georgia

The IMF has been involved with strengthening Georgian institutional capacity since 1992. In particular, the Fund provided technical assistance toward the establishment of a treasury function in the Ministry of Finance, and in the areas of tax administration, balance of payments statistics, and modernization of the Central Bank (the NBG), including monetary operations, foreign exchange market, banking legislation, bank supervision, accounting and auditing, payments system, and introduction of a national currency. In order to help the national authorities in strengthening the institutions to govern the economy, the Fund resident representative also assumed duty in Tbilisi on November 23, 1994.

Strengthening the domestic financial system was an early a priority of IMF programs as attested by the 1995 negotiated decision. Indeed, in their report on the economic situation in the country, IMF staff members referred to the Georgian financial system as "a rudimentary" one, in need of extensive technical assistance [IMF Archives, 1995c: 8]. In the words of the staff, "as a result of the absence of discipline and supervision in the immediate post-independence period the commercial banking system is in a perilous state. With the help of MAE (i.e. the IMF's Monetary and Exchange Affairs Department) technical assistance, discipline is being gradually established through the enforcement of new prudential regulations, closure of banks, and improved reporting and inspection procedures" [IMF Archives, 1995c: 8].

Another important example of the emphasis that the IMF placed on a strengthened institutional capacity can be found in the 1994 program. Under the framework of the program, indeed, the Government created a special Operations Division within the State Tax Inspectorate (STI) to monitor taxpayer compliance and to enhance the collection of tax arrears [IMF Archives, 1994a].

The development of a domestic regulatory framework able to withstand market forces also became a crucial part of IMF-sponsored structural measures in Georgia. In the 1996 IMF staff report, for instance, IMF staff members encouraged the authorities to give high priority to developing a legal framework for a market economy [IMF Archives, 1996a]. For instance, the IMF considered as prior actions, that is, actions necessary for the disbursement of its financial resources, an improvement of the domestic legal framework, including Parliamentary approval of new commercial banking and land laws. The revised commercial banking law would have included provisions for bank liquidation. The land law would have given landowners liberal rights of lease, sale, and inheritance [IMF Archives, 1996a].

At the end of the 1990s, then, the IMF started advocating an increasing number of structural policies aimed at fostering the development of the private sector and sustaining economic growth. In the 1998 program, for instance, the IMF encouraged national authorities to design policies such as the launching of urban and industrial land privatization; the removal of remaining trade restrictions; further steps to restructure the electricity sector; and a strengthening of commercial banks' prudential regulations. The program also targeted a deepening of judicial reform to secure an effective implementation of the many laws enacted by the Georgian parliament during the previous years [IMF Archives, 1998: 72].

In the staff report prepared in 1998, then, IMF members lingered on the problem of corruption, widespread across government institutions. In this connection, in order to continue receiving IMF financial assistance, Georgian national authorities publicly committed to fight domestic corruption [IMF Archives, 1998: 72]. In the Statement of Economic and Financial Policies, the Georgian authorities thereby pledged to adopt economic reform that would aimed "at making progress in fighting corruption, increasing accountability of executive public bodies, and boosting good governance" [IMF Archives, 1998: 70].

The fight against corruption also figured prominently in the first Interim-PRGF prepared by the Government in November 2000. Specifically, a working group was established to draft a national anti-corruption program. Such a program was meant to follow some strategic directions, including the liberalization of the business environment, the revision of the management of state resources to make it more effective, the optimization of public administrations. Still, the PRGF emphasized the need of strengthening the domestic law-enforcement and justice system so to contribute to anti-corruption activities [IMF Archives, 2000b: 22-24]. The 2000 and 2004 reform programs also emphasized the need for "a decisive attack on corruption" [IMF 2004].

Finally, to protect the most vulnerable groups during the transition period, IMF programs usually included the provision for the establishment of social safety net. This was true even in the early 1994 program when the Government increased nominal wages to take account of inflation targets. Still, in line with IMF advice, cash payments were given to the lowest-paid employees and to all pensioners. Special provisions were also made for children up to and including 16 years of age, single mothers, refugees, as well as students of the state higher educational institutions [IMF Archives, 1994a].

As already pointed out, the measures to improve the situation of the poorest people in the Georgian society grew in relevance over time, as economic stabilization was achieved and growth kick-started. The utmost example of the emphasis placed on the most vulnerable people in the country is certainly the adoptions of the Poverty reduction and Growth Facilities, in 2001 e in 2004. For instance, as Shigemitsu Sugisaki, IMF Deputy Managing Director presented the content of the PRGF approved by the IMF in January 2001, "Georgia's economic program for the next three years aims to lay the foundation for faster growth and poverty reduction" [IMF 2001]. Still, one of the centrepieces of the 2004 reform program was that of increasing core spending on social projects and infrastructure [IMF 2004].

4.2 - Moldova

Similarly to what had been done in Georgia, the IMF programs for Moldova also devoted a special attention to a number of structural reforms that could be of help in strengthening domestic institutions. For instance, the early 1993 program encouraged the National Bank of Moldova (NBM) and the Government to start close consultations with the Fund, the World Bank and the EBRD on specific measures to restructure the banking system, improve bank supervision, modernize accounting standards, and strengthen the capital adequacy requirement in all banks [IMF Archives, 1993]. Still, a crucial part of IMF assistance was to develop new central bank and commercial banking laws that will strengthen and clarify the NBM's ability to supervise the banking system.

Along with providing technical assistance to improve the functioning of domestic financial markets, the IMF also helped the national authorities in devising programs that could strengthen domestic institutional capacities in collecting and using taxes. According to one of the IMF staff reports, for instance, "priority ought to be assigned to improving the tax administration. Empowering the tax inspectorate to seize assets, including inventories, in case of non-payment of taxes is a necessary first step." In this connection, IMF staff stressed the need to proceed expeditiously with the establishment of a full-fledged Treasury [IMF Archives, 1995b: 16-17].

Creating a legal system appropriate for a market economy was another key concern in IMF-supported programs. In 1995, "major element of the structural reform program for 1995 is a review of key legislation to ensure compatibility with the requirements of a market economy. In particular, there is an urgent need to ensure that a clearly defined legislative basis exists for private firms to initiate bankruptcy proceedings against insolvent state enterprises" [IMF Archives, 1995a: 12]. A crucial part of the 1996 program, then, was that of creating a private market for land. Indeed, as of 1996, residential property and urban land were tradable, and land certificates, establishing farmers' right to land ownership had been distributed. However, sales of agricultural land were not still permitted [IMF Archives, 1996b].

As had been the case for Georgia, the relationship between the IMF and Moldova also helped the authorities to develop safety nets to reduce poverty and inequality in the country. Indeed, since the first adopted programs, the Government sought and obtained technical assistance on the design of a social safety net from several international actors including the Fund and the World

Bank with the overall objectives of protecting the most vulnerable. Specifically, the international technical assistance helped the establishment of benefits, including pension benefits, family allowances, and unemployment benefits. In addition, the Government strengthened the role of the Social Assistance Fund, with the aim of protecting those that might fall through the existing social safety net [IMF Archives, 1994b; IMF Archives 1993]. IMF staff also advised the Moldova authorities about how to prioritize among the multiple needs of the population. As one IMF staff report put it, "social safety net to be refocused to target most needy and promote economic restructuring" [IMF Archives, 1996b: 9]. Hence, the 1996 program outlined a strategy for restructuring social spending, in order to better target the most needy, while providing greater incentives for labour supply, mobility and retraining.

As already pointed out, the IMF decidedly shifted the focus of its programs to good governance and poverty reduction issues in the late 1990s, when economic stabilization and economic growth had been restored. At that time, making progress in improving the investment climate and modernizing Moldovan economic infrastructure became a dominant issue in the IMF-supported program. In this context, Moldova applied for the Fund's PRGF. The details of the program were discussed in Chisinau during July 12-26, 2000 and October 16-30, 2000. The mission met with President Lucinschi, Prime Minister Braghis, Speaker of Parliament Diacov, First Deputy Prime Minister and Minister of Economy and Reforms Cucu, NBM Governor Talmaci, Minister of Finance Manoli and other senior government officials and members of parliament, as well as representatives of NGOs.

With the PRGF, the issue of reducing poverty and inequality took central stage in the IMF-Moldova relationship. The underlying logic became that economic policies would have not only aimed at restoring growth, but also at improving social assistance and human development measures. In doing so, the measures designed to improve Moldova's long-run growth prospects dedicated special attention to the measures aimed at improving the business climate, promoting financial sector development and reducing poverty. Specifically, the Interim PRGF drafted in 2000 was built on three pillars. First, poverty reduction was regarded as dependent on economic growth and the creation of productive employment opportunities, especially in rural areas. The second pillar of the PRGF was that of improving social protection, by increasing the efficiency and equity of the social safety net. The third pillar focused on human development by increasing access to, and improving the quality of basic public services, such as primary health care and education.

From the perspective of the PRGF, privatization also took on a new dimension. That is to say, privatization was not solely regarded as a mechanism to promote the establishment of a market economy and a middle class but also to improve transparency in the Government's activities. As the 2000 PRGF reads, "privatization would also help to address governance and transparency issues in this sector" [IMF Archives, 2000a: 20]. In this connection, the IMF sustained national authorities in the decision to privatize domestic wineries and tobacco companies through an open-tender process. Likewise, the IMF encouraged the privatization of Moldtelecom following best international practices that include transparent processes and preparatory steps such as hiring an investment bank to assist in the sale [IMF Archives, 2000b: 3; IMF Archives 2000a: 23].

Furthermore, with the aim of improving transparency and good governance, the Moldovan authorities adopted a new Civil Code, drafted with German technical assistance, in October 2000. This would have helped strengthened the overall legal framework for defining property rights and contractual obligations [IMF Archives, 2000a; IMF Archives, 2000b].

The fight against corruption also gained importance in the IMF-Moldova relationship. For instance, in an IMF staff reports, IMF staff members identified in corruption one of the causes that impeded the attraction of "strategic investors" and called for the public sector reform agenda to include public administration reforms. Specifically, measures such as streamlining the structure of the government, civil service reform, and anti-corruption measures in public service delivery, as well as improving public

226

resource management, were regarded as crucial steps in the path of economic reform in the country [IMF Archives, 2000a: 5, 15].

In the 2006 PRGF, measures for improving the domestic system for private sector investments and for reducing poverty were still front and centre. As the IMF presented the newly adopted program, "the authorities' Economic Growth and Poverty Reduction Strategy Paper and the Moldova-EU Action plan provide a solid basis for the medium-term policy framework that will support conditions for durable, private sector-led, and pro-poor growth" [IMF, 2006]. Specifically, following the goal of strengthening economic growth and reducing poverty, the program envisaged a broad range of structural measures. For instance, public sector management had to be strengthened through improved corporate governance of state enterprises, privatization and public administration reform. The business environment was expected to be enhanced through the modernization of bankruptcy procedures, the streamlining of regulations, and the removal of restrictions on grain exports. Finally, the IMF invited the national authorities to strengthen the financial sector by improvements in transparency, a reduction in government interference, and the promotion of greater competition, including through the market access for foreign banks [IMF, 2006].

5 - Conclusions

In the speech delivered at the first meeting of the IMF, John Maynard Keynes spelled out his view about how the IMF and the World Bank were to perform. "If these institutions are to win the full confidence of the suspicious world, it must not only be, but appear, that their approach to every problem is absolutely objective and ecumenical." But if the two institutions would "grow up politicians", Keynes added, "the best that could befall – and that is how it might turn out – would be for (the IMF and the World Bank) to fall into an eternal slumber, never to waken or to be heard of again in the courts and markets of mankind" [as quoted in Harrod, 1951: 631-632]. Following Keynes' concerns, the founders of the IMF carefully drafted its Articles of Agreement mandating the organization to adopt its decisions based on technical and economic criteria, insulated from political concerns. This mandate – elsewhere defined as the doctrine of economic neutrality [Swedberg, 1986] – signals that the Fund's actions are carried out in isolation from political considerations. As a result, in contrast to other international actors analyzed in this book, the IMF does not pursue the goal of democracy promotion.

Recognizing the technical nature of IMF actions, this Chapter has nonetheless argued that the IMF may perform a number of actions that help shape the trajectory towards democracy. In particular, borrowing from the literature on the economic determinants of democracy, this Chapter has argued that IMF's policies to promote economic growth, institutional strengthening and good governance contribute to the creation of an environment conducive to democratic processes.

The Chapter has thereby tested these propositions by analyzing the activities that the IMF performed in its relationship with Georgia and Moldova since the early 1990s to present. Specifically, drawing on the findings positing a relationship between democracy, economic growth and institutional capacity, this Chapter has argued that IMF lending programs provided an interesting example of the activities and the mechanisms that an external actor such as the IMF can play in anchoring democratic processes. By reviewing IMF archival documents, the analysis carried out in this Chapter has thereby brought to the surface the IMF-supported measures within the frameworks of various lending programs in order to trigger economic growth and improving the domestic institutional setting. As has been shown, while the IMF initially focused on measures to promote economic growth via the traditional monetary and fiscal channels, in the late 1990s, economic growth became conceived as strictly correlated with strong domestic institutions, good governance and the reduction of social inequalities.

In conclusions, a few limitations to the analysis need to be mentioned. Although I carefully investigated the activities and mechanisms that the IMF employed to orient the economic and political trajectories in two hybrid regimes, I acknowledge that my empirical analysis is limited at the level of *design* and does not distil the causal effect of IMF actions on the democratic developments in Georgia and Moldova. In other words, the ultimate test of the democratic anchoring of IMF lending would be to assess its impact on the policies in member countries and to assess how the latter influenced democratic developments. Such an assessment is difficult for several reasons, including the multiple factors that influence a country's policies. The focus of this paper has therefore been more on the content and quality of democratic anchoring *design* rather than on the implementation of those policies at the domestic level.

Hence, it is plausible that further studies will refine or modify the findings presented in this Chapter. Nevertheless, the primary goal of this Chapter has been early stage theory building about the relationship between the IMF and democracy. In other words, I aimed at identifying a preliminary set of activities for future empirical research that may help explain how an important international actor, as the IMF is, can affect democratic and not only economic developments in its member countries.

Part III

Democratic Change Agents, Veto Players, and Foreign Policy Orientations

8

THE POLITICAL ECONOMY OF OLIGARCHIC STAGNATION. RUSSIA – IN TRANSITION TO WHERE?

Eugenia Baroncelli

1 - Introduction

With the launch of *perestrojka*, in February 1986, the then Soviet President Mikhail Gorbachev initiated a period of radical reforms, by opening the Communist Bloc to the Western democracies through the introduction of selected market-based elements in the Soviet planned economy, and by gradually opening institutions to citizens, through a cautious revision of the party-state-based centralism.

The main developments that followed the end of the Soviet system and of the bipolar contest with the United States (US), with the spreading out of the market-based liberal democracy to the majority of Eastern European and former Soviet countries, are largely known. Wide diffusion has also been given to the interpretation that the main Schools of International Relations (IR) have provided of these occurrences, both relative to domestic developments in the Union of Soviet Socialist Republics (USSR), and to its relations with the US, Western Europe (namely West Germany) and other former satellite states (namely Poland). Liberal and Cognitivist IR scholars have chosen to focus their attention on the role played, respectively, by a – supposedly – superior institutional performance of democratic institutions [Fukuyama, 1989], on the one side, and on processes of learning and change in foreign policy preferences by domestic and transnational political élite, on the other [Risse Kappen, 1995]. Contributions in the Realist vein have, on the contrary, emphasized the role played by structural variables (systemic

232

change and pressure, in particular) that, in their opinion, played a crucial role in pushing the USSR-US competition to the extreme [Gilpin, 1987; Oye, 1995]. Weakened by criticisms from both the Liberal and the Cognitivist camps, for having supposedly departed from its own methodological and substance claims, the Realist School has suffered an additional setback for not having anticipated the peaceful nature and voluntary elements in polarity change and systemic transition. The debate in the IR academic community has since then taken the route of a wider discussion on the respective roles of ideas, institutions and material factors in systemic change. What stands out clearly, and relevantly for our purpose here, is that all the three Schools posited a clear relation between internal and external factors (inside-out for Liberals, outside-in for Realists, mixed for Cognitivists) to understand the extraordinary changes that the USSR-Russia, and the world, have experienced since then. While these remarks may appear as self-evident from an IR perspective, little attention has been devoted so far to the role of external factors (and, more importantly, to the relation between internal and external factors) in democratic – domestic – regime transitions.[1]

Compared to the other former republics, or to the Eastern, Central and Southern European countries, the Russian case is important then in at least two respects. First, it was there that it all started. Looking at how events unfolded in the Russian Federation is then important to identify the features of the *primum movens*, in several cases a key source to study mechanisms of further democratic diffusion. Secondly, even without debating the difference between today's Russia and the unparalleled role of the USSR towards its sphere of influence prior to the events of 1989-1991, one should acknowledge that Russia currently enjoys a remarkable political clout as a regional power, in general, and on some neighbouring countries, in particular. The structural power that Russia still possesses, internationally and regionally, suggests using particular care in the exploration of the role played by external factors in the Russian transition, on the one hand, and in the investigation of the influence that Russia exerted on

---

[1] A notable exception is Magen and Morlino, 2008.

the transitions in neighbouring countries, on the other. While the second analytical question is directly addressed in other chapters [see Morini, this volume], we nonetheless note a seemingly inverse relation between regime consolidation in Russia and democratic effects in neighbouring countries.[2] With respect to the first analytical question, the role played by external factors that facilitated the Russian transition, this paper focuses on the peculiarly interactional nature of the internal-external dynamics. As argued in more detail below, the timing in Western aid policies, as well as the change in Russia's negotiation powers after the surge in oil prices in 2000, are crucial elements to understand the role played by external inducements to democracy [Åslund, 2007b; Fish, 2004].

Parallel to the debate on the Soviet collapse in IR studies, authors in comparative politics [Diamond, 1992; McFaul, 1997 and 2003; Bunce, 1999; Linz and Stepan, 1996, among the many] and institutional economics [Lipton and Sachs, 1992; Stiglitz, 2002] started to concentrate specifically on the study of domestic dynamics of transition in former-communist states, and to explore the theme of regime change, on the one side, as well as that of the evolution from planned to market economies, on the other. Only recently has an interest in the dialogue between these two strands emerged, in the attempt to deepen the study of the links between political and economic transition in post-communist regimes [Fish, 2005; Åslund, 2007; Lane, 2007]. Similarly to the other post-Soviet transitions analyzed in this book, Russia is peculiar as a case of "double transition", due to the simultaneous changes that occurred in its political and economic systems.[3] While such

---

[2] After the high democratic potential of demonstration effects in the early phases of the Soviet collapse and Russian regime building, the repression of Chechnyan separatism since the war of 1994 marked a clear shift away from the sympathetic stance towards democratic transitions in neighbouring countries. However, as explained below in this chapter, it was probably the existence of profound stateness problems that, not addressed at the federal level by Gorbachev, re-emerged with virulence during the Yeltsin's years, affecting at once democratic transition in Russia and Russia's stance towards transitions in its near abroad.

[3] See Linz and Stepan [1996: 244] on political transition and Åslund [2007b], among the many on economic transition. A contribution on the

similarity is shared by other cases of political transition in general (change in institutional rules and rule-making is highly likely to influence the management of the economic system), the case of the Soviet dissolution epitomizes almost to perfection the role that reciprocal influences between these two layers of change can play for the future of democracy.

This paper argues that the continuity in non-democratic practices across the Yeltsin and Putin's years has been accompanied by truly democratic experiments in the 1990s. Their failure in present times does not exclude that, as in the majority of transition cases, these democratic precedents will resurface in due course [Lipset, 1993; Hadenius and Teorell, 2005]. The core argument discussed below is that the peculiar nature of Russia's institutional hybridism is rooted in both long-term historical factors and short term institutional choices that were made at crucial junctures by the incumbent élite. Also, this contribution hypothesizes that the interaction between economic trends in oil prices and self-redistributing political-economy choices by the Kremlin will keep playing a determinant role in the future of Russia. Finally, it suggests that, over the medium-term, external incentives from powerful democratizers, such as the US and European Union (EU), should be better targeted if they are meant to have a lasting impact on the consolidation of a stronger democratic opposition in Russian civil society.

Section two sets the context for the subsequent analysis by briefly reviewing the key elements of the political and economic changes that have occurred since the dissolution of the Soviet Union (SU). In section three, after a discussion on the typological alternatives provided by existing contributions in the comparative and political economy literatures, the paper offers a critical assessment of the mixed nature of the Russian polity. In section four it identifies the main sources of such hybridism, arguing that these are to be found in Russia's stateness problems (conflicts on borders and identities) and institutional choices by the élite (deferred federal elections, a powerful presidency and weak

---

relation between economic and institutional change is provided by Açemoglu and Robinson [2005].

legislature, type and timing of economic reforms at the time of the transition, with chiefly non-redistributive management of the benefits from privatization). In the same section, the subsequent evolution from hybridism to a more consolidated form of authoritarianism is linked to elements of continuity in the long-seated tradition of *etatcratisme* that, it is argued, would be at the roots of the current "liberal disenchantment" and popular acquiescence to the state's continued pursuit of collusive schemes. Two external triggers have however accelerated the oligarchic and bureaucratic turns under Yeltsin and Putin, it is further argued: the "neglect of the West" and the alternate trends in oil prices. Section five discusses the alternative evolutions that await current Russian authoritarianism, by laying out the expected effects from the interaction of three set of factors: top-down élite-driven and systemic influences, the role of external triggers of change, and that of bottom-up instigators of democracy in Russian civil society. Section six concludes, by recapitulating the main arguments advanced in this paper and advancing hypotheses for future research.

2 - From the Empire's Dissolution to Putin's *Revirement*

According to the procedural interpretation of democracy, while only partially competitive, the elections of the Soviet Parliament in 1989 have been quoted to mark the change from an autocratic system to one in transition towards democracy in USSR-Russia. Gorbachev himself, while having maintained in principle the supremacy of the Communist Party, did not hesitate to label the reform towards the 1989 parliamentary election as democratic [Solnick, 1999: 795]. Similarly, numerous references can be found in Yeltsin's political rhetoric to the thesis of "democratic opposition" and "democratic alternative", suggesting that, in the first phase after the Soviet collapse, the expected outcome – at least from political élite – could not be but in the direction to democracy. According to some, this has happened without much attention to the contents of such rhetoric and, especially, without the necessary search for popular legitimation from citizens, who saw in that rhetoric the only alternative to the old Communist

236

regime [Solnick, 1999: 794-96]. In the cases of *perestrojka* and *glasnost*, it seemed evident that Gorbachev wanted to widen participation and promote pluralism in the existing system, while also pursuing openness and privatization of the economy. The first – and sole – President of the USSR was plausibly prevented from embarking on a more radically democratic track by several elements. The attacks to the central power from the Republics (especially the Baltic states), the pressures for a rapid transition to market economy and for the dissolution of the Communist Party all acted as powerful constraints to limit Gorbachev's freedom of manoeuvre [Brown, 1996]. The events that followed the end of the SU, and the separation of the Russian Republic in November 1991, with a declining Premier, unable or untimely in the adoption of democratic federal elections, in the midst of an economic crisis, mark Yeltsin's ascendance to power, and his election to the presidency of the newborn republic, which, since 1992 has become the actual Russian Federation.

The years up to 1993 were scattered by tensions between the Executive, which supported the option of liberal reform of the economic system, and the Legislative which, on the contrary, was favourable to preserve the main economic structures of the Soviet era [McFaul, 1995]. While also building a dangerous precedent towards the definition of the constitutional settlement of the new state the tug-of-war between Government and Congress[4] played a non marginal role in delaying/blocking the implementation of the economic reforms supported by the Executive [McFaul, 1995]. On October 1993, President Yeltsin chose to put a forceful end to the crisis, ordering the army to bombard the Parliament. The invasion of Chechnya in 1994, the uncertainties on the presidential elections in 1996, as well as the various reshufflings that Yeltsin made in the Executive between Spring and Summer 1999, further confirmed that the move from Soviet post-totalitarianism was not taking place in the direction of democracy.

---

[4] The reference is here to the self-attribution of disproportionate powers, following the Marxist model, by the Congress, on the one side, and to the recurrent direct appeals to the people made by Yeltsin, along the lines of the Latin American models of delegative democracy. See Linz and Stepan [1996: 396-397].

At the same time, openly preferring market economy over planned post-Soviet management, Yeltsin opted to proceed further in the direction that had been chosen by Gorbachev, by significantly liberalizing the Russian economy, integrating it into world markets, and by privatizing its productive system. Since 1994 however, Yeltsin had changed the initial approach to mass privatization of large state enterprises which, up to then, had been implemented mainly through the distribution of free vouchers (worth either cash or shares), and had substituted it with cash auctions. Small investors did not have the needed liquidity, however, and foreigners were prevented to take part to the auctions. In the end, a Consortium of the major Russian banks, formed by Vladimir Potanin of Oneximbank offered to acquire large shares of each company, which would be used as collaterals for the loan to the state (*loans for shares scheme*). The gains that the state derived from these sales, often transacted below their true value, were a needed injection of liquidity in public Russian coffers. The intermediation of these few, selected banks and their managers, that had emerged as national champions in key sectors of the Russian economy, was being consolidated as a typical clientele relationship between the political élite (the Executive and President Yeltsin) on the one side, and the economic élite on the other (financial oligarchs, who also benefited from privileged buying options in the privatization of state-owned enterprises). In the end, the auctions to sell the loans contracted by the state were largely controlled by the few financial oligarchs of the Consortium, who managed to block new entries, kept the bidding prices low and finally took control of the companies at ridiculously low prices.

When, during the electoral campaign for the presidential elections, in March 1996, Yeltsin started to lose on public support, he did not hesitate to resort to his connections with the privatization oligarchs to minimize the risk of defeat against his rival, the neo-Communist Zyuganov. In return for a substantial economic injection to his campaign, which he also strengthened by submitting the medias to strict controls, he allowed bankers and managers to reach majority shares in the largest state enterprises.[5] Yeltsin's victory, with a large margin in the second ballot (53.8% against 40.3% for Zyuganov) in July 1996, did not bring however the much hoped improvement in the country's economic situation, which in fact worsened considerably after the fall in commodity prices. Triggered by the Asian crisis, the vagaries in commodity markets ended in 1998 in a massive run against the rubble. The speculation hit a country that was plagued on its own by massive fiscal evasion, and lacked social safety nets almost totally. In spite of the International Monetary Fund (IMF) rescue package of July 1998, and of the several increases in interest rates to restore confidence in the rubble, the massive capital outflow forced the Government to devalue and convinced Yeltsin to ask again for external assistance.

While devaluation had some of the expected positive effect on Russian exports, the country was led out of the crisis by the increase in oil prices which occurred in 1999-2000. On the political side, the financial collapse of the Russian state had seriously exposed the Executive. Under fire from both the electorate and the Parliament, Yeltsin chose the road of successive reshufflings in the cabinet (first by calling Chernomyrdin, then substituting him with Kiriyenko –opposed by the Parliament in two votes – in April 1998, then reappointing in August of the same year Chernomyrdin, who was to be rejected by the Duma, and replaced with Primakov in September, then by removing Primakov to the benefit of Stephasin in May 1999, followed in August 1999 by the appointment of Vladimir Putin as Prime Minister).

---

[5] While these years had witnessed an end to the violent crushing of democratic attempts of 1991-1993, a gradual shift was also occurring away from Russia's chances to consolidate its incipiently democratic features [McFaul, 1995; Solnick, 1999]. The presidential elections of 1996 had not been cancelled, as feared by many, to avoid a fall in popular support to the President during the difficult days of the transition reforms. However, the elections of regional governors were postponed, and coverage was limited by strict controls of the media [Solnick, 1999: 804].

Many contributions have covered the events that occurred between 1993 and 1999, and have examined the interaction between Russia's economic policies, electoral cycles and institutional choices. On the one side, sympathetic readings have emphasized the virtues of Yeltsin's choice to open the Russian economy [Åslund, 2007b] and its good premises towards a possible institutionalization of the electoral contest with democratic rules [McFaul, 1999]. On the other side, critical readings have recalled the elements of continuity within the élite, and the anti-democratic connections in cases of new entries, which indeed occurred always in support to the existing regime [Solnick, 1999; Lane, 2007]. According to this interpretation, it was not the perception of the costs attached to an increasingly democratic environment that kept Yeltsin from interrupting the electoral routine, but his expectation that higher benefits would come from a prolonged stay in power, if that was backed by the support of the oligarchs that had emerged during the period of privatizations, and that could continue to help him to buy popular consensus.

However, an event that was "external" to the domestic political-institutional routine, the financial crisis of summer 1998, marked the end of the opportunistic pact between the government and the oligarchs, and opened a window of opportunity for a different course in the political evolution of Russia. On August 17 1998, the Russian government, unable to honour the debts that it had contracted in previous years through the emission of state bonds, financed through the loans for shares scheme by Russian citizens and Western lenders, declared its sovereign default. The financial crack of the Russian state tore down the oligarchs' privileged position: they saw their role further curtailed by Yeltsin himself, who, as seen above, formed a new government with a substantial presence of Communist ministers, under the guidance of former KGB Chief Yevgeny Primakov.

The years between 1999 and 2004 have witnessed the ascendance and consolidation of the power of Vladimir Putin, former KGB officer, designated as Prime Minister by Yeltsin since August 1999, temporary President after Yeltsin's resignation in December of the same year and, finally, President elect in March 2000, reconfirmed in his second mandate in March 2004. Taking a different approach to Russia's economic policy, Putin initiated the re-nationalization of some of the large state enterprises. He then appeared as the man that had successfully redressed the balance in favour of the citizens, by substantially circumscribing the rents and power positions that the oligarchs had accumulated during Yeltsin's presidency. The choice to bring some of the major companies of the country back under the state's control (energy, railway transport, war industries) and to promote them as national champions was, however, accompanied by the creation of privileged positions for a number of individuals in the President's entourage, largely former KGB officers and selected liberal bureaucrats that had worked with him in St. Petersburg [Shevtsova, 2007: 44].

During his first term, Putin chose to further pursue the track initiated by his predecessor, by adopting a new civil code and rationalizing the taxation and tariff systems, to prepare the entry of Russia in the World Trade Organization. Macroeconomic austerity and the rationalization of the taxation system (cuts in subsidies and pension schemes, centralization of taxation) had a definitely positive effect on the Russian economy, through increased revenue and the attainment of a surplus in the state budget. However, these effects gained a substantial boost from the increase in oil prices: while macroeconomic austerity was useful to restore confidence in the rubble, it was the change in oil markets that allowed Russia to increase substantially its foreign reserves [McFaul and Stoner Weiss, 2008].

With respect to chiefly political choices, Putin centralized power in the hands of the Executive, at the expense of the regional governors and of the economic oligarchs.[6] In May 2000 Putin introduced indeed relevant changes in the constitution. The

---

[6] To be sure, even if one of the most vocally quoted failures in Yeltsin's politics was his poor management of centre-periphery relations, -relations that he had not been able to guide towards a democratic and smooth transition- it was one of his men, the oligarch Anatoly Chubais who, in 1997, had used local governments and presidential representatives to keep provincial powers in check [Huskey, 2001].

high chamber in the Parliament (the Federal Council) was changed into a body of designated members – contrary to its previous elective nature. The reform also established that regional governors were to be nominated by the President, who was given the power to dismiss local legislative bodies if these rejected the appointed governors for two consecutive rounds of votes [Åslund, 2007b; Petrov, 2004]. At the end of 2003, near the conclusion of his first term, Putin's fiscal and administrative reforms towards centralization were accompanied by additional, increasingly arbitrary presidential measures against the economic élite.[7] Since the parliamentary elections of December 2003, and in spite of the earlier attempts to create new independent parties, the Duma became fully subservient to the Kremlin.[8]

In some respects, Putin has continued what had been initiated by Yeltsin in its foreign policy, by strengthening the repression of Chechnyan separatism, waging a second war against Grozny and manipulating popular consensus towards a carefully constructed image of national pride. However, Putin's foreign policy has been also marked by clear a change with respect to the ambiguities showed by Yeltsin's in the final period of his presidency in the relations with the Western partners. Yeltsin had shown trust in the US and Europe, at the proclamation of the end of Communism, by asking their financial and humanitarian aid, in 1992 and, again in 1998. Putin's first mandate was successful in

---

[7] The forced closure of NTV in 2002 and the subsequent closing of TV6, subsequently re-constituted as a private station thanks to the financing of Chubais and other oligarchs from the Yeltsin's years, are two cases in point. The prosecution and jailing into a forced labour camp of Mikhail Khodorkovsky, CEO of the Yukos oil company, that was officially declared bankrupt in October 2003, was another emblematic step in the gradual consolidation of regression to authoritarianism in Putin's Russia. See Shevtsova [2005: 227] and Åslund [2007b: 276-280].
[8] See McFaul, Ryabov and Petrov [2004: 296] and Shevtsova [2005: 285-293] who notes how the these elections were "free but not fair", arguing that the Kremlin had succeeded in exploiting its "administrative resources" to manipulate the competition process among candidate parties to the Duma (by openly sponsoring one party, United Russia, through all the available media outlets, and by creating new pro-Kremlin parties to steal votes from both the democrat and leftist camps).

foreign policy terms insofar as the President succeeded in defining Russia's role as a regional power in the post-Soviet space, while at the same time starting a seemingly constructive dialogue with both the US and the EU, which could possibly lead, beyond mere partnerships, to softer forms of integration.[9] Things changed since 2002-2003, when the choice between neo-conservative hopes of nationalistic reassertion clashed with their US counterparts, which envisaged a sheer junior partnership for Russia. While he carefully maintained personal high-level ties with several US and EU leaders, especially hinting at these special relationships to discourage anti-Kremlin surges in neighbouring states, Putin had Russia opposing the US decision to wage war against Iraq in the United Nations Security Council. More generally, as shown by his disagreement with NATO enlargement and US missile defence plans, Putin has openly criticized the projection of US military primacy in world politics in his second term. After the Beslan's tragedy, Putin also chose to mobilize anti-Western phobias to hide the failure of his Chenchnyan policy, resorting to a vague call against foreign terrorism [Shevtsova, 2005: 390-393].

As noted above, a sign of continuity has been Putin's pursuit of further accumulation of powers in the hands of the President. Both Yeltsin and Putin have enhanced the authoritarian features of the Russian regime, strengthening the role of the Executive and its freedom from competitively elected legislative bodies. However, the new President made it clear from the start that he rejected political pluralism. He gradually got rid of several potential competitors, by closing media channels owned by Yeltsinites, reforming the upper chamber in the Parliament as an arm loyal to the Kremlin, controlling votes in the Duma, redesigning the geographical and political map of the Federation's districts and appointing his loyals as governors. Such limitation of pluralism has been further pursued during his second mandate, through the adoption of laws that substantially

---

[9] To be sure, integration, especially in the EU, was chiefly pursued to gain Russia a direct influence on its decisions [Shevtsova, 2005: 336].

curtail the activities of NGOs and through a *de facto* public control of the media (all TV channels and almost all newspapers), which marked a clear weakening of previous democratic impulses and a drastic turn towards increased authoritarianism [McFaul and Stoner-Weiss, 2008].

The passage of powers to Medvedev, designated successor by Putin himself, and winner of the Presidential elections of March 2008, has not witnessed the departure of the old President, a Prime Minister that still has the primacy in the making of Russian politics. While Medvedev may appear to mark a change insofar as he does not share the same background as Putin's (he has a PhD in economics and has not had a past in the KGB-FSB), a year since his instalment, neither his domestic policies (further delays in the reform of the justice system, cosmetic benevolence towards democratic activists, wait-and-see attitudes in the Khodorkovsky farcical process) nor his foreign choices (oppositional stance towards the US on missile defence) have signalled the will to alter his predecessor's political formula.

3 - Transition Typologies and Russia: Conformity and Specificity

Definitional criteria may lead to oversimplification. However, they can help in making sense of an otherwise too complex reality. Studies in transition offer a number of typologies that capture the different dimensions in regime change. With respect to the state-society axis, transitions that have originated from civil society inputs (bottom-up) have been distinguished from those that have started from the redefinition of power shares within the dominant group or among the incumbent–competitor dynamic (top-down). While early contributions simplified the analytical setting to a dichotomous incumbent élite-opposition élite dynamic [Rustow, 1970; O'Donnell and Schmitter, 1986a], subsequent studies have deepened the knowledge on the inner workings of each of these two groups, and the influence that their composition effects were likely to have on transition [Przeworski, 1988]. In this respect, the degree of consensus between incumbent élite and opposition groups on fundamental issues such as national identity and geo-political borders of a state appears to be crucial in determining the solution in cases of stalled transitions (whereby higher consensus would lead to an expected easier transition towards democratic ends) [Rustow, 1971]. Looking at time characteristics of the transition process, the literature has distinguished between gradual and sudden transitions. With respect to the degree of completion in the transition process, complete transitions (mature and consolidated democracies vs. autocracies) have been coupled with incomplete transitions ("hybrid" [Morlino, this volume], "mixed" [Bunce and Wolchik, this volume], "anocratic" [Gurr, 1995], and "incoherent" [Polity IV, 2008] regimes).[10] Interestingly, as noted in this volume by Morlino, Bunce and Wolchik, post-authoritarian hybrid regimes are much higher in number compared to fully democratic regimes. Looking at the width of the overall transition process, and largely simplifying an altogether complex set of links between political institutions and economic choices, it is also useful to distinguish between mostly political transitions (institutional changes) and economic transitions (changes in the production and distribution systems and relations). Finally, looking at the relation between domestic (political system, social groups, economic system) and external variables, one could simplify by distinguishing between mainly internally-originated and externally-influenced transitions [on external factors see Dahl, 1971; Huntington, 1991: 108-123; Almond and Mundt, 1973: 626-629, on demonstration effect].

The comparative literature has then combined several of the above factors into typologies to interpret the complex combination of variables at different analytical levels and policy arenas: political, social, economic. Relative to their duration, sudden transitions towards democracy have been considered a necessary ingredient for consolidation, even when their immediacy was accompanied by the use of violence [Carothers,

---

[10] Also see Linz and Stepan [1996], Morlino [1998 and 2000], Diamond [1999], Whitehead [2002].

2007; Berman, 2007].[11] With respect to timing, the debate is open on the relative benefits that early changes in either of the two policy areas – economy and politics – could bring for democratization. On the one side, it has been argued that a solid economic system should come prior to any political transition towards democracy, even if this means tolerating longer periods of non-democratic rule [Myrdal, 1968; Huntington, 1991; Isham *et al.*, 1997]. Conversely, others have noted how differed democracy exposes peoples to the risk of missing sound opportunities for democracy in the name of an abstract time-sequencing [Carothers, 2007; Berman, 2007]. Finally, a number of scholars have supported the need of a simultaneous occurrence of democratic political transition and radical reforms of the economic system [Diamond, 1995; Bunce, 1999; McFaul, 2001].

While the long-term effects of the arms race with the US have played a role in the Soviet decline, relative to the weight of external influences on early change, the Russian transition was, as noted in the previous sections, the result of mainly domestic elements. The events that happened in Moscow between 1989 and 1991 were undoubtedly the first movers of the ensuing demonstrative transitions in the rest of Eastern Europe and of the former Soviet Empire. They indeed triggered the domino effect that was to re-model the overall geography, both internal and external, of the states on the Eurasian continent [Huntington, 1991: 98-100, 104-106].

Post-Communist transitions have been classified by Linz and Stepan [1996] as evolutions towards either democratic or authoritarian ends by post-totalitarian regimes (which these authors in turn considered as evolved sub-types of the totalitarian genus). The USSR of pre-*glasnost* and pre-*perestrojka* years has then been labelled as a case of "decay-induced post-totalitarianism" due to the "ossification of the apparatus, the gerontocratic leadership, the wooden language of the ideology, the loss of mobilization

---

[11] On the contrary, other authors have supported the thesis that gradual changes would be more promising for democratic stabilization [Przeworski, 1991; O'Donnell and Schmitter, 1996; Mansfield and Snyder, 2005 and 2007].

capacity, and the passivity of the population" [Linz and Stepan, 1996: 375]. Compared to cases of post-totalitarianism by choice (or originary societal mobilization), the case of Russia is marked, according to these scholars, by a less-than-voluntary approach to manage the transition on the side of the political élite. As such, the change occurred between 1989 and 1991 was the unexpected consequence of the ideological hollowing out in the praxis of management of power and mass mobilization, less and less pervasive when compared to pure totalitarianisms. While these remarks on the early involuntary nature of the transition have been further confirmed, there is little doubt that the Russian case is one of top-down, élite-guided regime change, according to some even "imposed" [Karl and Schmitter, 1994: 181]. With respect to its timing, the literature squarely places it in the camp of big-bang initiated transitions, moved then to the gray area of "protracted non-consolidation" [*Ibid.*].

Here then lies the first conundrum, as well as the crux in the transitology literature: how should one define the Russian regime? A particular case of post-Communist mixed regime [Bunce and Wolchik, this volume], 1990s Russia has also been compared to other "electoral democracies" [McFaul, Petrov and Ryabov, 2004: 5]. Elections occurred regularly then, results were not known beforehand – and were not overturned afterwards – and virtually all citizens were entitled to participate. In general, equality under the law and freedom of expression was largely guaranteed in the 1990s, even if these guarantees have become much looser overtime for certain categories (Chechens, radical democrats, Yeltsinites or "old" oligarchs that have not been co-opted indefinitely under Putin's second mandate) and individuals (opponents of the regime, and, more in general, of the Kremlin).

Thus, while there is agreement in the literature that Russia was not a full-fledged democracy in the 1990s, the shift from its Soviet and authoritarian past towards increased political openness was evident. As discussed in the previous section, Russia's transitioning regime has now moved to an increasingly authoritarian new era. A number of differently nuanced labels have been suggested to capture its (current) nature. All of them converge on one thing: in today's Russian regime the quantity and depth of non-democratic features vastly outweigh the number of democratic ones [McFaul, Petrov and Ryabov, 2004: 2-7]. Elections are free, as noted, but in general not fair. Electoral constraints on the Executive are virtually non-existent, and separation of civilian from military power is rarely guaranteed. In several elections Przeworskian uncertainty of outcomes has not been an option, and campaigning has been plagued by disparities in access to party formation and, more in general, civil society representation on the basis of either political or ethnic criteria. In the past five years, pluralism in the media has dramatically fallen, and so has the independence and fairness of the Judiciary. Coated into an "imitation (of) multiparty democracy" [Shevtsova, 2007] the essence of the Russian regime appears to be close to an "authoritarian order" [Bunce, this volume], marked by a high degree of uncertainty ["uncertainty in an authoritarian context", Morlino, this volume].

While today the Russian political regime is the result of the multiple changes that have occurred in the past twenty years, the roots of these different evolutions are at times located in a more distant past. The seminal work on consolidation by Karl and Schmitter [1994] has indeed been helpful in locating a key element in the explanation of the path followed by Russia in its political transition. The choice to postpone federal elections, the absent interest in the development of a multiparty system, and the generally low inclination towards a conciliatory management of the claims from the republics, which both Gorbachev and Yeltsin shared, played a crucial role in moving Russia and some of the other former republics away from a democratic trajectory. Other scholars, have on the contrary underlined the peculiarity of the Russian case, claiming a separate typological specificity for its "lost" or "frozen" transition [O'Donnell, 1996], also with respect to transitions in Southern European and Latin American countries [Bunce, 1995; Solnick, 1999]. Based on Rustow's seminal contribution [1971], these scholars have recalled the importance of stateness problems, as well as of ethno-nationalistic tensions, as possible elements that played against the development of

248

genuinely democratic institutions in Russia. Divergences on founding principles (borders, national identity) have created a higher risk that the stalemate on the institutional future of Russia moves from a situation of productive uncertainty [Przeworski, 1988] to an almost sterile soil for the growth of social and institutional democratic features.

On the one hand, the Russian is similar to other post-Communist contexts (such as Yugoslavia), and to transitions that occurred in other political settings (such as post-Franchist Spain and some Latin American countries). As in those cases, in the Russian case too the transition in the form of government was coupled with the issue of (re)definining the centre of state power. Different from the Spanish case, however, where competitive multiparty elections at the national level played a key role in preventing ethnic conflicts, and similarly to the case of Yugoslavia, the case of post-Soviet Russia is especially peculiar, as the country has inherited from the Federation highly politicized ethnic cleavages. According to Linz and Stepan [1996: 374-386], the choice that Gorbachev made, when he decided not to call competitive elections at the federal level prior to the creation of independent states, has played a key role in eroding Russia's bases for state power.

In spite of the popularity acquired with the elections of June 1991, Yeltsin chose to defer the issue of building democratic institutions, prioritizing on the contrary the pursuit of economic reforms (to stabilize the context towards the creation of a mixed economy with a "powerful private sector"). If in his memories he hints to the possibility of calling new elections for the Congress, which he quotes as a missed opportunity, there is no mention of the role that parties could have played as actors of democratic change (not even "Democratic Russia", the group that had contributed to his ascendance to power). Yeltsin's political agenda, in other words, lacked those ingredients of democracy building, as electoral competitiveness and multipartitism [Linz and Stepan, 1996: 390-400], that are essential for the constitutionalization of uncertainty that is characteristic of most transitions towards democracy [Przeworski, 1988: 1991].

Definitional issues on state borders and identities, as well as the choice to postpone federal elections on key founding principles played a crucial role in the early years of the formation of a hybrid regime in post-soviet Russia. Other elements however, were changing within the group of the reformist élite (the Yeltsinites), between them and the conservatives that were pressing for a comeback of Communism, and between the reformists and the oligarchs, that would have a key impact on the revirement towards authoritarianism.

The case of the Russian transition shows the importance that economic changes have on the redefinition of the institutional rules of the game. It also highlights the difficulty of separating economic from political-institutional factors in the study of regime change, and suggests how the heuristic division between policy areas (political-institutional, on the one side, and economic reforms on the other) should mostly be employed to improve the understanding of the effects that the interaction between different factors has on transitions. Time precedence (reforms of the economic system first, and of the political one afterwards), as well as dislocation in the duration of reforms (economic big-bang, political gradualism) have had a remarkable impact on the evolution of the Russian trajectory. Similarly, the oligarchic nature of privatization policies under Yeltsin shares some similarities with the strategy of re-nationalization pursued by Putin. In different ways both leaders have redefined the system through loyalty mechanisms that exhibit several neo-feudal traits [Åslund, 2007]. Economic change was also influenced by external factors. The lukewarm responses of the EU and US to Yeltsin's call for support during the crisis of 1991-92, have perhaps played a role in the President's political choices then, and have contributed to the gradual deterioration of democratic developments.

4 - The Russian Trajectory: History, Institutional Choices and the Political Economy of "Double" Transition

While certain features of the current Russian political situation may lead to suspect a further move towards a new "one party system" (United Russia, the Kremlin party par excellence, along with a host of smaller mock competitors financed by the Executive, since the 2003-2004 electoral cycle), this contribution argues that the current situation is rather one of bureaucratic authoritarianism [Shevtsova, 2007: 41], largely under the control of a single leader and his entourage (intelligence and security forces, bureaucracy and –selected- big business). What explains the evolution of the mixed regime towards this consolidating authoritarianism?

On the one side, the authoritarian essence of the Russian institutional evolution has been connected to historical elements, belonging to a "tradition" dating back to the pre-Bolshevik period [Shkaratan, 2007]. This interpretation tracks back to the Russian past the doubts that most citizens in today's Russia seem to retain about some characteristics of systems of diffused property rights under high degrees of wealth concentration. Such link, it has been hypothesized, would be at the basis of the popular consent to Putin's authoritarian politics, praised for having sanctioned through re-nationalizations and expropriations the privileged rents that had been gained by the oligarchs during the years of the Yeltsin's Presidency.

A similar argument, this time applied to the élite, is consistent with the reading of Linz and Stepan [1996: 400], according to whom the Russian undemocratic turn during Yeltsin's years should be ascribed to key constitutional and institutional choices, in the absence of a previous agreement on decision-making structures. In essence, the explanation of the Russian trajectory based on etatcratisme tracks its origins in three key elements: a tradition in institutional weakness, authoritarian discretion and opposition towards resource concentration in non-public hands, be they lawful or not. To be sure, however, as noted by Linz and Stepan [1996], the Russian's institutional weakness is a rather peculiar one: while carrying the usual baggage of problematic issues (the dual legitimation system of semi-presidentialisms, the resort to referenda as a populist tool) is here associated with the practice inherited from Communism of deferring all the power to the Soviets, a formula that obviously has been filled with higher substance in the very core of the former SU with respect to the other Republics. The hyper-legitimation of the Legislative implied by power concentration in the hands of the Soviets was, in essence, a powerful obstacle to the adoption of Western systems of inter-institutional horizontal accountability. As sketched in the previous section, shorter term effects such as the timing in the management of transition, since the years of Gorbachev's reforms, are also supposed to have negatively impacted on the chances for Russia's democratic development. The choice of gradualism that was made in that particular instance, combined with the characteristics of the existing proprietary structure (high levels in energy endowments, natural monopolies, concentration of private property in a few hands and tendency to an oligarchic management of the economy) created the ideal conditions for the perpetuation of a non-competitive context. It also offered to the political élite an option in collusive legitimation through the forming of an anti-democratic alliance. Such was the situation that, according to some, solved the stalemate on the future of foundational rule making for the new Russian state.

External factors have played a crucial role in the evolution of the Soviet transition first (since the first Gorbachev premiership), Russian then. In the first case, as shown by the Realist interpretation of the Soviet collapse [Oye, 1995], such external elements as the exasperation of the nuclear arms race since the early Eighties and the overall decline of the Soviet economy, have plausibly been key elements in the choice that Gorbachev made when he decided to gradually integrate the URSS into the world economy, through the promotion of incoming foreign direct investments and the support to trade ties beyond the area of CMEA and socialist countries (as with Cuba and Vietnam).[12] In the second case, others have noted how indecisiveness and bad timing on the side of the Western countries have played a non-negligible role in the authoritarian course steered by Yeltsin since the Fall of 1993 [Åslund, 2007b]. This is not to say that the failure of the reforms attempted by Yeltsin are the sole cause of the authoritarian revirement that occurred in Russia during those years. Similarly, it is not possible to explain the turning away

---

[12] See however the debate on first, second and third-image factors in explaining (international) systemic transition in Lebow and Risse-Kappen [1995].

from democracy that characterized Russian politics in mid-Nineties only based on the Western hesitancy about sending financial support to Yeltsin's reforms. To complete the picture it is perhaps necessary to look at other permanent elements of the system, Soviet first, and Russian later.

Among them, the presence of armed groups that enjoyed a privileged position, secret services (KGB first, KSF later) that were fully able to support themselves, and that possessed a knowhow on existing intelligence and espionage networks – consolidated since the years of post-totalitarianism – allows one to compare the Russian case to that of autocratic regresses that had occurred in Latin America between the Sixties and the Seventies (Argentina, Brazil, Chile). Added to the peculiar combination of stateness problems (ethno-territorial claims), and to the absence of a pre-existing democratic culture (absence of a tradition in horizontal inter-institutional accountability) even in the Russian pre-totalitarian years, their role explains the derailment towards soft authoritarianism that occurred at the turn of the new century, in the transition from Yeltsin to Putin.

The determinants of Russia's current stalemate are therefore to be sought both in long and medium-short term elements. As discussed above, the former primarily consist of a past of non-democratic experiences and of established rent positions that have endured across different regime changes, as in the case of the intelligence. The latter have been identified, respectively, with the effects of the arms race, the institutional selection at critical junctures, economic cycles and fluctuations in oil prices. Also, one should be aware that these factors were both domestic (the ideological changes undergone by the political élite between 1987-1991, their choices on constitutional orders and political reform) and international (the different stances of the US and the EU, the financial crisis of 1998).

Contrary to the tradition in comparative studies, which has endorsed the thesis of political primacy in post-Communist transitions, and which criticizes the economy-politics line of legitimation (a sort of reversed "pyramid of legitimacy" [Linz and Stepan, 1996: 435-439] from economic satisfaction to democratic consolidation), we think that it is neither possible, nor beneficial, to specify in advance the combination of political and economic factors that characterizes the trajectory of creation and consolidation in regime changes. Different from other former Soviet satellites, but similar to some of the former Soviet republics, the Russian case seems to support the thesis of a correlation in dimension and timing between welfare acquisition and political consensus on the side of the citizenry [Linz and Stepan, 1996: 445-449, on the period 1989-1994]. Between 1993 and 2000, much of the frustration about the social and economic conditions of the country has gradually been channelled to erode the consensus that supported the incumbent élite, to the benefit of older Communists and of new standard bearers of nationalism, coated in authoritarian tones. Leaded by President Putin, these latter have succeeded in gaining the praise for having brought Russia back on the tracks of growth, and for having increased its international prestige after the years of dependency from international aid. If such consensus is undoubtedly a key element in the current Russian regress to authoritarianism, then what is at stake analytically is not the primacy of either economic or political factors but the identification of the conditions under which the former factors prevail over the latter, as well as their consequences for the evolution of political change.

In the Russian case, the people's dissatisfaction after the economic crisis of 1998, and their critiques against the oligarchs, seem to originate from a poor management of the benefits of transition, and from a less-than-wise allocation of its costs. Gains from privatization were not distributed fairly across the different social groups – in fact the poorer were not affected at all. However, no alternative was given after the dismantlement of the social safety nets that had characterized the years of totalitarianism, when basic public goods were provided by the state through labour, health and education policies. In the hardships of the crisis, the lack of a substitute in such redistributive mechanisms was plausibly at the roots of the popular discontent and massive popular support for Putin in the elections of March 2000. The authoritarian, often violent, solution that was adopted to end the inter-institutional conflicts over power sharing and attribution (namely between the President, the Parliament and the Judiciary), as well as between the centre and the periphery of the country, has further exposed the limits of the existing institutional context, and its poor performance in providing checks on the action of the political élite in their search for a solution to the crisis.

While the lack of democratic precedents has undoubtedly played a role in leading Russia towards the non-democratic edge, the fact that constitutional systems of crisis management of a liberal-democratic type were not envisaged during those critical years is perhaps symptomatic. The faith in the – supposedly – beneficial effects of the market cannot be preserved indefinitely, especially when these effects are managed under rules that can be arbitrarily changed by those in power. Had federal elections been called before the degeneration of power conflicts at the centre, and before the deterioration of the Russian economy in the second half of the Nineties, nationalistic tensions in the peripheries may have been less severe. However, a genuine protection against the current authoritarian drift would have required a redefinition of the constitution along democratic and liberal terms, both with respect to the checks and balances at the centre, and with respect to reliable guarantees to private property for individual citizens. With respect to Gorbachev's choice, whether it was motivated by political myopia or, perhaps, by a genuine faith in the enduring unifying power of Socialism, one should not forget the difficulties that the Soviet leader faced when he was abandoned by his supporters when most in need of their contribution to redefine the rules of the system [Brown, 1996]. With respect to the institutional choices adopted by Yeltsin, the debate on the role of external hesitancy on the one side [Åslund, 2007b], and on the selfishness of his redistributive choices on the other [Lane, 2007], is still open.

What stands out from this picture is that a few elements that are considered key to help the move towards democratic consolidation were missing in the early years of the Russian transition. If, as noted by Przeworski, uncertainty within the group of reformist élite is a necessary condition to have a pacted transition towards democracy [Przeworski, 1991], such an uncertainty is not, however, a sufficient one. Interactional dynamics between political and economic élite at the moment of rule re-definition add a dimension that has been often ignored by models of transition and consolidation. Most often, these models classify the élite that are involved in the transition process (both incumbents-opposition leaders, and intra-group dynamics) by limiting their focus to the arena of political competition. The collapse of the Soviet state, which was ideologically connected to a quintessential level to the federation's productive system, created wide economic opportunities, absent in other authoritarian systems based on private – even if unequal – wealth distribution. Yeltsin's choice to redistribute asymmetrically the gains from privatization to the benefit of a few large banks, through the discriminatory management of *loans for shares* and other successive programs between 1995-97 has indeed contributed to create an oligopolistic power structure in the country. This certainly provided the political élite with a potentially wider – and more controllable – financial basis but it also ingrained a serious risk of instability, especially under the state's institutional weakness, both at the centre and in the regions.

In addition to the quoted role of external actors (lack of incentives from the EU and US' hesitancy) then, the absence of rules and resources at the centre, as well as the lack of experience in monitoring the implementation of privatization and economic opening, have created a situation where the surpluses in wealth that are typical of the early developments in emerging markets were easily appropriated by a small group. As seen above, these few would play a critical, but highly controversial role in the future of the country. Drivers of the Russian economic development after the demise of Communism, the oligarchs have indeed contributed to the creation of the self-redistributive system, and anti-competitive political control that currently characterizes the country. However, it was the Government that, under the two Putin's premierships, took advantage of the wide dissatisfaction in the society and penalized, by way of expropriation, re-nationalization or altogether suppression, some among the most productive Russian companies. An alternative course would have been that of altogether redesigning the rules of the game, according to higher thresholds on grounds of competition and redistribution, to the benefit of the whole Russian society. Evident in these occurrences is the theme of an authoritarian leadership that undermines its political adversaries and wins popular support through an exemplar punishment of the economic élite, preserving however the existence of corruption and regressive collusion between itself and the entrepreneurial élite. This recount shares, to be sure, a few elements with other instances of connection between elections and economic cycles in (already) democratic regimes (on the US *robber barons* at the end of the Nineteenth century see Åslund, 2007), a particular case of the more general question on the cumulability of political and economic power, a theme dear to the American political studies in the Sixties [Dahl, 1961; Polsby, 1963]. What should be noted here is that in the case of 1990s Russia the regressive effects of the capture of political élite have been particularly serious, perhaps because the oligarchs have enjoyed privileges for a rather long span of time, at the end of which there still was no system of property rights to limit their self-redistributing tendencies, and to grant them fair treatment even during demagogic upsurges. There was, in essence, no institutional framework to prevent a further drift to oligarchic patterns of self-redistribution.

5 - The Future of the Russian Regime: Economic Shocks, Systemic Resilience and Democratic Alternatives

What are the prospects that await the future of Russia's hybrid regime then? While no definite answers can be possibly given beforehand, the analytical avenues covered in the previous sections have provided several elements to ground a set of plausible hypotheses. Democratic alternatives to the ongoing context of predatory state, such as the one that seems to be consolidating in Russia these days, are closely linked to three sets of factors. First, top-down elements (both élite- and structural system-driven) will no doubt play a key role to move Russia away from authoritarian consolidation. The introduction of competition in both political and economic arenas (a radical improvement in the overall system of the rule of law, investment climate and privatization reform, diversification away from oil) will depend indeed, at first, on the will of political élite. However, much of these choices will be influenced by trends in economic cycles (oil prices, global crisis). Second, and partially linked to the previous point, the choice of large external actors will also matter. US foreign policy towards Russia, and EU's diversification strategies away from Russian oil will likely have an impact on the evolution of the Russian transition, even if these decisions will be chiefly influenced by the international state of affairs and, by system-wide trends in economic cycles. Third, threats to the further consolidation of the current authoritarian trend may come from below. While civil society in Russia suffers from several weaknesses (difficult environment, low impact), it has nonetheless remained the only independent ground to breed a genuinely democratic opposition.

Looking at the changes towards decreased democracy and increased authoritarianism that have marked the Yeltsin and Putin's years, one should not miss how the Russian system, even in the midst of institutional and economic shocks, at times violent ones, has enjoyed a substantial continuity with respect to oligarchic patterns in the management of the different sources of power. Slightly skewed towards the pluralist extreme, under Yeltsin, and more clearly biased towards the elitist pole, since the beginning of Putin's years, the Russian regime has constantly been marked by the presence of mechanisms of collusive self-redistribution of political and economic resources to small groups of individuals, selected on the basis of their loyalty to the Premier and to his ideas. In the case of the authoritarian turn under Putin's presidency, the erosion of the economic base that had undermined Yeltsin's position had been avoided thanks to the positive economic conjuncture at the international level, and to the skilful manipulation of large parts of the public opinion through a foreign policy marked by aggressive and nationalistic tones. However, with the exception of macroeconomic stability, that has until recently granted Russia noticeable growth rates and international economic prestige, internal stability has been bought with vast recourse to censorship and suppression of political and social pluralism, and through a careful nurturing of the personal popularity of Vladimir Putin. The existing state-based mechanisms to absorb social shocks have been dismantled, in spite of the worsening of the health conditions of large parts of the population (as in the case of the mounting rates in HIV-Aids diffusion), the exponential growth in poverty rates, and the overall deterioration of the quality of life for the majority of Russian citizens.[13] In the absence of a system for free and competitive expression of preferences, it is likely that, to grant the current Executive popular support, Putin and Medvedev will have to carefully mix coercion with selective distribution of the gains from economic growth, and namely, from oil sales.

In 2008 the Russian economy showed a sustained trend in growth (5.6% yearly rate) [World Bank, 2009]. However, with the global crisis still unfolding, Russian GDP is expected to fall by 4.5% in 2009 [World Bank, 2009].The future of the Russian economy appears to depend both on the price of crude oil and on the resilience of the current regime. High levels in oil prices played a key role in getting Russia out of the crisis of 1998. The downward fall to a half of their value in 2008 (USD 60 in July 2009, compared to USD 120 last year, [World Bank, 2009]) does not bode well for the endurance of patrimonial and oligarchic traits in the Russian regime. Sustained by a considerably high level of corruption and careful employment of violence, the system has to nonetheless keep producing resources to a level that is sufficient to meet popular demand.

In spite of the Kremlin's rhetoric on modernization and competitiveness achievements, data on recently re-nationalized state companies do not show a particularly positive performance [McFaul and Stoner-Weiss, 2008]. The management from former intelligence officers does not appear especially effective either [Åslund, 2007b]. Compared to the oligarchic arrangements that

---

[13] In 2006 73% of the Russian urban population lived below the poverty line, compared to 64% in the other countries in the ECA Region (Eastern Europe and Central Asia) [World Bank, 2007].

prevailed during the Yeltsin's years, the current power structure is marked by a strengthened role of the Executive and the President in the management of the economy. On the one side, power centralization implies a reduced risk for policymakers to be captured by economic élite. However, it seems that Russian market authoritarianism has not so far achieved any considerable reduction in corruption and corruption-induced additional costs. Ranking 120th out of a total of 181 surveyed countries, Russia has one among the worst investment climates in the world, not to say among the other fast-growing countries in the BRICs group [World Bank, 2009; The Economist, 2009: 59]. As in the case of other authoritarian regimes where political power is based on the rents extracted from strategic raw materials, there is always the risk that, with unfavourable economic conditions, under high levels of social and economic disparity, the regime's current military personalism will not be able to persist indefinitely. A coercive yet resourceful effort would be required through time to grant the combination of domestic growth and external assertiveness that has so far secured popular support to the Russian Executive, and that it will eventually erode the very – economic – bases of its power.

To such scenario of "extinction by implosion" a second can be added, of "frozen" or "trapped" transition, stopped at an intermediate step on the – theoretical – trajectory to democracy [see Pei, 2005, on China]. As in the case of the Chinese "market autocracy", the Russian system also experienced autocracy and Communist rule in its past, that, as seen above have brought about several constraints to the full development of key liberal and democratic principles. The absence of mechanisms to balance powers at the horizontal level, the habit of a collective property system of rights, are elements that were at the roots of the Russian/Soviet system, which could explain the difficulty that the regime has to exit the current hybrid phase of "soft authoritarianism". However, similarities between the two countries should be qualified by way of several, remarkable differences.

Russia has evolved from a Communist, post-totalitarian regime to a soft authoritarian one, through a semi-democratic interlude.

China, on the contrary, has experienced radical changes mainly in the economic realm, keeping its non-democratic institutional features largely intact. With respect to China, which has chosen a gradualist road to its economic transition, Gorbachev's gradualism in economic reforms has proved less than effective in curbing the dominance of former Party bureaucracies. The events that have followed the launch of *glasnost* and *perestrojka* have shown how, different from China, Russia had to undergo a radical change among political élite, to disclose transition for its economic system. Privatization of Russian large companies, the backbone of the Soviet productive system, as it has been observed by some, implied different outcomes compared to early agricultural reforms in China. In the case of Russia, however, change has allowed a new oligarchy, alternative to the Party nomenclature, to ally with non-Communist political élite. Up to 1999 the country underwent several experiments in democratic competition (parliamentary, presidential and, to some extent, regional elections), with opposition parties and civil society NGOs voicing almost freely their dissent through a plurality of independent media channels. Absent in the Chinese case, such democratic precedents will no doubt play a role in the future of the Russian transition.

This said, the move away from semi-democracy that has occurred in Russia since 1999 has brought the country closer to the authoritarian edge. The Russian oligarchs have provided support to a state that has prospered from restricted groups of self-redistributing agents. The financial collapse of 1998 has generated a new window of opportunity to redefine the rules of the game in a more democratic fashion. As seen above, however, such opportunity has been lost to the strengthening of collusive ties between the state and other oligarchies (intelligence and financial élite).

In the past, powerful external actors, particularly the US, have been officially either lukewarm or dismissive about Russian demands for support. Until the Iraq war of 2003, to Washington's ears, Russia spelt like an insolvent debtor, more than a potential democratizer. The situation has changed since then, on both US and Russian sides. Looking at the evolution of the Ukrainian transition, and at the countries that have experienced "coloured revolutions", an element of debate has been the role played by the external assistance in democratic transition that the EU and US have provided, and may provide towards similar aims in Russia. In spite of these hopes, however, there seems little evidence that the US has any intention to move from the current tones to a more confrontational diplomatic posture in its relations with Medvedev (a "good technocrat") and Putin.[14] Similarly the EU has not shown any intention to embitter its relations with Moscow on human rights issues, and individual countries, such as Germany, have secured regular provisions of gas through bilateral contracts with Russia. More seriously, different from Gorbachev and Yeltsin, Putin and Medvedev have actively discouraged external assistance towards democratic transition. Further deterioration of ethnic conflicts in territories that are strategic for both Russia and the West, such as the conflict with Georgia in summer 2008, may temporarily change the situation, but there is little chance that they can act as external triggers for regime change. In the wait of a less restrictive application of the existing controls on foreign financing to democratic NGOs, a chiefly domestic and élite-driven amendment, external actors should at least help democratic shifts with a better targeted diplomacy – not excluding open blame of human right abuses- in key international *fora*.[15]

---

[14] "We don't have the ability or even will to use coercive power to change Russia's behaviour", a Senior US administrative officer said shortly before Obama's trip to Russia [The Economist, July 4-10, 2009: 23]. Human rights issues have not been prominent in the agenda of the recent visit to Moscow of the US President either, which revolved around arms control, Iran, terrorism, Afghanistan, the world economy and climate change. See Financial Times, July 6, 2009.

[15] While the exclusion of Russia from some of these *fora* (such as the Council of Europe) has been advocated by human rights activists, self-exclusion from the negotiations of Russia to enter the WTO has been, on the contrary, threatened by Prime Minister Putin. According to the organization of the Regional Congress of NGOs, that was held in the Russian city of Penza, in December 2008, the Council of Europe openly showed its endorsement of Medvedev's policies on human rights protection by choosing as its co-organizer no less than the Federation Council, a patently governmental authority [Kommersant, December 3 2008].

As shown by the Ukrainian experience, a key element in the evolution towards democracy is the presence of bottom-up participation from civil society. In that case, however, social inputs were genuinely accepted and mobilized by reformist élite in the direction of increased democratic openness. Such acceptance is – to put it mildly – largely missing in Russia's current political élite who have, on the contrary, started a strategically managed rally of social consensus by creating and co-opting state-guided groups from civil society under the flag of "sovereign democracy" [Surkov, 2006]. Different from the totalitarian practices of the Soviet period, the Kremlin has embarked on a skilful management of inputs from civil society into channels that consolidate the status quo of soft authoritarianism. To this aim, former President Putin worked towards the creation of the Public Chamber in April 2004, and the adoption of the law of January 2006 on NGOs. In the former case, a consultative body that is nominally intended to channel inputs from civil society to state institutions in a host of areas of public relevance (constitutional policies, guarantees of the rights and freedoms of Russian citizens, social and economic development, civil society issues) ends up in being, at best, a mock, heterodirected mechanism to increase the visibility of largely non-political issues. At worst, thanks to its structure, functioning rules and membership, that are severely skewed towards the Kremlin loyals – its members are either directly appointed by the President or elected in turn by these people [Richter, 2007], the Chamber has become an additional information-gathering tool in the hands of the Executive.

In the latter case, procedural and substantial requirements of the 2006 Law on NGOs have drastically reduced the number of non-governmental organizations that are officially active on the Russian territory [Moscow Helsinki Group and Human Rights Without Frontiers, 2008].[16] Through such framing of consensus,

---

[16] The Law contains highly demanding registration and financing requirements, largely discretionary conformity assessments by the authorities – as well as substantial provisions that outlaw those foreign NGOs that are deemed to either

the Kremlin has significantly reduced social pluralism. More worrisomely, after the constitutional changes in the party system and electoral rules for the Federal Council have deprived the Legislative bodies of any remnants of their monitoring role over the Executive, such framing by the Kremlin has substantially impaired the locus of the remaining political opposition in Russia. At the same time it has ingrained in the public the perception of an increasingly competitive society, open to the many external inputs from globalization. Opinion polls report an apparent widespread support to Putin's strong hand (85% in July 2007, Levada centre) and a preference for security, stability and standard of living (75% in 2006) over democracy (13%) [reported in Shevtsova, 2007: 319]. According to some, such consensus is rooted in the – alleged – formation of a new middle class, which has seen its standards of life improving during the past eight years and that is consistently providing support to the Kremlin's "party of power" [Empirical Studies on Civil Society in Russia, 2007-2008, reported in Petrone, 2009].

If so, one may have to conclude that hopes of a democratic shift mainly lay in a top-down induced change, and that it would be up to the political élite (business representatives, and pragmatists among the federal authorities, according to some) to lead the change and revert the current Kremlin's approach to the peculiar redefinition of civil society borders. Alternatively, social upheavals may be triggered by an aggravation of the current global economic crisis. Growing economic disparities have worsened the situation and have increased the dissatisfaction among the poorest, so that the serious deterioration in quality of life and growing poverty levels may at some point percolate upwards in the form of pro-democratic radical political mobilization, in spite of the Executive's repression. Studies from centres that are independent from Kremlin-controlled pollsters [such as former Levada Centre, now VTsIOM, Mc Faul, 2004] have shown how several hundreds of independent pro-democracy

infringe the usual national security provisions – threat to sovereignty and territorial integrity – or pose a risk to Russian national unity and cultural heritage.

advocacy groups are in fact active over the whole Russian territory [Belyaeva and Proskuryakova, 2008]. In spite of their weak consolidation and low public awareness, especially due to the forced marginalization induced by the Law on NGOs of 2006, these groups are actively building democratic networks across the country. Some of them, such as the Moscow Helsinki Group and the Interlegal Foundation date back to the Soviet and early post-Soviet days, witnessing a long-seated heritage towards the protection of human rights in the Russian society.[17] They largely work in subterranean ways, when compared to their Kremlin-financed counterparts, that enjoy ample media coverage and substantial funding from the Executive, which is why, according to some advocates, their activity may have not been adequately understood so far, especially in political science academic circles outside of Russia.[18] In the absence of external support, largely curtailed by the law of 2006, extremely low funding and state-imposed constraints have further increased the costs of coordination, that were already particularly high due to the width in both the geographical and sectoral scope of their activities. In spite of the absence of mass demonstrations, especially after the massive repression of Kasparov's 'Other Russia' public meetings in the Spring of 2007, the activities of these groups in multiple areas (human rights protection, various health and community services) stand as an ongoing school for grassroots democracy.

Since the end of 2008, a decline in the restrictive application of the NGOs Law of 2006 has been recorded, mostly attributable to the adaptation lags that have followed bureaucratic changes at the ministerial level during the passage from Putin to Medvedev. The new President, however, has also opened the Presidential Council on Assistance in Development of Civil Society and Human Rights to several non-governmental human rights activists and, after consultations, has set up a Working group towards the revision of the Law of 2006. However, at the time of this writing,

---

[17] See http://www.mhg.ru and http://www.interlegal.ru.

[18] Author's interview with N. Belyaeva, Founder and President of Interlegal International, July 2009.

such revision, that should be coordinated by the Ministry of Justice, has not started yet. Noticeably enough, only one member of non-governmental human rights and democracy associations has been allowed as a party to the Working group, which is chaired by Vladislav Surkov, Putin's ideologue of the "sovereign democracy" concept that is precisely behind the Law that should be revised [Dzhibladze, 2009].

Finally, the chances of a democratic end to the current authoritarian stalemate will depend on two sets of political economy factors: the redefinition of the existing system of property rights and, more in general of the rule of law of the Russian system, and the trends in production cycles, at both domestic and international levels. The absence of a pre-defined system of property rights and a high level of discretion in the management of an economy are sustainable only to the point where economic resources from growth are high enough to "buy" popular consensus and to reward strategically chosen groups that are favourable to the incumbents. Such collusive system between the Kremlin and its new oligarchies (large banks, army and intelligence) may well endure for another long period of time in the absence of clear incentives towards a competitive context for all the economic actors, and of uniform treatment for previously acquired rent positions. As seen from post-1998 events, external shocks alone are not sufficient to induce democratic change in rule-making, even when situational incentives may lead in that direction (the oligarchs had indeed started to add elements of competition to their initial collusive approach to market capitalism but Putin's purge did not allow this adaptation to take place). The current economic crisis, an external shock that will likely force the élite to radically rethink their personalistic, softly authoritarian approach to redistribution may be a telling test on the institutional future of Russia. However, given the current situation, nothing would prevent that the change led the country further away from democracy. One may wonder what sort of adaptive mechanisms the Russian élite in power at the Kremlin may devise to keep the system alive, with the gradual disappearance of rents to buy popular consent, short of an increased resort to violent repression. The Ukrainian events suggest that popular mobilization and external support may be the key elements to tip the balance in the direction of democratic change. However, such shifts in domestic élite policies and price fluctuations are mainly short-term occurrences. Radical, favourable changes in the external international environment and consolidation of democratic opposition in Russian civil society may take a much longer time.

6 - Conclusions

This contribution has explored the history, nature and trajectory of the current Russian regime. As emerged from the analysis carried out in the previous sections, the signs of consolidation of the current authoritarian trend outnumber those in favour of a democratic shift. The initiator of all the post-Soviet transitions, Russia shared some of the original traits of other mixed regimes (above all free elections) but also developed, over time, several features that are considered symptomatic of authoritarian drifts, such as the preference for presidential over parliamentary features, the low interest for- and then open rejection of-multipartitism and, most of all, a tremendously weak drive towards the construction of an effective rule of law to guarantee basic liberal principles. In this study I have argued that the roots of these features are provided by the way in which Russian stateness problems and peculiar tradition in leadership styles have influenced the choices of political élite at key junctures during transition. The postponing of crucial institutional choices (on state building, through federal elections on founding constitutional principles, on regime building, through decisions on horizontal and vertical power balancing, as well as on the role of parties) to economic reforms has then set the course for the drift into the grey area of additional hybrid traits. Far from supporting the thesis of either economic or political primacy in the explanation of the shift of post-Communist Russia to the area of hybridism, this paper has argued the need to explore more in depth the internal links between institutional change and the political economy of a system, both with respect to the relations between political and economic élite, and with respect to their choices in leading rule change under conditions of systemic shocks. To this aim, the tradition of Russian self-redistributive authoritarianism has been identified here as a key long term-element that contributed to orient the élite' management of power in the Nineties, their response to the crisis of 1998, and the ensuing deterioration of the prospects for Russian democratization. Neither Yeltsin nor Putin have been able to redistribute evenly the gains from the privatization of the Russian economy. However, while the former has been sanctioned at some point through semi-democratic procedures, the latter has managed to reinforce the authoritarian traits that were latent in the Russian institutions and has consolidated a further move away from democracy. In the days of extreme weakness of the new Russian institutions, powerful external actors have been either dismissive (the US under Bush), detrimental (the IMF, in its advice on how to manage the financial crisis of 1998), or ineffective (the EU) in keeping Russia on democratic tracks.

The current consolidation of authoritarian traits, and the buying of popular consensus, has been mainly possible thanks to the rents that have accrued to Putin's government through the positive trends in oil prices. Social passivity to reforms that have reduced the scope for democratic opposition to only some portions of civil society has been guaranteed by the improvement in the overall macroeconomic situation of the country. However, if politicized, widespread corruption, personal security, a health system in disarray and widening income disparities will likely open serious cracks in that consensus. As discussed above, the patrimonial nature of Putin's and Medvedev's leadership, and the informal nature of most relationships among the élite, cast several doubts on the economic sustainability of the current situation. The current global economic crisis has already started to act as a structural trigger of adaptive change worldwide. This is no guarantee that self-redistributive muddling through at top levels will change, or that the slow process of consolidation of democratic opposition in Russian civil society will suddenly take a speedy turn. Similarly, external actors will have to deal with their priorities first, before they realize that another window of opportunity has opened to support Russia's move towards democracy. It may, and probably will, take some time before adaptation occurs away from authoritarianism. However, compared to 1998, memories of mismanagement and corruption from self-defined "democratic leaders", such as Boris Yeltsin, will be soon coupled with new memories of mismanagement and corruption from self-appointed "sovereign democratic leaders", as Vladimir Putin. Time will come for the Russian citizens when judging the performance of their leaders, effective or not, will be left to stable, certain rules that they have themselves freely defined, in their interest.

9

FROM VETO PLAYERS TO POTENTIAL CHANGE AGENTS: ECONOMIC ÉLITE'S SHIFTING INTERESTS AND UKRAINE'S ORIENTATION TO THE WEST

Rosaria Puglisi

1 - Introduction

Although inter-coalition instability and strife between majority and opposition continue to characterize Ukrainian politics and often result in political deadlocks and spectacular confrontations, the Orange Revolution marked a watershed in the fluid political scene of the post-Soviet country. It represented a distinctive step forward along the continuum from dictatorship to democracy described by Valerie Bunce and Sharon Wolchik in this volume. Massive élite and public opinion mobilization in the autumn of 2004, leading to the collapse of the 8 year-old regime of President Kuchma, allowed for the emergence of a pluralistic yet still contentious and highly conflictual political arena, where, in line with Bunce and Wolchik's definition, elections became more regular, free, fair and competitive, political institutions are representative, and civil liberties and political rights more guaranteed by law than they had been under President Yushchenko's predecessor. Still a mixed regime, a "halfway house" on the path to fully-fledged democracy, post-Kuchma Ukraine moved forward in the direction of a more consolidated democratic rule. Regardless of the political orientation of the parliamentary majority, the basic norms of political engagement became more widely accepted, unlikely to be thoroughly challenged and radically reformed. The most powerful, and hopefully long-lasting, consequence of the dismantling of the authoritarian architecture built to support and feed the Kuchma regime appears to be a basic consensus, within society as well as within the ruling élite, around the understanding of pluralism as a guarantee of individual rights and interests against potential opponents' attacks. Within this context, the shift from "veto players" to potential "change actors" made by powerful economic élite representatives who had been deeply entangled in a mutually beneficial rent-seeker/rent-giver relation with President Kuchma proved a significant strategic move. In keeping with March and Olsen's "logic of consequences" [1998], during the November-December 2004 street demonstrations and, especially, in the months following President Yushchenko's inauguration, influential economic leaders assessed costs and benefits arising from the new constellation of power. On the basis of their own calculations and as a result of unpublicized pacts made with the country's new leadership, they voted to stay rather than to go, to coexist with the new regime rather than to openly oppose it, to lobby for the consolidation of a rule of law, European Union (EU) oriented system, better able in their view to defend their personal business interests, rather than for the return to an unstable, transitional, Russian-leaning environment where, in their perception, their business would hardly progress. Far from appearing as a sign of a genuine conversion to democratic values or of what Morlino and Magen [2008a] call an "internalization of rules", the economic élite's reorientation bears nevertheless important consequences for the re-definition of Ukraine's both domestic and foreign policy priorities, leading, as it did, to the socialization of types of behaviour, political positions and business practices liable to influence societal changes at large. Against the background of a growing public opinion support for what the Yushchenko circle presented as Ukraine's European future, (a future dreamingly characterized by economic prosperity, increased individual and collective security and the triumph of rule of law over the arbitrariness that had marred the Kuchma years), the economic élite's adoption of pro-European positions in the aftermath of the Orange revolution was itself motivated by the twin purpose of attaining social legitimization and legal protection for their ownership rights. Faced by public contempt for the murky methods used to accumulate their capital under the previous regime and the potential risks of re-privatization ventilated by the Yushchenko leadership during the presidential campaign, some leading business representatives re-styled themselves as "national capitalists". In their new personas as socially responsible individuals interested in the well-being and economic progress of the country and its people, they started calling for Ukraine's political and economic integration into the international community and chose for their businesses practices that would make them more transparent and therefore better able to raise capitals on world stock exchanges. Although questionably a sign of internalized democratic rules, their option for internationally-accepted norms made economic élite potential change agents. In Finnemore and Sikkink's language [1998], Ukrainian economic leaders became "norm entrepreneurs", able to pressurize a political environment they were part of for the adoption of rules that would benefit them and their business activities, but would also contribute locking their country in a "virtuous spiral" of improved democratic practices and better standing within the international community.

This chapter looks at the shifting positions of the Ukrainian economic élite within the domestic political arena from the years of the Kuchma regime (1994-98) up until the first two years of the Yushchenko presidency (2007). In considering their implications for the consolidation of democracy in the country, the chapter examines changes in the business élite' opportunity structure and consequent cost-benefit analysis that turned them from veto players to potential change agents in the aftermath of the Orange Revolution. It discusses the role of external influences (the positive idea of Europe and the appealing business opportunities with Russia) in Ukraine's hybrid regime transition from an authoritarian to a democratic context and it offers some conclusion on the weight that specific group interests may play in this process.

2 - Veto Players: Business Élite under Kuchma

As many post-Soviet societies, following independence, Ukraine experienced the emergence of an oligarchic system. In the mid-

1990s, political influence, proximity to the sources of political power and control over political institutions allowed some powerful entrepreneurs to acquire exclusive authority over economic wealth and to secure property rights of former state assets undergoing privatization. In exchange, they provided support for the establishment and the consolidation of *a hybrid* regime, a *semi-authoritarian* structure revolving around the central figure of Ukraine's second President, Leonid Kuchma, thus giving rise to the "invisible politics" that ruled Ukraine between 1994 and 2004. Politically active social actors, the Ukrainian business élite entered into a "dominant coalition" with the institutional leadership of the country. Because of the stakes they held in the Kuchma regime, most of them fought, through lobbying and intriguing, for its preservation. As powerful veto players, they resisted the emergence of potential political and business opponents and undermined the country's chances of structural changes.

In the Kuchma years, business and political élite intertwined into a mutually dependent and mutually beneficial rent-seeker/rent- giver relationship. Powerful economic actors were provided with a political *krysha* (roof or protection) to conduct less than transparent deals, while political leaders received in exchange economic support to consolidate their positions of authority. In the years of the two Kuchma presidencies an oligarchic system emerged and consolidated thanks to the special privileges awarded by the President and his administration to the members of his inner circle. Closeness to the President guaranteed access to the administration, redistribution and utilization of state financial or administrative resources. The President's "personal rulership" played a somehow "integrative role" over a potentially heterogeneous political environment, temporarily unifying competing élite clans through the redistribution of material incentives and rewards.[1] Rather than ideology, the rule of law or the leader's charisma, the allocation of favours and economic benefits constituted the cement of this system, while a sense of loyalty and dependence informed formal

---

[1] On personal rulership see Roth, 1968; and on the effects of patrimonialism on fragmented societies see Heeger, 1974.

273

political and administrative relations [Bratton and Van de Walle, 1994].[2] Redistribution of resources, promises of privileged access to the privatization of strategic assets and management of profitable state enterprises were all used as currency to reward loyal supporters. Exclusion from all these opportunities served as a punishment for those who challenged the president's authority. Partial reform equilibrium sealed the alliance between the executive and parts of the economic élite.[3] Economic liberalization was pushed only as far as allowing the privatization of state assets, but not the correction of market distortions. The "selected introduction of market mechanisms" and the consequent generation of concentrated rents prompted a small group of actors, net winners under these conditions, to work actively for the preservation of the *status quo*. The business élite's accumulation of resources and the endurance of the Kuchma regime became mutually reinforcing phenomena, while the systematic extraction of rents imposed lasting effects upon the Ukrainian society. The allocation of income within a narrow constituency, the corruption of the state apparatus and the consequent expansion of the illegal economy, the lack of accountability and the resulting isolation of the political leadership weakened the capacity of the Ukrainian state [Hellman, 1998]. Asymmetrical control over the political institutions drew a line of divergent interests and possibilities between those who did and those who did not have access to the President. On the one hand, political power allowed big business representatives to shape the rules of the market to fit their own preferences, defending their newly acquired property rights and preserving their privileges. On the other hand, however, the systematic ousting from political institutions and mechanisms of resources redistribution of sections of the élite that had originally grown within his circle (like former Governor of the National Bank and 1999-2001 Prime Minister Viktor Yushchenko and 1999-2001 Deputy Prime Minister Yulia Tymoshenko) gave momentum to a

---

[2] See also Wallander, 2007 for a discussion on patrimonial authoritarianism in Russia.
[3] For an academic discussion of partial reform equilibrium, see Hellman, 1998; and Hellman *et al.*, 2003.

political opposition that made fighting against the corruption and the excesses of the Kuchma regime its electoral manifesto.

3 - From Veto players to Potential Change Actors: President Yushchenko and the Economic Élite

Separation between business and politics was one of the main slogans of the Orange Revolution. Coming to power as Prime Minister in January 2005, Yulia Tymoshenko promised the review of 3000 allegedly unlawful privatizations that had been carried out during the Kuchma presidency. In the immediate aftermath of the Orange Revolution, prominent oligarchs who had occupied central stage during the Kuchma years disappeared from the public scene. Fearing retribution and a challenge to their contested ownership rights, some took residence abroad, others simply kept a low profile, waiting for the storm to subside. In his 2006 annual address to Parliament, President Yushchenko proudly announced the dismantling of oligarchy in Ukraine. "The system of oligarchic control over the economy has been weakened and deprived of support by the state", he boosted [BBC, 2006a]. In fact, beyond belligerant threats and emphatic promises, the Yushchenko leadership did little to readdress the balance of power between business and politics. If the role and influence of big business representatives changed following the demise of the Kuchma regime, this was more the result of a number of different, accidentally related factors, than the outcome of a deliberate policy endorsed by the new President and his team. Itself plagued by internal, structural issues that weakened its determination to move against patronage networks, the Orange leadership failed to endorse a coherent approach to substantial reforms in this sphere. Orange's greatest (and only) success in their campaign towards fairer business-politics relations was the re-privatization of the steel giant Kyvoryzhstall. In a widely publicized auction, hailed by Ukrainian commentators as "the end of an era when well-connected tycoons ruled Ukraine" [BBC, 2005], the government sold Kryvorizhstall to the Indian company Mittal Steel for $4.84bn, equal to one fifth of the Ukrainian state budget. The plant had been firstly privatized in the run-up to the 2004 presidential elections by a consortium set up by Viktor Pinchuk (President Kuchma's son-in-law) and Rinat Akhmetov (Viktor Yanukovich's main financial supporter in the 2004 presidential race). The selling price in that case had been $800m. In spite of Interior Minister Lutsenko's announcement that 1700 legal cases had been opened for alleged violations of the privatisation process [Paskhaver and Verkhovoda, 2006], Kryvorizhstall was the only one to be finalized in court.[4] The looming perspective of large-scale re-privatizations created uncertainty in the Ukrainian business environment, affecting also those foreign investors President Yushchenko had tried to woo in the aftermath of the revolution. Writing in those days, a Financial Times commentator advised that, in order to avoid political distortions and to minimize investors' anxiety, the review of past privatization deals should be "limited in scope, governed by transparent rules and completed within a clearly stated and very brief time" [Financial Times, 2005].

Following Yulia Tymoshenko's dismissal from her Prime Ministerial post in the early autumn 2005, the Ukrainian authorities opted for an all-round forgive and forget strategy. The new Prime Minister Yurii Ekhanurov, rushed to reassure that Kryvorizhstall would be the last re-privatization and that he would resist popular pressure to reconsider previously made deals [Warner, 2005]. "The process of re-privatization in Ukraine is over, full stop. We had delivered on whatever promises and pledges given in Independence Square during the revolution", Prime Minister Ekhanurov remarked in November 2005 [Ekhanurov, 2005]. While attempts were made to work out a method of peaceful settlement of disputed privatizations, according to which, in exchange of a negotiated compensation, owners would be entitled to keep their privatized object, no peaceful settlement took ever place [Paskhaver and Verkhovoda, 2006]. The process of re-privatization was shut in the same way it had been emphatically opened, namely as a result of a political

---

[4] Pinchuk's minority shares in the insurance company Oranta were also returned to the state, while Pinchuk's contested property of Nikopol ferro-alloy plant remains to be adjudicated by the court [Paskhaver and Verkhovoda, 2006].

decision. The question of the "settlement of disputed privatizations" (or additional, possibly voluntary payments to be made by oligarchs to compensate the state for the acquisition of assets at below market prices) was not even touched during the meeting President Yushchenko held with 20 leading business representatives in October 2005 [Modra and Andrevskaya, 2005]. According to press reports, in a long, amenable speech, the President invited his guests to invest in industrial production, to pay taxes and to give up on corruption, but made no reference to past privatizations. Upon leaving the meeting, some of what the Ukrainian media were already calling "ex oligarchs" appeared ostensibly relieved that, as Rinat Akhmetov put it, "the word re-privatization does not exist anymore" [Modra, 2005]. The first "Council of the Oligarchs" (as the press dubbed the meeting) marked an important turn into relations between the Orange leadership and big business. Explaining the purpose of the gathering, Prime Minister Ekhanurov pointed out: "We really want these people to become truly devoted, with a national perception, [a] bourgeoisie, and [we want them to] be very sincerely involved in our business promotion and development" [Ekhanurov, 2005]. With the organization of the meeting, the President stretched out a friendly hand to business representatives and proposed them a truce: business would have to become socially responsible and, in exchange, no financial claim would be made to them to amend past mistakes. Disappointed Ukrainian observers judged the move a *pas faux* on the side of the President, another missed opportunity to set the previous record straight and recover additional badly needed budget resources.[5] The Orange leadership had also internal and structural reasons to avoid a frontal attack to oligarchic interests. A number of big and medium-sized businessmen (the minigarchs)[6] had played an active role in the revolution, standing by the President during the campaign and staffing his inner circle in the post-revolution

---

[5] Author's interview, Kyiv, November 6, 2006.
[6] The expression is Oleh Havrylyshyn's. Workshop on Business and State Relations in Russia and Ukraine, Jacyk Program for the Study of Ukraine and CERES, Toronto: November 30, 2006.

period. Allegations about their corruption and the wealth they had earned as a result of their proximity to President Yushchenko were widespread in the Ukrainian media [Leshchenko, 2006].

4 - A Changed Political Environment
The dismissal of the Tymoshenko's government in the autumn 2005, as a result of the Prime Minister's squabbles with Secretary of the Security and Defence Council Poroshenko was read by many as a sign that the oligarchic wing in the President's circle (the so-called lyubi druzy, the "dear friends") had prevailed. Mykola Tomenko, one of Tymoshenko's closest allies, accused President Yushchenko to "wobble between the interests of Ukraine and those of his personal friends". He claimed that a new Kuchma-like structure of power had emerged, with Yushchenko having become "hostage" of the old system. "Today the President's entourage tries to recreate the scheme tested during Kuchma's rule, when certain businessmen turned ministers ensured the wellbeing of the presidential family", Tomenko concluded [Tomenko, 2005]. Despite the persisting interconnection and mutual dependency between business and politics, Tomenko was, however, wrong on one account: Yushchenko's Ukraine was not Kuchma's Ukraine. Although not necessarily as a result of deliberate political moves induced by the Orange leadership, a number of key factors had changed. Branding it a "bourgeois revolution", a Ukrainian commentator encapsulated effectively the spirit and the significance of the social and political transformations that followed the 2004 events.[7] In addition to a widespread but ephemeral sense of empowerment among ordinary citizens, the Orange Revolution provoked substantial adjustments in the balance of power between institutions and in the interaction between institutions and élite. Hastily introduced in December 2004, as a compromise to resolve the constitutional impasse created by the rigging of the presidential elections, the constitutional reforms set in place dangerously unbalanced conditions of power. Even more dangerously, they failed to provide mechanisms to manage

[7] Author's interview, Kyiv February 9, 2007.

peacefully the awkward cohabitation between opposing President and Prime Minister. Despite their many serious shortcomings, however, the constitutional reforms produced, one single positive result: they contributed to the dismantling of the complex architecture of power grown around the presidency in the Kuchma years. Under Yushchenko, the presidency became one of the many competing centres of power, dispersing the presence and influence of economic interests over state institutions. Scattered conditions of power promoted a certain degree of pluralism and compelled conflicting economic forces to work towards broader coalition and consensus building. In the specific case of business-politics relations, the gradual but inescapable erosion of authority imposed to the presidency as a result of the constitutional reforms multiplied the number of access-points to political structures afforded to economic clans. Business became emancipated from the tight tutelage that President Kuchma had imposed on it, thus reversing a previously consolidated relationship of power. If before the revolution it was politics to rule business, the Orange Revolution gave the opportunity to big and medium businesses to take power directly in their own hands.[8] As a result of what became known as "the war of millionaires against billionaires", the monopolistic control of power employed by oligarchs before the revolution was broken and some form of competition was introduced in the system.[9] The 2006 parliamentary elections proved a remarkable opportunity for business groups to access en masse political institutions. Oligarchs and economic actors had gained increasingly wide representation in the legislative since independence, but the first elections since the Orange Revolution saw a real break-through [see Puglisi, 2003b]. Commentators painted the gloomy picture of a political process that had lost its ideological character and had become "monetized". With a price list set for all key posts, analysts reported that candidates would normally buy places in

---

[8] Author's interview, Kyiv February 9, 2007.
[9] Author's interview, February 15, 2007.

party lists from the party leaders.[10] Some blamed the recently introduced proportional representation for what they called the oligarchization of power [The Day Weekly Digest, 2006]. Former Deputy Speaker of Parliament and former Yushchenko's ally, Oleksander Zinchenko, predicted that oligarchs would end up controlling parliamentary factions. "It is obvious even now, he remarked, that money is playing the defining role as far as the March's parliamentary elections are concerned. All political parties or blocs include oligarchs and they, I can assure you, are playing key roles" [Interfax, 2006]. According to an urban legend widely circulated even by high-ranking politicians (including Yulia Tymoshenko), among its 450 members, the parliament elected in 2006 counted at least 300 dollar-millionaires [Khrush, 2006]. Oligarchs had obviously adopted different strategies of interaction with the institutional power. Previously withdrawn Rinat Akhmetov run and won a seat with Yanukovich' Party of the Regions, whereas Kuchma's son in law Viktor Pinchuk announced that his decision as to whether to take part in the elections or not depended on the guarantees that the Yushchenko leadership would provide in terms of protection of his property rights [Modra, 2005].[11] Eventually, he did not run.

With the appointment of the Yanukovich government in summer 2006, the emphasis shifted back to the uncontested primacy of business over politics. An atmosphere of *deja-vu* pervaded the corridors of power. Ukrainian observers labelled Yanukovich's "the new/old government" [Kremen and Smirnov, 2006]. Old faces of the Kuchma administration resurfaced in previously unthinkable permutations. New/old ministers and Prime Minister's advisors were deployed in a total turf war with the President and his circles for the control (both at a national and at a regional level) of the vertikal *vlasti* (the hierarchy of power

---

[10] Author's interview, Kyiv February 9, 2007.
[11] Pinchuk had been an MP in the two previous legislatures.

structures)[12]. Some of the first and most controversial steps of the Yanukovich's government gave a clear indication that the personal interests of influential business people would remain a factor to be reckoned with within the state administration. Plans for the restoration of free economic zones, the selective handing out of VAT reimbursement to export companies, the careful drafting of rules for the privatization of land and regional energy companies and the issuing of the 2007 state budget provided, in the eyes of some Ukrainian commentators, a serious blunder to the fate of Ukrainian liberalism and displayed the firm control of powerful economic actors over policy-making [see Soroka, 2006; Yatsenko, 2006a; Yatsenko, 2006b]. In a contradictory turn of events since the early days of the Orange leadership, a general climate of uncertainty and political strive contributed in securing oligarchic control over the institutions. As a counterbalance to the authority of Yanukovich's Party of the Regions, by its own admission a business party and a sound expression of the industrial interests of the so-called Donetsk clan, in autumn 2006 President Yushchenko sought himself support in a splintering faction of the Donetsk-group, Sergey Taruta's Industrial Union of Donbass (IUD). Faced by an Orange coalition in disarray, a lack of strategic thinking among his own team, a crumbling power base (his party Nasha Ukraina), and diving popularity rates, with the appointment of Vitalii Haiduk (IUD co-owner) as Secretary of the Security and Defence Council and Oleksander Chaly (former deputy Foreign Minister but also close to IUD's leadership) as deputy head of the Presidential Secretariat, the signal was given that a new alliance between the President and one of the most powerful financial-industrial groups of the country had been sealed.

---

[12] On the re-staffing of national and regional institutions with personnel loyal to PM Yanukovich, see BBC, 2006b; on Yushchenko-Yanukovich confrontational personnel policy see Mostovaya, 2006.

5 - Shifting the Cost-Benefit Balance: Social Legitimization and Economic Interests

The aftermath of the Orange Revolution saw the emergence of two parallel trends that altered substantially the opportunity structures in the Ukrainian political scene, imposed a shift in the cost-benefit balance of leading business representatives and turned them from veto players into potential change agents. Firstly, with the decline of the central role of the Presidency and the multiplication of access-points to the political system, Ukrainian politics became more pluralistic and, therefore, more fluid. This made political and economic actors more "open to new solutions and the possibility of substantial domestic changes" [Morlino and Magen, 2008]. Secondly, and probably more importantly, the lack of consequences in terms of property redistribution made business leaders less hostile towards the Yushchenko leadership and more inclined to take advantage of all the possibilities that the new environment offered.

The Orange Revolution and its aftermath produced a sea-wide effect in the economic élite's perception of time and space. They had previously viewed the 2004 presidential elections as their "end of history", a looming threat to their acquired power and property. Later, having survived the stormy days of the leadership change, economic élite representatives realized not only that their business empires were there to stay, but also that they themselves had a personal stake in the future of their country. As a result, the presence and influence of oligarchs on Ukrainian politics changed significantly. Following a period of meditative withdrawal, big businessmen reappeared on the country's social and political scene, reinvigorated and ready to engage in a full-scale campaign to clear off their names and build for them a publicly acceptable reputation. Having eluded threats of property redistribution, they chose to come out of the shadow they had lived in after the collapse of the Kuchma regime and to regain their public persona. Some went into parliament. Others stayed clear of official political positions but engaged in socially oriented and high profile projects. By and large, they worked to do away with the halo of corrupt, arrogant, even violent thugs that years of fast and easy capital accumulation had earned them.[13] The oligarchs' quest for recognition and social legitimization, a phenomenon that Harley Balzer [2003] has called "reutilization", went hand in hand with efforts to reject all negative connotations associated with the popular idea of oligarchs.[14] In an interview to the weekly *Korrespondent* in September 2006, Hryhorii Surkis, former member of the Parliament (MP) and business partner of Kuchma's head of the Presidential Administration Medvedchuk, noted: "We are used to say "oligarchs", but in other countries the word oligarch does not exist. Instead (expressions like) businessman, millionaire, billionaire (are used). These are the most law-observant members of society, they pay taxes, they create working places, they create progress (...)" [Paskhaver, 2006: 58-60]. Also Rinat Akhmetov, widely recognized as the richest man in Ukraine with a personal wealth estimated at $11.8bn and the most prominent financial supporter of Yanukovich's electoral race in the 2004 presidential elections contested vividly the label of oligarch. "I am not an oligarch, he said, oligarchs are in government. For them being in government is the only way of making money. I can tell an oligarch from afar. (...) Oligarchs have not found their place in business and they never will. (...) in business they look like cows walking on ice. I realized myself as a businessman and made my money a long time ago" [Ukraina TV, 2006]. Akhmetov became a member of parliament for the Party of Regions. Campaigning in his home constituency, he enunciated his motivation in taking up politics: "I want a government of economic growth, (...) I want to defend Ukraine's national interests, (...) I want Ukraine to become rich, (...) I want there to be no poor people in Ukraine" [Ukraina TV, 2006].

Unquestionably the most active of the Ukrainian businessmen in trying to create an image for himself as a philanthropist, Viktor Pinchuk made an explicit link between personal economic success, national responsibility and patriotism. He argued that

---

[13] See for example Korrespondent, 2006a: 22, or Kuzin and Penchuk, 2006.
[14] Reflecting a view common among the Ukrainian public, MP for the opposition party Bloc Yulia Tymoshenko Dmitrii Vydrin defined oligarchs as individuals who "try to take under control both money and state authority. Therefore if there are oligarchs, there is no state authority; [as], to a certain extent they have replaced it" [Vydrin, 2007: 23].

"the Ukrainian state owes its existence to the national business to a great extent", pointing out that the high development rates achieved in its post-independence years and the emergence of a "strong and united Ukraine" were twin results of national business' efforts. "If soon after independence, Ukraine had not had a young, powerful and ambitious economic force that tied itself to the national interest, its alternative history could have followed either a Central Asian or a neo-colonial path. We, the entrepreneurs (some of whom later would be called oligarchs) at once appreciated the value of independence" [Pinchuk, 2005].

Beyond the public makeover and the quest for a renewed social persona, however, the economic élite had substantial reasons to claim a personal interest in the future of the country. Not only political but also economic conditions had altered significantly since President Yushchenko's coming to power and this reflected in the businessmen's view of the world around them. The phase of primary capital accumulation that had characterized the Kuchma presidencies was over. The number and quality of assets expected to undergo privatization was now relatively insignificant in comparison to the deluge of the mid to late 1990s. In a phase of capital consolidation rather than capital expansion, big businessmen became aware that two conditions were to be satisfied if the recent positive trends experienced by the Ukrainian economy in general and their companies in particular were to be sustained. Firstly, a system of transparent and more or less universally applied norms ought to become predominant in Ukraine, thus carving in stone their ownership rights and granting their businesses the protection a court of law would provide. Secondly, industrial methods had to be dramatically modernized, plants upgraded, energy saving technologies introduced. A shift was required from an extensive to an intensive approach to economic growth. In short, the Ukrainian economy had to become part of the world economy to fully benefit of the market opportunities on offer; but in order for this to happen, securing a constant inflow of foreign and domestic investment was key.

After the years of double-digit negative growth that had followed the collapse of the Soviet Union, the Ukrainian economy started experiencing a positive trend at the turn of the new millennium. A positive but ephemeral conjuncture of increased foreign demand for major Ukrainian exports, i.e. metals, chemicals and machinery (+ 11% nominal growth in 2006 in comparison to a 5% decline in 2005), together with rising household consumption (+18% in 2006 in comparison to 2005) was responsible for the 7.1% GDP year on year growth recorded in 2006. Positive indicators had been registered already in 2001 (+9.2%), 2003 (+9.6) and 2004 (+12.1%).[15] In 2006, natural gas price hikes and political instability after the March parliamentary elections failed to impact negatively on the economy, as it was instead expected. A joke circulated in Kyiv that the Ukrainian economy performed better when feuding political forces turned their attention away from economic planning.

Cheaper production costs (related to lower raw material and labour force prices) had up to then proved the main source of competitive advantage for the Ukrainian industry on the world markets. Significantly, the metallurgical sector, 80% of whose production was export-oriented, played a crucial role in the country's economic renaissance, accounting for 41% of its 2005 exports [Korrespondent, 2006b: 39]. However, based primarily on raw-materials export, endowed with obsolete Soviet-era technology, dependent on massive energy consumption, the Ukrainian industry appeared fated to collapse if radical transformations were not introduced swiftly. That this pattern of development would be hardly sustainable in the long-term was evident to many, including big business representatives, many of which owed their own wealth to metal and metallurgy export.

With the wild business opportunities of the 1990s rapidly fading and the clear understanding that the legendary 700-800% annual revenues allowed by the unregulated and corrupt post-Soviet environment could no longer be replicated, leading business representatives inaugurated a two-pronged expansion strategy. They moved firstly towards the acquisition of assets abroad and, secondly, towards the capitalization of their companies on

---

[15] IMF data on GDP growth are available on http://www.imf.org.

285

international stock markets as channels through which to transform what economists defined their companies' "quality of growth".[16] Experts were indeed advising that, in order to maintain the economy's positive results, a shift had to take place from an extensive to an intensive model of development, i.e. from a model based on the exploitation of natural resources, to a model where technology and capital investment would lead to the production of added value goods; in other words, "from a Soviet to a European model of development".[17]

First among the leading Ukrainian business representatives, Rinat Akhmetov had turned his eyes to global financial markets even before the Orange Revolution. In an attempt to increase shareholder value and market capitalization, his companies had been gradually introducing international accounting standards. Foreign managers had been hired. Improving on transparency and corporate governance had become his System Capital Management's (SCM) stated objectives within a wider strategy aimed at creating "the most effective management structure for our business". SCM representatives were confident that the group would be listed on foreign stock exchanges within one year [Olearchyk, 2006]. International capital markets were increasingly seen by a number of Ukrainian companies as the main financial source for the gradual *perestroika* they had already started. Transparency and international credibility were seen as key for this purpose. In a *Financial Times* interview, *Finansy i Kredit* owner Kostyantin Zhevago explained: "Our goal is to look like any other company listed in the US or the UK. We understand we need to move fast and efficiently to remain competitive"[Olearchyk, 2006]. A number of medium-sized companies had already listed shares on the London Stock Exchange, while other large companies had established a partnership with international financial organizations, like the European Bank for Reconstruction and Development (EBRD) and the Japanese Bank for International Co-operation, willing to

---

[16] Author's interview, Kyiv, February 16, 2007.
[17] Author's interview, Kyiv, February 14, 2007.

fund their modernization efforts.[18] Acquisition of assets on foreign markets was the other element in the Ukrainian business' expansion strategy. Because of its growing engagement on the European markets, IUD was seen by some as the most powerful "agent for *Europeanization*" within the Ukrainian economic and political circles.[19] After its $468mn acquisition of the Huta Czestochova steel mill in Poland, in 2007 IUD was preparing to participate in a bid for the privatization of the Polish state energy company Elsen, originally part of the Huta Czestochova group. IUD Polish subsidiary, IUD Polska revealed also plans to acquire majority shares in the state-owned Gdansk Shipyards (3000 employers) and Gdynia Shipyards (6000 employees).

Ukrainian companies abroad proved active also in the banking sector. In 2007, Privat group opened a branch of its Privatbank in Lisbon, to service the large Ukrainian immigrant community in Portugal. A number of Ukrainian banks had also opened their representative offices abroad (rather than fully-fledged branches, allegedly a more complex administrative operation), VABank and Nadra in Budapest, Ukreximbank in New York and London, Forum in Prague, First Ukrainian International Bank in London and Moscow. Although strongly motivated by ambitious plans of business expansion, Ukrainian economic élite representatives' quest for Western markets was not, however, stirred by exclusively economic reasons. Opening up Ukraine to the international community was an integral part of their efforts towards social legitimization and business consolidation, as they needed, in the cynical words of a Ukrainian commentator, a "global environment", on which to spend the money they had

---

[18] In February 2007, Industrial Union of Donbass obtained credits for $150mn from the EBRD and $120mn from the Japanese Bank for International Co-operation for the upgrading of its Alchevsky metal plant [Ukrainska Pravda website, 2007].

[19] Author's interview, Kyiv, February 15, 2007. With one of its co-presidents sitting in the chair of Head of the Security and Defence Council (Vitalii Haiduk) and one of its previous advisors working as Deputy Head of President Yushchenko's Secretariat, IUD was well placed to enhance its agenda of Europeanization.

earned in the previous decade.[20] Promoting Ukraine's membership in the EU and widening Ukraine's investment opportunities on the world market became intertwined (although not generalized) themes in the discourse of big business representatives. Viktor Pinchuk's creation, the Yalta European Strategy (YES) proved an important instrument in an approach that YES Director Inna Pidluska defined of "soft integration".[21] Employing culture as the medium to create a more favourable environment to Ukraine's integration into the EU, Pinchuk's foundation focused on raising Ukraine's profile, both among the EU general public and the EU political and economic élite. A 2005 YES-promoted survey branded Ukraine "number one favourite candidate to accession in all European countries". With as many as 51% of the Europeans interviewed in the poll declaring themselves in favour of Ukraine joining the EU, the message sent by the YES leadership was that the idea of Ukraine as a potential member of the EU was becoming increasingly entrenched within the EU public. Any opposition raised by EU policy-makers amounted, therefore, to political speculation and did not reflect the majority will of the European people.[22] In its Agenda 2020, YES called unequivocally for Ukraine's membership in the EU by 2020. "Ukraine's future lies firmly in the European Union" – the document stated. "The country's tradition has been a profoundly European one. Its history is rich on the one hand and difficult on the other. The people of Ukraine cannot be taken to account for everything they had to endure in the past. All the more so, Europe should respect and honour the achievements of the Ukrainian people. Their aspirations should be treated as a voice in favour of a stronger and more active European Union".[23] More YES initiatives targeted political and economic decision-making circles. Since newly elected President Yushchenko's appearance at the 2005 Davos World Economic

---

[20] Author's interview, Kyiv, February 13, 2007.
[21] Author's interview, Kyiv, February 8, 2007.
[22] Details of the survey are available on YES webpage http://www.yes-ukraine.org.
[23] For the full text of Agenda 2020, see http://www.yes-ukraine.org.

Forum, Ukraine-related events had become a tradition of the Swiss resort to promote Ukraine's image and attract the world leaders' attention on issues key to the country's development. In 2007, Pinchuk treated the more than 300 prestigious guests who attended the YES-sponsored luncheon-conference "Where is Ukraine Heading?" to Ukrainian traditional dishes like borsch and cherry dumplings. During the event, to an audience including Latvian President Vaira Vike- Freiberga, EU Enlargement Commissioner Olli Rehn and former Polish President Alexander Kwasniewski, Prime Minister Yanukovich admitted: "The modernization of the Ukrainian economy is impossible without its integration into the world economic system" [Siruk, 2007]. Because of their increasing attraction towards the international arena and their interest in seeing Ukraine as a fully-fledged member of the international community, oligarchs came to be seen as primary consumers of globalization, the most powerful force to pull Ukraine onto the world scene.

6 - Democratic Example: the Idea of Europe and the Shadow of Russia

Within the new opportunity structure outlined by the Orange Revolution, the Ukrainian economic élite showed to be inclined to embrace new rules, institutions and policy choices, placing their country on a West-ward rather than East-ward geopolitical orientation. In line with the picture painted by Morlino and Magen [2008], rather than as a result of powerful external incentives (i.e. weak EU conditionality), business representatives opted for integration into the world economy in general and in the EU in particular because of the sheer economic advantages and the idealized perspectives of prosperity, security and rule of law protection that they saw in the process. Paradoxically and for the first time since independence, the selfish, individual interests of some business representatives came to overlap with the interests of Ukraine at large. The centuries-old Ukrainian foreign policy dilemma between Russia and the West acquired a new, unexpected and more sophisticated dimension, becoming a choice between two alternative models of economic development. In spite of the anxiety detected in the least developed industrial sectors, most likely to suffer of the liberalizing effects brought about by Ukraine's accession to the World Trade Organization (WTO) and the EU, in business circles, the idea of Europe was a generally positive one.[24] Talks with business representatives and their interviews in the press demonstrated that the EU was widely associated with increased efficiency, more advanced technology and higher legal and production standards. As an economic commentator summarized, the question both for the political and the economic élite was no longer "where to go?" but "how to get there?".[25] However, with no clear membership or association perspective in sight, Brussels appeared as a distant dream. Ukrainian analysts saw the government's efforts to keep the question of bilateral relations high on the EU agenda as unilateral ("You look like an idiot if you try to approximate with somebody who does not want to be approximated with you", one bitterly concluded) and were concerned that EU internal protectionism would either hamper trade opportunities for Ukrainian business or relegate Ukrainian companies to the subordinate role of subcontractors on the European markets.[26] Although positive, the idea of Europe was nonetheless a foggy one.

---

[24] Research conducted by a Ukrainian think tank highlighted misgivings and conflicting attitudes among different business sectors as for support towards the Ukrainian bid for membership in the WTO and perspectives for a still to come Free Trade Area with the EU. Well aware that formal membership of trading organizations would bring down quotas for Ukrainian products and thus enhance their industrial potential, sectors drawing heavily on export, like metallurgy or chemicals, lobbied actively for Ukraine's integration into the world markets. At the other end of the spectrum, however, the need to at best reform at worst abolish the system of state subsidies, as a precondition to WTO and EU membership, coupled with the expected requirement to adopt costly EU and international standards, provoked within the least technologically advanced sectors (i.e. agriculture, transport, selectively machine building) substantial concern.   Protectionism to keep out of the Ukrainian markets potentially powerful foreign competitors appeared as an attractive life-saving option also for sectors that were going through a phase of consolidation (i.e. banking and finance).   The Ukrainian version of the research paper coordinated by Olha Shumylo is available on http://www.icps.com.ua/doc/FTA_Impact_U.pdf.
[25] Author's interview, Kyiv, February 14, 2007.
[26] Author's interview, Kyiv, February 14, 2007.

The political élite had emphatically married a pro-European rhetoric, but observers doubted that they fully understood and were ready to implement the obligations deriving from a tighter association with the EU. Many were convinced that political statements served exclusively a short-term utilitaristic purpose and would unlikely go beyond a declaratory stage. "Fantasy" and "illusion" were the words most commonly used by Ukrainian commentators when referring to their government's promises to work towards the introduction of European standards in Ukraine.[27] EU officials characterized the Ukrainian élite's attitude towards EU integration as aimed at getting the "best of the two worlds", selectively emphasizing their rights to trade preferences, while overlooking their commitments towards the consolidation of democratic practices and rule of law.[28]

While striving towards an ideal that they could possibly not afford, they did not fully understand and were not entirely convinced to implement, the Ukrainian élite was affected by what an opposition MP defined as "political schizophrenia": "They aim towards EU standards, but they still live in an Asian satrapy".[29] If the EU appeared as a remote dream, Russia was, instead an immediate, short-term reality. Still the number one trading partner for Ukraine, Russia represented an important point of reference also in terms of business perspectives. In their strategy of expansion, Ukrainian companies showed to be ready to catch any opportunity at hand, willing to move, as a Ukrainian economist put it, "everywhere markets are".[30] For Ukrainian companies doing business with Russia was an easy option. Geographical proximity, the use of Russian as the region's *lingua franca*, a common historical past and shared economic habits established during the Soviet period made this relation comfortable; "like doing business with your brother", a Ukrainian analyst summarized.[31] However, similar foreign trade structures and overlapping industrial potential made Russia and

---

[27] Several interviews, Kyiv, February 2007.
[28] Author's interview, Kyiv, March 7, 2007.
[29] Author's interview, Kyiv, February 15, 2007.
[30] Author's interview, Kyiv, February 8, 2007.
[31] Author's interview, Kyiv, February 14, 2007.

Ukraine more likely competitors than allies on the world markets (significantly, also Russian metallurgy was heavily export-oriented).

The Russian industry's employment of obsolete technology and relatively wide availability of raw materials promised Ukrainian business a temporary relief against the urgency of industrial restructuring. Yet, failing to produce state-of-the-art-technology, the Russian model of extensive economic development, provided no incentive or instruments for Ukraine to catch up with the ongoing world-wide technological revolution.[32] Vague possibilities of largely profitable but unclearly regulated business deals (especially projects of co-operation for the exploitation and commercialization of energy resources from the Far-East of Russia) appeared as the swan song of post-Soviet wild capitalism, a style of doing business that, Ukrainians realized, would disappear in a structured and regulated economic environment. In Kyiv, the feeling was widespread that, apart from this sort of deals and a vast consumer market for Ukrainian agricultural products, Russia had little to offer, the type of cooperation it proposed had a temporary rather than long-lasting character and whatever it was prepared to trade would imply, most of all, a political price.

With estimated capital means several times larger than the Ukrainians', the presence of Russian businesses in Ukraine was perceived as a concrete risk for Ukrainian companies, because of their aggressiveness and rapaciousness, determination and capability to seize control of the most attractive Ukrainian assets. Ukraine's energy pipelines, for example, had been the constant objects of desire for Russia since the collapse of the Soviet Union. Fearing that losing control over some of the country's strategic assets would endanger Ukraine's security and sovereignty, Ukrainian nationalists had rejected several attempts made with the Kremlin's political support and the connivance of some Ukrainian political and economic forces to

---

[32] For an opposing view, pointing at information technology as one of the core factors in Russia' economic growth see Tsyganov, 2006.

establish a joint Russian-Ukrainian consortium to overlook the management of the pipeline network.[33]

In addition to Russian companies, Ukrainians were concerned about the Russian authorities' direct management and political use of economic affairs.[34] Moscow's wrangling even with trusty Belarus over gas prices had dispelled illusions that political loyalty would be rewarded with preferential energy rates. On the contrary, with a Russian ban on Ukrainian agricultural products pending and an attempted moratorium on the import of Ukrainian pipes, (unsuitable for import because allegedly containing radioactive material, when the metal used for its production was in fact imported from Russia), Ukrainians experienced on their own skin Moscow's tendency to play trade wars as an instrument of political pressure.[35] Through economic leverage on so many different levels, Moscow had been striving to keep Kyiv in its political orbit, preventing it from shifting West through an earlier WTO membership, tighter association with the EU (even in the form of a free trade area) or, even more worryingly, NATO accession. Co-operation within the four-sided Single Economic Space (SES), comprising Russia, Ukraine, Belarus and Kazakhstan, had been presented as an alternative to other international forms of economic co-operation. Since the Kuchma years, Ukrainian political élite had played skilfully SES perspective membership as a way to secure Russian political support. While pledging loyalty towards the organization, they had in fact systematically contrasted the practical implementation of agreements that, it was felt, risked diminishing Ukraine's sovereignty. By applying this ambiguous approach, Ukraine had

---

[33] On the latest scandal on a possible Ukrainian-Russian energy consortium and consequent last-minute legislation to prevent strategic assets to be sold off to Russia without consent of the main political institutions, see Eremenko, 2007.

[34] Reversing this argument, Dimitrii Trenin [2007] argues interestingly that Russian foreign policy decisions are instead dictated by private and corporate decisions. Daniel Treisman [2007] has forged the expression "silovarchs" to characterise a new business elite emerged from the network of security services and law enforcement veterans (the so-called *siloviky*) during the Putin's years.

[35] For more details on the pipelines moratorium, see Panova and Smirnov, 2006: 36-37.

undermined SES effective establishment, thus performing what a Ukrainian MP called a *tikhii sabotazh* (quiet sabotage).[36]

The Ukrainian position that integration in the SES would follow, not precede the creation of a Free Trade Area with the EU and would not go as far as the establishment of a custom union was dictated by two important considerations, significantly shared within Ukrainian political and economic circles, including Prime Minister Yanukovich.[37] Firstly, that a free trade area between Russia and Ukraine already existed on paper, but its practical functioning had thus far been obstructed by Russia's political use of trade disputes. Secondly, that setting up a custom union with Russia, Belarus and Kazakhstan would prevent the establishment of a custom union with the EU, which required trade concessions to be negotiated individually with single countries rather than the whole bloc [European Commission, 2003b]. Seen more as a political than an economic project, the SES had failed to capture also the economic élite's imagination.

On this complex chessboard of intertwining economic and political interests, Ukrainian big business played an ambivalent game. A journalist who interviewed several business representatives characterized them as "split personalities", looking East or West, speaking Russian or English, acting roughly or amiably according to the business opportunities they had set their eyes on.[38] Inclined to grab any possible short-term benefit deriving from the legendary economic deals the Russians

---

[36] Although counterintuitive, given President Kuchma's vocal support for SES and his enthusiastic signature of the SES founding agreement in the autumn 2003, this interpretation is widespread in Kyiv political circles. A demonstration of its credibility lies in the fact that, despite Russian attempts to depict the SES as an emerging EU-like structure, very little of what has been proposed has actually been translated into agreements and very little of what contained in those agreements has been eventually implemented [Author's interviews, Kyiv February 15, 2007].

[37] Although confirmed by Prime Minister Yanukovich during his visit to Brussels in September 2006, the position found some considerable opposition within the government, for example by Deputy Prime Minister Azarov, author's interview, Kyiv February 15, 2007.

[38] Author's interview, November 6, 2006.

could propose, most of them were, however, aware of the potential political costs that this closer interaction could imply. They were thus set to prevent Russians from irreversibly penetrating the fabric of the Ukrainian economy. Fearing but admiring their Russian counterparts, Ukrainian oligarchs thought they could outwit them or come to an agreement with them to extract the best possible deals for their own companies. Rinat Akhmetov's unconfirmed energy arrangement with Gazprom for the provision of 2bn cubic meters of gas over a 5 years- period at privately negotiated prices illustrates effectively this attitude.[39]

However, as close and attracted they might have felt towards Russian business, they were particularly wary of the risks that a closer interaction with Moscow might imply. If oligarchs of the early years might have thought of themselves as naturally inclined towards Russia, in 2007 Ukrainian businessmen's absolute priority was to preserve their independence while, at a the same time, enhance their business profits. It is better to make your money with the Russians and to protect them with the Europeans", an oligarch was anecdotally quoted as saying.[40] Confident that in Brussels' rather than Moscow's shadow they would be in a better position to maintain control over their country's economic wealth and promote their companies' growth, they became, in the words of a Ukrainian commentator, "instinctively European".[41] As a MP concluded, they felt the EU would offer them a "better *krysha*" (roof or mafia protection).[42]

---

[39] In early 2007, Metinvest, part of the SCM group, was granted a license allowing it direct access to foreign energy markets. The license gave Metinvest the possibility to buy 2 bn cubic meters of gas for a 5 years period at a set price, on either the Ukrainian or foreign markets, by-passing the intermediation of the highly contested Swiss-registered Rosukrenergo. Metinvest would then distribute the Russian gas to other SCM companies. The Ukrainian media speculated that 500 such licences had already been awarded, but besides Akhmetov's SCM, no company had the political weight to hold direct negotiations with Gazprom and the Kremlin to make the licence effective [Paskhover and Smirnov, 2006: 22-24].

[40] Author's interview, Kyiv, October 4, 2006.

[41] Author's interview, Kyiv, February 15, 2007.

[42] Author's interview, Kyiv, February 15, 2007.

7 - Conclusions

The political and economic transformations that occurred in Ukraine in the aftermath of the Orange Revolution changed the opportunity structures of a number of societal and economic actors in the country, causing them to shift alliances and embrace new political positions. Previously part of a "dominant coalition" with the President, interlocked in a mutually dependent and mutually beneficial rent-seeker/rent-giver relationship with him, big business representatives had acted in the Kuchma years as powerful "veto players". Because of the stakes they held in the regime, they had fought for its preservation, had resisted the emergence of potential political and business opponents and had undermined the country's chances of structural transformations. Viewing the leadership change expected to take place with the 2004 presidential elections as their "end of history", the looming threat to their acquired power and property, business representatives kept a low profile in the immediate aftermath of the Orange Revolution. Yet, the emergence of three parallel trends prompted them to reassess their cost-benefit balance and to shift from a hostile position towards the new leadership to different forms of participation in the newly emerged polity. From "veto players" economic élite representatives thus turned into potential "change agents".

Firstly, the dismantling of the complex power architecture that had supported and fed the Kuchma regime led to the multiplication of access-points to political power and, consequently, to the emergence of a pluralistic political structure that emancipated the economic élite from the tight tutelage they had been subject to in the previous years. Secondly, despite electoral promises to this effect, in the months following President Yushchenko's coming to power, the Orange leadership gave clear indications that ownership rights murkily acquired under the aegis of the previous regime would not be questioned. This dispelled the economic élite's worst fears and restored their confidence in the possibilities that their country still had in store for them. Thirdly, and probably most importantly, following an earlier phase of capital accumulation that had coincided with the post-Soviet transition and the two Kuchma presidencies, Ukrainian business was now undergoing a process of capital consolidation. Both in terms of ownership rights and in terms of capital investments. This new phase called for the adoption of a system of transparent and more or less universally applied norms that would grant businesses the protection that only a court of law would provide. Industrial methods had to be dramatically modernized as well, plants upgraded, energy saving technologies introduced. In the painful move from an extensive to an intensive approach to economic growth, from a Soviet to a European industrial model, the Ukrainian economy required membership in the world economy and an easier access to foreign and domestic capital investment.

Potential "change agents", economic élite representatives pursued a strategy aimed at legitimizing their presence and role in the eyes of the public opinion and at increasing the value of their industrial assets in Ukraine. This made them, in the words of Ukrainian commentators, "primary consumers of globalization" and "agents of *Europeanization*". Because of its promises of prosperity, security and rule of law protection, membership in the EU became for them a powerful magnet, an attractive example to follow, despite the weak conditionality (weak in comparison to the high expectations of the post-Kuchma Ukrainian society) proposed by Brussels. While in their respective cost-benefit balance, the business élite and the public opinion's assessment seemed to coincide on the understanding that increased pluralism and integration in the EU were good for Ukraine, this seemingly common approach has so far struggled to translate into effective permanent changes.

A step forward in Bunce and Wolchik's continuum from dictatorship to democracy, post-Orange Revolution Ukraine is still far from attaining a clean bill of health, both in terms of democratic achievements and membership in the EU. Despite widespread vocal support for these two objectives, Ukraine has to this day failed to complete the rule adoption-rule internalization-rule implementation-democratic rule of law circle described by Morlino and Magen [2008], with the majority of political and bureaucratic élite stuck in the first stage of this complicated process. Although ranked by Freedom House as a "free country", with reasonable perspectives of becoming a full democracy, the instability of the domestic political environment and the proved inclination of political actors to engage in spectacular and often fruitless confrontations qualify the Ukrainian transition (in the categorisation proposed by Morlino in this volume) as "uncertainty in a democratic context". While Ukraine satisfies the four conditions for a minimal definition of democracy (i.e. universal suffrage, free competitive and recurrent elections, multipartitism, different and alternative media sources), the quality of its democracy leaves the door open to speculations on its solidity and durability. Ukraine's appears as a fragile democracy, in the hands of a political élite so much engulfed in its internal disputes to become unable to deliver on the promises and expectations of its electorate.

In the specific case of business élite, their drive towards Western business standards and sympathy for the EU cannot be seen as an automatic guarantee neither of their deep democratic vocation nor of their full understanding of the costs and demands that a fully functioning democratic environment and EU membership impose. Because of their wider international exposure (wider than a number of top-ranking political figures), economic élite representatives could indeed become vehicles for the adoption of internationally-accepted business practices. However, the question as to whether, they could as well serve as instruments for the consolidation of political democracy in Ukraine rests on a knife edge. International experience also in the so-called second and third waves of democratizations in Latin America and Southern Europe in the 1970s and 1980s testifies of the important role played by some of these countries' economic élite in the processes of political transition from authoritarian to democratic regimes.[43] However, examples abound also of countries characterized by positive economic growth, a stable political and economic environment, oligarchs in power and no

---

[43] See, for example Cardoso, 1986: 137-153.

substantial democracy; Russia under Putin, being one of them. In the aftermath of the Orange Revolution, the influence of big businessmen on Ukraine's process of democratization has appeared scattered and ambiguous, highlighting business leaders' concern that instability might undermine the "country's value" and its perspectives of economic growth [Akhmetov, 2007]. However, while economic élite representatives have appeared more inclined towards forms of corporative democracy, where risks of instability and political challenges are effectively minimized, they have also demonstrated their determination in keeping in check the state's role in the management of the economy. This has helped guarantee a degree of economic pluralism and independence of the economic spheres *vis-à-vis* political decision-making and has significantly undercut (but not completely removed) chances that a Putin-like political system emerges in Ukraine. Contrary to the classical Barrington Moore's quote on the intertwining beneficial effects of economic growth and progress on the path towards democratization, however, the Ukrainian economic élite's striving towards improved economic performance may as well fail to result in an automatic move towards fully democratic institutions. This will be especially the case if democratic rules are not fully internalised and coherently implemented by the country élite and bureaucratic structures and if the latter continue failing to deliver on the electorate's expectations of good governance and stability.

10

MOLDOVA'S DEMOCRATIZATION: FROM IMMOBILITY TO REGRESSION

Alina Stanciulescu

1 - Introduction

After an initial opening towards democratization, Moldova has remained trapped in a sort of hybridization,[1] being unable either to democratize further or to decisively restrict liberties to resemble authoritarian regimes. The turning point out of this situation was represented by the 2001 victory of the Communist Party (PCRM) which formed the government as a result of what the international community recognized as democratic elections [OSCE, 2001]. Until the rise to power of the communists, Moldova was one of the most competitive regimes in the post-soviet space[2] and registered alternation in government as a result of free elections. The internal conflicts of the first legislatures, legislative deadlock and contrasts between President and Parliament, which were characteristic for the pre-2001 period, all account for Moldova's lack of progress towards more democracy. These conditions were brought to an end with the communists taking over the three main state institutions: the parliament, government and head of state. As a result, we have witnessed after 2001 a significant concentration of power into the hands of the President.[3] The sort of immobility on the continuum between democracy and authoritarianism which

---

[1] On hybrid regimes see for example Diamond [2002] and Morlino [2008].
[2] On pluralism "by default" in Moldova see Way [2002].
[3] Botan [2008] refers to it as the "vertical of power", as a result of Voronin holding the leadership of the governing party and the position of Head of State.

seemed to characterize Moldova before 2001 now seems to give way to an evolution towards the latter end.[4]

This chapter is organized as follows: the Introduction provides a brief insight of why the country falls into the category of hybrid regimes, section Two discusses the main contextual factors which account for Moldova's immobility after an initial opening towards democratization, section Three highlights two turning points in the evolution of the political regime which resulted in Moldova's moving away from the democratic type and closer to the authoritarian type of regime, sections Four and Five discuss the role of main institutional and social players in this process.

2 - Moldova's Hybrid Regime

The current regime in Moldova maintains an appearance of democracy but also displays features of authoritarianism. While a plurality of actors and interests exists, these are subordinated to the President and controlled through a variety of means such as appointments of loyal persons in key positions,[5] special favours in exchange for support, threats of judicial prosecution and use of other means of coercion, especially the police. The Communist Party has engaged in a series of activities aimed at reducing the salience of political opposition and at limiting the organization of dissent in the civil society. The short banning of the Christian Democrat Party (PPCD) opposition party, promoter of the mass manifestations against the regime in 2001, together with the threat of the lifting of immunity for the MPs which led those manifestations, as well as the denigration of independent civil society organizations and the creation of parallel organizations, and the control over the media are some of the current regime's means for political and social control.

But Moldova still maintains an appearance of democratic standards and a commitment to democratize at a rhetorical level. This strategy has a twofold objective: first, the democratic

---

[4] Freedom House rated Moldova in 2008 as semi-consolidated authoritarian regime (with a score of 5.00) downgrading it from the category of hybrid regime in 2007 (with a score of 4.96).

[5] For example, university rectors are appointed by the President.

elements introduced in the society through the legislation serve mainly at legitimizing the regime both internally and externally.[6] In many areas, Moldova has adopted European standards,[7] and most of the times these pieces of legislation have been adopted either unanimously or with a large majority. But the real problem is that the law remains mainly on paper. Élite and the population at large agree on the gap between written law and its enforcement. In the words of Lucinschi, ex-President of Moldova, "the law in the soviet mentality doesn't mean anything. It is always the boss to decide ... Laws are adopted according to what the EU says, but their application is soviet".[8] The problematic issue of law enforcement is, in the perception of the general population, the most important cause of the socio-economic situation in Moldova throughout the 2000s, as surveys show. From 2001 to 2008, the problem to which respondents referred the most often is law implementation [Barometrul Opiniei Publice (BOP), 2001-08]. But this facade adherence to EU standards is used by the regime as a means to have access to external funding.

Second, the same EU-compliant legislation may be used to punish or threaten with punishment political or social actors who may wish to change their allegiance from pro- to against the regime. In fact, political actors who do not agree with the rules of the game may be threatened that legislation will be applied

---

[6] In response to the recommendations of the Council of Europe's Parliamentary Assembly laid down in Resolution 1465/2005 on the functioning of democratic institutions in Moldova, the Parliament passed a great number of laws. Resolution 1572/2007 acknowledges the efforts of the Moldovan authorities : "welcomes the action taken to improve the functioning of democratic institutions, to increase the independence and efficiency of the judiciary, to ensure freedom and pluralism of the media, to strengthen local democracy, to improve economic performance, and to fight against corruption and trafficking in human beings and organs" and calls on the completion of decisive reforms so as to implement essential democratic practices.

[7] Voronin declared in December 2003, that EU integration is an objective of strategic importance and entrusted the government to implement structural reforms so as to meet the Copenhagen criteria and to harmonise national legislation to EU standards.

[8] Author interview with Mr. Petru Lucinschi, President of Moldova (1996-2001), Chisinau, April 2008.

against them. While at a formal level legislation exists, at a substantial level, the rule of law is mostly lacking: surveys show that only 10% of the respondents think that the judiciary treats everyone equally [Barometrul Opiniei Publice, 2003]. The actors supporting the government know that they may largely ignore the law without fearing that they will be prosecuted, but their behaviour may become punishable should their allegiance change. For example, corruption is a widespread phenomenon,[9] but most of the times it is left unpunished. The regime thus has a very strong weapon against defections, which consists precisely in the application of the law. As one representative of the opposition declared,[10] the government is very receptive to the accuses of corruption against opposition parties, while it is less so for accuses of corruption against their governing partners. Concern over the use of prosecution as a political weapon against important representatives of the opposition has also been expressed by external observers.[11] This use of law as a political weapon has led local analysts to conclude that the regime promotes a "dictatorship of law" [Botan, 2008].

3 - Stalling After an Initial Democratic Opening

There are many factors which may have contributed to the formation of a hybrid regime in Moldova and which resulted in Moldova being trapped in between democracy and authoritarianism. Among these factors, the difficulties of defining the nation and state are widely recognized as being serious obstacles to democratic consolidation [see for example Linz and Stepan, 1996; Ekiert et al., 2007; Bunce and Wolchik, this volume]. Moldova has had to deal with both the definition and consolidation of state boundaries, and with the issue of national identity and its relationship with the Romanian people and state.

---

[9] Moldova ranks 112 of 180 nations included in the Transparency International's Corruption Perception Index 2008.

[10] Author interview with Victor Osipov, Our Moldova Alliance, Chisinau, April 2008.

[11] See for example the Resolution of the Council of Europe no. 1465/2005, or Council of Europe Parliamentary Assembly Report 11374/2007.

303

In addition, the extreme economic difficulties, the weakness of parties and the absence of a political force strong enough to take the lead and promote reforms, plus the absence of a perspective of EU integration and the geographical proximity to the CIS did not favour Moldova's democratic path.

3.1 – Inter-Ethnic Tensions

While in itself ethnic diversity does not automatically correlate with poor democratic consolidation, it is the institutional choices and exploitation of such divisions that make ethnicity work against democracy. Ethnicity becomes relevant for democratization to the degree to which it becomes mobilized politically and in function of whether this mobilization is channelled towards a common goal or on strictly dividing ethnic grounds [Beissinger: 2008]. The ethnic composition of the Moldovan state has been used both by internal and external political forces to create antagonistic relationships between the various ethnic and linguistic groups. Internally, the disputes between the Moldovan or Romanian-speaking and other communities[12] regarding the settling of the national language was one of the causes of civil unrests. The state language law passed in 1989[13] declared Moldovan as the official state language, to be used in all spheres of the political, economic, social and cultural life. This and other manifestation of Moldovan nationalism as an anti-soviet reaction caused minority discontent. In the early 1990s, interethnic contrasts were being heated by all sides: ethnic Russians and Gagauz[14] who organized mass protests and the nationalistic requests of the Popular Front which promoted ethnic Moldovans and disregarded other minorities. Minorities reacted by suspending the application of central government edicts

---

[12] According to a population census in 2004, 75% are Moldovan native speakers, followed by 8% Ukrainians, 5% Russians, 4% Gagauz, 2% Romanians, 1% Bulgarians, and 1% of other nationality (National Bureau of Statistics of the Republic of Moldova, online at http://www.statistica.md.
[13] Law no. 3464 of 31.08.1989 on the statute of the state language of SSR Moldova; Law no. 3465 of 01.09.1989 on the functionality of languages spoken on the territory of SSR Moldova.
[14] Turkic ethnic group.

[Crowther, 1997: 294] in areas with non-Moldovan majority. Events culminated in the self-proclamation of two autonomous republics: the Gagauz republic around the Comrat city in August 1990 and the Transnistrian republic in September 1990.[15] In December 1991, the two republics, although not officially recognized, proclaimed Stepan Topal and Igor Smirnov presidents of the Gagauz and Transnistrian republics respectively.

Relations with the Gagauz Republic have been relatively easier, as in 1994, Moldova granted the region an autonomous status within the Moldovan Republic.[16] But relations with the breakaway Transnistria were complicated by the support offered by the Soviet military commanders to the separatists. The involvement of Russia in the separation of the Transnistrian region is not new and goes as far as 1924 when the Russian communist authorities created a Moldovan socialist republic centred on Tiraspol opposed to Bessarabia which had united with Romania in 1918. Bessarabia was eventually annexed to this republic in 1940 after the Ribbentrop-Molotov plan. Currently, ever since the 1992 civil war, Russian troops are stationed in the Transnistrian territories, notwithstanding Russia's official commitment to withdraw its troops.

The difficulty to find a national agreement on how to solve the matter, partly due to the huge asymmetry created by Russia's involvement, did not favour Moldova's path towards democracy. The Transnistrian issue only added to the political and economic transitions Moldova was facing and is still today viewed by Moldovan politicians as an impeding factor for the establishment of closer relationships with the EU and thus for further democratization.

---

[15] Unlike Gagauzia which was formed on ethnic bases (82% are Gagauz according to the 2004 demographic report of the National Bureau of Statistics, online at http://www.statistica.md), Transnistria was inhabited in 1989 by ethnic Moldovans (39%), Ukrainians (28%) and Russian (25%).
[16] On 23.12.1994 the Parliament of Moldova adopted a "Law on the Special Legal Status of Gagauzia".

3.2 – Identity Issue

In addition to the majority-minority and separatist tensions recalled above, the dispute around the existence of a distinct Moldovan language, different from the Romanian one and of a Moldovan identity different from the Romanian one contributed to further fragmentation within the population and political representatives [on the identity issue see King, 2003]. After independence, many intellectuals supported pro-Romanian views and so did a part of the population, but the majority favoured a pro-Moldovan identity, while the Russian-speaking minorities were in favour of a pro-Russian solution. The language issue is still today not settled and controversies are frequent both among linguists and especially among politicians, who bring it up at election times. Similarly, the post-soviet Moldovan state was debating two alternatives, if one excludes the idea of reuniting with Russia, discarded as soon as the pro-Romanian forces obtained a majority in the first independent legislature. The alternatives were either to reunite with Romania or to build an independent and sovereign Moldovan state. After the initial euphoria in the Romanian-Moldovan relations during the first 1990s, with the "flower bridges" which allowed for the first time Romanians and Moldovans to freely cross the Prut border, the pro-unification feelings were inhibited by separatist developments. The issue is today still relevant and is brought up in public discourse quite regularly. The absence of a general consensus among politicians and the population at large on the relationship between "Moldovan" and "Romanian" identities represents thus another dividing factor in Moldova.

3.3 – Economic Hardships

A third cause for the emergence of the hybrid regime is represented by the very difficult economic and social conditions experienced by the population since independence. The effects of land privatizations have had devastating effects, as the parcelling of agricultural land into small lots distributed to very poor farmers who lacked the resources to cultivate it resulted in large surfaces remaining uncultivated. Moldova being mainly an agricultural country, this meant that its economy was seriously hit by the collapse of agriculture. Moreover, Moldovan exports were largely dependent on the Russian market and Moldova was hit by the Russian economy crash in the 1990s. Economic difficulties certainly did not help create a strong attachment of the population to the ideals of democracy and market economy. Precisely when politicians talked about these ideals, the population was experiencing harsh economic conditions and ended up equating these ideals with their economic hardships. They became thus disenchanted with the democratic propaganda. As the two mandates of progressively reformist presidents – Snegur and Lucinschi – were characterized by extreme economic difficulties, this created a favourable environment for the communists who campaigned in 2001 on a platform which promised to restore collective farming and renationalize industry, as a way to oppose the devastating effects of privatization and economic liberalism initiated by their predecessors. Under very extreme conditions where salaries were paid in goods and people were obliged to barter [Motyl, 2008: 53], the population turned away from liberal discourses and chose to support a populist discourse.

3.4 – Weak Parties

The mixed regime in Moldova is considered to be a case of failed authoritarianism, generated as a result of élite fragmentation and state weakness which in practice meant that no political group was able to prevail over the others and impose its rule [Way, 2002]. The Moldovan party system has been very unstable and the Parliament has registered a very high turnover of political forces from one legislature to another. This was due both to the instability of the political offer – party/alliance instability in between elections, or to the very changing electoral fortunes of incumbents. The instability in the political offer may be traced back to various reasons: Moldova's lack of autonomous state development before 1991, and the absence of historical parties.[17] The emergence of

---

[17] Parties existed for a short period during the interwar and participated in the political life of Romania.

multiparty system after the declaration of independence from the former USSR in 1991 meant that all parties except the communist were completely new creations. This explains why they were very unstable, leader-centred and suffered frequent splits [Mosneaga, 2005a: 75-77].

Electoral support too was also very volatile. None of the main political forces in the 1994-1998 legislature succeeded in gaining representation in the subsequent elections: the Agrarians (PDAM) – which had obtained 43% of votes in 1994 and represented the main political force; the Socialists[18] – which were the second political force in 1994; the Peasant's and Intellectuals Block (BTI) which split and ran in separate alliances in 1998. The only exception is the PPCD which, in different electoral alliances,[19] succeeded in confirming its presence in Parliament. The 1998 elections brought to Parliament different political forces: the restored Communist Party (PCM) obtained the highest number of votes (30%) but was unable to form the government. Instead, the right-wing forces represented by the Democratic Convention (CDM), Movement for a Democratic and Prosperous Moldova (PMDP) and Party of Democratic Forces (PFD) formed the new government. Starting with the 1998 elections, this extreme pluralism which has characterized the Moldovan party system has also been increasingly associated with the presence of a dominant party – the PCM – which has succeeded in retaining a core electorate over subsequent elections [Mosneaga, 2005b: 93]. Among all political forces in Moldova, the communists have enjoyed constant support since 1998 when they obtained 30% of votes, consolidated to 50% in 2001 and 46% in 2005. The only other party which has succeeded in having continued parliamentary representation is PPCD.[20]

The very high turnover of political forces in Moldova is mirrored by a similar pattern of re-election rates for individual

---

[18] The Socialists ran in the Socialist Party and the "Unity-Edinstvo" Movement Bloc electoral block.

[19] Alliance of the Popular Christian Democratic Front in 1994 and CDM in 1998.

[20] PPCD failed to pass the electoral threshold in the April 2009 elections.

MPs. A study by Crowther and Matonyte [2007] shows that re-election rates to the Parliament have been extremely low, beginning with the first democratic election in 1994, with an average turnover close to 2/3. Moreover, experienced legislators, that is MPs who have leadership experience in parliamentary committees, commissions, and executive bodies were very few before 2001 and only starting with this legislature MPs holding leadership posts returned to Parliament in greater numbers.

This very unstable electoral support could have been the cause for the politicians' lack of activism and for their preference to "muddle through". In such an uncertain environment as the Moldovan electoral market, King could be right when he indentifies the lack of bold moves in strategic calculation on part of MPs, precisely that it was probably more secure not to "mess up" [King, 2000: 161]. But this behaviour could have also been simply dictated by the absence of experience of the MPs, many of them new in Parliament.

Directly connected to the instability of political forces in Parliament is the inability of the Parliament to consolidate itself as an institution in the post-communist institutional arena. Crowther [2007] identifies in the factional conflict which characterized the Moldovan Parliament the cause for the Parliament's incapacity to emerge as a stable institutional framework for democratic politics.

3.5 – A Foreign Policy in Between Two Attraction Poles

Moldova is a very small state caught between the EU and Russia. Its geographical position imposes Moldova a careful consideration of both of these attraction poles. As Lucinschi declared "Moldova needs to integrate into the EU but it cannot ignore Russia. If the EU and US do not ignore Russia, how could Moldova do that?".[21] Moldova acceded to the CIS in 1994, a choice which separated it from its more western neighbours which opted to strengthen their relationships with the EU. But at the same time Moldova signed the Partnership and Cooperation Agreement with the EU. In 1999 the

---

[21] Author interview with Lucinschi, Chisianu, April 2008.

309

government adopted its Program and "European integration" featured in its title,[22] but the change of government in November 1999[23] brought a reorientation of the foreign policy towards the CIS.[24] The 2001 campaign of PCRM bore a clear pro-Russian stance, but then slowly integrated in their discourses a more favourable position to the EU, until the declaration in 2003 of the EU as the main objective in foreign policy[25] and the signature in 2005 of the EU-Moldova Action Plan. In parallel with the rapprochement to the EU, the Moldovan-Russian relations have worsened: in 2003 they registered their coolest moments during Voronin's leadership, due to the failure of the Kozac Memorandum[26] on Transnistria. The two countries returned to more friendly bilateral relations in 2007 when an agreement to resume Moldovan exports to Russia[27] was reached.

Moldovan leaders have always tried to maintain a balance between the two attraction poles it borders – the EU and Russia. If the turn towards the EU is more recent, relations with Russia have always been considered strategic, if only due to Moldova's completely dependence on gas imports from Russia. As one representative of AMN declared "Moldova doesn't know what to

---

[22] Government Program for 1999-2002 "Rule of law, Economic revitalisation, European integration", April 1999.
[23] The centre right government led by Sturza is replaced by the communist-led government headed by Braghis after the approval of a censure motion.
[24] Government Program "Legality, Consolidation and Reforms – for the wellbeing of the Nation", January 2000.
[25] Voronin, declaration at the European Conference in Athens, April 2003.
[26] Promoted by a Russia, the plan proposed the formation of a federal Moldovan state and granted Transnistria disproportionate powers. This prompted mass demonstration in Chisinau and negative reactions from the OSCE. As a consequence, Voronin declined the signature and Putin had to cancel his visit. One month later, the European Commissioner for enlargement went to Chisinau and promised Moldova preferential treatment in the new European Neighbourhood Policy (ENP). A few days later Voronin declared European integration an objective of strategic importance.
[27] Russia had suspended in 2006 Moldovan wine exports officially on sanitary reasons, in practice in reaction to Moldova's introduction of new custom rules for Transnistria.

choose: more European democracy or cheaper Russian gas".[28] Moreover, Russia has until recently[29] represented the main market for Moldovan exports.[30] Together with the Russian involvement in the Transnistrian issue, these elements cannot be neglected in Moldova's foreign policy orientation. Illustrative is Voronin's declaration in 2006: "the same way that the European option constitutes a political factor for Moldova's development, the friendship and strategic partnership with Russia determines the future of my country".[31] Notwithstanding the closing-in of the relations between Moldova and the EU over the years, the perspective of joining the EU, which proved to be a strong democratization factor in Central and Eastern Europe, has lacked for Moldova, which was too small and too far away from Western Europe to arouse interest: the new neighbourhood policy of which Moldova is part, is not an enlargement policy.

4 - Turning Points: 2000-2001

The period of immobility which characterized Moldova's hybrid regime after the initial opening towards democratization came to an end in the 2000-2001 period. Several events have marked important turning points in the evolution of the Moldovan regime: the 2001 elections which brought to power the Communist Party and the 2000 constitutional change from a semi-presidential to a parliamentary type of regime.

While classical theorists of democracy argued that parliamentary systems are more likely than presidential systems to sustain democracy [Linz, 1990], this has not been the case in Moldova, which has moved from a semi-presidential to a parliamentary regime in 2000. The sole constitutional design in force in Moldova since 2000 is not sufficient to explain the power

---

[28] Author interview with Victor Osipov, Alianta Moldova Noastra, Chisinau, April 2008.

[29] Only in 2008 Romania surpassed Russia as the main destination of Moldovan exports according to the National Statistics Bureau, online at http://www.statistica.md.

[30] 80% of Moldovan wine is exported to Russia. In 2006, Moldova was severely hit by the Russian ban on import of wine from Moldova.

[31] Voronin, Chisinau, 27 January 2006, http://www.president.md.

patterns which have developed among institutions, but it needs to be interpreted in the context of the political actors who activate within the constitutional framework and enact those rules. Therefore, the analysis of the constitutional change from a premier-presidential to a parliamentary system may not disregard the simultaneous consolidation of executive powers in the hands of the President thanks to his leadership of the majority party in the 2001 legislature, namely PCRM.

The constitutional amendment introduced in 2000 and replacing the direct election of the President with election by Parliament coincided in practice with the concentration of power in the hands of the President. The amendment aimed at avoiding that a populist figure appealed to the electors and manipulated them into granting more powers to the President, as both Snegur and Lucinschi had tried,[32] and as a reaction, political parties in Parliament thought to introduce a strong parliamentary control over the election of the President. This move was intended as a limit to any future presidentialist tendencies. But in practice, the effect was the opposite, due to one important coincidence: the new President Voronin was at the same time leader of PCRM which had an absolute majority of seats in the Parliament. As Roper rightly noted, "Voronin's presidential authority does not come from his (new) constitutional powers but from the fact that he is the leader of the parliamentary majority faction" [Roper, 2008: 123]. By controlling an absolute majority of seats in Parliament, and by heading the most united and cohesive party in the legislature, the new President had no obstacle to passing legislation.

The strong grip of President Voronin and PCRM continued after the 2005 elections, when the communists, although short of the majority needed to elect the President, were nonetheless able to do so. One of the reasons is to be found in the constitutional provision requiring the dissolution of the Parliament in case of the impossibility to elect the new President after three unsuccessful attempts. This might have "obliged" MPs from opposition parties to cast a vote in support of a presidential

---

[32] Both had initiated popular referendums for allowing more powers to the President.

candidate they did not approve, in order to avoid early parliamentary elections as had happened in 2001. Another reason is the ability of PCRM to attract some of the fragmented and divided opposition forces into collaboration.[33]

With Voronin president for two mandates and PCRM in government for two mandates (2001-2005 and 2005-2009), there seems to be a stabilization of the appeal of the communists and their leader to the population, which resulted in a lower turnover of political élite and the beginning of a sort of continuity of political élite/party in power positions. Thus, the condition identified by Way [2002] as a cause for Moldova's mixed regime – precisely that no group was able to prevail over the others – is now slowly disappearing. If we add to this lower turnover of political forces the strategies used to attract their main opponents into collaborative relations in the Parliament – by "stealing" their opponents main card, that is, rapprochement with the EU, at least at a rhetorical level – the control over the media especially outside the main cities, and the unequal application of the law, we have enough signs which suggest that the regime is evolving towards more authoritarianism. The return to a parliamentary republic design in practice coincided with increased power for the President and an increased control of PCRM over the state institutions.

5 - Inter-Institutional Dynamics: Towards More Democratization?

As discussed in section Three, Moldova's hybrid regime has resulted from the simultaneity of several contextual factors. But the main state institutions have also played their part in the process, although there has been a significant variance in the role played by various institutional actors – President, Parliament, and Constitutional Court – in the democratization process. This section focuses on agency and discusses the inter-institutional dynamics from the point of view of democratic advancement.

Over the years, the influence of the main state institutions in the democratization process in Moldova has not been constant and this was due both to their activism but also to their prerogatives

---

[33] Three opposition parties supported the election of Voronin for a second mandate.

as specified in the Constitution. A significant redrawing of attributions happened with the 2000 constitutional amendment, which replaced Moldova's semi-presidential design in favour of a parliamentary design, through the introduction of the parliamentary election of the Head of State.

If we analyze the interactions between *Parliament* and *President* in Moldova since the beginning of the '90s we note two elements: first, as already noted, the legislature has been very fragmented and divided and political forces present in Parliament were usually unable to obtain representation in two subsequent elections.[34] Second, due to this high turnover of political forces but also MPs, no political force was strong enough to prevail in Parliament and push through reform, in whatever direction. This has been for a long time one of the causes for the legislative blockage and subsequent lack of significant improvements in reforms. Due to its fragmentation, the Parliament was unable to legislate and thus it did not assume a prominent role. Moreover, the weakness of the parliamentary majority deprived the various cabinets of continuous support for the policy-making and led to cabinet instability.[35] But neither were the first two Presidents more successful in asserting their role. They frequently clashed with the Parliament over the direction of reforms, and notwithstanding their attempts at increasing their powers through the modification of the Constitution, they both failed to do so.

The initial design of the newly instituted Soviet Socialist Republic (SSR) Moldova was that of a parliamentary republic where the Parliament elected the President.[36] However, in 1991, the Parliament passed a law providing for the direct election of the President. This decision to move towards a semi-presidential system was the result of internal fighting between the political forces in the first SSR Moldovan Parliament and of the

---

[34] Some parties did succeed in obtaining parliamentary representation but in different electoral blocks.
[35] After independence, there have been 11 cabinets until 2009. During the same period, there have been five legislatures.
[36] Law no. 250-XII of September 3rd 1990 instituted the office of President to be elected by Parliament.

consequent inability of the Parliament to legislate [Roper: 2008]. As a way out of this immobility, the position of the President was strengthened. But the mandates of both Snegur and Lucinschi, both directly elected, have still been characterized by legislative inefficiency and contrasts between the President and Parliament, which led both of them to argue for a presidential system. Both however met the Parliament's resistance, which in 2000 opted for a return to the parliamentary election of the Head of State.

The first President, Snegur, lacked support in Parliament due to his contrasting opinions with the dominant parliamentary majority, the Popular Front of Moldova: while the latter supported reunification with Romania, Snegur supported the idea of an independent Moldovan state. Relationships between the two institutions were also tense due to the attempts of both the President and the parliamentary majority to control the government, as a result of the provision according to which members of the government are appointed by the President and confirmed by the Parliament (art. 98 of the Constitution). The Parliament was itself divided on the issue of statehood, between those who supported the idea of a sovereign Moldovan state and those who supported the idea of a rapid reunification with Romania; in addition, there were the pro-Russian forces that were in favour of closer relations with Moscow. With President Snegur himself rather isolated, the Parliament divided along state and identity issues, and the Popular Front adopting a policy of obstructionism, the political arena lacked a strong player able to push through reforms. The legislative process was very slow. This paralysis could only be brought to an end by the early dissolution of the Parliament and early elections.

In order to facilitate consensus in Parliament, the 1994 legislature was to count only 1/3 MPs compared to the previous Parliament.[37] Also to overcome the difficulties of passing legislation, one of the first acts of the second legislature (1994-1998) was to adopt a new Constitution on July 29th, 1994. It increased the powers of the President who could dissolve the Parliament if the latter did not

---

[37] 104 instead of 380 MPs.

succeed in forming the government or if it blocked legislation for three months. The President could also call for popular referendums. These new provisions were the result of a learning process on inter-institutional interactions. A Constitutional Court was also created. The various attributions[38] of the Court made it, at that time, a potentially strong and independent player. Although it seemed that the second legislature enjoyed a more united majority, the agrarians soon split into confronting factions. The short collaboration between the President and the agrarians in Parliament was also due to end soon, due to the divergence over the name of the state language, which led Snegur to exit the party in 1995 and take his supporters with him. As a result of the difficult experience of the first independent legislative activity, Snegur campaigned at the end of his first mandate for a more presidential state, where the President would have greater power in policy-making, but he failed to gain support in the Parliament for his initiative.

Lucinschi, winner of the 1996 presidential elections and a centrist, was confronted with a left wing Parliament until the 1998 elections when a loose coalition government was formed.[39] However, like previously, this parliamentary majority was very unstable as it brought together parties holding very different views. Infighting and reciprocal corruption charges further increased the divisions in the coalition government, which led to Cabinet instability.[40] As a result, Lucinschi, like his predecessor,

[38] Among its attributions, the Constitutional Court is the only authority responsible for constitutional review, reviews initiatives aimed at revising the Constitution, solves cases of non-constitutionality of judicial acts, ascertains the circumstances justifying the dissolution of Parliament, the suspension from office of the President of the Republic of Moldova or the interim office of the President of the Republic of Moldova, as well as impossibility of the President of the Republic of Moldova to exercise his duties for more than 60 days (art. 135 of the Constitution).
[39] Electoral Block "Democratic Moldova Convention" (CDM), Electoral Block "For a Democratic and Prosperous Moldova" (PMPD) and Democratic Forces Party (PFD).
[40] After the resignation of Prime Minister (PM) Ciubuc, Urechean fails to gain the Parliament's investiture. A new majority dominated by the communists installs Sturza as the new PM. After ten months, the same majority withdraws its confidence and votes in a new government headed by Braghis.

became promoter of the idea of a Constitutional modification in the direction of a presidential regime and, at the same time, engaged in harsh critiques of the Parliament. The consultative referendum approved Lucinschi's idea but the participation was below the minimum threshold. Lucinschi nonetheless pushed forward with his idea, but met the opposition of almost all forces in Parliament. As a result, the Parliament passed a law[41] which replaced the direct election of the President with election by Parliament.[42] This modification of the Constitution enjoyed very high support among MPs[43] and their declared objective was to contrast authoritarianism[44] but at the same time to increase the coordination between the two main institutions. As a result, the design of power relations was changed: instead of an independent president which enjoyed direct popular legitimacy, an indirectly elected president dependent on the parliament was preferred. The choice of the Moldovan MPs was contrary to that of many ex-soviet republics which chose presidential forms of government. On that occasion, political parties played an important role in limiting the President's attempt to extend his powers. However, as already discussed, during Voronin's mandates, the constitutional modification did not bring about democratic consolidation, but became associated with a reduction of the political pluralism and an almost completely President – dominated Parliament.

The absence of a dominant player and the high competition between players (adversarial relations between President and Parliament, incumbents lost to their contenders, high turnover of parties and MPs), which had characterized Moldova's political system during the first decade of its independence, was shaken after the 2001 elections which brought some significant changes in the power relations. PCRM's victory in the 2001 parliamentary

---

[41] Law no. 1115-XIV of July 5th 2000.
[42] According to the new constitutional provisions, in order to elect the President, 61 votes are needed.
[43] Adopted with 97 out of 101 votes.
[44] Author interview with PPCD representative, Chisinau, April 19th, 2008.

elections[45] and the appointment of their party leader as Head of State put an end to this situation of high competition between weak political actors and marked the beginning of a communist domination of the political arena. With PCRM, the Moldovan political system overcame the situation of extreme volatility and the policy making did benefit from a constant input, though not towards the democratization of Moldova, but towards an increased control over politics of the incumbents. Under the strong leadership of their president, the parliamentary majority for the first time stayed together during the term and the legislative efficiency increased significantly. But this more united legislative majority which had lacked during the previous legislatures, did not act as a check for the activity of the government or the President, but became a "voting machine of the President".[46] The election of Voronin as President of the Republic while he maintained his party leadership meant that the power balance between the President and Parliament was now weighting more on the President's part.

This power configuration between President and Parliament continued also after the 2005 elections although with some differences. In the 2005 elections the Communists obtained 45,98% of votes and only 56 seats out of 101. This simple majority did not allow them anymore to elect the President by themselves, for which 61 votes are needed. Under these circumstances, they had to negotiate with other forces in the Parliament. This represented an important occasion for opposition parties to increase their role in Parliament. In fact, as a condition for their support to the election of the President, a part of the opposition forces[47] signed with Voronin an agreement which committed the government to work towards the fulfilment of the EU Action Plan. As March and Herd [2006] pointed out, it is the fact that the Parliament still elects the President to have safeguarded a role for the Parliament. The 2005 elections proved

---

[45] PCRM obtained 50,07% of the votes which ensured them an unprecedented large majority of 71 out of 101 seats.

[46] Author interview with Oazu Nantoi, IPP, Chisinau, April 13, 2008.

[47] PPCD, the social liberals (PSL) and the democrats (PDM).

that the Parliament is not completely devoid of power, as opposition parties made their voice heard when directly negotiating with the majority party for the election of the Head of State. As such, the Parliament has remained a latent locus of power [March and Herd, 2006], which it uses however only on occasion of the election of the Head of State.

Apart from the 2005 moment when the *opposition* successfully negotiated with the governing party an agreement which committed the government to work towards EU rapprochement, during the communist rule, the Parliament has had a fragmented and weak opposition. There are very few other examples when the opposition acted together [Cashu, 2005], but the norm is that the Parliament very rarely checked on the activities of either the President or government, being reduced to a mere "voting machine", that is, an institutional setting which only serves to pass the legislation indicated by President Voronin. The most important and recent example on a change of attitude of the opposition parties is represented by their successful boycott of the election of Voronin's successor for state presidency after the April 2009 elections. With just one vote short of the minimum which allowed them to elect the new President, the communist party was unable to install a successor to Voronin, due to the opposition vow to force anticipated elections in reaction to the alleged electoral fraud registered in April.[48]

The above analysis highlights that until the rise of Communists to power, there have been two constants in the interactions between the President and Parliament in Moldova: the first is a much divided Parliament; the second is the adversarial relations between President and Parliament. Moreover, there is another feature that characterizes all three Moldovan Presidents: they all attempted to concentrate more powers in their hands. Pointing to the fragmentation and division of parliamentary parties, Snegur

[48] Opposition politicians have rejected the OSCE and other international organisations conclusions on the fairness of the April 2009 elections and have accused the government of major fraud. Massive demonstrations against the electoral fraud took place in Chisinau and ended in violence and with the intervention of police forces.

and Lucinschi were in favour of more power for the President as a way to ensure more efficiency and to overcome legislative blockages. But they failed to obtain the Parliament's support. The attempt to modify the constitutional design to their advantage appears to have been the dominant strategy employed by the major political actors. The system for the election of the President is one example, but the modifications to the electoral law[49] points to the same conclusion. The power concentration which both Snegur and Lucinschi failed to realize through constitutional modification was instead reached with Voronin's double leadership as Head of State and leader of the majority party.

Taking advantage of their power positions, the communists acted so as to increase even more their grip on power. Their main strategy in the political arena was to attract other players into their sphere of influence. One of the most obvious cases is the PPCD, an opposition party once the hardest opponent of PCM, which changed its position from overtly anti-communist[50] to collaborationist with the communists. But while many local observers accuse PPCD of abandoning its ideals and of collaborating with the communists,[51] it may also be seen as a strategic move to obtain from the communists support for their legislative proposals and advantages in the local constituencies where they rule, or as a player which is in fact capable of negotiating with the majority party, as the 2005 agreement demonstrates. However, this change of course of PPCD has had devastating consequences on the electoral fortunes of the party, which failed to gain representation in the July 2009 elections.

---

[49] As an attempt to reduce the role of opposition parties, the communists modified the electoral law (law no. 718-XII of 17.09.91 regarding parties and other socio-political organisations) in April 2008 by raising the threshold for parliamentary representation from 4% to 6%. This high threshold together with the prohibition of pre-electoral alliances favour big parties and mergers. Another provision states that after the 2009 elections only parties which have obtained parliamentary representation will benefit from state funding.

[50] Iurie Rosca, leader of PPCD, was one of the most important political figures of the anti-communist manifestations in Chisinau in 2002. In 2005 he was elected vice-President of a communist-dominated Parliament.

[51] Author interview with an investigative journalist, Chisinau, April 2008.

Another actor which has sometimes proved important in the democratization process is the *Constitutional Court*. On several occasions, the Court has played an important role in mediating conflicts between the different branches of government especially in the period 1994-2000 [Way, 2002; Way, 2003]. But the importance of the Court has decreased since the communist victory. In fact, the control the communists gained over appointments to the Court since 2001[52] offers to date little insurance against a full politicization of the Court.

One indicator of the importance of the Constitutional Court in the legislative arena is the quantity of referrals it receives. Imperfect as it might be, this indicator shows that in less than fully democratic states, low number of referrals to the Constitutional Court are indicative of malfunctioning of this institution. If we use this indicator, the role of the Constitutional Court in Moldova has decreased during transition and especially during the communist rule. The reason for the decreasing number of referrals is to be found in the increasing subordination of the Court to the regime. As a prominent lawyer commented,[53] "the possibility to win against the government before the Constitutional Court is null ... The Court is completely subdued by the regime. This is why it is wiser to wait for the composition of the Court to change in order to raise issues of constitutionality".

As this section has shown, the interactions between the Parliament and President have not been particularly fruitful during Moldova's transition mainly as a result of the lack of consensus on the one hand among the parliamentary parties, on the other hand between the parliamentary majority and the President. Not only have the first two Presidents frequently found themselves at odds with the parliamentary majority, but the parliamentary majority itself has been much divided on the direction of reforms. This meant that no actor was able either to push through the reform process alone, nor to round up a coalition of forces committed towards a common goal.

---

[52] Of the six judges, two are appointed by the Parliament, two by the President and two by the Superior Council of the Magistracy.

[53] Author interview with Vitalie Nagacevschi, President of the Association "Jurists for Human Rights", Chisinau, May 2008.

Until 2001 the division of the political élite has been one impeding factor for democratization in Moldova. With the rise to power of the communists in 2001, the strong leadership of Voronin ensured that the two institutions – Parliament and President – would engage in more collaborative relations. Voronin in fact succeeded in maintaining a strong influence over most of his party's parliamentary faction insuring an unprecedented legislative efficiency. However, this "imposed collaboration" between the President and Parliament did not lead to more democracy, but to a subordination of the Parliament to the President.

6 - Weak Civil Society and the Creation of "Parallel Organizations"

If the President-Parliament relations have not been conducive to democratization due to their frequent confrontations and to the absence of a strong player committed to democratize, the role of civil society organizations as "change agents"[54] has been very reduced due to two main reasons. The first is connected to their role in the soviet society, where trade unions and similar organizations were the main providers of recreational services for the population. Moreover, instead of functioning as bottom-up organizations, they were top-down channels of participation through which the regime ensured its followers' support. Therefore, the civil society organization lacked the experience of really representing their members in relations with the authorities and of transmitting the demands of the society to the political decision makers. This is still true today, where "it is not the trade union to contact the party and lobby it but it is the party to contact the trade union for support".[55] The second reason is to be found in the strategy, lately used by the communists, of creating *"parallel"* *organizations* and discrediting and discouraging participation in the independent civil society organizations.[56]

The advent to power of the communists in 2001 has been accompanied by actions aimed at taking over the arena reserved

---

[54] Change agents or norm entrepreneurs make pressure on domestic rulers to adopt democratic rules [Finnemore and Sikkink, 1998].
[55] Author interview with Victor Osipov, AMN, Chisinau, April 2008.
[56] *Ibid.*

for civil society organizations, in an attempt to control their activities and channel them into specific directions. As a result, the potential of civil society as change agents in Moldova is rather small. The most important causes for this situation are the creation of "parallel" organizations and the pressures on members of the independent organizations to change affiliation. Many civil society organizations such as the union of journalists, the union of writers, trade unions have a double representation in Moldova. This means that, besides the independent civil society representations created from grass roots, the regime has created parallel organizations which ensure the support to government policies. The existence of such parallel organizations, loyal to the regime, has divided the social forces in almost every domain. One of the results of this is the lack of strikes against the regime; with very few exceptions, there have been no important manifestations of social forces against the regime, and one of the causes may be traced back to this division of the organizations representing the social forces.[57]

These parallel organizations also serve to legitimize the regime to the members of these organizations and to the public at large. Intrinsically connected to this function, the parallel organizations also have the function to delegitimize the "other" organizations, the independent ones, and to deter people from joining them. In fact, they benefit from privileged contacts with the authorities compared to their independent counterparts and were granted benefits that the other associations did not enjoy.[58] Moreover, the pro-government mass media gives constant and massive coverage to these loyal organizations and to their "successful" dialogue with

---

[57] There are other causes as well of the absence of strikes notwithstanding the serious economic difficulties in Moldova during the transition years. One cause could be the predominant mentality of the blue collars, legacy of the previous communist soviet regime, that of waiting for problems to be solved from the centre and without any personal involvement – author interview with the National Confederation of Trade Union representatives L. Manea, O. Budza, P. Chiriac, Chisinau, April 2008. The lack of individual initiative in the socio-political sphere is a widespread characteristic in Moldova.
[58] Author interview with Victor Osipov, AMN, Chisinau, April 2008.

the authorities. But instead of pushing for greater inclusiveness and democracy, these loyal organizations' main aim is to obtain advantages for their members while not annoying the regime.

One very telling example is the split of the historical trade union, the General Federation of Trade Unions of Moldova into two organizations: CSRM – The Confederation of Trade Unions in Moldova and *Solidaritatea* or CSLS – The Confederation of Free Trade Unions. At the time of the break, *Solidaritatea* argued that it withdrew from the Federation due to financial scandals, while CSRM argued that the new organization was created to weaken the trade union and to support the PCRM [Moldova Azi, 2007]. Local observers support the idea that the split was in fact orchestrated by the Communists and that the resulting *Solidaritatea* was their puppet organization [Moldova Azi, 2007]. During the parallel coexistence, CSRM has publically and repeatedly accused the government of intimidating actions and of exercising pressures over trade union members to change affiliation in favour of the *Solidaritatea*. CSRM has even brought these accusations before the International Labour Organization Committee for free association. In June 2007, in an unexpected move, the two trade unions merged. Local analysts commented that this represented the absorption by the communist trade union of the independent trade union [Moldova Azi, 2007].

The above considerations are valid for organizations representing workers. But the situation is different for the associations of the patronage, which represent relatively big[59] economic interests in Moldova and the majority of which are foreign investors. Foreign investors have easy access to the Moldovan government[60] and are known to obtain from the government particular deals or legislation that favour their interests. However, these economic actors are themselves interested in a certain degree of rule of law which is necessary for

---

[59] The measure is relative to the wealth of the country and the almost disastrous economic situation of the non-industrial sectors. Therefore, the term of big industry used in the Moldovan context is not comparable to any European standard.

[60] Author interview with T. Botorovschi from the Ministry of Foreign Affairs and European integration, Chisinau, April 2008

their economic activities to function well. The main aspect economic actors are interested in is the predictability of the juridical, but not only, effects of their actions. The independence of the judiciary is an issue on which foreign investors insist.[61]

The NGO sector in Moldova, although quite developed,[62] does not support common actions but is very dispersed in their activities, and as a result their potential influence on policy-makers is rather limited. Moreover, the government only recently started to invite civil society organizations (CSOs) to collaborate in the drafting of legislation and policy and mainly as a result of EU's insistence on the issue. But even when consultations are called, local observers report that few NGOs respond and many are unable to provide any expert advice [IDIS, 2009: 14]. This, in turn, has negative consequences, as the government then uses these joint sessions to legitimize the policy-making process to EU authorities, while imposing their own views on the matter. While their main activities are largely to criticize the government, or to monitor compliance with Moldova's international commitments, NGOs' voices are very rarely listened to by the government. Moreover, according to an independent report [IDIS, 2009: 15], the authorities frequently accuse civil society experts of irresponsibility due to their criticism which is interpreted as an attempt to harm the image of Moldova abroad.

7 - Conclusions

Displaying both democratic and authoritarian features, Moldova was until recently and like most post-soviet states a case of mixed regime; for many years it didn't seem to evolve towards any of the two ideal types. Various contextual factors contributed to this situation. Among these, the particular geographical position, in the proximity of two big political entities, Russia and the EU (which also represent two fundamentally different types of political regime) and their policy towards Moldova (Russian support in favour of a separatist region and neglect on the EU's side for more than a decade since Moldova's

---

[61] Author interview with T. Botorovschi from the Ministry of Foreign Affairs and European Integration, Chisinau, April 2008.

[62] There were 7000 NGOs in 2007 according to IDIS, 2009: 14.

independence, if we consider the first serious sign of EU interest towards Moldova being the signature of the EU-Moldova Action Plan) is one of the explaining factor of the non-evolution of the regime towards either democracy or authoritarianism. Moldova's feeble democratization and liberalization reforms during the 1990s combined with weak institutions and political parties, lack of rule of law, and extreme poverty seemed to indicate the possibility that the hybrid regime could become permanent. Externally obliged to find a balance between two political giants compared to the very small Moldova, and internally torn in political fighting between parties and institutions on matters related to both internal reforms and external policy, Moldova had no real chance to move away from the status quo. The absence of a strong domestic actor (party, leader or institution) to push forward either towards more democratization or more authoritarianism was rightly indicated as the cause for Moldova's failed transformation in an authoritarian state [Way, 2002].

The post-2001 events demonstrate how right this explanation was. The coming to power of a united party under a strong leadership that of the communists under Voronin, altered the delicate balance of the highly competitive and pluralist political arena which had characterized Moldova so far. The appearance of a strong party and a strong leader and the constant electoral support they have enjoyed so far provided the input that the Moldovan regime lacked in order to move closer to one of the two ideal types. The communists' successful attempts at reducing the space for the political opposition and also for the organization of dissent in society, together with their attempts at controlling the media and limiting the access of opposition to the media are indicative of the direction towards which the country is heading. At the same time, the adoption of a high number of legislation in accordance with EU standards, and the adoption of the EU-priority in the official rhetoric may only indicate that a long term hybridization in Moldova is very likely.

Externally, a stronger hand on the EU's side in its monitoring of Moldova's fulfilment of its obligations as well as closer contacts between the European Parliament and Moldovan opposition parties, could help push through democratization in Moldova even in the absence of an accession perspective. Internally, the 29 July 2009 parliamentary elections confirmed PCRM as the dominant party, but the party failed to gain a majority of seats in Parliament, which impeded them to elect Voronin's successor as Head of State. Whether the opposition parties which obtained representation in the July 29 elections will be able to form a coalition government and to push Moldova on its path towards democracy remains to be seen. The experience of government at local level by coalitions of opposition parties, which have proved very fragmented, does not allow us to be too optimistic about their collaboration. The boycott of the election of Voronin successor's by opposition parties after the April 2009 elections and the subsequent anticipated elections held in July 2009 represents the first prove that opposition parties may overcome their divisions and work towards a common goal. The mass manifestations accusing electoral fraud in the April elections could provide the incentive opposition forces need to push through a change of route for Moldova.

11

REGIME DEVELOPMENT IN BELARUS AND THE ROLE OF INTERNATIONAL FACTORS

Anastassia Obydenkova

1 - Introduction

Belarus, as the last dictatorship in Europe, presents a unique example of regime development. The political regime of Belarus has fluctuated from a more or less democratic institutional setting, being a hybrid regime in the middle of the 1990s, to an authoritarian one. An attempt to understand the formation and consolidation of the political regime in Belarus effectively will support the aims of this volume, which are to examine and explain how regimes move towards democracy or autocracy. In this chapter I intend to identify the sort of political regime established in Belarus and to answer two research questions: (1) why this particular type of regime was formed in Belarus; (2) how this regime evolved over time and what factors may explain its path.

Belarus did not simply switch from a Soviet totalitarian regime to a new authoritarian regime. There was a stage, between the dissolution of the Soviet Union and Lukashenko's authoritarian regime, when it was a hybrid regime. At the beginning of the 1990s, Belarus had pro-democratic tendencies. The first presidential election of 1994 was competitive and democratic, with all candidates having the same opportunity and rights. However, free fair democratic elections of 1994 became the first step towards authoritarianism. Thus, Belarus presents an interesting case study as it allows one to see the possible developments of a hybrid regime and its path to authoritarian regime. Moreover, in modern Belarus there is still a sharp contrast between some formal democratic institutions and authoritarian rule. Therefore, this chapter will also examine the disparities between the democratic formality and the authoritarian reality of the political regime of Belarus.

We assume that there is a possibility of democratization in all cases. The process of regime development may take the reverse order – from hybrid regime to an authoritarian one and then back to hybrid, which eventually might be followed by a democratic regime. That is another reason why it is important to examine the case of Belarus within the theoretical framework of hybrid regimes.

2 - The Formation of Lukashenko's Regime and Its Crisis

The contextual explanation of the origin of a hybrid regime provides a good analytical framework for examining the phenomenon of Belarus. The Belarusian regime appeared from totalitarian Soviet regime and retained quite a few of its institutional settings. This section will examine the process of change undergone by this state and the consequences for the institutional set-up that emerged. There are two stages to be distinguished in the development of the political regime in Belarus. The first period is 1994–2003, the second from 2004 onwards. The first period is the formation of the regime of Lukashenko – establishing the main institutions governing the politics of the state. It was based on the strong support of the population of Belarus. The second period is the crisis of the political regime and losing the support of the population for Lukashenko and his regime.

There have been a few factors which contributed to the establishment of the present political regime. Among the most important are: the wide support of the electorate for Lukashenko and his anti-corruption platform which dominated in the 1990s; economic and political support for Russia and the union with Russia; maintenance of a socialist economy; and a certain nostalgia the population had for the Soviet Union. To understand this phenomenon of Belarus, we should recall that, unlike other post-Soviet republics, Belarus had the shortest period of real independence, which lasted only for nine months. At all other times, the territory of modern Belarus belonged either to the

329

Russian Empire or to the Great Duchy of Lithuania.[1] Thus, in Belarus, the national identity was not so well formed and developed as in the case of other post-Soviet states [see Gapova, 2002; Marples, 1999].

From 1994, the political regime of Belarus was supported by the majority of the population. People provided a wide support to a *person*. This electoral mood was combined with general post-Soviet distrust for *faceless institutions*, such as parliament. Partly, this reflected the long-lasting traditions of the Tsarist regime and Soviet Union, when the leader, whether it be a tsar or chair of the party, would have "direct" communication with the people and would seize their support. Examples of this phenomenon could be found in Yeltsin´s Russia, in Turkmenistan, and in Belarus [Obydenkova, 2008a]. This can be described as a regime of direct power and direct connection – "president – people" – and it made the role of other political institutions insignificant. All other political élite, both "rightist" and "leftist", became "enemies of the regime of Lukashenko" and were gradually eliminated from politics. The people supported Lukashenko in person and all his decisions regarding the referenda and change of the Constitution in 1996. From 1996, the Parliament became a purely nominal institution controlled by the President [see Deyermond, 2004].

Then, Lukashenko passed a law seizing control over all financial flaws, i.e. over large and medium-sized private enterprises. This deprived political opposition of financial sources and support. The parliamentary elections held in May 1995 were not particularly successful nor very democratic. The restrictions placed on the mass media and on the candidates' expenditures during the campaign led to a shortage of information about the candidates and almost no political debate before the elections [see Krivolap, 2006]. The main problem was the lack of voter turnout. After the second round, the legislature

---

[1] Belarus was only declared independent after World War I (on 25 March 1918) and independence was already ended on 1 January 1919, when the Soviet regime was proclaimed in Smolensk. After a period of joint Lithuanian-Belarusian Soviet regime, Belarus joined the USSR on 30 December 1922 as a Soviet Socialist Republic.

had only 120 elected deputies and was still missing the 174 members necessary to form a new parliament. Another round of elections was discussed, but the government claimed to have no money to finance them. This marked the beginning of a very weak parliament and also demonstrated a certain public apathy towards matters that concerned the legislative branch [see Kazakevich, 2006; Melyantsou, 2006].

The most powerful impact on the formation of the current political regime in Belarus was through the referenda. One of the major factors which defined the following development of political regime was the Referendum of 1996 which led to a change in the Constitution. The amendments of the Constitution, according to Lukashenko, would expand the power of his office. This was a turning point in post-Soviet politics in Belarus. A May 1995 national referendum was the first step in the amendment process. Out of the four questions, one asked if the president could disband Parliament if the members violated national law. The vote, which several Supreme Soviet deputies protested, resulted in 77% in favour of the provision regarding the dismissal of the legislature by the president.[2] Two years later, Lukashenko scheduled the first referendum that would potentially alter the Constitution.

In 1996 Lukashenko unilaterally established the referendum after the Supreme Soviet refused to support the measures or set up a date for the vote. An earlier attempt by the Supreme Soviet to establish their own referendum in September 1996 was struck down as "inconsistent with the Constitution" by the Constitutional Court. The referendum amended the Constitution mostly to strengthen the power of the presidency. Amongst the changes made were the following: (1) the Supreme Soviet, the unicameral parliament of Belarus, was abolished. The Supreme Soviet was replaced by the National Assembly, a bicameral parliament; (2) the term of President Alexander Lukashenko

---

[2] Other questions on the ballot, such as the national flag and national emblem, didn't affect the Constitution as a whole, but their status has been decided by the Constitution.

was extended from 1999 to 2001 [see Badrihanov, 2006; Behterev, 2001; OSCE, 2001]. During the referendum, 84% of the approximately 7.5 million voters approved the amendments. Other changes included the expanding role of the Council of Ministers, which allowed it to deal with issues related to development of economic, social and political spheres within Belarus. The results of the 1996 referendum led to the exclusion of opposition parties from the new Parliament and resulted in the amendment of the constitution that took key powers off the Parliament.[3]

Two important findings stem from this. First, the Parliament was very weak from the beginning of Belarus's independence. The decisions of the Parliament (then, the Supreme Soviet) had never been taken into account by the executive branch. Secondly, the Constitutional Court, which had the power to cancel the laws and decrees of the President, had been always supportive of any decision, decree or law passed by the President [Behterev, 2001; OSCE, 2001; Bruce, 2005]. Thus, with a weak Parliament, strong presidency, and judicial branch serving in the role of the executive, autocracy became deeply enrooted in political institutions and legal texts. The regime was fully formed after the election of 2001. Political opposition was completely eliminated and the restrictions on the freedom of mass media were increased as never before.

The next referendum, initiated again by the President, was held in 2004 to lift the restriction on the number of terms for president. Previously, Lukashenko had been limited to two terms and thus would have been constitutionally required to step down after the next presidential election, due in 2006, but this referendum opened the way for him to stay in power without any limits on the number of terms [Badrihanov, 2006; Forrester, 2004; Aleksandrenkov, 2006]. The voter turnout for the referendum was nearly 90%, with 77.3% of the voters agreeing to eliminate term limits. The changes were implemented on October 17,

---

[3] Due to problems associated with transparency and ballot stuffing, the European Union, United States and several other nations did not recognize the results of the vote.

2004.[4] Two years later, Lukashenko ran in the 2006 election and won 83% of the vote during the first ballot [Aleksandrenkov, 2006; Krivolap, 2006; Melyantsou, 2006].

Table 33. Ratings of regime transition for Belarus

	2001	2002	2003	2004	2005	2006	2007	2008
Electoral Process	6.75	6.75	6.75	6.75	7.00	7.00	7.00	7.00
Civil Society	6.50	6.25	6.50	6.75	6.75	6.75	6.50	6.50
Independent Media	6.75	6.75	6.75	6.75	6.75	6.75	6.75	6.75
Governance	6.25	6.50	6.50	6.50	N/A	N/A	N/A	N/A
National Democratic Governance	N/A	N/A	N/A	N/A	6.75	7.00	7.00	7.00
Local Governance	N/A	N/A	N/A	N/A	6.50	6.50	6.50	6.75
Judicial Framework and Independence	6.75	6.75	6.75	6.75	6.75	6.75	6.75	6.75
Corruption	5.25	5.25	5.50	5.75	6.00	6.25	6.25	6.25
Democracy Score	6.38	6.38	6.46	6.54	6.64	6.71	6.68	6.71

Note: The ratings are based on a scale of 1 to 7, with 1 for the highest level of democratic progress and 7 for the lowest level. The Democracy Score is an average of ratings for the categories tracked in a given year. With the 2005 edition, Freedom House introduced separate analysis and rating for national democratic governance and local democratic governance.

Source: Freedom House, *Country Report: Belarus (2005);* and Freedom House, *Belarus: Nations in Transit Ratings and Averaged Scores,* www.freedomhouse.org

In this context, it is interesting to trace the changes in regime development in Belarus through the democracy rating of Freedom House. To recall from the first chapter, the classification

[4] Like the 1996 referendum, the validity of the vote was brought into question. According to the OSCE, many polling places went without independent observers. The OSCE believed that the standards of the vote did not meet OSCE requirements for "free and fair elections". Data from other NGOs indicate that 50% of voters did not participate in the referendum.

of political regimes offered by Morlino, based on the rating of Freedom House, is as follows: semi-consolidated democracies (rating between 3.00 and 3.99), transitional or hybrid regimes (4.00–4.99) and semi-consolidated authoritarian regimes (5.00–5.99). If we now look at the rating of transition made by Freedom House for Belarus, then, we will find that Belarus initially belonged to the third group of "semi-consolidated authoritarian regimes" and evolved into a purely authoritarian one.

The rating of Freedom House for Belarus (see Table 33) is available for the whole period 2001–2008. However, it still captures some fundamental changes and presents an accurate summary of internal dynamics of Belarus for this particular period.

In the 1990s, the rating for measurement of different aspects of the regime – for example, civil society was still 5.25 – and then rose gradually up to 6.50 in 2008. Electoral process was more transparent and democratic in 1997 and was recognized as completely undemocratic in 2008. The issues of corruption were under relatively better control in the period of 1999–2004. If the rating had been available for the very beginning of the 1990s, it would demonstrate even greater disparities in the transformation of the regime and consolidation of authoritarianism in Belarus.

Since his election in 1994 Lukashenko has consolidated power steadily. He used the referenda to make the most radical changes in the Constitution and established a new political regime. The November 1996 referendum to amend the 1994 Constitution was the most important critical point in the development of the regime as it allowed the President to seize control over the Parliament.

What secured electoral support for Lukashenko? The political support of the population was based on two main factors. In the 1990s, the first aspect was the idea of union with Russia, which formed a significant part of Lukashenko's both electoral campaigns. The perspective of such a union was extremely popular among the population. Thus, when in 1990 Belarus declared its national sovereignty and independence from the Soviet Union, the referendum of March 1991 referendum held throughout the Soviet Union showed that 83% of the population of Belarus wanted to preserve the Soviet Union. This partly confirms the hypothesis that difficulties in defining the nation state may play a role in establishing a non-democratic regime.

The second aspect was the establishment of socio-economic stability in the society. It implied the maintenance of big industries, factories, and plants, preservation of high employment of the population and relatively high pensions, and other social benefits. The price of it was the absence of privatization and state control over the economy.[5] Controlled media advertised the regime as the guarantee of social security which was juxtaposed later in 2000s to Russian 'pro-capitalist' reforms, social chaos and insecurity.

The economy of Belarus was based on "market socialism" rather than market economy. This means that the State retains much of the provisions of the national companies. Trade in Belarus stays mainly within the post-Soviet states and with Russia as the main trade partner, partly due to the Russia and Belarus free-trade agreement. Trade with other countries amounted to less than 25% of the total volume of Belarusian trade. One of the major sources of this well-being was significant economic support coming from Russia which was the main destination of Belarusian exports.

Another source of financial stability and some economic growth of Soviet-type economy in Belarus was the favourable rate Belarus was charged by Russia for gas compared to European countries and other post-Soviet countries.

To sum up, the regime established in Belarus had the following peculiarities. First, extensive donations from Russia provided Belarus with market and natural resources, and, thus, with necessary financial resources for realization of socio-economic programmes. Secondly, socio-economic stability favourable to population, significant social spending and social packages (e.g. pensions) provided the support of the population. In turn, support of the population allowed Lukashenko to retain power in his own

---

[5] Higher Economic Court of the Republic of Belarus, Statistics, http://www.court.by.

hands, eliminate political opposition, and avoid sharing power through actual balance of power as required by the Constitution. However, the regime of Lukashenko went down along with his popularity among the people. The rating of Lukashenko fell rapidly after 2003. According to different social questioners, the support for Lukashenko fell from 40% to 50% at the beginning of the 2000s to only 14–19% in 2003.

This process was paralleled by the worsening relationship with Russia. The idea of integration with Russia was always pictured as expansion of the developed social system of Belarus to Russia. However, integration implied the emergence of Russian private business in Belarus which would eventually lead to a significant change from socialism to capitalism in Belarus with clear predominance of Russian private enterprises. That would not only break the social system itself but the whole ideology and popularity of image of Lukashenko.

The ideology was significantly changed to a defence of population against "close" and "far away" vicious neighbours, in other words against both Russia and the West. The new idea was that Belarusians are the "best Slavs", who have kept their best traditions and values in contrast to those Slavs who have sold themselves to capitalism and Western values. This ideology brought the rating of Lukashenko a little up to 30% of the support of the population. However, support of the population of Belarus for the personal regime and charisma of Lukashenko has gone down radically and may lead to the beginning of wider dialogue between different social groups of Belarus and foreign actors. At the same time the government is now far less resistant to changes in its foreign policy course and is also considering changes in its economic system, ideology and political values.

3 - Formality and Reality

What sort of regime is Belarus? To answer this question, we have to delineate the main institutions governing the present political life of the state. In the case of Belarus, it is important to distinguish between formal institutions and the informal aspect of politics – the way the institutions really function. In the formal description of the institutions, provided by the Constitution, one can find the division of powers.

Formally, there is the balance of powers established between executive, legislative and judicial branches in Belarus. The President of the Republic of Belarus is the official head of the state, the head of the army and the highest government official. The President has the Council of Ministers, led by a prime minister, to advise him on what needs to be done.

The National Assembly has two chambers. The House of Representatives has 110 members elected in single-seat constituencies elected for a four-year term. The Constitution outlines the formal democratic character of the election as "the basis of universal, equal, free, and direct electoral suffrage by secret ballot" (art. 91). It is a majoritarian system, with the outcome decided by overall majorities in single-member constituencies. The functions of the House are to consider draft laws and the other business of government; it must approve the nomination of a prime minister (art. 97); and may deliver a vote of no-confidence on the government (art. 97). The second chamber is the Council of the Republic. It has 64 members, 56 members indirectly elected and 8 members appointed by a president.

Both the House of Representatives and the Council of the Republic have balancing powers. The House of Representatives has the formal power to appoint the Prime Minister of Belarus, make constitutional amendments, call for a vote of confidence on the prime minister and make suggestions on the foreign and domestic policy of Belarus. In addition, each chamber has the ability to veto any law passed by local officials if it is contrary to the Constitution.

In its turn, the Council of the Republic has the power to select various government officials, conduct an impeachment trial of the President and the ability to accept or reject the bills passed from the House of Representatives. The main functions of the Council are the following: making the laws for Belarus; approving the state budget; granting powers to the executive and judicial levels of government; exercising control functions; and even helping carry out foreign policy.

The Constitutional Court of Belarus is the highest court in Belarus. It deals with matters involving the Constitution and the legality of certain laws passed by the government. The court has the power to declare any law unconstitutional. Thus, the Constitutional Court can announce the laws passed by the President unconstitutional and, thus, it could balance the power of the President. However, in reality the Constitutional Court plays according to the rule of Lukashenko. Only from April to May 2007, the Court reviewed 101 decrees and laws and all of them were deemed as constitutional. The Constitutional Court, just like both branches of the Parliament, is the supporter of Lukashenko. However, it could be one of the crucial democratic change agents in the future.

If analyzed from a legal perspective, Belarus could be characterized as a presidential republic, with the balance of power, and some of other democratic norms and principles, such as referendum and elections. However, the political reality is very different from the one described in legal texts and in the Constitution of Belarus.

In an analysis of the overall political situation in Belarus, the contrast between formality and reality is striking. While even the amended constitution of 1996 outlines a number of democratic rights, in practice they are all neglected, ignored and even prohibited and prosecuted. Thus, one can find in Belarus potential democratic change agents rather than real ones, such as political parties of the opposition, civil society organizations, mass media, NGOs, and trade unions that play little role or no role at all in political life of the state.

338

The institutional mechanisms of expressing the will of the population are formally guaranteed by the Constitution. Section 3 of the present Constitution is divided into two chapters dealing with the organization and running of elections. The first chapter of Section 3 deals with the Belarusian electoral system and the second chapter details the organization of national referendums. Both referendum and election could be institutional tools for democratization of Belarus in future.

For example, national referenda are described by the Constitution as elections whereby citizens can determine whether a specific legal text can become official law or not. For this to take place, one of the following conditions must be met: the President wishes to hold one, both houses of the National Assembly request to hold one, or the citizens petition for it. If the National Assembly calls for a plebiscite, a majority is needed in both chambers for it to be official. If the citizens request a plebiscite, they must gather 430,000 signatures from eligible voters across the country. Additionally, over 30,000 people from each region must sign the petition, including the capital Minsk. Once either condition is met, the president *must* issue a decree setting the date of the national plebiscite.

Political parties could be democratic change agents as well. However, their role by now is just as insignificant as that of the Parliament. In Belarus, while there are political parties that either support or oppose President Lukashenko, the majority of the seats in the National Assembly are filled by those not affiliated with any political parties ("non-partisans"). However, there are three political parties who hold seats in the House of Representatives: the Communist Party of Belarus (8 seats), the Agrarian Party of Belarus (3 seats), and the Liberal Democratic Party of Belarus (1 seat). The other two parties that pledged their support to Lukashenko, the Belarusian Socialist Sporting Party and the Republican Party of Labour and Justice, did not secure any seats in October 2004 election.[6]

---

[6] See, for example, "Minsk gotov k peremenam" at http://charter90.org/bel/news/2006/03/07/gotov.

Opposition parties, such as the Belarusian People's Front (BPF) and the United Civil Party of Belarus (UCPB), did not gain any seats. The UCPB and the BPF are some of the parties that comprise the People's Coalition 5 Plus, a group of political parties who oppose Lukashenko. Several organizations, including the OSCE, declared the election un-free due to opposition parties' negative results and the bias of the Belarusian media in favour of the government. However, in constitutional as well as political terms, the House is of marginal importance. At the 2000 election, it took four rounds of voting before all the seats were filled; in the end, 86% of the elected deputies were independent, and the remainder were the representatives of parties traditionally loyal to the President [OSCE, 2000].

However, the OSCE/ODIHR Election Observation Mission reported that the 13–17 October 2004 elections fell significantly short of OSCE commitments. Universal principles and constitutionally guaranteed rights of expression, association and assembly were seriously challenged, calling into question the Belarusian authorities' willingness to respect the concept of political competition on a basis of equal treatment. According to OSCE/ODIHR, principles of an inclusive democratic process, whereby citizens have the right to seek political office without discrimination, candidates to present their views without obstruction, and voters to learn about them and discuss them freely, were largely ignored.

Government restrictions on freedom of speech and the press, peaceful assembly, religions and movement all increased in 2001.[7] Despite the constitutional provisions, a 1998 government decree limited citizens' right to express their own opinion. Although independent media remain widely available in Minsk, the authorities stepped up their campaign of harassment against the independent media. The authorities continued to restrict the right to a free press through near-monopolies on the means of production of newsprint; means of distribution on national level

---

[7] On the role of mass media in democratization, see Obydenkova, 2008a; Obydenkova, 2008b; Obydenkova, 2007; Pastukhov, 2001.

broadcast media, such as television and radio, and by denying accreditation of journalists critical of the regime. Freedom of assembly is restricted under former Soviet law, which is still valid.[8] Belarus has a tight grip controlling the media. Control over the media ranged from monetary fines, confiscation of equipment, and harsh restrictions on independent TV stations by the State Control Committee. In 2003, restrictions grew harsher, giving authorities control to shut down media stations.

The constitution provides for the right of workers – except state security and military personnel – to voluntarily form and join independent unions and to carry out actions in defence of workers' rights, including the right to strike. In practice, however, these rights are again limited. The Belarusian Free Trade Union (BFTU) was established in 1991 and registered in 1992. Following the 1995 Minsk metro workers strike, the President suspended its activities. In 1996 BFTU leaders formed a new umbrella organization, the Belarusian Congress of Democratic Trade Union (BCDTU), which encompasses four leading independent trade unions and is reported to have about 15,000 members.

The Belarusian government is also criticized for human rights violations and its actions against NGOs, independent journalists, national minorities and opposition politicians. During the rule of the current administration in Belarus, there have been several cases of persecution, including the disappearance or death of prominent opposition leaders and independent journalists. NGOs are often closed for minor reasons, usually to do with technical matters. The NGOs most affected are those relating to human rights [see Pershai, 2006; Pastukhov, 2001].

As this observation shows, it is quite difficult to find truly democratic change actors within Belarus. In the case of Belarus it is necessary to distinguish between "internal", or national, agents and "external", or international, ones. It is more complicated to address the issue of *national* "democratic change agents" in the

---

[8] It requires an application at least 15 days in advance of the event. The local government must respond positively or negatively at least 5 days prior to the event. Public demonstrations occurred frequently in 2001, but always under government oversight.

way they are described by Finnemore and Sikkink [1998] as "change agents" or "norm entrepreneurs". The role of president fits perfectly this definition which was elaborated later by Morlino and Magen [2008a] of a "change agent" with the only condition that it is not a democratically oriented change agent. The definition goes as follows: "(democratic) change agents or "norm entrepreneurs" not only mobilize to pressurize decision-makers to adopt (democratic) rules..., but they also engage domestic decision-makers in process of persuasion and social learning to redefine their interests and identities" [parentheses are made by the author]. As far as national democratic agents are concerned, it is difficult indeed to find them within modern Belarus – political parties, Parliament, Constitutional Court and other institutions are meaningless, mass media is suppressed, NGOs and trade unions are almost non-existent. However, the role of *external* democratic change agents presents quite an interesting case study. Among the international agents is, in the first place, the European Union.

4 - International Aspects: Relations with Russia and the EU

International factors played an important role in the regime development in Belarus. Among all other post-Soviet states, Belarus seems to have been most influenced by the interplay of internal and external factors. This interplay is an important factor in the regime transition of any state in general and in post-Soviet context in particular [see Obydenkova, 2008b; 2006; and 2005]. However, the case of Belarus is still unique as it demonstrates high dependence on some external factors. In other words, the understanding of regime formation of Belarus is possible only within the analysis of this interplay, i.e. tight interconnection between national and international politics.

The foreign policy of any state is multi-faceted and complicated. It is not the purpose of this section to go into detail of every aspect of Belarusian foreign policy, but only to outline its main peculiarities. Due to its historical legacy and geopolitical location, the main focal points of foreign policy of Belarus are the relationship with its two biggest neighbours – Russia and the

EU. Belarus foreign policy is balancing between these two geopolitical giants.

4.1 - Russia

From the very beginning of his presidency, Lukashenko sought to develop a closer relationship with Russia. Russia and Belarus signed an association treaty for the two countries that provided for economic and military cooperation and political convergence (1996), agreements on the formation of political union (1997), and on a common united state (1999) [see Deyermond, 2004; Bruce, 2005; Obydenkova, 2008c]. In return for his political loyalty of Belarus, Lukashenko expected to be subsidized economically with low gas prices. In addition, Russia developed strong trade links with Belarus. Due to the structure of Belarusian industry, Belarus relied heavily on Russia both for export markets and for the supply of raw materials and components. The following table demonstrates Russian exports to and imports from Belarus, as compared with a number of other countries throughout in the period from 1995 to 2004.

Table 34. Russia–Belarus: Economic trends of the 1990s and 2000s

	1995	2000	2001	2001	2003	2004
Russian exports (development in %, 1995=100)						
Belarus	100	187.8	183.4	199.7	256.4	375.8
Ukraine	100	70.3	73.9	82.3	106.2	150.7
Poland	100	263.7	248.8	220.4	273.6	337.6
Germany	100	148.7	148.1	129.8	167.8	214.2
US	100	107.6	97.3	92.4	97.5	152.6
Russian imports (development in %, 1995=100)						
Belarus	100	169.8	181.4	182	223.3	295.8
Ukraine	100	55.2	58.1	48.8	67.1	92.1
Poland	100	54.2	72.8	98.4	129.7	174.9
Germany	100	60.1	89.6	101.8	125.0	163.1
US	100	82.8	122.8	112.5	111.7	120.7

Source: Summarized by Federal Service of State Statistics website http://www.gks.ru) and Russian Analytical Digest 04/06, p. 6

The table also demonstrates the striking difference between the changes in imports from and exports to Belarus as compared with the changes to one post-Soviet country (Ukraine), to one

Eastern European state (Poland), Western European one (Germany) and the US. In terms of trade, about a half of Belarusian exports used to flow to Russia. The introduction of free trade between Russia and Belarus in mid-1995 led to a spectacular growth in bilateral trade.

However, Russia's political backing for Belarus was not absolute. Putin's presidency in Russia brought about some changes in Belarus–Russia relations. Putin decided to de-ideologise foreign policy with Belarus and to put it on more pragmatic terms. There were three areas of conflict: (1) finalizing the Constitutional Act creating a Union state and the timeline for its implementation (was drafted and approved during 2005–2006, but was never put to a referendum); (2) adopting a single currency for use in both countries; and (3) raising the price for Russia energy sold to Belarus (from 01/01/2007).

The framework for the Union of Russia and Belarus was set out in the numerous treaties.[9] The integration treaties contained commitments to monetary union, equal rights, single citizenship, and a common defence and foreign policy. However, despite the declarations, the integration was a virtual process and was marked by a number of economic and political conflicts. Belarus was not actually willing to implement these treaties. The main obstacle to the agreed union has been Lukashenko's personal refusal to approve the conversion of the Russian Central Bank into a single emission centre. This would have implied conceding essential aspects of Belarusian sovereignty. No agreement on *implementation* of these treaties was given by Lukashenko [see Deyermond, 2004; Sahm, 2006: 1-3].

During Putin's second term in presidency, Russia aimed to place the bilateral relationship with Belarus purely on principles of market economy. In 2006, both Russian political leadership and Gazprom declared that Belarus should pay "European prices" for gas deliveries from 2007 onwards [see Sahm, 2006: 3; Deyermond,

---

[9] Among these are the Treaty on the Formation of a Community of Russia and Belarus (1996), the Union Charter (1997), and the Treaty of the Formation of a Union State (1999).

2004]. Russia demanded higher prices for its energy supplies and a 50% share in the Belarus gas pipeline monopoly Beltransgaz. Belarus agreed to sell Russia 50% of the stock in Beltransgaz and Russia agreed with the evaluation made by Belarus of the stock in $5 billion and agreed to pay half of this price over the course of four years [see Bruce, 2005 and Aleksandrov, 2007: 12]. The cost of transporting Russian gas also rose.[10]

4.2 - European Union

Following the recognition of Belarus as an independent state in December 1991 by the European Community, EC/EU–Belarus relations initially experienced a steady progress.[11] Belarus signed the Partnership and Cooperation Agreement (PCA) in 1995, thus, committing to political, economic and trade cooperation. Some assistance was provided to Belarus within the framework of the TACIS programme and also through various aid programs and loans. Between 1991 and 1995, fifty million Euros was donated to the improvement of Belarus, in the specific areas of production, distribution, energy, and transport.

Between 1996 and 1999, Belarus was also a beneficiary of the Tempus programme. Tempus was concerned with the academic exchanges between the EU and Belarus, focused on renewing the higher education programs in Belarus, and more specifically reorganized the structure of the system, as well as enhanced areas of study that were essential in improving the Belarusian social and economic life.[12] Tempus also focused on improving the Belarusian education system.

There had been no specific strategies, only some official documents and speeches, such as "The Enlargement of the EU and Possible Consequences for Belarusian Foreign Trade Interests" and "Current Requirements of the EU-Belarus

---

[10] The conflict over gas prices was followed by the conflict over oil prices. Overall, the increase in energy prices increased Belarus trade deficit with Russia, which was $6.2 billion in 2006 [Aleksandrov, 2007: 12].

[11] Commission of the European Communities, European Neighbourhood Policy Strategy Paper 2004, sections 564, 565, 566, 567, 568, 569, 570.

[12] Country Strategic Paper National Indicative Programme: Belarus (2005–2006).

Relations with the EU". After Lukashenko came to power, most of these initiatives were reversed.

The relationship between the EU and Belarus collapsed in 1996 when the EU refused to recognize the results of the referendum which increased the powers of the Belarusian president. The EU did not recognize the 1996 constitution, which replaced the 1994 constitution. The Council of the European Union decided in 1997 to freeze its relationship with Belarus: the PCA was not implemented, nor was its trade-related part; Belarusian membership in the Council of Europe was not supported; bilateral relations at the ministerial level were suspended and EU technical assistance programs were frozen.[13] In addition, the EU did not recognize Lukashenko as the legitimate leader after his term expired in 1999.

Furthermore, the European Union excluded Belarus from its European Neighbourhood Policy (ENP), which was originally designed to establish a "ring of friends" in the Union's geographical proximity.[14] Brussels has claimed this exclusion to be a direct response to the establishment of an authoritarian regime under President Lukashenko.

However, there have still been some initiatives of the EU's attempting to improve the situation in Belarus. Thus, for example, one of the most crucial programs in this period was the Civil Society Development Programme (CSDP). The CSDP, enacted from 2002 to 2003, targeted the development of mass media, civil society, education, NGOs, and democratic institutions. The development of the independent mass media is a particularly important issue within the authoritarian context as it is one of the

---

[13] Acknowledging the lack of progress in relation to bilateral relations and the internal situation following the position adopted in 1997, the EU adopted a step-by-step approach in 1999, whereby sanctions would be gradually lifted upon fulfilment of the four benchmarks set by the Organization for Security and Co-operation in Europe. In 2000, some moderately positive developments toward the implementation of recommendations made by the OSCE were observed but were not sufficient in the realm of access to fair and free elections.

[14] See, for example, Commission of the European Communities, European Neighbourhood Policy Strategy Paper 2004, sections 564, 565, 566, 567, 568, 569, 570.

potential tools of regime turnover towards democratization [see Obydenkova, 2007; 2008b; Mickiewicz, 2008].

Between 2004 and 2006, the EU assisted Belarus in strengthening border control, attempting to decrease the trafficking of people and drugs between Belarus and its neighbouring countries.[15] The improved policies and practices against trafficking and stronger border control led to other policies strengthening laws, such as fighting organized crime. EU-Member states also provided individual assistance to help Belarus better fit the necessary requirements, especially in the areas of civil society, independent media, cultural activities, and youth exchanges.

Belarus's economy is dependent on trade with the EU. Particularly after the spoiling relationship with Russia, Lukashenko became more attentive to the EU. The Belarusian leadership tried to improve its relationship with the EU. Lukashenko made a number of statements about the potential role that Belarus could play in combating illegal migration, blocking drug- and human-trafficking, and the arrival of illegal migrants on EU territory [Aleksandrov, 2007: 13].

However, the major obstacle in the EU–Belarus relationship remains the absence of actual attempts at democratization of the political regime of Belarus on the part of Lukashenko. In addition, the EU still does not recognize the results of Belarus's 2006 presidential election. Thus, the overall relationship between the EU and Belarus remain overall frozen.

4.3 - Alternatives in Foreign Policy of Belarusian Élite

The gas and oil conflicts between Belarus and Russia were the realization of Russia's decision to place its relations with the former Soviet republics in terms of market economy. The main cost of this was important for Belarus as it was virtually deprived of its most significant economic partner and political ally. Belarus has sought to move away from Russia, but it has few

---

[15] See, for example, Country Strategic Paper National Indicative Programme: Belarus (2005–2006).

options because of its poor relations with the West and lack of bilateral ties with other post-Soviet countries.

In contrast, the multilateral participation of Belarus in the parallel integration process within the Commonwealth of Independent States (CIS) was remarkable [Obydenkova, 2008c]. Belarus not only participated in the CIS, but is also involved in a number of other sub-regional forms of cooperation in Post-Soviet space – Single Economic Space (SES), Alma-Ata Declaration, EvrAzEs.[16] A number of structures regulating Belarus-Russia Union State were also established: the Supreme State Council, Permanent Committee, Council of Ministers, etc. Inter-institutional structures were created on the national level (sections for the CIS and Union State within the MFA, a commission for the CIS in Parliament) and inter-institutional level (summits, inter-parliamentary assembly, executive committee, etc.). However, despite the recent crisis in its relationship with Russia over gas prices, Russia remains the largest and most important partner for Belarus both in the political and economic fields [Deyermond, 2004].

In a new turn, the Belarusian leadership has increased its contacts with Azerbaijan, Ukraine and tries to improve its relationship with Poland and the Baltic countries. Belarus also has signed a contract with Venezuela to jointly develop a Venezuelan oil deposit [Aleksandrov, 2007: 13]. Belarus also tries to establish long-term economic and military collaboration with China [Ibid.]. Beijing signed a number of different agreements with defence enterprises in Belarus and named Belarus its strategic partner. However, despite all recent changes in foreign policy of Minsk, Russia still remains the most

---

[16] Institutional mechanisms regulating Belarus' participation in the post-Soviet cooperation were much better developed. Within the Ministry of Foreign Affairs (MFA), new departments were established: the Department for Russia and the Union State, the Department for CIS and EvrAzEs. A permanent commission for international affairs and relations with the CIS was also created. A number of inter-organizational structures have appeared, e.g. only within the CIS are Council of Heads of States/Governments, Council of Ministers, Inter-parliamentary Assembly CIS [see Obydenkova, 2008c].

important partner of Belarus in trade, and its most influential political ally. Belarus is still dependent on Russian economy, trade, and political leadership.

5 - Conclusion

There are a number of factors which have contributed to the formation of the non-democratic regime in Belarus. The first one is the very short period of real independence of Belarus as a state (only nine months) and the legacy of totalitarian regime. The second factor was the political apathy of the population and, as a result of low turnover at the election, a weak parliament. The degree of political competition and contestation during the early 1990s was also very low. Another reason was the institutional selection in the early period of transition in the 1990s, which also contributed to the formation of a strong presidency and weak parliament.

The period 1991–1994 was marked by political and institutional stagnation. The political opposition was weak and lacked the necessary popularity among people. Soviet nomenclature remained in power all through the transition period. All this resulted in institutional stagnation, absence of reforms, and the absence of any pro-reform initiative coming from the Parliament in Belarus. The last factor is one of the most important explanatory variables in different outcomes of regime transition in Belarus and, for example, in Ukraine. The introduction of Lukashenko's new reforms only reinforced the enormous power of the president vis-à-vis Parliament. Lukashenko eliminated political opposition through the dissolution of Parliament and replaced "challenging" deputies with the more "tolerant" ones, thus, depriving the opposition of any power. In contrast, in Ukraine the opposite trend took place. The 1996 Constitution of Ukraine limited the powers of the executive branch and strengthened the Parliament. It allowed for further pro-democratic development of the state. In contrast to Belarus, the Ukrainian president became accountable to Parliament.

Another important factor is the widely spread pro-Russian mood of the population in Belarus. This makes the case of Belarus quite different from other post-Soviet states. The idea of union with Russia was the main issue of pre-electoral campaigns of the two most popular candidates for presidency in the election of 1994 – Kubevich and Lukashenko [Ioffe, 2003; Goujon, 1999]. This is an important factor which makes a crucial difference once Belarus is compared with, for example, Ukraine and Moldova. The people of the last two states were far less supportive of the role of Russia in their national politics and economy. On the contrary, both Ukraine and Moldova are marked by increasing nationalism. This nationalist mood was also quite strong in all Caucasian and Central Asian post-Soviet states.

What sort of hybrid regime was Belarus? It is difficult to classify the case of Belarus and to put it in the specific group of hybrid regimes. The reason is that Belarus was a fluctuating regime; it had a short period which can properly be described as hybrid, in the beginning of the 1990s, and a further development of the regime was consolidation of the authoritarian regime. It can be concluded that the case of Belarus sustains two main hypotheses: that institutional inertia of the previous regime plays an important role in the formation of a hybrid regime, and that "the survival of authoritarian veto players (as Lukashenko) points towards a single solution"; in the case of Belarus that is a protected autocracy [see Morlino, this volume].

The case of Belarus also contributes to the studies of regime transition by highlighting the importance of the international context. Initially Belarus enjoyed the same status within the programmes of the EU targeted at post-Soviet states. However, it became isolated from Europe after the constitutional change of 1996, which was not recognized by the EU as a democratic reform. At the same time, its main partner was neighbouring Russia, which provided for political and economic support. Thus, the case of Belarus is probably the best example among all other post-Soviet states which demonstrates the importance of the interplay of national and international factors.

Since independence, Georgia has alternated between two types of hybrid regime: that which is described by Morlino [this volume] as a "democracy without law" and that which is defined as "limited democracy". The first of these two types would be the most accurate label during the period 1992-95, when the newly-returned Head of State Eduard Shevardnadze had yet to fully consolidate his authority and rival cliques of former communists, nationalists and mafia groups vied for control of the state apparatus. It could also probably be applied to the period 2001-2003, when President Shevardnadze's political party, the Citizens Union of Georgia (CUG), had splintered and the government, the parliament and even the presidential administration itself was driven by factionalism and was no longer capable of governing. Throughout the rest of Georgia's post-independence history, while political parties and other interest groups have been legal and have been able to operate reasonably freely, the presidential administration and its associated "party of power" (first the CUG under Shevardnadze and subsequently the United National Movement under his successor Mikheil Saakashvili) have deployed extensive administrative resources to ensure that neither parliamentary nor presidential elections are truly competitive, effectively foreclosing the possibility of a rotation of power through the ballot box. During these periods, Georgia would qualify better as a "limited democracy."

In this chapter I argue that the way the political regime in Georgia developed depended both on institutional and other structural legacies from the past and on the way state and society were reconfigured during the early years of independence [see Bunce and Wolchik, this volume]. The chapter begins by tracing the evolution of the Georgian regime from the last days of communism to the presidency of Mikheil Saakashvili and then goes on to identify a number of structural and conjunctural factors that explain why the regime has evolved in the way it has.

1 - Legacies of Communist Rule

The organizational legacy of the Soviet state had a major impact on the formation of new political regimes in all former Soviet republics during the 1990s. The organizational structure of state and Communist Party organs in the USSR was marked by the near subordination of the former to the latter. While the ministries would carry out the day-to-day implementation of Party policy, they would operate under the close supervision of the relevant department of the Communist Party Central Committee [Simis, 1982: 13-21]. This would apply at all-Union level (i.e. at the level of the USSR), at republican level and even at local level. Similarly, the representative bodies (soviets) at all levels would merely rubber stamp the decisions made by the relevant Party organs. At each level, all-Union, republican and local, the Communist Party leadership (personified in the first secretary of the relevant party organ) would have the final say about the decisions that were to be taken. As we shall see later on in the chapter, by the mid-1990s the presidential administration in Georgia had begun to take on very many of the same features as the Communist Party had previously.

Another Soviet organizational legacy was the administrative-territorial structure of each republic. This structure was based on the principle of ethno federalism. According to this principle, the USSR was divided territorially into a hierarchical system of administrative units and sub-units. At the top of the hierarchy were the fifteen union republics, which enjoyed the formal right to secede from the USSR, even though this was not a feasible scenario until the very last days of Communist rule. Other smaller regions or sub-units that were deemed to "belong" to a particular nationality were given the status of "autonomous republic," "autonomous *oblast* (province)" or "national *okrug* (district)" – in descending order of autonomy – within a given union republic.

These regions were typically established as "national homelands" for a particular national group or (in rare cases) a religious group. Each union republic was entitled to its own flag, its own language, its own administrative structure, and its own "official" culture. Autonomous republics and autonomous provinces were also granted most of these attributes but not the right to secede. By 1990, there were also twenty autonomous republics, ten autonomous *okrugs* and eight autonomous *oblasts*. The Soviet state collapsed along the fault-lines of this federal structure as all fifteen union republics became independent and many of the sub-units (autonomous republics and autonomous *oblasts*) began demanding greater autonomy from their union republics. Georgia contained within its territorial structure two autonomous republics (Abkhazia and Adjara) and one autonomous *oblast* (South Ossetia). This division would be crucial to the reconfiguration of state power in the 1990s.

Also highly relevant in terms of legacies are the attitudinal norms that were prevalent amongst the Soviet political and economic élite, which were framed by the principle of the arbitrary exercise of power by rulers over the ruled. The concept of the "dictatorship of the proletariat", as formulated by Lenin and Stalin, was the "rule – unrestricted by law and based on force – of the proletariat over the bourgeoisie" [Jowitt, 1992: 66]. While the principle of arbitrary repression over society reached its apogee during the purges of the late 1930s and later began to dwindle, the fulfilment of goals set by the Party leadership continued to take precedence over the observance of the law. This particularly applied to the industrial and agricultural sectors, where over-centralization and over-regulation meant that the fulfilment of plans and production targets depended on the ability of economic managers to "bend the rules", i.e. to circumvent the laws and decrees emanating from Moscow. Very often this would involve informal deals with other actors in the sector or with Party officials whose job it was to supervise state enterprises. As a result, economic actors found that they could break the rules with relative impunity, providing they gained the connivance of the local Party boss. By the 1980s corrupt practices pervaded the entire hierarchy of the Communist Party of the Soviet

Union (SU).[1] Over time, the ubiquity of rule-breaking and corruption came to be used as an instrument of control that was exploited by power brokers as those in charge of supervising Soviet industry, most notably Party bosses, were able to blackmail those they supervised by collecting compromising material or *kompromat* on them. The instrument of blackmail against the backdrop of ubiquitous and unavoidable rule-breaking was used by superiors to ensure the loyalty and obedience of subordinates and reinforced the hierarchical and arbitrary nature of power relations within party and state élite [Gregory, 1989: 521; Simis, 1982: 44-45].

Another legacy of the Soviet period was the lack of autonomy of civil society. Although there were a plethora of cultural, youth and sports associations, these were no more than auxiliary organizations of the all-pervasive Communist Party and had no autonomous existence outside the Party. In the SU there was no effective civil society because the totalitarian legacy meant that there was no room for the kind of social discourse that would allow for the independent articulation of group interests and the development of the kind of social and political identities that form the basis of a strong civil society or a stable party system [Hanf and Nodia, 2000: 44-45]. Moreover, the Party state had done everything in its power to *eradicate* social subsystems that were independent of it. The only form of collective identity that was unwittingly reinforced by the Soviet system was ethnic identity. In parallel with the territorial division of the Soviet Union outlined above was a bureaucratic classification of individual citizens in which an individual's nationality was registered in his or her passport and could even determine where he or she was allowed to live and work. Nationality had become, in Brubaker's words, "an obligatory ascribed status" [Brubaker, 1996: 18] and in the 1990s would come to form the basis for "uncivil" rather than "civil" society.

---

[1] Georgia's ruling elite under First Secretary V.P. Mzhavanadze blatantly sold ministerial posts until Mzhavanadze's dismissal in 1972. Mzhavadnadze's wife is also believed to have been involved in the illicit smuggling of precious stones [see Simis, 1982: 34–43].

Turning now to specific legacies, Georgia was one of those republics of the USSR in which nationalist discourse became increasingly prevalent even within official cultural organizations such as the Georgian Writers' Union.[2] During the 1970s a small but active dissident movement began to campaign against perceived cultural Russification. Like in the Baltic republics and Armenia, but in contrast to the Central Asian republics and Belarus, popular demonstrations demanding increased sovereignty (and eventually independence) from the USSR began to take hold as restrictions on freedom of expression were lifted in the late 1980s. Georgia's national liberation movement, led by intellectuals, former dissidents and even criminals, would pose an insurmountable challenge for the Georgian Communist Party at the close of the 1980s.

2 - An Open-Ended Transition: From Gamsakhurdia to Saakashvili

2.1 – The Rise and Fall of Gamsakhurdia

The events of 1989-92 were characterized by a progressive fragmentation of state organizations within Georgia that would have major implications for the kind of regime that would emerge afterwards. This chain of events was set in motion on 9 April 1989 when Soviet forces violently dispersed a pro-independence demonstration in Tbilisi that had been organized by former dissidents, leaving nineteen people dead and hundreds injured. This move backfired spectacularly as recriminations led to the resignation of Georgian Party boss, Jumber Patiashvili, and the Communist Party lost all vestiges of legitimacy in the eyes of a large majority of the population. As a result, the *de facto* coalition that developed in the Baltic republics between a reformist communist leadership and the leaders of a broad national

---

[2] For example, there was uproar at the Eighth Congress of the Georgian Writers' Union in April 1976, when one well-known delegate to the conference, Revaz Japaridze, drew tumultuous applause for a forceful speech fiercely critical of a suggestion by the Georgian Minister of Education that school subjects be taught in Russian. Even Georgian First Secretary Eduard Shevardnadze was heckled by the writers when he attempted to calm the situation [Suny, 1988: 309].

movement (or Popular Front) was not possible in Georgia, where any form of compromise with the authorities came to be seen by nationalist leaders as treachery. As a result, the national opposition became highly radicalized and moderate voices were completely sidelined, making it no longer possible to create a Popular Front along Baltic lines [Wheatley, 2005: 45]. In contrast to the Baltic republics, it was the *radical* opposition that gained the upper hand in Georgia, not the (relative) moderates.

By 1990, momentum in public rallies had swung behind one of the leaders of the radical opposition, literature professor Zviad Gamsakhurdia, who championed the interests of ethnic Georgians and demanded Georgia's independence from the USSR. However, unlike the Popular Fronts in the Baltic republics, Gamsakhurdia was not able to unite Georgia's national liberation movement. A divisive figure, he alienated both moderate intellectuals and fellow dissidents Giorgi Chanturia and Irakli Tsereteli, both of whom had established their own political parties (the National Democratic Party and the National Independence Party respectively). When Gamsakhurdia's "Round Table-Free Georgia" bloc defeated the incumbent Communists in elections to the Georgian Supreme Soviet on 28 October 1990, Chanturia and Tsereteli did not participate in the elections having elected instead their own alternative body, the National Congress. The National Congress had armed support; it was backed by Jaba Ioseliani, the leader of an infamous paramilitary organization called the *Mkhedrioni* (Horsemen). The fragmentation of anti-communist forces and the increasing militarization of society would lead to Gamsahkhurdia's defeat after just fourteen months by an unlikely alliance of former communist nomenclature, intellectuals, paramilitary groups and his former "comrades in arms" from the National Congress. Gamsakhurdia fled Tbilisi on 6 January 1992. His legacy was a bitter civil war in the autonomous region of South Ossetia (see the following paragraph), where mobilization by Georgian military units to "liberate" ethnic Georgians living in the region from the control of the Ossetian élite in January 1991 had led to an equally fierce counter-mobilization by Ossetians. The war only ended in July 1992, after Georgia had lost most of the territory of South Ossetia to Ossetian separatists.

2.2 – The Return of Shevardnadze

Following Gamsakhurdia's ouster, real power rested with the paramilitary leaders who had forced him out and who had control of many of the weapons that had been bought or stolen from Soviet military depots as the USSR collapsed. First among equals were Ioseliani, whose *Mkhedrioni* enjoyed the unswerving loyalty of a generation of young men, and Tengiz Kitovani, whose National Guard had originally been loyal to Gamsakhurdia but had split from the former leader when he had attempted to subordinate it to the Ministry of Internal Affairs. A splinter group of the National Guard, still loyal to Gamsakhurdia, controlled much of western Georgia and other smaller armed groups (some affiliated to nationalist political parties) also roamed freely.

It was against this backdrop that, under Ioseliani's initiative, the paramilitary leaders decided to invite former first secretary of the Georgian Communist Party Eduard Shevardnadze back to Georgia to chair a newly-formed State Council, which was set up to run the now independent republic until new elections could be held. As it was the intention of the paramilitary leaders that Shevardnadze should be no more than a figurehead to attract foreign donor money, the latter was unable to consolidate his authority in the short term, or even halt the continuing fragmentation of his country. In August 1992, Georgian forces entered Abkhazia under Kitovani's initiative, purportedly to clear western Georgia of pro-Gamsakhurdia militias (called Zviadists) and to rescue top officials who had been taken hostage, but the real aim was to wrest authority from the ethnic Abkhaz élite that now had almost full control over the autonomous republic and to grab the lucrative economic resources that Abkhazia possessed (most notably tourism and agricultural products such as citrus fruit). Like the war over South Ossetia, the war over Abkhazia was lost by the Georgian side; in September 1993 Georgian forces were driven out of the Abkhaz capital Sukhumi and most ethnic Georgians were forced to flee the autonomous republic.

Following this defeat, Kitovani and Ioseliani's power began to ebb away and Shevardnadze began to consolidate his authority. Most importantly, he reinforced and revitalized the old Georgian

358

Ministry of Internal Affairs (MoIA), of which the police were the most visible and influential part. As a union-republic ministry during the Soviet period[3], the MoIA had not been "decapitated" by the collapse of the Soviet state and could therefore be restored relatively easily. In September 1993 he dismissed Ioseliani's *protégé* as Minister of Internal Affairs and, after briefly occupying the post himself, appointed a loyalist, the former KGB general Shota Kviraia, as minister. In re-establishing the police as the major source of coercive authority, Shevardnadze was often forced to co-opt members of paramilitary groups into the force. However, from 1995, the MoIA remained loyal to the president, both under Kviraia, and under his powerful successor, Kakha Targamadze (minister from 1995-2001), under whose stewardship the MoIA was to gain a reputation for corruption and extortion.

Shevardnadze was attempting to consolidate control over an élite that was both deeply divided and fragmented. It was divided geographically in the sense that Abkhazia and South Ossetia had effectively broken away and Adjara was controlled by a local leader whose loyalty to the centre was questionable (see below), and at the same time it was fragmented into rival patronage networks. The fragmentation of the élite had accelerated during the last days of communist rule and during the Gamsakhurdia period, and power was now dispersed among patriotic and nationalist militias, networks of former Soviet power brokers and elements of the former Soviet security forces. This fragmentation and division meant that Shevardnadze was not able to establish full hegemonic control, and the partial regime consolidation that did occur would inevitably be based on factional pluralism.

Once he had re-established the MoIA as a (more or less) effective instrument of state coercion, defeated the paramilitaries and established a degree of control over most regions,

---

[3] In the USSR there were two categories of ministries: all-Union ministries and Union-republican ministries. All-Union ministries had no counterparts at republican level. The Ministry of Defence was an all-Union ministry. Union-republican ministries, on the other hand, existed at the level of the republic, although they also had their counterparts at all-Union level, which would exercise a supervisory role.

Shevardnadze's position was far more secure. He now sought to reactivate the old networks (Party, Komsomol[4] and police) with which he was familiar during his time as First Secretary. These networks were to form the basis of the state administration both in the capital and in the regions. He also placed Georgia's most important economic assets (most notably the banking sector) into the hands of a group of trusted associates, most of whom were close to his own family. The formal landmark that defined Shevardnadze's (partial) consolidation of power was the passage of the new Georgian Constitution in August 1995. The Constitution abolished the post of prime minister and Shevardnadze occupied the newly (re-)established post of president, winning the November 1995 presidential elections with almost 75% of the vote.[5]

Another tool Shevardnadze used to consolidate his authority both within his rudimentary state bureaucracy and within the fractious parliament was the establishment of the CUG as a "party of power". The CUG was set up in November 1993 by Shevardnadze and the reform-minded leader of the Green Party, Zurab Zhvania (see below). It was a "broad church" that out of necessity would include most of the key players in Georgia, including former communist apparatchiks, intellectuals and young pro-western reformers. The logic of establishing a "party of power" was in many ways predicated on the model of the old Communist Party with which Shevardnadze was clearly familiar. It was, in a sense, a de-ideologized reproduction of the old Party.

After the passage of the Georgian Constitution in 1995, power rested primarily with the presidential administration or State Chancellery. Instead of a prime minister, there was a state minister, who was also the head of the State Chancellery. From 1995-98 this post was held by Nikoloz Lekishvili and from 1998-2000 by Vazha Lortkipanidze. Both men had held leading

---

[4] KOMSOMOL refers to the official communist youth organization, the Communist Youth League (KOMmunistichieskii SOiuz MOLodiozhi in Russian).
[5] Shevardnadze had been made head of State by the Georgian Parliament in November 1992 after having been elected as Chairman of Parliament unopposed by popular suffrage in the elections of October 1992.

positions in both the Communist Party and Komsomol structures and both had large networks of former Party and Komsomol associates on which they could draw. The State Chancellery, although it had little power on paper, very much resembled the old Central Committee; its departments, and even the individuals who manned them, were in many ways a reproduction of the old Party bureaucracy.[6]

By the end of 1995, Shevardnadze had all but eliminated the paramilitaries. In late 1993 he had pledged that Georgia would join the Commonwealth of Independent States (CIS) – which the country's leaders had hitherto refused to join – to win the backing of Russian President Boris Yeltsin, and used both military force and the threat of Russian military intervention to defeat Gamsakhurdia's supporters in western Georgia. Tengiz Kitovani was arrested in January 1995, after leading a faction of some one thousand lightly-armed supporters in a quixotic attempt to retake Abkhazia. Ioseliani was also arrested following an assassination attempt against Shevardnadze in August 1995. By the end of 1995, the National Guard and the *Mkhedrioni* had been effectively neutralized.

Although Shevardnadze had made major steps towards consolidating his authority after the chaos of the early 1990s, the high degree of fractionalization within the political élite meant that he was never able to complete this process of consolidation and was forced to retain power by maintaining a delicate balance between various alliances of actors with conflicting aims. These included his own inner circle of family and close associates, as well as various networks of former Communist Party bosses and

---

[6] Within the State Chancellery, one of the most powerful posts was that of secretary of the Security Council, held by Nugzar Sajaia from the Council's inception in 1996 until his suicide on 25 February 2002. The Security Council was chaired by the President and consisted of eight other members, including the State Minister, the Foreign Minister, the Defence Minister, the State Security Minister and the Minister of Internal Affairs. Its task was to oversee all matters of defence and security. Sajaia had previously held equivalent posts in the Communist Party of Georgia; he had been head of the department of administrative structures and later head of the department of organizational Party work in the Central Committee of the Georgian Communist party.

Komsomol activists and Zhvania's "Young Turks". Meanwhile, the autonomous republic of Adjara remained firmly under the control of Aslan Abashidze, a local potentate, who had been appointed by Gamsakhurdia but had not called for the separation of Adjara from the rest of Georgia. Shevardnadze also had no control whatsoever over the former autonomous territories of Abkhazia and South Ossetia, which had been lost during the civil wars of the early 1990s. Inevitably his balancing act was not to last forever.

Given the plurality of power centres with which he was forced to reckon after he returned to Georgia, Shevardnadze sought allies from outside his immediate circle. Aware of the need to attract much-needed foreign capital into the country, he encouraged the emergence of a younger group of politicians into the limelight. The key figure he brought in was Zhvania, who in November 1993 helped him establish the CUG (see above). After the CUG won the largest number of seats in the 1995 parliamentary elections, Zhvania was elected Chairman of Parliament. He brought into the CUG leadership and into parliament a number of like-minded associates, most of whom were young English speakers who had close ties to western-based international organizations and western universities. Amongst this group was Mikheil Saakashvili, a Columbia University Law specialist whom Zhvania had invited back from the US. Although former nomenklatura figures close to Shevardnadze dominated the CUG in the regions, the parliamentary leadership of the party was drawn mainly from Zhvania's and Saakashvili's associates.

Nevertheless, this "power-sharing agreement" was a precarious one; Zhvania's camp could find little common ground with Shevardnadze's former Party appointees and at times entered into open conflict with Aslan Abashidze, who set up his own electoral bloc to challenge the CUG in the 1999 parliamentary elections. Shevardnadze sought to placate Abashidze by assuring him that he would retain control over Adjara's (mainly informal) economy and by promising to enshrine the words "autonomous republic of Adjara" in the Georgian constitution. Moreover, Shevardnadze felt instinctively closer to his old comrades than to the "young pretenders". Following his re-election as president in 2000 with the help of significant electoral fraud (after Abashidze had withdrawn his candidature at the last minute as a result of the president's assurances), the president appeared to rely more and more on his own inner circle and on the various networks of former Communist Party and Komsomol officials. This led to the increasing alienation of Zhvania's supporters.

Matters came to a head in September 2001, when Saakashvili resigned as Minister of Justice, after having publicly accused a number of state officials of corruption. Almost simultaneously Shevardnadze left his position as Chairman of the CUG, a post he had held since 1993. On 1 November, Zurab Zhvania resigned as Chairman of Parliament after a bungled attempt by officials from the Ministry for State Security to raid the premises of the independent television station, Rustavi-2 (which supported Zhvania and Saakashvili's camp), ostensibly on the pretext that the company owed the state unpaid taxes. The CUG then began to disintegrate and Zhvania and Saakashvili went into opposition. Shevardnadze dismissed their associates from government positions and henceforth relied on an ever narrower circle for support. Above all, these consisted of trusted associates and family friends. In late 2001, he appointed as state minister Avtandil Jorbenadze, who was close to his family. In 2002 he merged the Ministries of Finance and Tax and Revenues, both of which had been briefly under the control of Zhvania's associates, and put Mirian Gogiashvili, the son of an old friend, in charge of the new merged ministry. Finally after Kakha Targamadze had resigned simultaneously with Zhvania following the incident over Rustavi-2, the new Minister of Internal Affairs was Koba Narchemashvili, who – according to press reports – was the godson of Shevardnadze's wife, Nanuli.[7]

By 2003, the process of power consolidation that Shevardnadze had undertaken with a considerable degree of success in the 1990s had gone into reverse gear. Gradually, his hold on the

[7] "Khaburzania and Narchemashvili – New Members of the President's Team", in *Civil Georgia: Online Magazine* (Main Topic, 23 November 2001) at www.civil.ge.

political and economic levers of power weakened. His family no longer had full control over the country's economy as more independent players – most notably the business tycoon, Badri Patarkatsishvili, who had made large sums of money in the oil, automobile and media business in Russia – began to buy up real estate and media outlets in Georgia. Moreover, power – and significant financial resources – had accrued to the third sector, which mainly consisted of foreign sponsored NGOs. This sector was strongly supported by Saakashvili and Zhvania, who now appeared to represent a viable opposition force (even though they had formed separate opposition parties). Moreover, following the collapse of the CUG, Shevardnadze could barely cobble together a majority in parliament. His élite was now not only totally disengaged from society, but also disconnected from much of the strata of political actors, bureaucrats and intelligentsia that had supported him ten years previously.

2.3 – Saakashvili at the Helm

After the peaceful protests (known as the Rose Revolution) that forced Shevardnadze from office after flawed parliamentary elections in November 2003, political posts were divvied up amongst supporters of the "triumvirate" that had led the protests – Mikheil Saakashvili, Zurab Zhvania and parliamentary chairperson Nino Burjanadze – with Saakashvili's and Zhavania's supporters coming to wield far more influence that Burjanadze's. The presidency (to which Saakashvili was elected in January 2004) remained the principal locus of state power and, despite the abolition of the State Chancellery, probably became even more powerful than it was before. Even on paper, the powers of the president were boosted; as a result of constitutional amendments passed in February 2004, he now had the right to order the preterm dissolution of parliament – a right that Shevardnadze had never had. At the same time, the post of prime minister was (re)created and given to Zurab Zhvania. The cabinet that took shape in 2004 was roughly equally divided between those loyal to Zhvania and those aligned with Saakashvili. Most were young and oriented towards the West, many having worked or studied abroad or having been involved in Georgian NGOs or international donor organizations. In November 2004, Saakashvili's party, the National Movement, and Zhvania's United Democrats united to form the United National Movement (UNM) after having won a large majority of seats (and 66% of the vote) as a single electoral bloc in repeat parliamentary elections held in March. The UNM was fashioned as a "ruling party" in much the same way as the CUG before it. Within the twenty-member ruling council, Saakashvili's supporters had ten members, Zhvania's supporters, eight, and Burjanadze's supporters, two. The parliamentary chairperson, Nino Burjanadze, did not formally join the party although she pledged her support for it.

After Zhvania's untimely death in February 2005, power at national level fell into the hands of a number of closely-knit networks of young, mainly western-educated friends and associates of Saakashvili's from western-funded NGOs or international organizations, as well as former colleagues with whom he had worked during his time as Justice Minister. In particular, an influential network made up of figures who had previously run the "Open Society—Georgia Foundation" (Soros Foundation) and an NGO called the Liberty Institute rose to prominence. These individuals had actively planned the Rose Revolution and had helped mobilize the population for Shevardnadze's overthrow. The most prominent amongst them were Kakha Lomaia, Minister for Education and former head of the Soros Foundation, as well as Giga Bokeria and Givi Targamadze, previously of the Liberty Institute, who had both entered parliament in 2004. They were also close associates of Minister of Internal Affairs Vano Merabishvili, who had himself been the head of an NGO in the late 1990s. The influence of these individuals did not derive so much from their official positions, but from the close connections they developed with Saakashvili as a result of their work in the NGO sector during the Shevardnadze period. By 2006 Bokeria and Targamadze dominated parliament through their control over the UNM, wielding more informal influence even than parliamentary chairperson Nino Burjanadze. Saakashvili's reliance on close networks of associates carried with it certain risks, as it had for Shevardnadze. The promotion of one network over and above all others led to the disillusionment and defection of many of Saakashvili's erstwhile allies, including Salome Zourabishvili, foreign minister from 2004 to 2005, Gogi Khaindrava, State Minister for Conflict Resolution from 2004 to 2006, Irakli Okruashvili, briefly Minister for Internal Affairs and then defence minister from 2004 to 2006, and Koba Davitashvili, a former close ally of Saakashvili's who had occupied the number one slot in the party list of the National Movement in the disputed November 2003 parliamentary elections. Moreover, over a dozen members of parliament who had been elected in repeat parliamentary elections in 2004 through the National Movement's party list left the party. These disaffected former members of Saaakashvili's entourage formed the core of a burgeoning opposition movement.

By October 2007, amid popular disillusionment towards Saakashvili's autocratic style and perceived economic inequalities, this opposition managed to bring over 50,000 protesters out onto the streets of Tbilisi in sustained protests that at times seemed to threaten the very survival of the government. After the protests had been quelled by the imposition of a nine-day state of emergency in November, Saakashvili faced criticism both internally and externally over the manner in which this had been done (which included the beating up of opposition leaders and the destruction of the premises of the main opposition television channel, Imedi).

As a result of the November events, Saakashvili was forced into a temporary tactical retreat. He declared pre-term presidential elections for 5 January 2008 and, in his bid to secure re-election· moved some of his more unpopular associates to less prominent positions.[8] However, following a disputed victory in the presidential elections in which official figures gave him victory in the first round with 53.41% of the vote but the opposition claimed that he had won by electoral fraud, he felt that he could re-assert his authority. As opposition unity foundered and street protests dwindled, the UNM used its two-thirds majority in parliament to pass constitutional changes to reduce the number of MPs elected proportionally from 150 to 75 (while preserving all 75 seats elected in single mandate constituencies) in a deliberate attempt to ensure the ruling party the maximum number of seats in the forthcoming parliamentary elections. This move was taken unilaterally without opposition support. Buoyed by the administrative resources it had at its disposal and by disarray within opposition ranks, the UNM won the parliamentary elections held on 21 May 2008 with 59.18% of the vote and 119 out of 150 seats. The opposition denounced the vote as fraudulent and most opposition members of the Parliament (MPs) boycotted the new parliament.

Saakashvili's election victories filled him with a new sense of confidence, which may have prompted him into making his ill-fated attempt to regain control over the breakaway enclave of South Ossetia on the night of 7 August 2008. It would appear likely that the political leadership in the Russian Federation had prepared for the eventuality of war in South Ossetia and had made strategic military contingencies with this end in mind. In many ways it would seem that the Russian leadership had goaded Saakashvili into launching a military assault on the enclave so that Russia could subsequently reinforce its grip on both South Ossetia and Abkhazia. However, most observers also agree that Saakashvili's decision to launch a military attack on Tskhinvali on the night of 7 August was ill thought-out and foolhardy. The result was the deaths of around six hundred people on both Georgian and South Ossetian sides and the

---

[8] He removed Lomaia from the Cabinet and appointed him instead as head of the National Security Council. Bokeria was made deputy minister for foreign affairs—a relatively low-ranking position.

temporary occupation by Russian troops of broad swathes of Georgian territory. Large numbers of Russian troops remain in Abkhazia and South Ossetia, and following the Russian Federation's decision to recognize the "independence" of the two enclaves in late August 2008, both remain under the firm control of Moscow.

Although the country rallied around Saakashvili in the short term and even opposition leaders put aside their differences with the Georgian president during the seven-week period of Russian occupation, questions soon began to be asked about Saakashvili's role in starting the hostilities. Opposition protests resumed in November 2008, and intensified in April 2009 with permanent rallies staged outside parliament and other strategic locations.

3 - Explaining Georgia's Hybrid Regime

In Georgia, the nationalist élite that challenged the communist authorities during the last few years of communist rule were strong, but at the same time radicalized and highly fragmented internally. On assuming power, Gamsakhurdia's new élite were faced with counter-mobilization from the side of the élite of the two ethnic enclaves. As a result, the new regime could not consolidate and remained highly fragmented, leading to the near collapse of state power as civil war engulfed the country. Eduard Shevardnadze, the seasoned Soviet power-broker, was able to put the bits and pieces together to a certain extent by relying on the power of clientelist networks that he had inherited from the communist period, but was never able to achieve complete consolidation. His successor, Mikheil Saakashvili, had more success in consolidating power, but his reliance on a narrow circle of advisors led to poor decision-making, culminating in the disastrous conflict with Russia over South Ossetia, which undermined his credibility both amongst his own citizens and amongst his American and Western European allies.

This brief vignette of Georgia's political development since 1988 highlights the role of three factors that have proved crucial to Georgia's transition: the role of élite actors, most notably the extent to which the élite is factionalized; the role of institutions, both formal and informal, that determine the incentive structures in which political actors operate; and finally, the role of the international community in providing leverage over Georgian political leaders to prevent an authoritarian consolidation of power.

Turning first to the role of élite, experience in the post-Soviet space shows that outside the Baltic republics, where a democratic system was installed relatively rapidly, the consolidation of power by one or other élite faction normally leads to the establishment of an authoritarian regime. Such a process occurred in the Central Asian republics, Azerbaijan, Belarus and, most recently, Russia. Hybrid regimes in post-Soviet countries such as Georgia, Ukraine and Moldova are most often the result of the incapacity of leaders to consolidate power. These regimes exhibit what Lucan Way describes as *pluralism by default* in which "political competition survives not because leaders are especially democratic or because societal actors are particularly strong, but because the government is too fragmented and the state too weak to impose authoritarian rule in a democratic international context" [Way, 2002: 127]. This state of affairs often proves temporary (as in the Russian Federation), and can give way to a more authoritarian system when one faction of the political élite is able to impose its hegemony over all others. In this section I will assume that the successful consolidation of power by the political élite or some faction thereof in a post-Soviet setting is likely to result in increased authoritarianism.

The chain of events that led to Gamsakhurdia's victory and his subsequent overthrow are of crucial importance to the subsequent evolution of the Georgian political élite. First of all, the disastrous decision made by the communist authorities in Georgia (with the backing of Moscow) to use disproportionate force against demonstrators on 9 April 1989 prevented the establishment of a *de facto* coalition between reform-minded communist leaders and a broad-based and (relatively) moderate Popular Front of the sort that existed in the Baltic republics. While in the Baltic republics the Popular Front was allowed to organize and develop into a relatively coherent organization, in Georgia compromise between the communist authorities and the opposition became impossible after 9

April and there was no space for any moderate opposition. Instead the radical opposition dictated the pace of events, and derived its momentum from the support it obtained in street rallies through the populist rhetoric of Gamsakhurdia and other radical leaders. However, it lacked organizational capacity, and ultimately broke apart due to the conflicting ambitions of its leaders. Even the conflicts that occurred in the periphery (i.e. in South Ossetia and Abkhazia) were partly predicated by the emergence and subsequent fragmentation of the radical opposition at the centre; the war in South Ossetia was partly triggered by Gamsakhurdia's single-minded campaign to integrate South Ossetia into the rest of the country and to break the power of the local élite, while the war in Abkhazia began in the wake of the total collapse in state power that occurred in the aftermath of Gamsakhurdia's downfall. The way communist system in Georgia broke down therefore had a major impact on the subsequent configuration of the Georgian political élite and the capacity of the new leaders to restore state power.

The events set in motion by the breakdown of communist rule led to a situation of "pluralism by default" in which the political élite was fragmented and no single part had the capacity to consolidate power over other parts. This situation prevailed throughout the first half of the 1990s. While Shevardnadze was eventually able to achieve a partial consolidation of power in the late 1990s, the coalition that united the ruling CUG was necessarily a broad one and began to fall apart in 2001, in the second year of Shevardnadze's second term as president. The high degree of political competition and contestation during the transition had thus made it impossible for Shevardnadze to consolidate an authoritarian system of government. This was in contrast with Azerbaijan, where the relative weakness of alternative centres of power was no match for President Heidar Aliyev's well-organized networks of former Communist Party officials and Aliyev was able to consolidate power relatively easily. In Shevardnadze's Georgia the emergence of a hybrid rather than an authoritarian regime was therefore predicated by the fragmentation of the political élite.

Although touted as a victory of "civil society", the success of the Rose Revolution in 2003 was not so much the result of a successful mobilization from below, but was instead the outcome of a carefully orchestrated mobilization from above by the most powerful dissident faction of the erstwhile political élite, that of the former justice minister Mikheil Saakashvili. The fundamental variable that explains the Rose revolution was not civil society, but the continued fragmentation of the élite. Several years later, when Saakashvili's administration faced popular protests of a similar scale calling for his resignation, there was no repetition of the "revolutionary" scenario. This was because Saakashvili's élite, while narrow in terms of the number of individuals actively participating in decision-making, remained relatively coherent and immune from fragmentation and was better equipped to resist public protests than its predecessor.

Although many prominent individuals broke away from Saakashvili's circle and formed their own opposition parties during the period 2004-2008 (see above) they were not able to divide the state bureaucracy (which remained firmly subordinate to the presidency). Given the unchallenged dominance that Saakashvili enjoyed in the aftermath of the Rose Revolution, he had far more freedom than Shevardnadze in appointing and nominating his own people to positions of power. While in the beginning of his term of office he was forced to accommodate prime minister Zurab Zhvania, Zhvania's untimely death left his supporters leaderless and more or less dependent on the president. By the time the UNM came to nominate candidates for the parliamentary elections of May 2008, Saakashvili and his associates had a free hand in nominating their loyal followers as future MPs.[9] One year after these elections, the UNM had lost just one MP, a telling testimony to the lack of independence of the new parliamentary majority. In the equivalent period after the

---

[9] Indeed they were able to ignore the objections of parliamentary chairperson Nino Burjanadze, who refused to participate in the elections in protest against the failure to include her own associates on the UNM party list. However, this was considered a price worth paying as Burjanadze already had few effective levers of control within the political elite.

1999 parliamentary elections, the ruling CUG had already lost around a dozen MPs and would soon splinter completely into rival factions.[10] This testifies to the success of Saakashvili in consolidating power in comparison with his predecessor, Eduard Shevardnadze. By 2008 the political élite was, unlike previously, relatively coherent and monolithic.

Another key determinant of élite behaviour is the incentive structure in which élite actors operate. This structure determines which behaviours are rewarded with success (principally political and economic power) and which lead to failure. It is defined by the institutions, formal and informal, that constitute the rules of the political game.[11] Looking first at formal institutions, these can be considered both as dependent and as independent variables; in other words institutions constrain the behaviour of leaders, but leaders can themselves mould the institutions that determine the behaviour of future leaders [Wise and Brown, 1999: 27]. The institutional choices made by leaders are therefore highly important in determining the future contours of the regime [see also Bunce and Wolchik, this volume]. In this regard, one tool that both Shevardnadze and Saakhashvili used in their efforts to consolidate power was the institutional choice of a strong presidency. This allowed both presidents to create a powerful administration that could supervise and control both the legislative and executive branches of government. Symptomatic of the weakness of the (formal) executive branch under Shevardnadze was the fact that the 1995 constitution abolished the post of prime minister and made all ministers individually responsible to the president. The bodies that had real executive power were the presidential administration, which fulfilled more or less the same supervisory role as the Central Committee of the Communist Party had previously, and the National Security Council (made up of

---

[10] Including a prominent group of businessmen who later formed their own party called the New Rights, as well as a number of other prominent MPs including Nino Burjanadze.

[11] Douglass North defines institutions as "the rules of the game in a society or, more formally, are the humanly devised constraints that shape human interaction" [North, 1990: 3].

Shevardnadze's most trusted officials, see footnote 5), which was a kind of latter-day politburo. Although the State Chancellery as a formal organization was abolished under Saakashvili, the presidency still represented the main locus of power and was further strengthened by the 2004 constitutional amendments. During Saakashvili's administration the key decision-makers derived their influence not so much from their formal positions, but more from their personal proximity to the president.

The establishment of a party of power is another example of institutional selection that is relevant to the Georgian case. The logic of such a party is to secure a dominant position in parliament and to ensure that state employees, businessmen, and intellectuals can join the main networks of power. During Shevardnadze's administration, continuing divisions within the CUG meant that this institution was only able to provide a parliamentary majority for a limited period of time. The UNM under Saakashvili was far more coherent and fully subordinate to the president. It was therefore able to ensure that the president and his entourage had a compliant parliament that did not question executive orders. The lack of an effective body that could monitor and control executive decision-making allowed the executive to take unilateral steps that were not in the best interests of the country. The decision to intervene militarily in South Ossetia in August 2008 is the clearest example of such misguided and unchecked decision-making.

Another institution that plays a central role in any transition to democracy is that of elections [see Bunce and Wolchik, this volume]. The capacity of elections to articulate the will of voters in a (relatively) neutral manner depends on the incentives of those who participate in elections and those who manage them to ensure a fair and transparent contest. The key question here is whether incumbents are prepared to countenance the possibility of electoral defeat. The incentive structures experienced by political actors as they contemplate such a prospect is elegantly described by Weingast, who argues that incumbents will subvert the electoral process and cling to power if they calculate that the costs of accepting defeat are greater than the costs of subversion. He argues that they will only cede defeat "when the expected gains from accepting the loss exceed those from subverting" [Weingast, 1997: 255]. In the Georgian context, defeated incumbents may not only face political oblivion as a result of electoral defeat; the tendency of power-holders to act arbitrarily means that once defeated they may later risk prosecution for their deeds while in office (as occurred with some of Shevardnadze's acolytes in the aftermath of the Rose Revolution), further discouraging them from ceding power. Moreover, it is not only the president and the national leadership of the state that face strong incentives to maintain the *status quo*. The high level of dependency of both the election administration and the state administration at local level on the president and his networks has meant that the local level bureaucrats who manage the elections depend on the top leadership of the state for their jobs and are unlikely to favour a result that may lead to their dismissal.[12] There is therefore a very strong incentive for them to "deliver the right result" through the use of administrative resources or even electoral fraud.

In many countries, political parties reduce uncertainty by providing political leaders with the institutional backing to carry on fighting after the loss of one election in the hope of winning the next. However, the very high levels of electoral volatility observed in Georgia over successive parliamentary electoral cycles (averaging 52% per cycle from 1992-2008 according to Pedersen's index[13]) mean that the probability that a party that performs well in one election will be able to repeat its performance in the next is limited. This is because the party system in Georgia is poorly-

---

[12] The district election committees in practice remain highly dependent on the central election commission, whose members are nominated by the president. Before 2006 all state administrators at district level (*gamgebelis*) were appointed by the president. Although reforms in local government that came into effect in 2006 gave the elected district councils the right to appoint the *gamgebeli*, all councils were dominated by the UNM and *gamgebelis* still required an informal recommendation from the centre.

[13] Pedersen's index is calculated as half the sum of the percentage change in electoral support (in terms of votes, rather than the number of deputies elected) between two consecutive parliamentary elections for each party or bloc (discarding spoilt ballot papers and votes "against all").

institutionalized, consisting of a "party of power" that is wholly dependent on the figure of the president but lacks any kind of ideology, and a plethora of small opposition parties, most of which are narrow factions led by former members of the political élite who have broken with the president and his entourage.[14] None of these parties have stable roots in society and their fate depends on that of their leaders. For a "party of power" such as the CUG or the UNM, which depends for its identity and even its existence on its proximity to power, electoral defeat is likely to spell the party's demise, encouraging incumbents to take a short-term perspective and subvert the electoral process. For opposition parties too, electoral defeat may prove fatal, encouraging their leaders to dispute the official results of elections and take their protests onto the street. This is what occurred after the parliamentary elections in November 2003, resulting in Shevardnadze's resignation, and again after elections in 2008, although on this occasion the opposition failed to achieve its goal.

Overall, the purpose of elections in Georgia is not to give voters the opportunity to replace their governments, but to confer legitimacy on the incumbent regime. The ruling party and the incumbent political élite are normally able to draw on the resources of the state in order to ensure victory. This is achieved by a variety of means, ranging from more or less legitimate campaigning, supported in most cases by largely favourable media coverage, to the use of "soft" administrative resources, such as providing electricity, fuel, and other public goods shortly before elections, to outright falsification and fraud. However, if opposition leaders also have

---

[14] At the time of writing, there were seven such parties: the Democratic Movement–United Georgia (led by former parliamentary speaker Nino Burjanadze), the Movement for a Fair Georgia (led by former prime minister Zurab Noghaideli), Movement for United Georgia (founded by former defence minister Irakli Okruashvili), Georgia's Way (led by former foreign minister Salome Zourabichvili), the Party of the People (led by Saakashvili's former close ally, Koba Davitashvili), the Party of Women for Justice and Equality (led by former ruling party MP Guguli Maghradze), and the Party of the Future (led by former presidential advisor Gia Maisishvili). Saakashvili's National Movement was once such a party too, as it was formed in 2001 after his resignation as Shevardnadze's justice minister.

sufficient financial and bureaucratic resources, they may challenge this "victory" on the streets, threatening the government's continued hold on power. For this reason, since Georgia gained independence in 1991 power has changed hands in Georgia through pressure in the streets, but never through the ballot box.

Also highly relevant are *informal institutions*. During Shevardnadze's term as president, as previously, ubiquitous violation of the law by state bureaucrats was used as a means of informal control. Within the state bureaucracy, subordinates' behaviour was controlled by the threat of arbitrary sanctions from above. In part, the persistence and even deepening of the kind of Soviet "organizational culture" identified at the beginning of the chapter was facilitated by budgetary constraints and the consequent shrinkage of the (formal) state which meant that official salaries were insufficient to maintain even a basic standard of living. The result was that corruption became a necessity for virtually all those working in state organizations, further reinforcing the effectiveness of top-down, informal levers of control.

The new Georgian government that came to power after the Rose Revolution was fairly successful in rooting out low level corruption. The "license to be corrupt" that had been granted during the Shevardnadze period to most low and middle-level bureaucrats in exchange for their loyalty was withdrawn, and was replaced by increased official salaries. Nevertheless, corruption persisted in the top highest echelons of power, and, as previously, high officials were only brought to account for corruption if their loyalty to the leadership appeared to be in doubt. The most revealing case in this respect was that of Saakashvili's former defence minister, Irakli Okruashvili, who was arrested for corruption and extortion on September 27, 2007, just two days after he had appeared on television to announce the formation of a new opposition party and to accuse President Saakashvili of plotting to murder the businessman and media tycoon, Badri Patarkatsishvili. Okruashvili's arrest came a few days after the arrest his client, Mikheil Kareli, the former governor of Shida Kartli province, once again on charges of extortion, after he had been involved in a clash with the local police and fired from his position. The point was not whether Okruashvili and Kareli were guilty of extortion; indeed, there was significant evidence that they had been involved in wrongdoing, and Kareli, in particular, had been accused by his opponents of tolerating smuggling activities from South Ossetia as early as 2004. This incriminating evidence or *kompromat* (see above) was used against them, however, only when they established themselves as opponents of the incumbent regime.

The fact that the old Soviet-era institution of *kompromat* as a means to intimidate and silence opponents still persisted despite the root and branch replacement of personnel that the Rose Revolution had brought about highlights the fact that institutions – in particular informal institutions – are "sticky," or resistant to change [North, 1990: 6 and 37]. In many ways, the Rose Revolution was little more than an exercise in "repackaging", in which the faces at the top changed but the rules of the game remained more or less the same. The hierarchical norms within the élite, predicated as they were on loyalty to the leader and the threat of blackmail to ensure compliance, remained intact. Such norms, or informal institutions, can endure for decades, if not generations. It is this "institutional stickiness" that is central to the explanation of why post-Soviet hybrid regimes such as Georgia remain so resistant to democratic change.

The arguments outlined above suggest that Shevardnadze's failure to consolidate an authoritarian regime can be ascribed to his incapacity or unwillingness to curtail the relative autonomy of rival factions within the political élite. However, his successor, Mikheil Saakashvili, faced no such constraints and was able to achieve more or less full control over the bureaucracy of the state through his own informal networks and through his ruling party, the UNM. Many of his opponents have described his regime as authoritarian in nature and even many independent observers agree that the independence of the media and the judiciary has declined since the Rose Revolution. Indeed Georgia's Freedom House score for press freedom confirms this trend, declining from 54 in 2003 to 60 in 2008 (on a scale of 1 to 100 from "free" to "not free"). Nevertheless, it would be a mistake to describe Georgia as a fully authoritarian regime, as many of the formal attributes of democracy are still in place. Although the 2008 presidential and parliamentary elections were far from free and fair and administrative resources were deployed extensively by the ruling party, outright falsification of the results probably boosted the incumbents' share of the vote by no more than several percentage points. Even media freedom, while declining, was still ranked higher than all of Georgia's post-Soviet neighbours in 2008, with the exception of the Baltic republics and Ukraine.

For a country such as Georgia, which lacks primary commodities such as oil or gas, outright authoritarianism may undermine prospects for external funding and foreign direct investment. While the informal institutions that define how power is exercised and perceived in Georgia are "sticky" and hard to change (see above), Georgian leaders can tinker with the formal institutions by endowing the regime with a number of procedural features of democracy (such as superficially competitive elections) but still leave the fundamental (informal) authoritarian dynamic intact. Georgia is probably more vulnerable to pressure from western powers than other post-Soviet states because of its self-perception as a European nation and the desire, shared by most of the political class and the majority of citizens as well, to integrate into Euro-Atlantic structures. Since the Rose Revolution Georgia's political leaders have used the slogans of western democracy and integration into western structures as a mantra and are constrained at least to pay lip service to democratic principles. If the explanation for the hybrid regime under Shevardnadze was the fragmentation of the political élite, Georgia's hybrid status under Saakashvili may be ascribed to "soft" pressure from the west.

However, international leverage on Georgia to democratize has so far proved limited because the international community has little to offer Georgia in terms of meaningful incentives for change. European Union (EU) membership is out of the question; growing resistance to the enlargement process amongst many EU member states have effectively put Turkey's bid for EU membership on hold and even the prospects of membership for successor states of

Yugoslavia such as Macedonia, Bosnia and Serbia look increasingly uncertain. Georgia (along with Ukraine and Moldova) is much further down on the list of potential members than any of these states. Similarly, the West and NATO do not have much to offer Georgia in terms of security guarantees given their reluctance to jeopardize their links with Russia. Even the apparently warm embrace afforded to Saakashvili by so-called neo-conservatives within the Bush administration offered little in terms of substance and the misguided belief that he would receive US support may have encouraged the Georgian president to act impulsively in his dispute with Russia over the breakaway territories. The fact that Georgia was denied a Membership Action Plan (MAP) at two successive NATO summits in 2008 is a clear indicator of the West's limited commitment to Georgia's security. It is also worthy of note that no meaningful conditionality was attached to a possible MAP for Georgia; little weight was given to democratic reforms (or the lack thereof) in the decision of whether or not to grant the MAP.

4 - Conclusion

Georgia's development as a hybrid regime has been conditioned by the factional pluralism that was inherent to the Georgian political élite during the Shevardnadze administration, which was in turn conditioned by the way the communist regime was dismantled. This factional pluralism bore little relevance to democratic pluralism as élite factions had few links with society and proved incapable of aggregating the interests of citizens in the way that political parties do in developed democracies. While the narrow political clique that governed the country under the Saakashvili administration was able to gain control of most, if not all, levers of power, the authorities maintained a democratic facade to court the support of Western allies.

The institutional matrix that has defined the incentives for both high and low level state bureaucrats in Georgia has hardly been conducive to the development of a flourishing democratic system either. Formal institutions (including the constitution, electoral laws and other legal codes) have been adopted and amended willy nilly by those in power, while the informal institutions that reward unquestioning loyalty, blackmail and vote-rigging have remained an ingrained part of the organizational culture of the Georgian political élite since the Soviet period.

In terms of the old debate as to whether it is actors that determine the process and outcome of regime change [O'Donnell and Schmitter, 1986; Karl and Schmitter, 1991] or whether it is instead cultural, socioeconomic, or institutional preconditions [Lipset ,1960; Almond and Verba, 1963; Diamond, 1992; Linz and Stepan, 1996], the Georgian case seems seem to show that both are important. Structural legacies, in particular the informal institutional framework of the Soviet state, as well as the organizational structure of society, appear to have played a major role in the transition process. Here we have in mind the peculiar norms of loyalty enforced by blackmail within state structures as well as the incapacity of society to organize itself around competing (non-ethnic) social identities. However, there was still room for political actors to make a major impact on the process through guile, innovation and blunder. For example, the disastrous decision made by the communist authorities in Georgia (with the backing of Moscow) to use disproportionate force against demonstrators on 9 April 1989 undoubtedly radicalized the population and ensured the victory of Gamsakhurdia and his demagogic and divisive policies, leading to civil strife and further complicating the prospects for a smooth and successful democratic transition. Similarly, the manner in which Shevardnadze put together his "coalition" and his skill in bringing together diverse actors first helped bring order to his damaged country but in the long run led to his downfall. Finally, the strategies employed by the main actors (both government and opposition) in the run up to the Rose Revolution helped ensure the outcome of that upheaval and the subsequent domination of Saakashvili's close circle.

While in part the decisions made by actors depend on their subjective preferences, élite actors are strongly constrained in their behaviour both by the incentive structures that are determined by institutions and by the structure of the society in which they are embedded. Here we return to the point made in the beginning of this chapter about the weakness of civil society. The absence of strong grassroots organizations capable of articulating and aggregating the interests of citizens has meant that political leaders derive their influence through their populist appeal to a large mass of the population, rather than through their leadership of stable and institutionalized organizations. Thus, social organizations – or what is commonly known as civil society – play little role in determining the evolution of the political regime. It is true that at certain critical junctures – the Rose Revolution being a prime example – society appears to mobilize; however, it is unable to do so autonomously. NGOs represent a narrow, urban élite and have few links with society at large. As such they do not constitute civil society and make little contribution to the democratization process.

The Georgian case illustrates best of all how the formal attributes of democracy can be maintained sufficiently in order to placate western critics while the informal dynamic provides citizens with few levers to influence the way they are governed. In Georgia democracy has been a kind of "selling point" that the authorities use to portray the country as a western-leaning republic deserving both of international financial assistance and of support against its neighbour, Russia. The juggling act that is necessary between preserving power, on the one hand, and portraying Georgia as a democracy on the other is however, difficult to maintain. Eduard Shevardnadze ultimately failed in this endeavour and at the time of writing his successor too appeared to be facing a hard choice: whether to establish a fully authoritarian form of government and risk western opprobrium and the possible withdrawal of much needed investment and support against Russia, or whether to embark on the path of regime change and risk political oblivion.

References

Akhmetov, R. (2007), quoted in *Ukrainska Pravda website*, April 3.

Aleksandrenkov, J. (2006), 'Issledovanija prezidentskih voborov v Belarusi: obzor osnovnih istochnikov' (Analysis of the Elections of the President in Belarus: Review of Main Sources of information), in *Politicheskaia sfera*, 7, pp. 19–32.

Aleksandrov, O. (2007), 'The Crises in Russian-Belarusian Relations', in *The Russian Analytical Digest* 15 (7), pp. 11–14.

Almond, G.A. and Mundt, R.J. (1973), 'Crisis Choice and Change: Some Tentative Conclusions', in G.A. Almond, S.C. Flanagan, and R.J. Mundt, eds. *Crisis, Choice and Change*, Boston, Little Brown & co., pp.626-229.

Almond, G.A. and Verba, S. (1963), *The Civic Culture: Political Attitudes and Democracy in Five Nations*, Princeton, Princeton University Press.

Anderson, L. (1987), 'The state in the Middle East and North Africa', in *Comparative Politics*, 20, p. 118.

Åslund, A. (2002), *Building Capitalism. The Transformation of the Former Soviet Bloc*, Cambridge, Cambridge University Press.

Åslund, A. (2007a), *Russia's Capitalist Revolution. Why Market Reform Succeeded and Democracy Failed*, Washington DC.

Åslund, A. (2007b), *How Capitalism Was Built: The Transformation of Central and Eastern Europe, Russia, and Central Asia*, Washington DC, Peterson Institute for International Economics.

Åslund, A. and McFaul, M. (2006), *Revolution in Orange: The Origins of Ukraine's Democratic Breakthrough*, Washington, DC, Carnegie Endowment for International Peace.

Averre, D. (2007), 'Sovereign Democracy and Russia's Relations with the European Union', in *Demokratizatsiya*, 4, pp. 115-122.

Badrihanov, E. (2006), 'Zagovor protiv Lukashenko' (Plot against Lukashenko), http://www.vzglyad.ru/politics.

Balzer, H. (2003), 'The Routinization of the New Russians?', in *The Russian Review*, 62 (1), pp. 15-36.

Baracani, E. (2008), 'EU Democratic Rule of Law Promotion', in A. Magen and L. Morlino, eds. *International Actors, Democratization and the Rule of Law: Anchoring Democracy?*, London, Routledge, pp. 53-86.

Baracani, E. (2010), 'The US and EU Strategies Compared in Promoting Democracy', in F. Bindi, ed. *Foreign Policy of the*

European Union, Washington, Brookings Institution Press, pp. 303-318.

Barbarosie, A. (2001), 'Understanding the Communist Electoral Victory in Moldova', in *Transition: Newsletter about Reforming Economies*, Feb.-March: 9-10.

Barnett, M.N. and Finnemore, M. (2004), *Rules for the World: International Organizations in Global Politics*, Ithaca, Cornell University Press.

Barometrul Opiniei Publice (2001-08), 'What should be done in order to improve the socio-economic situation in our country?' (Ce ar trebui intreprins pentru a imbunatati situatia socio-economica din tara noastra?).

Barometrul Opiniei Publice (2003), 'Does the judiciary treat everyone equally and punishes the guilty whoever they are?' (Sistemul judiciar trateaza egal pe fiecare si pedepseste vinovatii indiferent de cine sunt ei), April.

Barro, R.J. (1996), 'Democracy and growth', in *Journal of Economic Growth*, 1 (1), pp. 1-27.

BBC (2005), 'UT1 TV', as reported in BBC Monitoring Research in English, 24 October 2005.

BBC (2006a), 'UT1 TV', as reported in BBC Monitoring Service in English, 9 February 2006.

BBC (2006b), 'The Friar's Greed...', in *Ostrov website* (Donetsk), August 31, as reprinted in BBC Monitoring Service in English, September, 5.

Behterev, U. (2001), 'Bankruptcy as a method of rehabilitation', in Белорусский *рынок (Byelorussian Market)*, http://www.kay.by.

Beichelt, T. (2007), 'Democracy Promotion in Eastern Europe in the Context of the European Neighbourhood Policy', EUSA Tenth Biennial International conference, Montreal, Canada, May 17-19.

Beissinger, M.R. (2008), 'A New Look at Ethnicity and Democratization', in *Journal of Democracy*, 19 (3), pp. 85-97.

Belyaeva N. and Proskuryakova, L. (2008), *Report for Russian Federation. Civil Society Diamond: CIVICUS Civil Society Index Shortened Assessment Tool*, Interlegal Foundation, Research centre for Public Pulicy and Global Governance, Moscow.

Benardo, L. and Neier, A. (2006), 'Russia: The Persecution of Civil Society', in *New York Review of Books*, 53 (7), pp. 35-37.

Berger, H. - G. Kopits - I. Szekely (2007), 'Fiscal indulgence in Central Europe: loss of the external anchor', in *Scottish Journal of Political Economy*, 54 (1), pp. 116-135.

Berglof, E. and Roland, G. (1998), 'The EU as an 'outside anchor' for transition reforms', Site Working Paper n. 132.

Bertil, N. (2008), *The rebuilding of Greater Russia: Putin's foreign policy towards the CIS countries*, London, Routledge.

Bielasiak, J. (2005), 'Party Competition in Emerging Democracies: Representation and Effectiveness in Post-Communism and Beyond', in *Democratization* 12 (3), pp. 331-356.

Bogaturov, B. (2007), 'Nastojašcaja doktrina', in *Nezavisimaja gazeta*, May 28th.

Boix, C. and Stokes, S. (2003), 'Endogenous democratization', in *World Politics*, 55 (1), pp. 517-549.

Bordačev, T. (2005), 'Russia's European Problem: Eastward Enlargement of the EU and Moscow's Policy, 1993-2003', in Antonenko O. and Pinnick K., *Russia and the European Union*, Routledge, London.

Botan, I. (2008), 'Party institutionalization and elections', in *Governing and Democracy in Moldova*, VI (111), pp. 1-15.

Börzel, T.A. and Risse, T. (2000), 'When Europe Hits Home: Europeanization and Domestic Change', in *European Integration on line Papers*, 4 (15).

Boughton, J.M. (2000), 'Michel Camdessus at the IMF: A Retrospective', in *Finance & Development*, 37 (1).

Boughton, J.M. (2001), *Silent revolution: the International Monetary Fund, 1979–1989*, International Monetary Fund, Washington, DC.

Bratton, M. and Van de Walle, N. (1994), 'Neopatrimonial Regimes and Transitions in Africa', in *World Politics*, 46 (4), pp. 453-489.

Brooker, P. (2000), *Non-Democratic Regimes. Theory, Government & Politics*, New York, St. Martin's Press.

Brown, A. (1996), *The Gorbachev Factor*, Oxford University Press, New York.

Broz, J.L. and Hawes, M.B. (2006), 'Congressional Politics of Financing the International Monetary Fund', in *International Organization*, 60 (2), pp. 367-399.

Brubaker, R. (1996), *Nationalism Reframed: Nationhood and the National Question in the New Europe*, Cambridge, Cambridge University Press.

Bruce, C. (2005), 'Friction or Fiction? The Gas Factor in Russian-Belarusian Relations', Chatham House Briefing Paper, REP BP 05/01, http://www.chathamhouse.org.uk/pdf/research/rep/BP0501gas.pdf.

384

Brzezinski, Z. and Sullivan, P. eds. (1997), *Russia and the Commonwealth of Independent States: Document, Data and Analysis*, Armonk, New York, M.E: Sharpe.

Bunce V. (1995), Should Transitologists Be Grounded?, in *Slavic Review*, 54 (1), pp. 111–127.

Bunce, V. (1999a), 'The Political Economy of Post socialism', in *Slavic Review* 58 (4), p. 756.

Bunce, V. (1999b) *Subversive Institutions: The Design and the Destruction of Socialism and the State,* Cambridge Studies in Comparative Politics, Cambridge, UK; New York, Cambridge University Press.

Bunce, V. (2000), 'Comparative Democratization: Big and Bounded Generalizations', in *Comparative Political Studies* 33 (6-7), pp. 703-734.

Bunce, V. (2003), 'Rethinking Recent Democratization: Lessons from the Post-communist Experience', in *World Politics* 55 (2), p. 167.

Bunce, V. (2004a), 'Comparative Democratization: Lessons from Russia and the Post-socialist World', in M. McFaul and K. Stoner-Weiss (eds.), *After the Collapse of Communism: Comparative Lessons of Transition,* Cambridge, Cambridge University Press, pp. 207-231.

Bunce, V. (2004b), 'Status Quo, Reformist and Secessionist Politics: Explaining Variations in Centre-Regional Bargaining in Post-communist Ethno federations', paper presented at the Workshop on Nationalism and Secession, Cornell University, April 24 and at the Workshop on Eastern European Politics, Harvard University, Centre for European Studies, May 14.

Bunce, V. (2005a), 'The National Idea: Imperial Legacies and Post-communist Pathways in Eastern Europe', in *East European Politics and Society*, 19 (3), pp. 406-442.

Bunce, V. (2005b), 'Promoting Democracy in Divided Societies', paper presented at the Joint conference of the Peace Studies Program [Cornell University] and the Peace Research Institute Frankfurt. Frankfurt, Germany, October 10-11.

Bunce, V. (2006a), 'Global Patterns and Post-communist Dynamics', in *Orbis* 50 (4), pp. 601-620.

Bunce, V. (2006)b, 'Democracy and Diversity in the Developing World: The American Experience with Democracy Promotion', in J. Escheverri-Gent (ed.), *Difference and Inequality in the Developing World,* Washington, D.C., American Political Science Association.

Bunce, V. – McFaul, M. - Stoner-Weiss, K. eds. (2007), *Waves and Troughs of Post-communist Reform,* unpublished book manuscript.

Bunce, V. and Watts, S. (2005), 'Managing Diversity and Sustaining Democracy in the Post-communist World', in P. Roeder and D. Rothchild (eds.), *Sustainable Peace: Power and Democracy After Civil Wars*, Ithaca, NY, Cornell University Press, pp. 133-158.

Bunce, V. and Wolchik, S. (2006), 'International Diffusion and Post-communist Electoral Revolutions', in *Communist and Post-Communist Studies*, 39 (3), pp. 283-304.

Bunce, V. and Wolchik, S. (2008), *American Democracy Promotion and Electoral Change in Post-communist Europe and Eurasia*, unpublished book manuscript.

Burkhart, R. and Beck, M.L. (1994), 'Comparative Democracy: The Economic Development Thesis', in *American Political Science Review*, 88, pp. 903-910.

Burnell P. ed. (2000), *Democracy Assistance: International Co-operation for Democratization*, London.

Burnside, C. and Dollar, D. (1997), *Aid, Policies, and Growth*. Policy Research Working Paper N° 1777. World Bank, Development Research Group, Washington, DC.

Burnside, C. and Dollar, D. (1998), *Aid, the Incentive Regime, and Poverty Reduction*. Policy Research Working Paper N° 1937. World Bank, Development Research Group, Washington, DC.

Camdessus, M. (1994), *Supporting Transition in Central and Eastern Europe: An Assessment and Lessons from the IMF's Five Years' Experience*. Speech Given at the Second Annual Francisco Fernández Ordóñez Address, Madrid. 21 December.

Camdessus, M. (1995), *The IMF in a Globalized World Economy--The Tasks Ahead*. Third Annual Sylvia Ostry Lecture, Ottawa. 7 June.

Cardoso, F.H. (1986), 'Entrepreneurs and the Transition Process: The Brazilian Case', in G. O'Donnell, P.C. Schmitter, and L. Whitehead, eds. *Transitions from Authoritarian Rule. Comparative Perspectives*, Baltimore, The John Hopkins University Press, pp. 137-153.

Carnaghan, E. (2007), *Out of Order: Russian Political Values in an Imperfect World*, Pennsylvania, Pennsylvania State University Press.

Carothers, T. (1999), *Aiding Democracy Abroad: The Learning Curve*, Washington, DC, Carnegie Endowment for International Peace.

Carothers, T. (2000), 'Taking stock of democracy assistance', in Cox, M. - Ikenberry, G.J. – Inoguchi, T. eds., *American Democracy Promotion. Impulses, Strategies, and Impacts*, Oxford, Oxford University Press, pp. 181-199.

Carothers, T. (2002), 'The End of the Transition Paradigm', in *Journal of Democracy*, 13 (1), pp. 5–21.

Carothers, T. (2006), 'The Backlash against Democracy Promotion', in *Foreign Affairs,* 85 (2), pp.55–68.

Carothers, T. (2007a), 'Misunderstanding Gradualism', in *Journal of Democracy,* 18 (3), pp. 18-22.

Carothers, T. (2007b), 'The "Sequencing" Fallacy', in *Journal of Democracy,* 18 (1), pp. 12-27.

Cashu, I. (2005), 'Analysis: Why an Orange Revolution is Unlikely in Moldova', *RFERL,* March 6.

Chong, A. and Calderón, C. (2000), 'Causality and Feedback Between Institutional Measures and Economic Growth', in *Economics and Politics,* 12 (1), pp. 69-81.

Chwieroth, J.M. (2008), 'Normative Change From Within: The International Monetary Fund's Approach to Capital Account Liberalization', in *International Studies Quarterly,* 52 (1), pp. 129-158.

Collier D. and Levitsky, S. (1997), 'Democracy with Adjectives: Conceptual Innovation in Comparative Research', in *World Politics,* 49 (3), pp. 430-451.

Coricelli, F. (2007), 'Democracy in the Post-Communist World: Unfinished Business', in *East European Politics & Society,* 1, pp. 82-90.

Council of the European Union (1999), 'Regulation (EC, Euratom) No 99/2000 of 29 December 1999 concerning the provision of assistance to the partner States in Eastern Europe and Central Asia', *Official Journal of the European Communities,* L 12/1, 18.1.2000.

Council of the European Union (2009), 'Joint Declaration of the Prague Eastern Partnership Summit, Prague', 7 May 2009.

Council of the European Union and European Parliament (2006), Regulation (EC) No 1638/2006 of 24 October 2006 laying down general provisions establishing a European Neighbourhood and Partnership Instrument'.

Cox, M. - Ikenberry, G.J. - Inoguchi, T. eds. (2000), *American Democracy Promotion: Impulses, Strategies, and Impacts.* Oxford, Oxford University Press.

Croissant, A. and Merkel, W. (2004), 'Introduction: Democratization in the Early Twenty-First Century', in *Democratization,* 11 (5), pp. 1-9.

Crowther, W. (1997), 'The Politics of Democratization in Post-Communist Moldova', in K. Dawisha and B. Parrott eds. *Democratic Changes and Authoritarian Reactions in Russia, Ukraine, Belarus, Moldova,* Cambridge, Cambridge University Press, pp. 282–330.

Crowther, W. (2007), 'Development of the Moldovan Parliament One Decade after Independence: Slow Going', in *The Journal of Legislative Studies,* 13 (1), pp. 99–120.

Crowther, W. and Matonyte, I. (2007), 'Parliamentary élite as a democratic thermometer: Estonia, Lithuania and Moldova compared', in *Communist and Post-Communist Studies,* 40 (3), pp. 281-299.

Crystal, J. (1995), *Oil and Politics in the Gulf: Rulers and Merchants in Kuwait and Qatar,* Cambridge, Cambridge University Press.

Dahl, R.A. (1971), *Poliarchy. Participation and Opposition,* New Haven, Yale University Press.

Dawisha, K. and Turner, M. (1997), 'The Interaction between Internal and External Agency in Post-Communist Transitions', in Dawisha, K. (ed.), *The International Dimensions of Transition in Russia and the New States of Eurasia,* Amronk (NY), M.E. Sharpe.

Deyermond, R. (2004), 'The State of the Union: Military Success, Economic and Political Failure in the Russia-Belarus Union', in *Europe-Asia Studies* 56 (8), pp. 1191–1205.

Diamond, L.J. (1992), 'Economic development and democracy reconsidered', in *American Behavioral Scientist,* 35 (4-5), pp. 450-499.

Diamond, L.J. (1999), *Developing democracy: toward consolidation,* Baltimore, Johns Hopkins University Press.

Diamond L.J. (2002), 'Thinking about Hybrid Regimes', in *Journal of Democracy,* 13 (2), pp. 25-31.

Diamond L.J. (2008), *The Spirit of Democracy. The Struggle to Build Free Societies throughout the World,* New York, Times Books, Henry Holt and Company.

Diamond, L.J. – Linz, J.J. – Lipset, S.M. (1989), 'Introduction', in Diamond, L. – Linz, J.J. – Lipset, S.M. eds., *Democracy in Developing Countries: Latin America,* Boulder, Lynne Rienner.

Diamond, L.J. and Morlino, L. (2004), 'An Overview', in *Journal of Democracy,* 15 (4), pp. 20-31.

Diamond, L.J. and Morlino, L. (2005), *Assessing the Quality of Democracy,* Baltimore, John Hopkins University Press.

Dimitrov, M. (2008), 'The Resilient Authoritarians', in *Current History,* 107, pp. 24-29.

Dimitrova, A. (2002), 'Enlargement, Institution-Building and the European Union's Administrative Capacity Requirement', in *West European Politics,* 25 (4), pp. 171-90.

Dimitrova, A. and Pridham, G. (2004), 'International Actors and Democracy Promotion in Central and Eastern Europe', *Democratization,* 11 (5), pp. 91-112.

Di Tommaso, M.L. - M. Raiser - M. Weeks (2007), 'Home grown or imported? Initial conditions, external anchors and the determinants of

388

institutional reform in the transition economies', in *The Economic Journal*, 117 (520), pp. 858-881.

Dodini, M. and Fantini M. (2006), 'The EU neighbourhood policy: implications for economic growth and stability', in *Journal of Common Market Studies*, 44 (3), pp. 507-532.

Dzhibladze, Y. (2009), *Situation of NGOs and Freedom of Association in Russia: Latest Developments*, Centre for the Development of Democracy and Human Rights, Materials for the EU-Russia Consultations on Human Rights, Brussels, 25 May, http://www.mhg.ru.

Easton, D. (1965), *A Systems Analysis of Political Life*, New York, Wiley.

EIDHR (2009), 'Compendium of activities funded under EIDHR 2000-06 per country', EIDHR website.

Ekhanurov, Y.I. (2005), speech at the Carnegie Endowment for Peace, Washington, 1 November, published in the Ukraine Action Report, n. 597, article 1.

Ekiert, G. – Kubik, J. – Vachudova, M.A. (2007), 'Democracy in the Post-Communist World: An Unending Quest?', in *East European Politics and Societies*, 21 (1), pp. 7-30.

Ekman, J. (2009), 'Political Participation and Regime Stability: A Framework for Analyzing Hybrid Regimes', in *International Political Science Review*, 30 (1), pp.7-31.

Energy Information Administration (2009), *EIA World Nominal Oil Price Chronology: 1970-2007*, http://tonto.eia.doe.gov.

Epstein, D. - Bates, R. - Goldstone, J. - Kristensen, I. - O'Halloran, S. (2006), 'Democratic Transitions', in *American Journal of Political Science*, 50 (3), pp. 551–569.

Eremenko, A. (2007), 'Zakon 'O Trube': kak zalatats' dyry', in *Zerkalo Nedeli on the web*, 5, February 10-16.

European Commission (2003a), 'Communication on Wider Europe - Neighbourhood: A new framework for relations with our Eastern and Southern Neighbours'.

European Commission (2003b), 'Reactions to Draft Agreement establishing a Single Economic Space by Russia, Ukraine, Belarus and Kazakhstan', Information to the Press circulated by the Delegation of the European Commission to Ukraine, September 17.

European Commission (2004), 'Communication on European Neighbourhood Policy Strategy Paper'.

European Commission (2007), 'Furthering human rights and democracy across the globe', Luxembourg.

389

European Commission (2008), 'Communication from the Commission to the European Parliament and the Council on the Eastern Partnership', Brussels, 3.12.2008, COM (2008) 823 final.
European Commission (2009), 'Vademecum on financing in the frame of the Eastern Partnership', 16 December 2009.
European Union (2007), 'Country Strategy paper, 2007-2013: Russian Federation'.
Featherstone, K. (2004), 'The political dynamics of external empowerment: the emergence of EMU and the challenge to the European social model', in A. Martin and G. Ross eds. *Euros and Europeans: monetary integration and the European model of society*, Cambridge, Cambridge University Press, pp. 226-247.
Fenger, M. (2009), 'The Diffusion of Revolutions: Comparing Recent Regime Turnovers in Five Post-communist Countries', in *Demokratizatsiya*, forthcoming.
Financial Times (2005), 'Ukraine: An Exemplary Start', 26 October, editorial comment.
Financial Times (2009), 'Obama must be firm on foreign policy', 6 July by Gideon Rachman (electronic edition).
Finer, S. E., (1970), *Comparative Government*, Harmondsworth, Penguin Books.
Finkel, S. - Perez-Linan, A. - Seligson, M. – Azpuru, D. (2006), 'Effects of US Foreign Assistance on Democracy Building: Results of a Cross-National Quantitative Study', Final Report, USAID, January 12, Version No. 34.
Finnemore, M. and Sikkink, K. (1998), 'International Norm Dynamics and Political Change', in *International Organization*, 52 (4), pp. 887-917.
Fischer, S. (2005), 'The EU's Strategy of 'New Neighbourhood' and its Impact on International Relations of the Former SU', paper presented at the annual meeting of the International Studies Association, Honolulu, March 1-5.
Fish, M. S. (1998a), 'Democratization's Prerequisites', in *Post-Soviet Affairs*, 14 (July-September), pp. 212-247
Fish, M. S. (1998b), 'The Determinants of Economic Reform in the Post-communist World', *East European Politics and Societies*, 12 (Winter).
Fish, M. S. (2002), 'Islam and authoritarianism', in *World Politics*, 55, pp. 4-37.
Fish, M. S. (2004), 'Weak Parliaments and Democratic Fragility', paper presented at the conference on "Democratization by Elections? The Dynamics of Electoral Authoritarianism." Division de Estudios Politicos, CIDE, Mexico City, April 2-3.

Fish, M.S. (2005), *Democracy Derailed in Russia: The Failure of Open Politics,* Cambridge, Cambridge University Press.

Fish, M. S. (2006), 'Stronger Legislatures, Stronger Democracies', in *Journal of Democracy,* 17 (1), pp. 5-20.

Fishman, R. (1990), 'Rethinking State and Regime: Southern Europe's Transition to Democracy', in *World Politics,* 42 (3), pp, 422-440.

Flikke, G. and Godzimirski, J.M. (2006), 'Words and Deeds. Russian Foreign Policy and Post-Soviet Secessionist Conflicts', NUPI Report, http//www.nupi.no.

Forbrig, J. and Demes, P. eds. (2007), *Reclaiming Democracy: Civil Society and Electoral Change in Central and Eastern Europe,* Washington, D.C.: German Marshall Fund.

Forrester, S. – Zaboroska, M.J. - Gapova, E. (2004), eds. *Over the Wall / After the Wall: Post-communist Culture through a Western Gaze,* Bloomington: Indiana University Press.

Francois, J.F. (1997), 'External bindings and the credibility of reform in Regional Partners', in A. Galal and B. Hoekman eds., *Global Markets: Limits and Possibilities of the Euro-Med Agreements,* London, Centre for Economic Policy Research, pp. 35-48.

Fritz, V. (2007), *State-Building: A Comparative Study of Ukraine, Lithuania, Belarus, and Russia,* Budapest, Central European University Press.

Frye, T. (2002), 'The Perils of Polarization: Economic Performance in the Post-communist World', in *World Politics,* 54 (April), pp. 308-337.

Fukuyama, F. (1989), 'The End of History?', in *The National Interest,* 16 (Summer), pp. 3-18.

Fukuyama, F. (2004), *State-Building: Governance and World Order in the 21st Century,* Ithaca (NY), Cornell University Press.

Gagnon, V.P. (2004), *The Myth of Ethnic War: Serbia and Croatia in the 1990s,* Ithaca, N.Y., Cornell University Press.

Gans-Morse, J. (2004), 'Searching for Transitologists: Contemporary Theories of Post-Communist Transitions and the Myth of a Dominant Paradigm', in *Post-Soviet Affairs,* 20 (4), pp. 320–349.

Ganzle, S. (2007) 'The European Neighbourhood Policy: Extending Governance Beyond Borders?', University of British Columbia.

Gapova, E. (2002), 'On Nation, Gender, and Class Formation in Belarus... and Elsewhere in the Post-Soviet World', in *Nationalities Papers,* 30 (4), pp. 639–662.

Gapova, E. (2004), 'The Nation in Between; or, Why Intellectuals Do Things with Words?' in S. Forrester, M.J. Zaboroska and E. Gapova,

391

eds, *Over the Wall / After the Wall: Post-communist Culture through a Western Gaze,* Bloomington: Indiana University Press, pp. 65–79.

Geddes, B. (2007), 'What Causes Democratization?', in C. Boix and S.C. Stokes, eds, *The Oxford Handbook of Comparative Politics,* Oxford, Oxford University Press, pp. 317-336.

Gelman, V. (2005), 'Political Opposition in Russia: A Dying Species?', *Post-Soviet Affairs,* 3.

Gelman, V. (2008), 'Out of the Frying Pan, Into the Fire? Post-Soviet Regime Changes in Comparative Perspective', in *International Political Science Review,* 29 (2), pp.157–80.

Gershman, C. and Allen, M. (2006), 'The Assault on Democracy Assistance', *Journal of Democracy,* 17 (2), pp. 36-51.

Gibson, J.L. (2001a), 'The Russian Dance with Democracy', in *Post-Soviet Affairs,* 17 (2), pp. 101-128.

Gibson, J.L. (2001b), 'Social Networks, Civil Society, and the Prospects for Consolidating Russia's Democratic Transition', in *American Journal of Political Science* 45 (1), pp. 51-68.

Goldstone, J. – Gurr, T.R. – Harff, B. - Levy, M. - Marshall, M. – Bates, R. - Epstein, D. - Kahl, C. - Surko, P. – Ulfelder, J.C. – Unger, A. (2000), *State Failure Task Force Report: Phase III Findings.*

Goujon, A. (1999), 'Language, Nationalism and Populism in Belarus', in *Nationalities Papers,* 27 (4), pp. 661–677.

Grabbe, H. (2006), *The EU's Transformative Power: Europeanization through Conditionality in Central and Eastern Europe,* New York, Palgrave Macmillan.

Green, A. (2007), 'Democracy and Donor Funding: Patterns and Trends', in *Eastern European Studies Newsletter,* Wilson Centre, September-October, pp. 5-11.

Gregory, P.R. (1989), 'Soviet bureaucratic behaviour: khozyaistvenniki and apparatchiki', in *Soviet Studies,* 41 (4), pp. 511-525.

Grilli di Cortona, P. (2009), *Come gli Stati diventano democratici,* Roma, Laterza.

Gros, D. (2001), 'Who needs and external anchor?', CEPS Working Document n. 161.

Hadenius, A. and Teorell, J. (2007), 'Pathways from Authoritarianism', in *Journal of Democracy,* 18 (1).

Haerpfer, C.W. (2008), 'Support for Democracy and Autocracy in Russia and the Commonwealth of Independent States, 1992-2002', in *International Political Science Review,* 29 (4), pp.411-432.

Haggard, S. and Kaufman, R.R. (1995), *The political economy of democratic transitions,* Princeton, Princeton University Press.

Hale, H. (2004), 'Divided We Stand', in *World Politics*, 56, pp. 165-173.

Hale, H. (2005a), 'Regime Cycles, Democracy, Autocracy and Revolution in Post-Soviet Eurasia', in *World Politics*, 58 (October), pp. 133-165.

Hale, H. (2005b), *Why Not Parties in Russia? Democracy, Federalism and the State*, Cambridge, Cambridge University Press.

Hale, H.E. (2006), 'Democracy or Autocracy on the March? The Coloured Revolutions as Normal Dynamics of Patronal Presidentialism', in *Communist and Post-communist Studies*, 39, (3), pp. 305-329.

Hamilton, D. and Mangott, G. eds. (2007), *The new Eastern Europe: Ukraine, Belarus, Moldova*, Washington, Centre for Transatlantic Relations.

Hanf, T. and Nodia, G. (2000), *Georgia Lurching to Democracy. From Agnostic Tolerance to Pious Jacobinism: Societal Change and Peoples' Reactions*, Baden Baden, Nomos Verlagsgesellschaft.

Hanson, S.E. (2007), 'The Uncertain Future of Russia's Weak State Authoritarianism', in *East European Politics and Societies*, 21 (1), pp.67-81.

Harrod, R.F. (1951), *The Life of John Maynard Keynes*, London, Easton Press.

Hassner, P. (2008), 'Russia's Transition to Autocracy', in *Journal of Democracy*, 19 (2), pp. 5-15.

Heeger, G. (1974), *The Politics of Underdevelopment*, London, Macmillan.

Helliwell, J.F. (1994), 'Empirical Linkages between Democracy and Economic Growth', in *British Journal of Political Science*, 24 (2), pp. 225-248.

Hellman, J.S. (1998), 'Winners Take all: The Politics of Partial Reform in Post-communist Transitions', in *World Politics*, 50 (2), p. 203-234.

Hellman, J.S. – Jones, G. - Kaufman, D. (2003), 'Seize the State, Seize the Day: State Capture and Influence in Transition Economies', in *Journal of Comparative Economics*, 31, pp. 751-773.

Herz, J. ed. (1982), *From Dictatorship to Democracy. Coping with the Legacies of Authoritarianism and Totalitarianism*, Greewood Press, Westport.

Higley, J. - Pakulski, J. - Wesolowski, W. (1998), *Élite and Democracy in Eastern Europe*, New York, St. Martin's Press.

Hite, K. and Cesarini, P. eds (2004), *Authoritarian Legacies and Democracy in Latin America and Southern Europe*, Notre Dame, University of Notre Dame Press.

Howard, M.M. and Roessler, P.G. (2006), 'Liberalizing Electoral Outcomes in Competitive Authoritarian Regimes', in *American Journal of Political Science* 50, (2).

Huber, E. – Rueschemeyer, D. – Stephens, J.D. (1993), 'The Impact of Economic Development on Democracy', in *Journal of Economic Perspectives*, 7 (3), pp. 71-85.

Huntington, S.P. (1991), *The Third Wave: Democratization in the Late Twentieth Century*, Norman, University of Oklahoma Press.

Huntington, S.P. (1997), *The Clash of Civilization and the Remaking of World Order*, New Delhi, Viking.

IDIS (2009), *100 most urgent problems of Moldova in 20*08, Chişinău, 2009

IMF, (1996), *Partnership for Sustainable Global Growth*. Interim Committee Declaration. Washington, DC 29 September.

IMF, (1997), *Good Governance. The IMF's Role*. International Monetary Fund, Washington, DC.

IMF, (2001), *IMF Approves US$141 Million PRGF Loan for Georgia*, Press Release 01/4, 12 January 2001.

IMF, (2004), *IMF Approves US$144 Million PRGF Arrangement for Georgia*, Press Release 04/107, 4 June 2004.

IMF, (2006), *IMF approves US$118.2 Million Arrangement Under the Poverty Reduction and Growth Facility with Moldova*, Press Release No. 06/91. 5 May 2006.

IMF Archives, (1993), *Republic of Moldova - Request for Stand-By Arrangement and Purchase Under the Systemic Transformation Facility- Letter of Intent*. EBS/93/177. 16 November 1993.

IMF Archives, (1994a), *Republic of Georgia - Request for Purchase Under the Systemic Transformation Facility - Statement of Economic Policies and Technical Annex* EBS/94/221. 16 November 1994.

IMF Archives, (1994b), *Staff Report for Second Review Under the Stand-by Arrangement, and Request for Purchase Under the Compensatory and Contingency Financing Facility*. EBS/94/225. 28 November 1994.

IMF Archives, (1994c), *Staff Report on Request for Purchase Under the Systemic Transformation Facility*. EBS/94/221 Sup.1. 30 November 1994.

IMF Archives, (1995a), *Staff Report for Request for Stand-by Arrangement*. EBS/95/26. 1 March 1995.

IMF Archives, (1995b), *Republic of Moldova - Request for Stand-By Arrangement*. EBS/95/26. 2 March 1995.

IMF Archives, (1995c), *Staff Report on Request for Use of Fund Resources Under a Stand-by Arrangement and Second STF Purchase.* EBS/95/101. 13 June 1995.

IMF Archives, (1995d), *Staff Report on Request for Use of Fund Resources Under a Stand-by Arrangement and Second STF Purchase* EBS/95/110 Sup. 3. 15 June 1995.

IMF Archives, (1996a), *Enhanced Structural Adjustment Facility Policy Framework Paper. 1996-1998.* EBS/96/21. 9 February 1996.

IMF Archives, (1996b), *Staff Report for the Request for an Extended Arrangement* EBS/96/68. 3 May 1996.

IMF Archives, (1998), *Staff Report for the 1998 Article IV Consultation and Request for the Third Annual Arrangement Under the Enhanced Structural Adjustment Facility.* EBS/98/118. 10 July 1998.

IMF Archives, (2000a), *Staff Report for the 2000 Article IV Consultation and Request for a Three-Year Arrangement Under the Poverty Reduction and Growth Facility.* EBS/00/249. 1 December 2000.

IMF Archives, (2000b), *Interim Poverty Reduction Strategy Paper - Staff Assessment.* EBD/00/110. 4 December 2000.

IMF Archives, (2000c), *Joint Staff Assessment of the Interim Poverty Reduction Strategy Paper.* EBD/00/111. 4 December 2000.

IMF Fiscal Affairs Department, (1999), *Should Equity Be a Goal of Economic Policy?* Economic Issues N° 16. International Monetary Fund, Washington, DC.

Inglehart, R. F. and Welzel, C. (2005), *Modernization, cultural change, and democracy: the human development sequence*, New York, Cambridge University Press.

Inkeles, A. and Smith, D. H. (1974), *Becoming Modern: Individual Change in Six Developing Countries*, Cambridge Mass, Harvard University Press.

Interfax (2006), January 16.

Ioffe, G. (2003), 'Understanding Belarus: Questions of Language', in *Europe-Asia Studies*, 55 (7), pp. 1009–1047.

Ioffe, G. (2004), 'Understanding Belarus: Economy and Political Landscape', in *Europe-Asia Studies*, 56 (l), pp. 85-118.

Jamal, A.A. (2007), *Barriers to Democracy: The Other Side of Social Capital in Palestine and the Arab World*, Princeton, Princeton University Press.

James, H. (1995), 'The Historical Development of the Principle of Surveillance', in *IMF Staff Papers*, 42 (4).

Joint Statement (2003) of the Twelfth EU-Russia Summit in Rome on 5-6 November 2003, Annex I 'The Common European Economic Space Concept Paper'.

Joint Statement (2005) of the Fifteen EU-Russia Summit, Moscow, 10-11 May 2005, Annex I 'Road Map for the Common Economic Space'.

Jowitt, K. (1992), *New World Disorder: The Leninist Extinction*, Berkeley and Los Angeles, University of California Press.

Kagarlitsky, B. (2005), *Upravlyaemaya demokratia: Rissia kotoraya nam navyazali*, (Managed Democracy that Has Been Imposed upon Us), 575.

Kamhi, A. (2006), 'The Russian NGO Law: Potential Conflicts with International, National and Foreign Legislation', in *International Journal for Not-for-Profit Law*, 9 (1), pp. 1-16.

Kantor, V. (1999), 'Fenomen russkogo evropeytsa', in *Nauchnye doklady*, Moscow, MONF, IMEMO, n° 101.

Karatnycky, A. (2005), 'Ukraine's Orange Revolution', in *Foreign Affairs*, 84 (2), pp. 35-52.

Karl, T. (1995), 'The Hybrid Regimes of Central America', in *Journal of Democracy*, 6 (3), pp. 72-86.

Karl, T. and Schmitter P.C. (1991), 'Modes of transition in Latin America, Southern and Eastern Europe', in *International Social Science Journal*, 128, pp. 269-84.

Kasparov, G. (2007) 'Battling KGB', in *Journal of Democracy*, 18 (2), pp.115-119.

Kazakevich, A. (2006), 'Political cartography of Belarus in results of presidential; elections in 1994–2006', in *Politicheskaia sfera*, 7, pp. 5–19.

Kelley, J. (2006), 'New win in Old Wineskins: Promoting Political Reforms through the New European Neighbourhood Policy', in *Journal of Common Market Studies*, 44 (1), pp. 29-55.

Keukeleire S. and J. MacNaughtan (2008), *The Foreign Policy of the European Union*, Basingstoke, Palgrave Macmillan.

Khrush, T. (2006), 'How to stop the Oligarchisation of Power', in *The Day Weekly Digest*, n. 2, January 31.

King, C. (2000a), *The Moldovans: Romania, Russia and the Politics of Culture*, Stanford, Hoover Institution Press.

King, C. (2000b), 'Post-Communism. Transition, Comparison and the End of Eastern Europe', in *World Politics*, 53, pp. 143-172-

King, C. (2003), 'Marking time in the middle ground: Contested identities and Moldovan foreign Policy', in *Journal of Communist Studies and Transition Politics,* 19 (3), pp. 60-82.

Knack, S. (2004), 'Does Foreign Aid Promote Democracy?', in *International Studies Quarterly*, 48, pp. 251-266.

Knight, A. (2008), 'The Truth about Putin and Medvedev', in *New York Review of Books*, 55 (8), pp. 11-14.

Koinova, M. (2009), 'Diasporas and Democratization in the Post-Communist World', in *Communist and Post-Communist Studies*, 42, pp. 41-64.

Kommersant (2008) *NGO Congress Off to a Loud Start*, December 3, online edition at http://www.kommersant.com.

Kopstein, J. and Reilly, D.A. (2000), 'Geographic Diffusion and the Transformation of the Post-communist World', in *World Politics*, 53, pp. 1-37.

Korrespondent, (2006a), 'Akhmetov idiot na Kiev', March 4, p. 22.

Korrespondent, (2006b), March 18, p. 39 (quoting Ukrainian State Statistic Department Data).

Kozyrev, A. (1992), 'Russia and Human Rights', in *Slavic Review*, 51 (2), pp. 287-293.

Krastev, I. (2005), 'Russia's Post-Orange Empire', in *Open Democracy*, October 20, pp. 1-4.

Krastev, I. (2006), 'Democracy's Doubles', in *Journal of Democracy* 17 (2), pp. 52-62.

Kremen, T. and Smirnov, A. (2006) '100 dnei zastoya', in *Korrespondent*, 44 (233), November 11, pp.18-22.

Krivolap, A. (2006), 'Novie media I aktualnaia politika vesno – 2006' (New Media and Cultural Policy of the Spring 2006), in *Politicheskaia sfera*, 7, pp. 48-53.

Kubicek, P.J. (2000a), 'Regional Polarization in Ukraine: Public Opinion, Voting and Legislative Behaviour', in *Europe-Asia Studies*, 52, (2), pp. 273-294.

Kubicek, P.J. (2000b), *Unbroken Ties: The State, Interest Associations, and Corporatism in post-Soviet Ukraine*, Ann Arbor, University of Michigan Press.

Kubicek, P.J. (2002), 'Civil Society, Trade Unions and Post-Soviet Democratization: Evidence from Russia and Ukraine', in *Europe-Asia Studies*, 54 (4), pp. 603–624.

Kubicek, P.J. (2003), *The European Union and Democratization*, London, Routledge.

Kubicek, P.J. (2005), 'The EU and Democratization in Ukraine', in *Communist and Post - Communist Studies,* 38 (2).

Kunter, B. (2007), 'Belarus: Do no Harm - Requirements for the External Promotion of Democracy', in *Osteuropa* 57, (1).

Kuzin, S. and Penchuk, B. (2006), *Donetskaya Mafiya. Antologiya*, Kyiv, OAO Poligrafkniga.

Kuzio, T. (2005a), 'From Kuchma to Yushchenko: Ukraine's 2004 Presidential Elections and the Orange Revolution', in *Problems of Post - Communism* 52, (2), p. 29.

Kuzio, T. (2005b), 'Ukraine's Orange Revolution', in *Journal of Democracy*, 16 (2), pp.117-130.

Kuzio, T. ed. (2009), *Democratic revolution in Ukraine: from Kuchmagate to the Orange Revolution,* London, Routledge.

Landman, T. (2003), 'Map-Making and Analysis of the Main International Initiatives on Developing Indicators on Democracy and Good Governance', paper, Human Rights Centre, University of Essex.

Landman T. (2005), *Protecting Human Rights. A Comparative Study*, Washington, Georgetown University Press.

Lane, D. (2007), ed. *The Transformation of the State Socialism. System Change, Capitalism or Something Else?*, Houndmills, Basingstoke: Palgrave Macmillan.

Lavigne, M. (1999), *The Economics of Transition. From Socialist Economy to Market Economy*, Basingstoke, Palgrave.

Leblang, D.A. (1996), 'Property Rights, Democracy and Economic Growth', in *Political Research Quarterly*, 49 (1), pp. 5-26.

Leblang, D.A. (1997), 'Political Democracy and Economic Growth: Pooled Cross-Sectional and Time-Series Evidence', in *British Journal of Political Science*, 27 (3), pp. 453-472.

Lebow, R.N. e Risse-Kappen, T. (1995), *International Relations Theory and the End of the Cold War,* New York, Columbia University Press.

Leshchenko, S. (2006), 'Viktor Yushchenko's Political Orbits', in *Ukrainska Pravda website*, January 20 (as reported in BBC Monitoring Service in English, 5 February 2006).

Levitsky, S. and Way, L.A. (2002), 'Elections without Democracy: The Rise of Competitive Authoritarianism', in *Journal of Democracy,* 13 (2), pp. 51-65.

Levitsky, S. and Way, L.A. (2005), 'International Linkage and Democratization', in *Journal of Democracy*, 16(3), pp. 20-34.

Levitsky, S. and Way, L.A. (2006a), 'Linkage versus Leverage', in *Comparative Politics*, 38 (4), pp. 379-400.

Levitsky, S. and Way, L.A. (2006b), 'Linkage and Leverage: How do International Factors Change Domestic Balances of Power?', in Schedler, A. ed., *Electoral Authoritarianism: The Dynamics of Unfree Competition*, Boulder, Lynne Rienner.

Levitsky, S. and Way, L.A. (2007a), 'Linkage, Leverage, and the Post-Communist Divide', in *East European Politics and Society*, 21 (1), pp.48-66.

Levitsky, S. and Way, L.A. (2007b), *Competitive Authoritarianism: The Origins and Evolution of Hybrid Regimes in the Post-Cold War Era,* unpublished book manuscript.

Li, Q. and Reuveny, R. (2003), 'Economic Globalization adn Democracy: An Empirical Analysis', in *British Journal of Political Science,* 33 (1), pp. 29-54.

Liakhovich, A. (2007), 'Power Poles: an Examination into the Dynamics of the Current Relationship between Russia and Belarus', Belarus Public Policy Fund (Pontis foundation and the Belarusian Institute for Strategic Studies).

Linden, R. (2002), *Norms and Nannies: The Impact of International Organizations on the Central and East European States,* The New International Relations of Europe, Lanham, Md., Rowman & Littlefield Publishers.

Linz, J.J. (1964), 'An Authoritarian Regime: the Case of Spain', in E. Allardt and Y. Littunen (eds.), *Cleavages, Ideologies and Party Systems,* Helsinki, Westermarck Society, pp. 291-342.

Linz, J.J. (1990), 'The Perils of Presidentialism', in *Journal of Democracy,* 1 (1), pp. 51-69.

Linz, J.J. and Stepan, A. (1996), *Problems of Democratic Transition and Consolidation: Southern Europe, South America, and Post-Communist Europe,* Baltimore, Johns Hopkins University Press.

Lipset, S.M. (1959), 'Some social requisites of democracy: Economic development and political legitimacy', in *American Political Science Review,* 53 (1), pp. 69-105.

Lipset, S.M. (1960), *Political Man: The Social Bases of Politics,* expanded edition, New York, Doubleday.

Loukoianova, E. and Unigovskaya, A. (2004), 'Analysis of Recent Growth in Low-Income CIS Countries', in *IMF Working Paper, WP/04/151.*

Lust-Okar, E. (2004), 'Divided They Rule: The Management and Manipulation of Political Opposition', in *Comparative Politics,* January, pp. 159-179.

Lust-Okar, E. (2007), 'Elections in Authoritarian Regimes: Catalysts for, or Obstacles to, Reform?', paper delivered at the workshop "Democratization by Elections?", University of Florida, Gainsville, November 30-December 2.

Lyall, J. (2006), 'Pocket Protests: Rhetorical Coercion and the Micropolitics of Collective Action in Semiauthoritarian Regimes', in *World Politics,* 58 (3), pp. 378-412.

399

Lynch, M. (2001), 'Globalization and international democracy', in *International Studies Review*, 2 (3), pp. 91-101.

March, J.G. and Olsen, J.P. (1998), 'The International Dynamics of International Political Orders', in *International Organization*, 52 (4), pp. 943-969.

Magen, A. and Morlino, L. eds. (2008), *International Actors, Democratization and the Rule of Law. Anchoring democracy?*, London, Routledge.

Magen, A. - Risse, T. - McFaul, M. eds. (2009), *Promoting Democracy and the Rule of Law: American and European Strategies*, New York, Palgrave Macmillan.

Main, S.J. (2006), *The Bison and the Bear: Belarusian and Russian Relations 2003-2006*, Central & Eastern European Series, Conflict Studies Research Centre.

Malfliet, K. – Verpoest, L. – Vinokurov, E. eds. (2007), *The CIS, the EU and Russia*, Basingstoke, Palgrave.

March, L. and Herb, G.P. (2006), 'Moldova between Europe and Russia: Inoculating against the Coloured Contagion', in *Post-Soviet Affairs*, 22 (4), pp. 349-379.

Marples, D.R. (1999), *Belarus: A Denationalized Nation*. Post-communist States and Nations. Amsterdam, Harwood Academic Publishers.

Marples, D.R. (2004), 'The prospects for democracy in Belarus', in *Problems of Post-Communism*, 51 (1), pp. 31-42.

Marx, A.W. (2003), *Faith in Nation: Exclusionary Origins of Nationalism*, Oxford; New York, Oxford University Press.

Mauro, P. (1997), 'Why Worry About Corruption?', in *Economic Issue* No. 6. International Monetary Fund, Washington, DC.

McFaul, M. (1995), 'State Power, Institutional Change and the Politics of Privatization in Russia', in *World Politics*, 47 (2), pp. 210-243.

McFaul, M. (2002), 'The Fourth Wave of Democracy and Dictatorship: Noncooperative Transitions in the Post-communist World', in *World Politics* 54 (2).

McFaul, M. (2004a), 'Meddling in Ukraine: Democracy is not an American Plot', in *Washington Post*, December 21.

McFaul, M. (2004b), 'Political Parties', in M. McFaul, N. Petrov and A. Ryabov *Between Dictatorship and Democracy*, Washington DC, Carnegie Endowment for International Peace, pp.105-134.

McFaul, M. (2005), 'Transitions from Post-communism', in *Journal of Democracy* 16, (3).

McFaul, M. (2007), 'Importing Revolution: Internal and External Factors in Ukraine's 2004 Democratic Breakthrough', in Bunce, V. –

400

McFaul, M. - Stoner-Weiss, K. eds., *Waves and Troughs of Post-communist Reform,* unpublished book manuscript.

McFaul, M. and Stoner-Weiss, K. (2008), 'The Myth of the Authoritarian Model: How Putin's Crackdown Holds Russia Back', in *Foreign Affairs,* January/February.

Melyantsou, D. (2006), 'Spontaneous groups in post-electoral period', in *Politicheskaia sfera,* 7, pp. 32–42.

Mendelson, S.E. (2004), 'The Seven Ingredients: When Democracy Promotion Works', in *Harvard International Review* 26, (2).

Mendelson, S.E. and Gerber, T. (2005), 'Local Activist Culture and Transnational diffusion: An Experiment in Social Marketing among Human Rights Groups in Russia', unpublished manuscript.

Mendelson, S.E. and Glenn, J.K. (2002), *The Power and Limits of NGOs : A Critical Look at Building Democracy in Eastern Europe and Eurasia,* New York, Columbia University Press.

Merkel, W. (2004), 'Embedded and Defective Democracies', in *Democratization,* 11(5), pp. 33-58.

Mickiewicz, E. (2008), *Television, Power, and the Public in Russia,* Cambridge, Cambridge University Press.

Millennium Challenge Corporation, (2006), *Board Meeting Summary, June 16, 2006,* http://www.mcc.gov.

Millennium Challenge Corporation, (2007), *Congressional Notification Transmittal Sheet, August 24, 2007,* http://www.mcc.gov.

Millennium Challenge Corporation, (2009a), *Georgia: An Overview,* http://www.mcc.gov.

Millennium Challenge Corporation, (2009b), *Moldova: An Overview,* http://www.mcc.gov.

Millennium Challenge Corporation, (2009c), *Ukraine: An Overview,* http://www.mcc.gov.

Ministry of Foreign Affairs of the Republic of Belarus, (2009), Bilateral Cooperation: United States, www.mfa.gov.

Mitckih, N. (2004), 'Bankruptcy in 'homeopathic doses' and on optimal schema for economy of Belarus', in *Anti-crisis Control and Heightening of Competitiveness of the Republic of Belarus Economy,* Minsk, Byelorussian State University, pp. 86–87.

Modra, S. (2005), 'Akhmetov: Ya bolshe lyublyu chai pit' doma. Surkis: Ya ne mogu byt' vragom prezidenta, Pinchuk: by ne khotelos vnov' idti v deputaty', in *Ukrainska Pravda website,* October 15.

Modra, S. and Andrevskaya, A. (2005), 'Yushchenko pokazal eks-oligarkham mesta ikh byloi lobbistkoi slavy', in *Ukrainska Pravda website,* October 10.

401

Moldova Azi (2007), 'Subordination through merger' (Subordonarea prin unificare), 15 June, http://www.azi.md.

Momani, B. (2004), 'American politicization of the International Monetary Fund', in *Review of International Political Economy*, 11 (5), pp. 880-904.

Momani, B. (2005), 'Recruiting and Diversifying IMF Technocrats', in *Global Society*, 19 (2), pp. 167-187.

Morlino, L. (1998), *Democracy between consolidation and crisis. Parties, groups, and citizens in Southern Europe*, Oxford, Oxford University Press.

Morlino, L. (2003), *Democrazie e Democratizzazioni*, Bologna, Il Mulino.

Morlino, L. (2004), 'Good and Bad Democracies: How to Conduct Research into the Quality of Democracy?', in *Journal of Communist Studies and Transition Politics*, 20 (1), pp. 5–27.

Morlino, L. (2008a), 'Democracy and Changes: How Research Tails Reality', in *West European Politics*, 31(1-2), pp. 40-59.

Morlino, L. (2008b), 'Régime hybrides ou régimes en transition?', in M.S. Darviche (ed.), *Penser la dynamique des régimes politiques*, Paris, L'Harmattan, pp. 1–24.

Morlino, L. (forthcoming), 'Are There Hybrid Regimes? Or is Only and Optical Illusion?', in *European Political Science Review*.

Morlino, L. and Magen, A. (2008a), 'Methods of Influence, Layers of Impact, Cycles of Change: A Framework for Analysis', in Magen A. and L Morlino (eds.), *International Actors, Democratization and the Rule of Law. Anchoring Democracy*, London, Routledge.

Morlino, L. and Magen, A. (2008b), 'Scope, Depth and Limits of External Influence - Conclusions', in Magen and Morlino, *International Actors, Democratization and the Rule of Law. Anchoring Democracy*, London, Routledge.

Moscow Helsinki Group and Human Rights Without Frontiers (2008), *Control and Punishment: Human rights implications of Russian legislation on NGOs*, Report by the MHG and HRWF, Moscow and Brussels, http://hrwf.net.

Mosneaga, V. ed. (2005a), *Moldoscopie. Probleme de analiza politica Mosneagă*, Chişinău, USM.

Mosneaga, V. (2005b), 'Parties and party system in Moldova: 1990-2002', in A. Kulik, and S. Pshizova eds. *Political Parties in Post-Soviet Space: Russia, Belarus, Ukraine, Moldova and the Baltics*, Praeger, Westport, Connecticut.

Mostovaya, Y. (2006), 'Self-destruction Strategy', in *Zerkalo Nedeli on the Web*, 39 (618), October 14-20.

Motyl, A.J. - Ruble, B.A. – Shevtsova, L. (2005), eds *Russia's Engagement with the West*, Armonk and London: M.E. Sharpe.

Motyl, N. (2008), 'Moldova in Transition: from Survival to Rebirth', in A. Kurkov ed. *Histories of Hope*, London, EBRD.

Muller, E.N. (1995), 'Economic Determinants of Democracy', in *American Sociological Review*, 60 (6), pp. 966-982.

Mungiu-Pippidi, A. (2007), 'Disputed Identity as Inescapable Pluralism: Moldova's Ambiguous Transition', paper presented at the Project on Democratic Transitions, Foreign Policy Research Institute, February 8.

Nodia, G. (1996), 'How Different Are Post-Communist Transitions?', in *Journal of Democracy*, 7 (4), pp. 15-29.

North, D. (1990), *Institutions, Institutional Change and Economic Performance*, Cambridge, Cambridge University Press.

Obydenkova A. (2005), 'Puzzles of the European Regional Integration and Cooperation: Interplay of 'Internal' and 'External' Factors', in R. Di Quirico ed. *Europeanization and Democratization. Institutional adaptation, Conditionality and Democratization in European Union's Neighbour Countries,* Florence, European Press Academic Publishing, pp. 199–222.

Obydenkova, A. (2006), 'Democratization, Europeanization and Regionalization beyond the European Union: Search for Empirical Evidence', in *European Integration Online Papers,* 10 (1).

Obydenkova, A. (2007), 'The International Dimension of Democratization: Test the Parsimonious Approach', in *Cambridge Review of International Affairs*, 20 (3), pp. 473–490.

Obydenkova, A. (2008a), *Democratization, Regionalization and Europeanization in Russia: Interplay of National and Transnational Factors,* Germany, VDM Verlag.

Obydenkova, A. (2008b), 'Europeanization and Democratization: Trans-national impact on Sub-national Democratization?', in *European Journal of Political Research*, 3 (47), pp. 221–246.

Obydenkova, A. (2008c), 'Reintegration vs. Regional Cooperation? Some Puzzles in Post-soviet Eurasia in the context of Comparative Regionalism', The Leonard Davis Institute for International Relations Working Paper, The Hebrew University of Jerusalem.

O'Donnell, G. (2004), 'Human Development, Human Rights and Democracy', in G. O'Donnell, J. V. Cullel and O. Iazzetta, *The Quality of Democracy. Theory and Applications*, Notre Dame, University of Notre Dame Press.

O'Donnell, G. and Schmitter, P.C. (1986a), *Transitions from Authoritarian Rule: Tentative Conclusions about Uncertain Democracies*, Baltimore, Johns Hopkins University Press.

O'Donnell, G. and Schmitter, P.C. (1986b), 'Political Life After Authoritarian Rule: Tentative Conclusions About Uncertain Transitions', in G. O'Donnell, P.C. Schmitter and L. Whitehead eds. *Transitions from Authoritarian Rule: Comparative Perspectives*, Baltimore, Johns Hopkins Press.

O'Donnell, G. – Schmitter, P.C. - Whitehead, L. eds. (1986), *Transitions from Authoritarian Rule*, Baltimore, Johns Hopkins University Press.

Olearchyk, R. (2006), 'Ukrainian Billionaire Oligarchs Eager to Westernise', in *Financial Times*, October 31.

Önis, Z. and Bakir, C. (2007), 'Turkey's political economy in the age of financial globalization: the significance of the EU anchor', in *South European Society and Politics*, 12 (2), pp. 147-164.

Organization for Economic, Co-operation and Development, (2007), *OECD Glossary of Statistic Terms*, http://stats.oecd.org/glossary/detail.asp?ID=6043 (accessed 5 May 2009).

Organization for Economic, Co-operation and Development, (2009), *IDS Online-DAC Database - Destination of Official Development Assistance and Official Aid - OECD.Stat*, http://www.oecd.org.

OSCE (2001), Office for Democratic Institutions and Human Rights – Republic of Moldova, Parliamentary Elections 25 February 2001, Final Report, http://www.osce.org.

Ottaway, M. (2003), *Democracy Challenged: The Rise of Semi-Authoritarianism,* Washington, Carnegie Endowment for International Peace.

Oye, K. (1995), 'Explaining the End of the Cold War: Morphological and Behavioral Adaptations to the Nuclear Peace', in R.N. Lebow, and T. Risse-Kappen, eds. *International Relations Theory and the End of the Cold War,* New York, Columbia University Press, pp. 57-84.

Pandey, S.K. (2007), 'Asia in the Debate on Russian Identity', in *International Studies*, 44 (4), pp.317-337.

Panova, K. and Smirnov, A. (2006), 'Zheleznaya khvatka', in *Korrespondent*, June 22, pp. 36-37.

Papaioannou, E. and Siourounis (2008), 'Economic and social factors driving the third wave of democratization', in *Journal of Comparative Economics*, 36 (3), pp. 365–387.

Paskhaver, O. and Verkhovoda, L. (2006), 'Privatizatsiya do i posle oranzhevoi revolutsii', Working Paper Tsentr Sotsialno-ekonomicheskikh Issledovanii, Kyiv, CASE Ukraina.

Paskhover, A. (2006), 'Delo Pakhnet Miliardom', in *Korrespondent*, 38, September 30, pp. 58-60.

Paskhover, A. and Smirnov, A. (2006), 'Pryamo v gaz, in *Korrespondent*, September 16, pp. 22-24.

Pauly, L.W. (1999), 'Good governance and bad policy: the perils of international organizational overextension', in *Review of International Political Economy*, 6 (4), pp. 401-424.

Peel, Q. (2006), 'Putin's gas logic is in short supply', in *The Financial Times*, 5th January pp. 2-12.

Pershai, A. (2006), 'Questioning the Hegemony of the Nation State in Belarus: Production of Intellectual Discourses as Production of Resources', in *Nationality Papers,* 34 (5), pp. 623–635.

Peterson, P.G. (2002), '*Public Diplomacy and the War on Terrorism'*, in *Foreign Affairs*, 81 (5), pp. 74-94.

Petrone, L. (2009) *La retorica della società civile al servizo della democrazia sovrana nella Russia di Putin*, unpublished manuscript.

Petrov, N. (2004), 'Federalism', in M. McFaul, N. Petrov, N. and A. Ryabov, eds. *Between Dictatorship and Democracy,* Washington, Carnegie Endowment for International Peace, pp.213-238.

Pevehouse, J.C. (2005), *Democracy from Above: Regional Organizations and Democratization*, New York, Cambridge University Press.

Pinchuk, V. (2005), 'We, the National Capitalists', in *Zerkalo Nedeli on the web*, December 17-23.

Pirchner, H. (2005), *Reviving Greater Russia? The future of Russia's borders with Belarus, Georgia, Kazakhstan, Moldova and Ukraine*, Lanham, MD, University Press of America.

Plokhy, S. (2008), *Ukraine and Russia: representations of the past,* Toronto, London, University of Toronto Press.

Polikanov, D. and Timmins, G. (2004), 'Russian Foreign Policy under Putin', in C. Ross, ed. *Russian Politics under Putin,* Manchester, Manchester University Press, pp. 223-35.

Polity IV (2008), 'Political Regimes Characteristics and Transitions, 1800-2008, User's Manual', http://www.systemicpeace.org/polity.

Pop-Eleches, G. (2007), 'Between Historical Legacies and the Promise of Western Integration: Democratic Conditionality after Communism', in *East European Politics and Societies*, 21 (1), pp. 142-161.

Pridham, G. (2005), *Designing Democracy. EU Enlargement and Regime Change in Post-Communist Europe*, Basingstoke, Palgrave.

Pridham, G. - Herring, E, - Sanford, G. eds. (1997), *Building Democracy? The International Dimension of Democratization in Eastern Europe*, London, Leicester University Press.

Przeworski, A. (1991), *Democracy and the market. Political and Economic Reforms in Eastern Europe and Latin America*, Cambridge, Cambridge University Press.

Przeworski, A. and Limongi, F. (1993), 'Political Regimes and Economic Growth', in *The Journal of Economic Perspectives*, 7 (3), pp. 51-69.

Przeworski, A. and Limongi, F. (1997), 'Modernization: theories and facts', in *World Politics*, 49, pp. 155-183.

Przeworski, A. - M. Alvarez - J.A. Cheibub - F. Limongi (2000), *Democracy and Development: Political Institutions and Well-Being in the World, 1950-1990*, Princeton, Princeton University Press.

Puglisi, R. (2003a), 'Clashing Agendas? Economic Interests, Élite Coalitions and Prospects for Cooperation between Russia and Ukraine', in *Europe-Asia Studies*, 55 (6), pp. 827–45.

Puglisi, R. (2003b), 'The Rise of the Ukrainian Oligarchs', in *Democratization*, 10 (3), pp. 99–123.

Quinlan, P.D. (2007), 'Back to the Future: An Overview of Moldova and Voronin', July 20.

Ragin, C. (2000), *Fuzzy-Set Social Science*, Chicago, The University of Chicago Press.

Ragin, C. (2008), *Redesigning Social Inquiry: Fuzzy Sets and Beyond*, Chicago, The University of Chicago Press.

Reddaway, P. and Glinski, D. (2001), *The Tragedy of Russia's Reforms. Market Bolshevism against Democracy*, Washington DC, United States Institute of Peace Press.

Remmer, K. (1985-86), 'Exclusionary Democracy', in *Studies in Comparative International Development*, 20 (winter), pp. 64-85.

Risse-Kappen, T. (1994), 'Ideas do not Float Freely: Transnational Coalitions, Domestic Structures and the End of the Cold War', in *International Organization*, 48 (2), pp. 185-214.

Robertson, G. (2008), 'Managing Society: Protest, Civil Society, and Regime in Putin's Russia', unpublished manuscript, University of North Carolina, Department of Political Science.

Roessler, P.G. and Howard, M.M. (2007), 'Measuring and Analyzing Post-Cold War Political Regimes', paper presented at the workshop 'Democratization by Election?.' University of Florida, November 30 – December 2.

Roper, S. (2008), 'From semi-presidentialism to parliamentarism: Regime change and presidential power in Moldova', in *Europe-Asia Studies*, 60:1, pp. 113-126.

Rose R. (2000), 'Uses of Social Capital in Russia: Modern, Pre-Modern, and Anti-Modern', in *Post-Soviet Affairs* 16, (January–March).

Rose, R. and Munro, N. (2008), 'Do Russians see their future in Europe or the CIS?', in *Europe-Asia Studies*, 60 (1), pp.49-66.

Ross, M. (2001), 'Does oil hinder democracy?', in *World Politics*, 53, pp. 325-361.

Roth, G. (1968), 'Personal Rulership, Patrimonialism and Empire-Building in the New States', in *World Politics*, 20 (1), pp. 194-206.

Rouquié, A. (1975), 'L'Hipothèse "Bonapartiste" et l'Emergence des Sistèmes Politiques Semicompetitifs', in *Revue Française de Science Politique*, 25.

Rustow, D.A. (1970), 'Transitions to Democracy: Toward a Dynamic Model', in *Comparative Politics* 2, (3), pp. 337-363.

Ryabov, A. (2008), 'Tandemocracy in Today's Russia', in *Russian Analytical Digest*, 49, pp. 2-6.

Sahm, A. (2006), 'Integration – A Path to Self-Assertion? Relations between Belarus and Russia in the International Context', in *The Russian Analytical Digest,* 4.

Sakwa, R. (2003), 'Putin's Foreign Policy: Transforming the East', in Gorodetsky, G. ed. *Russia Between East and West: Russian Foreign Policy on the Threshold of Twenty-First Century*, London, Frank Cass.

Sannikov, A. (2002), *'Russia's Varied Roles in Belarus'*, in Balmaceda, M. *et al.* eds. *Independent Belarus: Domestic Determinants, Regional Dynamics, and Its Implications for the West*, Cambridge, HURI Press, pp. 222-231.

Sarna, A. (2006), 'Politicheskaia reclama – 2006: vlasti i oppozitcii' (Political advertisement 2006: authority and opposition), in *Politichnaia Sfera,* 7, pp. 63–74.

Schedler, A. (2002), 'The Nested Game of Democratization by Elections', in *International Political Science Review / Revue Internationale De Science Politique,* 23 (1), pp. 103-122.

Schedler, A. ed. (2006), *Electoral Authoritarianism: The Dynamics of Unfree Competition*, Boulder, Lynne Rienner.

Schedler, A. (2007), 'Blunt Manipulation, Incisive Protest Explaining Election Outcomes under Authoritarian Rule', paper delivered at the workshop "Democratization by Elections?", University of Florida, Gainsville, November 30-December 2.

Schimmelfennig, F. (2003), *The EU, NATO and the Integration of Europe: Rules and Rhetoric,* Themes in European Governance, Cambridge, UK; New York, Cambridge University Press.

Schimmelfennig, F. (2005), 'Strategic Calculation and International Socialization: Membership Incentives, Party Constellations, and Sustained Compliance in Central and Eastern Europe', in *International Organization,* 59 (4), pp.827-60.

Schimmelfenning, F. (2007), 'European Regional Organization, Political Conditionality, and Democratic Transformation in Eastern Europe', in *East European Politics and Societies,* 21 (1), pp. 126–141.

Schimmelfennig, F. and Scholtz, H. (2007), 'EU Democracy Promotion in the European Neighbourhood: conditionality, Economic Development, and Linkage', paper presented at the EUSA Tenth Biennial International Conference, Montreal, Canada, May 17-19.

Schimmelfennig, F. and Sedelmeier, U. (2005), *The Europeanization of Central and Eastern Europe,* Cornell University Press.

Schmidtke O. and Yekelchyk S. eds. (2008), *Europe's last frontier? Belarus, Moldova, and Ukraine between Russia and the European Union,* New York, Houndmills, Palgrave.

Schmitter, P. C. and Brouwer, I. (1999), 'Conceptualizing, Researching, & Evaluating Democracy Promotion and Protection', EUI Working Paper SPS No. 99/9, European University Institute, Firenze.

Schmitter P.C. and Karl, T.L. (1993), 'What Democracy is... and is Not', in L. Diamond and M. Plattner (eds.), *The Global Resurgence of Democracy,* Baltimore, Johns Hopkins University Press.

Schmitter, P.C. and Karl, T.L. (1994), 'The Conceptual Travels of Transitologists and Consolidologists: How Far to the East Should They Attempt to Go?', in *Slavic Review,* 53 (1), pp.173–185.

Sedelmeier, U. (2005), 'EU Identity Formation through Enlargement Policy Practice', paper presented at the Conference on "Towards a Transnational and Transcultural Europe."

Sestanovich, S. (2007), 'Putin's Invented Opposition', in *Journal of Democracy,* 18 (2), pp.52-62.

Shevtsova, L. (2005), *Putin's Russia,* Washington, Carnegie Endowment for International Peace.

Shevtsova, L. (2007), *Russia – Lost in Transition,* Washington, Carnegie Endowment for International Peace.

Simis, K. (1982), *USSR: Secrets of a Corrupt Society,* New York, Simon and Schuster.

Silitski, V. (2005a), *The Long Road from Tyranny: Post-Communist Authoritarianism and Struggle for Democracy in Serbia and Belarus*, unpublished book manuscript.

Silitski, V. (2005b), 'Is the Age of Post-Soviet Electoral Revolutions Over?', in *Democracy at Large*, 1 (4), pp. 8-10.

Silitski, V. (2005c), 'Pre-empting Democracy: The Case of Belarus', in *Journal of Democracy*, 16 (4), pp. 83-97.

Silitski, V. (2006), 'Another Contagion: Pre-emptive Authoritarianism in the Former SU following the Coloured Revolutions', paper presented at the Conference "Waves and Troughs of Post-communist Transitions: What Role for External Versus Domestic Variables?", Centre on Democracy, Development and Rule of Law, Stanford University, April 28-29.

Silitski, V. (2007a), 'Different Authoritarianisms: Distinct Patterns of Electoral Change', in *Forbrig and Demes*, pp. 155-173.

Silitski, V. (2007b), 'Contagion Deterred: Pre-emptive Authoritarianism in the Former SU', in Bunce, V. – McFaul, M. - Stoner-Weiss, K. eds., *Waves and Troughs of Post-communist Reform,* unpublished book manuscript.

Sirowy, L. and Inkeles, A. (1990), 'The Effects of Democracy on Economic Growth and Inequality: A review', in *Studies in Comparative International Development*, 25 (1), pp. 126-157.

Siruk, M. (2007), 'Promoting The Ukrainian Way', in *The Day Weekly Digest*, 3, January 30.

Smith, G. – Law, V. - Wilson, A. – Bohr, A. – Allworth, E. (1988), *Nation-Building in the Post-Soviet Borderlands: The Politics of National Identities,* Cambridge, Cambridge University Press.

Smith, H. (2005), *Russia and Its Foreign Policy*, Helsinki, Kikimora Publications.

Smolski, A. (2006), 'Tendencies and Problems of Economic Insolvency. Bankruptcy–institution development in Belarus: 1991–2005', Working Paper, Belarus, Vitebsk State Technological University

Solnick, S.L. (1999), 'Russia's «Transition»: Is Democracy Delayed Democracy Denied?', in *Social Research*, 66 (3), pp.789-824.

Somaini, E. (2009), *Geografia della democrazia*, Bologna, il Mulino.

Soroka, S. (2006), 'Budget Azarova: Smertitel'ny vystrel po liberalizovannoi ekonomike', in *Ukrainiska Pravda website*, September 20.

Spector, R.A. and Krickovic, A. (2007), *The Anti-Revolutionary Toolkit*, unpublished manuscript, University of California, Berkeley, Department of Political Science and Institute for International Studies.

Stiglitz, J.E. (2002), *Globalization and its Discontents*, New York, W.W. Norton and Company.

Stoner-Weiss, K. (2001), 'The Limited Reach of Russia's Party System: Underinstitutionalization in Dual Transitions', in *Politics & Society*, 29 (3), pp. 385-414.

Stoner-Weiss, K. (2006), *Resisting the State: Reform and Retrenchment in Post-Soviet Russia*, New York: Cambridge University Press.

Stoner-Weiss, K. (2007), 'When the Wave Hits a Shoal: The internal and External Dimensions of Russia' Backslide from Democracy', in Bunce, V. – McFaul, M. - Stoner-Weiss, K. eds., *Waves and Troughs of Post-communist Reform*, unpublished book manuscript.

Suny, R.G. (1988), *The Making of the Georgian Nation*, Bloomington, Indiana University Press.

Surkov, V. (2006), Transcript of a speech by the Deputy Head of the Administration of the President, aide to the president of the Russian Federation, Vladislav Surkov, prepared for the staff of "United Russia", 7 February 2006, http://www.edinros.ru.

Swedberg, R. (1986), 'The Doctrine of Economic Neutrality of the IMF and the World Bank', in *Journal of Peace Research*, 23 (4), pp. 377-390.

Teorell, J. and Hadenius, A. (2003), 'Global and Regional Determinants of Democratization: Taking Stock of the Large-N Evidence', paper presented at the conference on "Democratic Advancements and Setbacks: What Have we Learnt?", Uppsala, Sweden, June 11-13.

Teorell, J. and Hadenius, A. (2007), 'Election as Levers of Democracy: A Global Inquiry', paper presented at the workshop "Democratization by Election?", University of Florida, November 30 – December 2.

Thacker, S.C. (1998), 'The High Politics of IMF Lending', in *World Politics*, 52 (1), pp. 38-75.

The Day Weekly Digest (2006), number 2, January 31.

Tomenko, M. (2005), 'Changes are Only About to Begin, or is the Second Phase of the Orange Revolution Possible?', in *Ukrainska Pravda website*, September, 30.

Tovias, U. and Ugur, M. (2004), 'Can the EU anchor policy reform in third countries', in *European Union Politics*, 5 (4), pp. 395-418.

Treisman, D. (2007), 'Putin's Silovarchs', in *Orbis*, Winter, pp. 141-153.

Trenin, D. (2007), 'Russia Redefines Itself and its Relations with the West', in *The Washington Quarterly*, 30 (2), pp 95-105.

Tsyganov, A.P. (2006), 'Projecting Confidence, not Fear: Russia's Post-Imperial Assertiveness', in *Orbis*, Fall, pp. 667-690.

Tudoroiu, T. (2007), 'Rose, Orange, and Tulip: The Failed Post-Soviet Revolutions', in *Communist and Post-Communist Studies*, 40 (3), pp. 315–342.

Ugur, M. (1999), *The European Union and Turkey: An Anchor/Credibility Dilemma*, Aldershot, Ashgate.

Ukraina TV (2006), 20 February (as reported in BBC Monitoring Service in English, 20 February).

Ukrainska Pravda website (2007), February 2.

U.S. Department of State – Bureau of European and Eurasian Affairs (2009), *Belarus: U.S. Relations*, www.state.gov.

U.S. Department of State – Bureau of European and Eurasian Affairs, (2008), *United States-Ukraine Charter on Strategic Partnership*, http://merln.ndu.

U.S. Department of State – Bureau of European and Eurasian Affairs, (2009), *United States-Georgia Charter on Strategic Partnership*, http://merln.ndu.edu.

U.S. Department of State – Bureau of European and Eurasian Affairs, (2001-2009), *FY 2000-2008 U. S. Assistance to Eurasia*, http://www.state.gov.

U.S. Department of State – Bureau of Political-Military Affairs (2009), *Security Assistance Funds administered by the Bureau of Political-Military Affairs*, http://www.state.gov.

U.S. Agency for International Development, (2005), *The NGO Sustainability Index for Central and Eastern Europe and Eurasia*, Washington, DC.

U.S. Agency for International Development, (2008-2009),*Congressional Budget Justification for Foreign Operations, Fiscal Year 2008 and 2009,* http://www.usaid.gov.

Vachudova, M.A. (2005), *Europe Undivided: Democracy, Leverage, and Integration after Communism*, Oxford, Oxford University Press.

Vachudova, M.A. (2006), 'Democratization in Post-communist Europe: Illiberal Regimes and the Leverage of International Actors', Working Paper 69, Centre on Democracy, Development, and the Rule of Law, Stanford, September, http://cddrl.stanford.edu.

Vahl, M. (2007), 'EU-Russia Relations in EU Neighbourhood Policies', in K. Malfliet, L. Verpoest and E. Vinokurov – eds. – *The CIS, the EU and Russia*, Basingstoke, Palgrave, pp. 121-141.

Van Houtven, L. (2002), 'Governance of the IMF. Decision making, Institutional Oversight, Transparency and Accountability', in *Pamphlet Series* No. 53. International Monetary Fund, Washington, DC.

Van Wersch, J. and De Zeeuw, J. (2005), 'Mapping European Democracy Assistance: Tracing the Activities and Financial Flows of Political Foundations', working paper, The Hague, Netherlands Institute of International Relations 'Clingendael', Conflict Research Unit.

Verdery, Katherine (1993), 'Whither "Nation" and "Nationalism"?', *Daedalus*, Vol.122, No. 3, 1993.

Vinokurov, E. (2007), 'The EU-Russia Common Economic Space and the Policy-Taker Problem', in K. Malfliet, L. Verpoest and E. Vinokurov – eds. – *The CIS, the EU and Russia*, Basingstoke, Palgrave, pp. 221-234.

Vreeland, J.R. (2003), *The IMF and economic development*, Cambridge, Cambridge University Press.

Vydrin, D. (2007), 'Esli est' oligarchy, to net vlast', in *Profil' Ukraina*, February 12, p. 23.

Wallander, C. (2007), 'Russian Transimperialism and Its Implications', in *Washington Quarterly*, 30 (2), pp. 107-122.

Warner, T. (2005), 'Sale Ends Ukrainian 'Re-privatisations'', in *Financial Times*, 26 October.

Way, L.A. (2002), 'Pluralism by Default in Moldova', in *Journal of Democracy*, 13, (4), pp. 127-141.

Way, L.A. (2003), 'Weak States and Pluralism: The Case of Moldova', in *East European Politics and Societies*, 17 (3), pp. 454-482.

Way, L.A. (2004), 'The Sources and Dynamics of Competitive Authoritarianism in Ukraine', in *Journal of Communist Studies and Transition Politics*, 20 (1) , pp. 143–161.

Way, L.A. (2005a), 'Rapacious Individualism and Competitive Authoritarianism in Ukraine, 1992–2004', in *Communist and Post-Communist Studies*, 38 (2), pp. 191–206.

Way, L.A. (2005b), 'Authoritarian State Building and the Sources of Regime Competitiveness in the Fourth Wave: The Cases of Belarus, Moldova, Russia, and Ukraine', in *World Politics* 57, (2), pp. 231-261.

Way, L.A. (2005c), 'Ukraine's Orange Revolution: Kuchma's Failed Authoritarianism', in *Journal of Democracy,* 16.

Way, L.A. and Levitsky, S. (2007), 'Pigs, Wolves and the Evolution of Post-Communist Competitive Authoritarianisms 1992-2005', in Bunce, V. – McFaul, M. - Stoner-Weiss, K. eds., *Waves and Troughs of Post-communist Reform,* unpublished book manuscript.

Weede, E. (2007), 'The Impact of Democracy on Economic Growth: Some Evidence from Cross-National Analysis', in *Kyklos*, 36 (1), pp. 21-39.

Weingast, B. (1997), 'The political foundations of democracy and the rule of law', in *American Political Science Review*, 91 (2), pp. 245-263.

Wheatley, J. (2005), *Georgia from National Awakening to Rose Revolution: Delayed Transition in the Former Soviet Union*, Aldershot, Ashgate Publishing.

White, S. and McAllister, I. (2007), 'Belarus, Ukraine [and Russia]: East or West?', paper presented at the 39th Annual convention of the AAASS, New Orleans, November 15-18.

White, S. – McAllister, I. – Light, M. (2002), 'Enlargement and the New Outsiders', in *Journal of Common Market Studies*, 40, (1), pp. 135-53.

Whitehead, L. ed. (1996), *The International Dimensions of Democratization: Europe and the Americas*, Oxford, Oxford University Press.

White House – Office of the Press Secretary, (1992), *Freedom Support Act of 1992 Fact Sheet*, http://www.fas.org.

Wigell, M. (2008), 'Mapping "Hybrid Regimes": Regime Types and Concepts in Comparative Politics', in *Democratization*, 15(2), pp. 230-250.

Wilson, A. (2005), *Virtual Politics: Faking Democracy in the Post-Soviet World*, New Haven, Yale University Press.

Wilson, K. (2006), 'Party-System Development under Putin', in *Post-Soviet Affairs*, 22, pp. 314-348.

Wise, C.R. and Brown T.L. (1999), 'The separation of powers in Ukraine', in *Communist and Post-Communist Studies*, 32, pp. 23-44.

World Bank, (1998), *Assessing Aid. What Works, What Doesn't and Why*. Policy Research Report N° 18295. World Bank, Washington, DC.

World Bank, (2007), *World Development Indicators*, http://web.worldbank.org.

World Bank (2009), *Russian Economic Report 18: Refocusing Policy on Households*, ECA, http://web.worldbank.org.

Yatsenko, N. (2006a) 'Billions of Illusions. Coalition's Omnipotence and the President's Veto: Can This Fragile Construction Guarantee Ukraine's Transparent and Effective Economic Development?', in *Zerkalo Nedeli on the web*, 47, December 9-15.

Yatsenko, N. (2006b) 'Full Speed Ahead, Anticrisis Coalition Initiates the Revival Free Economic Zones and Techno-Parks', in *Zerkalo Nedeli on the Web*, 29, July 29-August 4.

Youngs, R. (2004), *International Democracy and the West: The Roles of Governments, Civil Society, and Multinational Business*, Oxford, Oxford University Press.

Zakaria, F. (1997), 'The Rise of Illiberal Democracy', in *Foreign Affairs*, 76 (6), pp. 22-43.

Zaprudnik, J. (1993), *Belarus: At a Crossroads of History*, Boulder, Westview Press, pp. 229–245.

413

Zhuplev, A. (2008), 'Economic Internationalization of Russia: Roots, Trends, and Scenarios', in *International Political Science Review*, 29, (1), pp.99-119.

Zielonka, J. and Pravda, A. eds. (2001), *Democratic Consolidation in Eastern Europe, International and Transnational Factors*, Vol. 2, Oxford, Oxford University Press,.

Zimmerman, W. (2007), 'Normal Democracies' and Improving How They Are Measured: The Case of Russia', in *Post-Soviet Affairs,* 23 (1), pp.1–17.

**Other European Press Academic Publishing
Publications:**

International Politics and Economics

Roberto Di Quirico	*Building on Borrowed Bricks*
Ilkka Saarilahti	*40 vuotta Euroopan Union Budjetointia Yleisen taloisarvion kehitys vuosina 1968-2008*
Ilkka Saarilahti	*Les procèdures budgètaires de l'Union europèenne de 2004 à 2008*
Antonio De Chiara	*Multinationals Corporations*
Roberto di Quirico	*Europeanisation and Democratisation*
Jan van der Harst	*The Atlantic Priority*
Baroncelli -Varvesi	*Europe in Progress*
Xiaojie Xu Petro	*Petro Dragon's Rise*
Minoru Nakano	*New Japanese Political Economy and Political Reform*
Ryuji Mukae	*Japan's Refugee Policy: to be of the World*

European Press Academic Publishing (EPAP)
Publications on:
http://www.e-p-a-p.com
http://www.europeanpress.eu
orders@e-p-a-p.com

www.ingramcontent.com/pod-product-compliance
Lightning Source LLC
Chambersburg PA
CBHW051722260326
41914CB00031B/1689/J